Europe

Praise for the book

Ageing in Society brings forth exciting new questions, fresh perspectives, and a necessary critical approach to key issues – this is indeed an authoritative introduction. The book will inform students in ways that so many texts in the area, satisfied with comfortable bromides, do not.

> Jaber Gubrium, Editor of *Journal of Aging Studies,*
> University of Missouri-Columbia

This completely revised third edition of *Ageing in Society* presents one of the most comprehensive pictures of ageing today. The book offers the reader cogent discussions of the most up to date perspectives and evidence available. The contributors are all leading experts in their fields – comprising a range of important disciplines as they apply to ageing. *Ageing in Society* is a cutting edge text on one of the most important subjects facing the modern world – a must for all students of ageing.

> Mike Bury, Emeritus Professor of Sociology, University of London

The third edition of the comprehensive textbook *Ageing in Society* extends its scope to include continental Europe, allowing broader as well as deeper insights into recent trends in gerontology. Gerontologists and practitioners are urged not to stop reading before they have reached the insightful last chapter 'Ageing into the future'!

> Professor Dorly Deeg, Editor-in-Chief of *European Journal of Ageing*, VU University Medical Centre

Ageing in Society

European Perspectives on Gerontology

3rd edition

edited by
John Bond
Sheila Peace
Freya Dittmann-Kohli
Gerben J. Westerhof

S SAGE Publications

London ● Los Angeles ● New Delhi ● Singapore

Contents

List of boxes

List of figures

List of tables

List of contributors

Janet Askham is Professor of Social Gerontology at the International Policy Institute, King's College, London, UK and Director of Research at the Picker Institute Europe.

Jan Baars studied sociology and philosophy in Amsterdam and is Professor of Interpretive Gerontology at the University for Humanist Studies in Utrecht and Professor of Philosophy of the Social Sciences and the Humanities at Tilburg University in the Netherlands.

John Bond was trained as a sociologist. He is Professor of Social Gerontology and Health Services Research in the Institute of Health and Society and Institute for Ageing and Health, based at Newcastle University.

Peter Coleman is Professor of Psychogerontology at the University of Southampton, and was editor of the BSG's journal Ageing and Society 1992–1996 and co-editor of the first two editions of its textbook Aging in Society: An Introduction to Social Gerontology, 1990 and 1993.

Freya Dittmann-Kohli studied Psychology in Marburg and Berlin. She did empirical research on lifespan psychology at the Max-Planck-Institute for Human Development and Education and has the Chair for Psychogerontology at the Radboud University Nijmegen, Faculty of Social Sciences, where she directed large-scale survey studies in Germany and the Netherlands on the second half of life.

Dieter Ferring is Professor at the University of Luxembourg and Director of the Integrative Research Unit on Social and Individual Development (INSIDE).

Daniela Jopp was trained as a psychologist at Free University of Berlin, Germany, and is now DFG Post-doctoral Research Fellow at the Adult Cognition Lab, Georgia Institute of Technology, Atlanta, USA.

Tom Kirkwood is Professor of Medicine and Director of the Institute for Ageing and Health at Newcastle University, UK.

Franz Kolland is Professor of Sociology at the Faculty of Social Sciences and Humanities at University of Vienna and Head of the Research Group of Social Gerontology.

Ralf Krampe is Professor and Psychologist at the Center for Developmental Psychology, University of Leuven, Belgium.

Harald Künemund is Professor for ageing research and methodology and Director of the Institute of Gerontology at the University of Vechta, Germany.

Giovanni Lamura is Senior Researcher at the Department of Gerontological Research, Italian National Research Centre on Ageing, Ancona, Italy.

Alfons Marcoen was Professor of Developmental Psychology at the Catholic University of Leuven, Belgium.

Lynn McInnes is Senior Lecturer in Psychology and Panel Manager for North East Age Research at Northumbria University, Newcastle upon Tyne, UK.

Heidrun Mollenkopf is a retired Senior Research Associate at the former German Centre for Research on Ageing, University of Heidelberg, Germany.

Gerhard Naegele is Professor of Social Gerontology and Director of the Institute of Gerontology at the University of Dortmund, Germany.

Ann O'Hanlon completed her masters and doctoral degrees in psychology at the University of Southampton. She is now based at the Royal College of Surgeons in Ireland where she coordinates the multisite cross-disciplinary Healthy Ageing Research Programme (HARP). She is also an executive member of the BSG.

Frank Oswald is Senior Research Scientist and Deputy Chair of the Department of Psychological Ageing Research, Institute of Psychology, University of Heidelberg, Germany.

Sheila Peace was trained as a human geographer and is Professor of Social Gerontology in the Faculty of Health and Social Care at the Open University, UK. She is currently a member of the Executive Committee of the BSG and is co-editor of the second and third editions of the textbook Ageing in Society.

Chris Phillipson was trained as a sociologist, is a Professor of Applied Social Studies and Social Gerontology at Keele University, UK, and is a former President of the British Society of Gerontology.

Gregorio Rodriguez Cabrero is Professor of Sociology at the University of Alcalá (Madrid), Spain. He is Director of the Spanish Journal of the Third Sector.

Emmanuelle Tulle is a Lecturer in Sociology in the School of Law and Social Sciences at Glasgow Caledonian University, UK.

Christina Victor is Professor of Social Gerontology and Health Services Research and Head of the School of Health and Social Care at the University of Reading, UK.

Hans-Werner Wahl is Professor of Psychological Ageing Research and Chair of the Department of Psychological Ageing Research, Institute of Psychology, University of Heidelberg, Germany.

Alan Walker is Professor of Social Policy and Social Gerontology at the University of Sheffield, UK, and Director of the UK New Dynamics of Ageing Programme and of the European Research Area in Ageing.

Rudi Westendorp is Professor and Head of the Department of Gerontology and Geriatrics at Leiden University Medical Center, University of Leiden, the Netherlands.

Gerben Westerhof is Associate Professor in the Behavioural Science Institute at the Radboud University Nijmegen, the Netherlands.

Acknowledgements

Every effort has been made to trace all the copyright holders, but if any have been inadvertently overlooked the publishers will be pleased to make the necessary arrangement at the first opportunity.

We are grateful to the following for permission to produce copyright material:
The World Health Organisation for Figures 1.1 and 1.2.
The United Nations for Figure 1.3. The United Nations is the author of the original material.
Table 6.1 is reproduced from Blaxter (1990) *Health and Lifestyles*. London: Routledge.
The Crown Copyright Office for Figure 6.3.
The Centre for Policy on Ageing for Table 10.1, which is reproduced from L. A. Kellaher (2002) Is genuine choice a reality? The range and adequacy of living arrangements available to older people. In: K. Sumner (ed.) *Our Homes, Our Lives: Choice in Later Life Living Arrangements*. London: The Centre for Policy on Ageing and The Housing Corporation.
Professor Carl Eisdorfer for Figure 10.2, which is reproduced from C. Eisdorfer and M. P. Lawton (eds) (1973) *Psychology of Adult Development and Aging*. Washington DC:. American Psychological Association.
The authors F. Oswald and H.-W. Wahl, and Springer Publishing for Figure 10.3.

We would like to thank the contributors for their part in the development and completion of this volume. This enterprise would not have been possible without the support of the British Society of Gerontology, particularly John Vincent and Julia Twigg for their encouragement and support. We would especially like to express our gratitude to Cath Brennand for her hard work and support throughout the last five years. Cath not only managed the work of the four editors but efficiently assured the quality of the finished manuscript, managed the reference data base and assisted in the editing and proof reading.

1

The ageing world

Sheila Peace, Freya Dittmann-Kohli,
Gerben J Westerhof and John Bond

INTRODUCTION

Over the past two centuries a gradual transformation has taken place across the world; the population has been ageing due to the on-going decline in fertility coupled with increasing longevity. This global phenomenon will continue to dominate the twenty-first century even though different world regions will experience demographic change at different rates. It is predicted that in the developed regions of the world, including Europe, a third of the population will be aged 60 years or over by 2050; while in the less developed regions the older population will make up almost 20% (United Nations, 2002). These changes also mask dramatic differences. The developed world will have gradually moved to this position supported by relative socio-economic advantage, while within less developed regions the ageing population will have evolved at a faster rate and within a far less well developed infrastructure. This is not a recent discovery; the Population Division of the United Nations has reported on this trend over the past 50 years (United Nations, 1956; United Nations, 1999) identifying the important need for recognition in language which states that population ageing is 'unprecedented', 'pervasive', 'profound' and 'enduring' (United Nations, 2002, p. xxviii). Gradually the number of older people will exceed the number of younger people, and amongst the older population there will be an increase in the oldest old. These changes will impact upon all aspects of human life – from family composition, living arrangements and social support to economic activity, employment rates and social security – and to transfers between the generations. While the ageing of the population will be unique within every country and characterised by specific cultural experiences where older people will occupy particular roles as leaders, experts, grandparents; the global nature of ageing will also lead to some common experiences that are characterised because of the years lived.

AGEING IN EUROPE

The ageing world reflects the balance between declining fertility and increasing longevity, but as can be seen from Figures 1.1 and 1.2, the balance varies between different parts of the world leading to very different profiles. Dramatically, the figures indicate both the length of time in which European countries have experienced population ageing but also how this continent sits alongside Western Pacific nations in terms of the increase in life expectancy, with the Americas not very far behind. During the second half of the twentieth century, countries represented by the European Union have witnessed not only a decline in fertility – with particularly stark declines in Greece, Spain, Ireland, Poland and Portugal between 1980 and 2000 (OPOCE, 2002) – but perhaps more importantly an increasing life expectancy reflecting improvements in the lives of many Europeans throughout the twentieth century. These trends affect not only the proportion of those living over 65 years of age but more especially the number of the oldest old aged 80 years and over. Indeed, apart from Japan, the EU countries currently have the most pronounced trend in terms of population ageing and this pattern varies between countries. It is expected that by 2015 the average age will have reached 50 years in parts of eastern Germany, northern Spain, central France and northern Italy (Walker, 1999a), and it is estimated that, by 2050, 29.9% of the European population will be over the age of 65, with the proportion of the oldest old (aged 80 years or more) by this time being greatest in Italy (14.1%), Germany (13.6%) and Spain (12.8%) (Eurostat News Release, 2005). However, there is always variation within overall trends and in comparing data across Europe we can see that in some eastern Mediterranean countries the population is ageing at a slightly slower rate (OPOCE, 2002).

Worldwide data show that the majority of older people are women as life expectancy continues to be higher for women than men. In 2000 there were 63 million more women than men aged 60 or older, and this increase was greater within older age groups (see Figure 1.3). This imbalance between the genders in later life is seen throughout Europe.

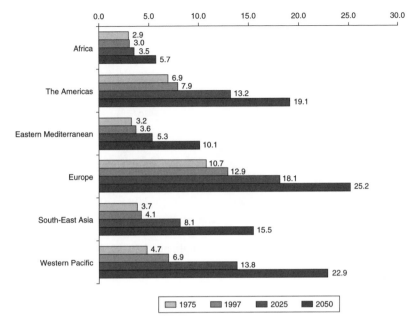

Figure 1.1   Proportion of people aged above 65, (percentage of total population)

Source: WHO World Atlas of Ageing (1998) p. 25

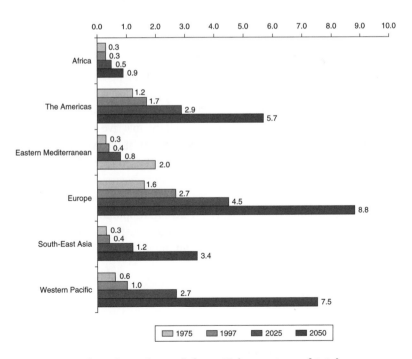

Figure 1.2   Proportion of people aged above 80 (percentage of total population)

Source: WHO World Atlas of Ageing (1998) p. 28

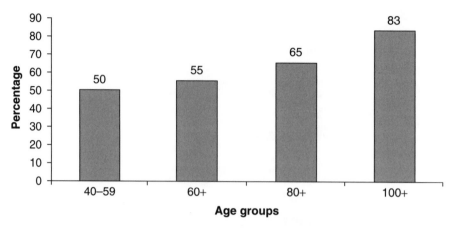

**Figure 1.3   Proportion of women among people aged 40–59, 60+,
80+ and 100+ years, world.**

Source: (United Nations, 2002 p. xxx)

The higher life expectancy of women is particularly prominent within the 25 nations of the European Union where women live on average 6 years longer than men (81.2 years for women compared with 75.1 years for men). As a result of this greater life expectancy, in 2004 women made up 59% of those aged 65 years or more and, as seen in Table 1.1, Latvia had the highest number of women in this age group (68%) and Greece and Cyprus the lowest (55% each).

Given these changes in demography, it is not surprising that Europe is witnessing a projected growth in the old-age dependency ratio (the population aged 65 years and more who are economically inactive as a percentage of the population aged between 15 and 64 who are part of the working population). The ratio rose from 24.9% in 2004 to 52.8% in 2050 for the 25 countries in the European Union (see also Chapter 6).

These statistics provide a brief overview of current demographic trends, but they provide little background to the context in which this population is ageing – people who form different cohorts and different generations. To provide this backcloth first we need to establish the parameters for defining Europe and its characteristics.

IDENTIFYING EUROPE

The context and changing nature of Europe can be defined in many ways. Here, attention is given to the natural and material environment; to the cultural mix; to the

Table 1.1 Percentage of women among those 65 years or more in 2004.

	Life expectancy at birth 2004[a]		Share of women among those aged 65 years or more, 2004	Fertility rate 2004	Women's age at first child	
	Women	Men			1994	2004[b]
EU25	**81.2**	**75.1**	**59.3**	**1.50**	**26.8**	**28.2**
Belgium	81.7	75.9	58.8	1.64	26.9	27.6
Czech Republic	79.2	72.6	61.3	1.22	22.9	26.3
Denmark	80.1	75.4	57.8	1.78	27.2	28.4
Germany	82.1	76.5	60.3	1.36	27.3	28.8
Estonia	76.9	66.0	67.0	1.40	23.4	24.6
Greece	81.4	76.6	55.3	1.29	26.4	27.9
Spain	83.8	77.2	57.8	1.32	28.1	29.2
France	83.8	76.7	59.2	1.90	27.9	28.4
Ireland	81.2	76.4	56.5	1.99	27.1	28.0
Italy	82.5	76.8	58.8	1.33	27.7	28.3
Cyprus	81.7	76.6	55.3	1.49	25.2	27.2
Latvia	76.2	65.9	67.7	1.24	23.3	24.7
Lithuania	77.7	66.3	65.6	1.26	23.0	24.8
Luxembourg	82.2	76.0	59.3	1.71	27.8	28.7
Hungary	77.2	68.7	63.2	1.28	23.6	26.3
Malta	80.7	76.7	58.0	1.37	NA	NA
Netherlands	81.4	76.9	58.4	1.73	28.2	28.9
Austria	82.1	76.4	61.4	1.42	25.4	27.0
Poland	79.2	70.6	62.1	1.23	23.6	25.5
Portugal	81.4	74.9	58.2	1.40	25.6	27.1
Slovenia	80.7	73.5	62.6	1.25	24.6	27.5
Slovakia	78.0	70.3	62.4	1.24	22.8	25.3
Finland	82.2	75.3	60.9	1.80	26.9	27.8
Sweden	82.6	78.3	57.2	1.75	27.1	28.6
United Kingdom	80.7	76.2	57.7	1.74	28.2	29.7

Some of the data are estimations.
NA: Data not available.
[a]2003: EU25, Belgium, Estonia, Italy, Malta, United Kingdom.
[b]1997: Belgium, 2002: Estonia, Greece, Spain.
Source: Eurostat News Release (2006).

political boundaries, reflecting some of the tensions that exist between historical conflict and economic development; and finally to unification and diversity.

Natural and material Europe

The great Eurasian land mass has commonly been defined as stretching from the Arctic Ocean in the north and the Scandinavian peninsula to the Atlantic Ocean in the west where the North Sea provides the link to the United Kingdom and Eire, to the Mediterranean Sea and Strait of Gibraltar which separate southern European countries from the African continent, and on to the eastern markers of the Urals, the Ural River and the Caspian Sea which have conventionally separated Europe from Asia. This is a continent of great diversity in terms of climate, the dominance of the Alpine mountain chain, and the human development of fertile plains alongside its central river systems from the Volga to the Danube to the Rhine to the Thames.

It can be seen geographically as up to fifty countries that can be divided into a number of regions – eastern Europe, south-east Europe, central Europe, southern Europe, western Europe, Scandinavia and the British Isles/UK – ranging across a vast mix of rural and urban landscapes. There are 18 cities having populations exceeding one million inhabitants, and areas of dense population are seen in contrast to the rural hinterland of the northern continent (Eurostat News Release, 2004). Already the variation in rural and urban living can lead to lifestyles that can be described as more peasant-like or more metropolitan while at the same time there are also cultural stereotypes attached to regions known as Mediterranean, Scandinavian or Alpine. Given this breadth, is there a European culture?

Cultural Europe

Diversity is a central part of European culture. History has shown that it has been the scene of kingdoms and empires that have moved through periods of conflict and stability to create more cohesive nation states. Whilst the Greek and the Roman civilisations have influenced and underpinned the development of cultural traditions through language, literature and political processes and structures, adoption of the Christian religion has also been central both to periods of conflict and the regional adoption of particular religious ideologies. Whilst Roman Catholicism is the chief religion of southern and western European countries, Protestantism is dominant in the UK, Scandinavian countries and parts of northern Europe. But these are not the only orthodoxies; the Orthodox Eastern Church predominates in eastern and south-eastern Europe, and the Muslim faith is central to parts of the Balkan Peninsula and Transcaucasia. Indeed, whereas certain religions may be dominant in particular areas, migration has also led to the spread of a variety of religious groups especially within urban and metropolitan centres.

Across Europe national identities may commonly involve particular religious traditions, but the impact of recent political history also nurtures aspects of identity formation, and politics and religion are often intertwined. During the twentieth century, Europe not only witnessed two world wars but also saw the rise and demise of two ideological blocs, for and against communism, in what was known as the 'cold war'. Here opposition was seen between western European countries influenced by the USA in opposition to communist countries of eastern Europe dominated by the USSR. In more recent times the breaking-up of the Soviet bloc in the early 1990s led to both the democratisation of former communist countries and to ethnic nationalism within the region of the former Yugoslavia. Consequently, a number of countries have been transformed from states with centralised economies towards more market-based economies – countries such as Estonia, Latvia, Lithuania, Slovakia and Slovenia, where the suppressed national cultures are now becoming more visible.

Stability, continuity and change are key factors when defining the context of Europe. International migration has been a dominant experience across the continent for a number of centuries. People have moved not only between countries but also between continents. For different nations this can be seen as part of both an historic colonial past and a recent past; whilst for individuals and groups emigration may have been prompted by the desire for asylum, employment and an improved quality of life. Such experience gives the European continent a very different historical and cultural profile from that of younger continents.

Migration patterns are also subject to on-going development influenced by political, economic and demographic trends. Warnes *et al.* (2004, p. 311), commenting on the European experience, says:

> Only in the last half-century has the net movement reversed, and since the 1980s another radical change has occurred: Greece, southern Italy, Spain and Portugal, which through most of the twentieth century were regions of rural depopulation and emigration to northern Europe, the Americas and Australia, have become regions of return migration and of immigration from eastern Europe and other continents (Fonseca et al., 2002; King, 2002).

So, in contrast to the national unity of the states in North America, cultural diversity both within and between countries in Europe is historic and on-going. Nevertheless, political unity between many European countries has been seen by some as an advantage and a strength.

Political boundaries

A period of conflict from the late nineteenth century through to the mid twentieth century brought a number of western European political leaders to consider that stability and peace could be secured only through developing economic and political unity. This led to the setting up of the European Coal and Steel Community (ECSC) in 1951 with six members – Belgium, West Germany, Luxembourg, France, Italy and the Netherlands. The success of the ECSC led them to sign the Treaties of Rome in 1957 establishing the European Atomic Energy Community (EURATOM) and the European Economic Community (EEC) through which they removed trade barriers between them and formed a 'common market'. In 1967 these three institutions merged into a single Commission establishing the European Parliament, leading to direct elections for members from each country in 1979 (see Box 1.1).

Box 1.1   The development of the European Union

European Commission (EC) 1967

- The EC was formed from a merger of the European Economic Community (Common Market); the European Coal and Steel Community, and the European Atomic Energy Community (EURATOM).
- Denmark, Ireland and UK join in 1973; Greece joins in 1981; Spain, Portugal join in 1986.

Treaty of Maastricht, 1992 creates the European Union, 1 November 1993

- Belgium (EUR), Denmark, France (EUR), Germany (EUR), Greece (EUR), Ireland (EUR), Italy (EUR), Luxembourg (EUR) the Netherlands (EUR), Portugal (EUR), Spain (EUR), United Kingdom of Great Britain and Northern Ireland.

1 January 1995

- Austria (EUR), Finland (EUR) and Sweden join in 1995.
- Turkey is considered as a candidate country in 1999.

Treaty of Nice, 2003, establishes new rules governing size and ways of working for EU institutions.

1 May 2004

- Ten new countries join the EU to become the EU-25.
- Cyprus (Greek part), Czech Republic, Estonia, Hungary, Latvia, Lithuania, Malta, Poland, Slovakia, Slovenia.
- Croatia is accepted as a candidate country in 2004.
- Bulgaria and Romania to join the EU in 2007.

(EUR) Countries currently adopting the European currency

Source: Europa (2006)

New forms of co-operation concerning defence and inter-governmental co-operation between member states were introduced through the Treaty of Maastricht in 1992, leading to the creation of the European Union (EU). In 1993, 12 nation states were united – growing to 15 in 1995 – and the development of economic and political integration has led to a wide range of common policies from agriculture to consumer affairs, from energy to transport, each leading to on-going debate concerning the development of national and European policy. Removing barriers to trade between the nations should lead to a 'common market' in which goods, services, people and capital can move freely. Throughout the 1990s this system has evolved, developing greater freedom of movement and greater mobility for EU citizens.

Alongside these developments, 1992 also saw the introduction of a single European currency managed by the European Central Bank. This was adopted by

12 of the 15 countries to replace their national currencies (Sweden, the UK and Denmark did not adopt the euro). The development of monetary union comes at a time when European unity is also growing through the membership of many eastern European countries and there have been moves towards establishing a new EU constitution (Europa, 2006). Consideration of a future for the EU-25 and beyond to include an ever wider spread of culturally diverse nations leads to a recognition of the contrasts that will emerge in terms of wealth and welfare, national ideology, common security, foreign policy, and the tensions that will exist between nationalism and federalism.

SOME CRUCIAL QUESTIONS

Above we have outlined some of the features of the European context in which individual and population ageing has occurred. But looking at these data raises some crucial questions concerning feminisation, diversity and ageism, and how the ageing individual captures his or her own sense of the life course within such diverse societies. It is to these issues that we now turn briefly, before outlining how this text will approach the topic – ageing in society.

Feminisation

Whilst we can see that the increased life expectancy of women has made later life more of a women's world than a man's, the profile of the ageing population is changing leading to different roles and relationships (Arber et al., 2003). In some European countries the difference in life expectancy between women and men is narrowing (Barford et al., 2006) and it is now becoming more common for people to spend longer periods of time as couples from late middle age into older ages. In contrast, it is the world of the oldest old that is most likely to be feminised. The present generations of older women may more commonly experience aspects of deprivation; indeed the feminisation of later life has led to a widespread attitude to older women of being socially invisible and of leading a tucked-away life of little impact to public life.

However, cultural variation exists in terms of lifestyles both within and between regions of Europe. For example, there are differences in the living arrangements between those living in southern, middle and northern Europe and those living in former communist countries and western Europe. In both southern and eastern European countries, living with family members is more common for older people of both genders (Iacovou, 2000). In many other parts of Europe very old women are increasingly living alone at the end of life, often spending their latter days in long-term residential care. Cultural factors will impact upon living arrangements, and the development of different forms of housing and care – such as co-housing, extra-care housing, home sharing – may attract some older women willing to move or share accommodation later in life (Peace and Holland, 2001b). However, the need for long-term care or end-of-life care will still remain and differences in life expectancy will continue to make this particularly a women's issue while many women will still continue to care for older men.

Increasingly, younger generations of older women are becoming more aware of their position within the older population and more conscious of a need to voice their concerns and convey skills and expertise across the generations (Bernard *et al.*, 2000; OWN Europe, 2006). The everyday lives of older men and women may vary enormously. Immense change in family life, educational status, employment patterns, and financial security within different European countries has influenced identity formation and the experience of everyday life. Many women in late middle age already perceive themselves as not being inferior, less able, or of less worth than men – obtaining visible positions in the professions, in science, in the mass media and in political and economic life. This has encouraged them to claim and take up leadership roles, and to use their particular outlook on interpersonal relations, human development, and norms and values to influence and develop a more humane society. In the future change may be seen across cultural groups; for example, the lives of older Muslim women in Europe may increase the will to support a female identity that is free, able and self-determined.

Diversity

Of course, gender forms only one aspect of diversity and it is important to reflect on these issues when considering the situation of older migrants in Europe – groups whose diversity adds to the complexity of the ageing population (Warnes *et al.*, 2004). In particular, two groups are recognised: first, the millions of economic migrants (guest workers), often with colonial links, who have moved into and across Europe during the twentieth century, especially after the Second World War (Warnes *et al.*, 2004). These are people from the Caribbean, the Indian subcontinent, north Africa, and east Asia who have subsequently 'aged in place' (Burholt, 2004). Unlike their host populations, some (but not all) members of these groups often had little education and took low-paid manual work which could lead them to experience a life of disadvantage. In later life their situation is complex for they may suffer from a cumulative disadvantage: poor language skills, incomplete work history leading to a lack of eligibility for health and welfare services, diverse caring responsibilities; financial insecurity, social isolation or lack of immediate kin or cultural group. Consequently, they may be subject to double and triple jeopardy through issues associated with age, gender and ethnicity.

In the UK, for example, the 2001 Census data show that people from black and minority ethnic groups have a younger age structure than the white population. The white population has over 16% of people aged 65 or over compared with 9% of the Black Caribbean population who were part of the first large-scale migration to Britain during the 1950s. As Figure 1.4 shows, other groups have a different profile reflecting their immigration to the country throughout the twentieth century.

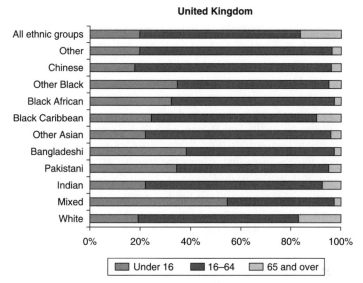

Figure 1.4   Age distribution in the United Kingdom: by ethnic group 2001/02

Source: National Statistics, 2002

In contrast, the other group that is expanding rapidly in Europe are northern Europeans, in their fifties or sixties, who permanently or seasonally migrate to southern Europe. This group are predominantly property owners with occupational pensions who are able to finance their moves to a warmer climate and take advantage of technological, political and economic changes such as low-cost transport, and on-line banking, purchasing and shopping (Warnes, 2001). This group demonstrate an ability to support kin financially at a distance and to offer social and emotional support; they are also seen as willing to move again through return migration to their country of origin, which may be due to a need for health and welfare services, and end-of-life care.

Warnes also identifies under-researched migrant groups, including return labour migrants moving from northern to southern Europe or from Britain to Ireland (Rodriguez *et al.*, 2002), and those older Europeans moving internationally to live near or with relatives across the world as well as within Europe. Commenting on people receiving their pensions in a different country, Warnes (2004, p. 312) states:

> There are a third more British pensioners in Germany than in Cyprus, Gibraltar, Greece, Malta and Portugal put together, while among German pensioners there are more in Switzerland and in Austria than in Spain or in Italy, Portugal and Greece combined.

What is obvious from this comment is the cultural diversity of older people across Europe (indicative of the overall demography). In taking this analysis further, Warnes *et al.* (2004) offer a typology of older migrants highlighting strengths and weaknesses in terms of 'human capital', indicating potential areas of resource and needs in terms of finance, health, emotional support and long-term care, and demonstrating the potential for inter-generational involvement.

Ageism

In recognising the strengths and weaknesses of various groups of older people we are also drawn to consider how these attributes may be influenced by the continuing pervasive ageism that affects the lives of all. Discrimination towards people because of their age is seen most explicitly in terms of definitions of age for pensions and state benefits and the field of employment where jobs have been defined in terms of a young market despite the need to use the skills of the older workforce (Taylor, 2003). Recognition of a range of issues has led the concept of age discrimination to be acknowledged formally. In May 2001, the National Service Framework for Older People was introduced in Britain where the first standard aims 'to ensure that older people are never unfairly discriminated against in accessing NHS and social care services as a result of their age' (Department of Health, 2001). In the EU, the European Council Directive 2000/78/EC (27 November 2000) has established a framework for equal treatment in employment and occupation which recognises age alongside gender, sexual orientation, race, disability, religion or belief as potential grounds for discrimination. The member states of the EU had until 2006 to develop national law relating to this directive. In the UK, the Equality Act 2006 underpins the establishment of the Commission for Equality and Human Rights (CEHR) from October 2007 (CEHR, 2006). This Commission will bring together the work of three existing commissions, the Equal Opportunities Commission (EOC), the Commission for Racial Equality (CRE) and the Disability Rights Commission (DRC), and for the first time will also provide a national body tackling age discrimination.

However, the pervasive nature of ageism is not clear-cut (Bytheway, 1995) and more likely to be implicit than explicit; it is found in the limitations of negative attitudes, different forms of exclusion, and the harm caused by judgements made against people because of their age that reflects how both individuals and society feel about getting older – a fear of ageing (see Chapters 6 and 11). Research has begun to examine the nature and breadth of ageism throughout society. In the UK, the Research on Age Discrimination (ROAD) project, a partnership between Help the Aged and the Open University, is beginning to identify the diversity of situations in which discrimination appears from hairdressing to service delivery, from access to public toilets to 'what to wear' – facets of everyday life (Open University and Help the Aged, 2006). In Europe, the Alliance for Health and the Future has undertaken research in eight countries identifying examples of age discrimination, from health and social care, to employment, to pensions and financial services, and in areas of public participation, education and leisure (Alliance for Health and the Future, 2006). These studies are beginning to show that finding ways to develop a more age-inclusive society needs to acknowledge the impact of multiple discrimination that can jeopardise the lives of many older people.

The ageing individual

When thinking of factors that lead to forms of exclusion, the vulnerability of the individual to being seen as a frail person in need of support and care can be central. Our experience of the lifecourse is based on time within a given society and for the ageing population the periods spent in middle age and third age are seen to be expanding, developing and changing. We could argue that as long as someone can live independently many aspects of society may be available to them. We know that, in the main, older people wish to live in their own homes within the community even though some people may move to be with children. How far people wish to remain integrated and involved with the people and place in which they live is very much an individual decision although technological development may allow for greater accessibility and assistive living. It is only a small proportion of older people who decide to live within age-segregated housing communities and at present this decision is made by only certain people (Croucher *et al.*, 2006). In the main, people wish to live in settings that are familiar in some way and which say something about their own identity and the society in which they live.

Increasing life expectancy will also lead to greater diversity amongst the very old and the fourth age should not be seen as just one of decline. This is a population of survivors demonstrating great strengths which continues to be dominated by older women. Those with different levels of vulnerability and frailty will range from those who have lived with on-going chronic physical health conditions to those who are beset with mental health problems. Although they may come to need an increasing level of care, how they are treated is perhaps the most decisive issue and the ultimate test of ageism for many people having to face end-of-life care within places that become institutionalised and no longer person-centred.

WAYS FORWARD

It is with the views of the ageing individual in mind that we move on to consider how this text addresses issues raised. However, first it will have been recognised that our brief has been not only to centre on the ageing world – and in particular the lives of older people living across the European continent – but also more importantly to bring together European authors – biological and social scientists with an interest in ageing and later life. All of the chapters involve both British and European authors who have been able to develop discussions incorporating a wide range of research and experience.

The topic is complex, multidisciplinary and holistic and it is through these terms that we embrace the whole person. We are concerned not only with experiences of older people but with ageing as a process. Together these two perspectives allow us to capture the complexities of the individual within society. Consequently, there is a need for a text which at a primary level allows the reader to engage with specific disciplines in order to provide a baseline for going on to develop further complexity. For this reason the book is divided into two parts, the aim being for the reader to consider all chapters within Part One before reading the chapters in Part Two. The first part consists of five chapters, including this introduction. Chapters 2, 3 and 4 allow the reader to focus clearly on particular disciplinary approaches to studying ageing: biological, psychological and sociological. Here we consider why and how we age, enabling the reader to integrate the differing perspectives.

Chapter 5 offers a different baseline for guiding the reader through the second part of the text by focusing on the evidence base and the variety of research methods, both quantitative and qualitative, that are commonly used in gerontology. It is a multidisciplinary subject in which different disciplines engage with data through populations, samples, methods and forms of analysis which are more or less embracing of positivism, more or less theoretically driven, and more or less open to subjective interpretation of meaning by both researcher and researched. In recent years the complexity of human ageing seen through the individual within society has led researchers to use multi-method approaches to research which have led to the triangulation of data, allowing for conflict as well as indefinite triangulation to occur. The discussion of methodology is essential to understanding the detailed analysis to follow.

In the second part of the book the aim has been to do two things: first, that every chapter should offer a unique in-depth contribution to the discussion of its topic; and second, that the chapters be cumulative and that there be a sequence to the way in which topics have been chosen and ordered. Chapters 6–10 consider specific aspects of the lives of older people as a group – their health, financial security, work, personal relationships and the context in which they live. The research discussed draws upon both national and international survey data as well as more detailed ethnographic material sometimes underpinned by particular theoretical debates which allow the authors to consider the impact on individual ageing through a specific lens. However, this more individualistic view is further developed in Chapters 11–13 where a more psychological perspective unpacks the ageing world in more depth.

If read as a whole, this text should enable the reader to undertake a journey and to arrive at a point where it is possible to look forward to how the ageing individual within the context of European society will face the future. Our own view of how we see the future of ageing is presented in Chapter 14.

2

The biology of ageing

Rudi G. J. Westendorp and
Thomas B. L. Kirkwood

INTRODUCTION

Although human ageing has many dimensions, at its heart it is a biological process that we share with a very broad range of animal species. If we are to understand ageing we must therefore comprehend at least the broad principles of its biology, since these provide the fundamental matrix upon which social and other factors are based. There is a particular importance in addressing the biology of ageing now, at a time when many preconceptions about the ageing process, such as that it is an essentially fixed, ineluctable part of our biological make-up, are being challenged. This challenge is coming from two directions. First, the continuing increases in life expectancy (Oeppen and Vaupel, 2002) show that – contrary to all predictions – life expectancy has not settled at some ceiling imposed by genetic programming. Second, new biological understanding of the basic mechanisms of ageing reveal that the process is intrinsically more malleable than most of us have yet appreciated (Kirkwood, 2005).

In this chapter we make a brief survey of some of the key features of the biology of ageing, looking at why and how we age, at the blend between genetic and non-genetic factors influencing longevity, and at the relationship between normal ageing and disease. We conclude with a brief discussion of the implications of these features for the future of human ageing.

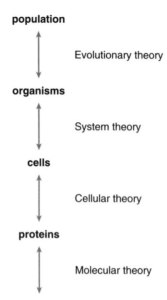

population

Evolutionary theory

organisms

System theory

cells

Cellular theory

proteins

Molecular theory

Figure 2.1   Ageing needs to be understood at a hierarchy of biological levels

From a biological perspective ageing is extremely complicated, affecting the functions of the body at all levels, from molecules to populations (see Figure 2.1). In order to understand ageing, its effects at all of these levels need to be understood.

WHY DO WE AGE?

Our species adapts to its environment. This notion not only underlies the brilliant insights of nineteenth-century Darwinian thinking, which have shaped our knowledge of why we are as we are, but it is an ongoing reality that can be observed in current populations around the world. Climates in polar and tropical regions are very different, and the people who survive there have adapted to those extreme environments. Tens of thousands of years and thousands of generations have passed since *Homo sapiens* emerged as a species in the middle of Africa and began its migration to the rest of the world. The mechanism underlying this success has been the continual drive, underpinned by natural selection, to survive even under the most adverse of conditions.

From the Darwinian point of view we have no difficulty in understanding the biology of birth, development and reproduction. However, it is much harder to understand the later end of the lifespan – why we become frail, diseased and more likely to die as we grow older (see Figure 2.2). Is such deterioration necessary, is

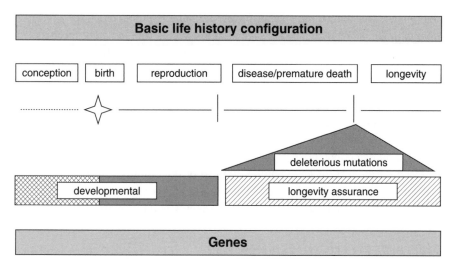

Figure 2.2   Genetic architecture of the human life history

it inevitable? For example, why do we become less able to get around, more likely to fall, and more likely to die from the post-operative complications of a hip fracture? What is it about the passage of time that renders older cells and organs more vulnerable to disease? Can the clues to these puzzles be found in the context of our adaptation to the environment?

The idea that natural selection has played its part in shaping our ageing process is reinforced by the evidence that ageing and longevity are influenced by genes (Finch and Tanzi, 1997). First, the lifespans of human monozygotic twin pairs are statistically more similar than lifespans of dizygotic twins, pointing clearly to a role for genetics. Second, there are significant differences in lifespan between different genetically inbred strains of any given laboratory animal, such as the mouse. Third, studies of simple organisms like fruit flies, nematode worms and yeast have identified gene mutations that affect duration of life. However, although genes influence longevity, it has also been shown that genes account for only about 25% of the variance in human lifespan (Finch and Tanzi, 1997; Cournil and Kirkwood, 2001). We need to look rather carefully at the evolutionary logic that might have shaped the genetic component of ageing, weak as the latter is.

Lack of an evolutionary programme for ageing

Many adhere to the view, often implicitly assumed, that ageing and death are simply the terminal phase of the developmental process, driven by genes like early development. If pressed to explain why it should be so, this notion is often justified on the grounds that ageing evolved as some kind of evolutionary necessity – to clear older generations out of the way as a form of inbuilt population control. However, there is in fact scant evidence that ageing plays such a role in nature, or that such an evolutionary pressure could have worked. The reason is simple. Animals in nature die young. Only rarely do they survive long enough to reveal significant ageing. Out of a population of newborn wild mice, for example, nine out of ten of them will be dead before 10 months even though half of the same animals reared in captivity would still be alive at 2 years (Austad, 1997). Thus, ageing in mice is seen only in protected environments, and a similar statement would have applied to primitive human populations, before the advent of civilisation.

Based on the lack of an evolutionary need or opportunity to evolve genes for ageing, we are required to look elsewhere than strict genetic programming for an understanding of the genetic contribution to ageing and longevity.

Genes with late deleterious effects

The first evolutionary scenario that is not founded on the idea of a programme explained ageing through the accumulation of late-acting deleterious germ-line mutations. Medawar (1952) reasoned that mutations with late age-specific effects are subject to weaker selection than mutations with early age-specific effects, since the proportion of individuals alive must decline with increasing age *even if there is no intrinsic increase in the tendency to die.* Phrased otherwise, mortality due to extrinsic causes is a sufficient explanation why only a small proportion of the original birth cohort survives until older age. Thus, in the course of evolution there has been the opportunity for random accumulation of late-acting deleterious mutations in the genome. In humans, the theory suggests, these deleterious genes have become apparent in developed countries at a time when mortality at young age has largely disappeared, and large proportions of the population do survive up to ages far beyond those that would have been common among our ancestors. This is the so-called 'demographic transition'. As an example of a gene with a late-acting deleterious effect, Medawar cited the case of the gene for Huntington's chorea, a genetically induced fatal neurodegenerative condition which does not usually become apparent until a person is past reproductive age, putting the gene effectively beyond the reach of natural selection. Medawar's concept is now known as the 'mutation accumulation' theory.

A second scenario, suggested by Williams (1957), is also founded on the idea of late deleterious gene effects but introduces the idea of trade-offs. A gene with a beneficial effect on fitness early in life would be selected for, even if the same gene produced detrimental effects on fitness late in life. As an example, Williams cited a hypothetical gene regulating calcium deposition which might favour bone growth during development but lead to calcification of the arteries in later life. Williams' concept is now known as 'antagonistic pleiotropy' (pleiotropy referring to the property of a gene that has different effects in different contexts). Another example is that heterozygote carriers of the cystic fibrosis gene have a selective advantage of resistance to cholera but render the carriers at risk of disabling pulmonary and gastrointestinal disease later in life (Gabriel *et al.*, 1994)

Although the mutation accumulation and antagonistic pleiotropy concepts have played an important role in shaping evolutionary thinking about ageing, tests of the actions of mutation accumulation have largely proved negative (Kirkwood and Austad, 2000), while verified instances of individual genes with antagonistically pleiotropic effects remain few in number (Leroi *et al.*, 2005).

The disposable soma theory

Another approach to explaining evolution of ageing comes from considering the logic of how much organisms should be expected to invest in maintenance and repair systems that underpin bodily survival. In spite of a formidable array of survival mechanisms, most species appear not to be programmed well enough to last indefinitely. The key to understanding why this should be so, and what governs how long a survival period should be catered for, comes from looking once more at the data from survival patterns in wild populations. If 90% of wild mice are dead by 10 months, any investment in programming for survival much beyond this point can benefit at most 10% of the population. This immediately suggests that there will be little evolutionary advantage in programming long-term survival capacity into a mouse. The argument is further strengthened when we observe that nearly all of the survival mechanisms required by the mouse to combat intrinsic deterioration (DNA damage, protein oxidation, etc.) require metabolic resources. Metabolic resources are scarce, as evidenced by the fact that the major cause of mortality for wild mice is cold due to insufficient energy to maintain body temperature. From a Darwinian point of view, the mouse will benefit more from investing any spare resource into thermogenesis or reproduction than into better DNA repair capacity than it needs.

This concept, with its explicit focus on evolution of optimal levels of cell maintenance, is termed the 'disposable soma theory' (Kirkwood, 1977, 1997). In essence, the investments in durability and maintenance of somatic (non-reproductive) tissues are predicted to be sufficient to keep the body in good repair through the normal expectation of life in the wild environment, with some measure of reserve capacity. Thus, it makes sense that mice (with 90% mortality by 10 months) have intrinsic lifespans of around three years, while humans (who probably experienced something like 90% mortality by age 50 in our ancestral environment) have intrinsic lifespans limited to about 100 years. The distinction between somatic and reproductive tissues is important because the reproductive cell lineage, or germ line, must be maintained at a level that preserves viability across the generations, whereas the soma needs only to support the survival of a single generation. As far as is known, all species that have a clear distinction between soma and germ line undergo somatic senescence while animals that do not show senescence, such as the freshwater Hydra, have germ cells distributed throughout their structure (Martinez, 1998).

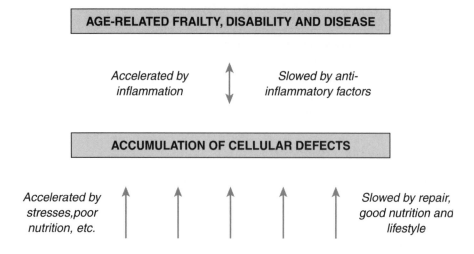

Figure 2.3   Molecular damage and ageing

Source: adapted from Kirkwood (2005)

HOW AGEING IS CAUSED

The evolutionary explanation of ageing, particularly in the form of the disposable soma theory, provides a bridge between understanding not only why ageing occurs but also how ageing is caused in molecular and cellular terms. In essence, it predicts that ageing is nothing more nor less than the gradual, lifelong accumulation of subtle faults in the cells and organs of the body. These faults, as we shall see in a later section, arise from many causes and affect many targets. Faults arise on a continual basis and most are put right. However, since there has been insufficient selection to evolve higher efficiency of repair, some slip through the net. Thus, although the driving force in ageing is the accumulation of damage, genetic regulation plays its part through evolving how hard the brakes are put on this accumulation by investing effort in maintenance and repair.

The defects that cause ageing start to arise very early in life, probably even *in utero*, but in the early years both the fraction of affected cells and the average burden of damage per affected cell are low. However, over time the faults increase, resulting eventually in age-related functional impairment of tissues and organs (see Figure 2.3). This view of the ageing process makes clear the life-course nature of the underlying mechanisms. Ageing is a continuous process, starting early and developing gradually, instead of being a distinct phase that begins in middle to late life. The view also helps us to re-examine the sometimes controversial relationship between 'normal ageing' and age-related disease (see Box 2.1).

Box 2.1   Understanding the complex causes of normal ageing and its intrinsic variability

A key question in the life science perspective on ageing is whether it is meaningful to think of a 'normal' ageing process, as distinct from the collection of age-related disorders and diseases with which the conventional medical model has been primarily concerned. We examine this question in the light of the distinction between 'component causes' and 'sufficient causes' as originally developed by Rothman (1976). Here, we apply the distinction between component and sufficient causes to describe the ageing process (Izaks and Westendorp, 2003).

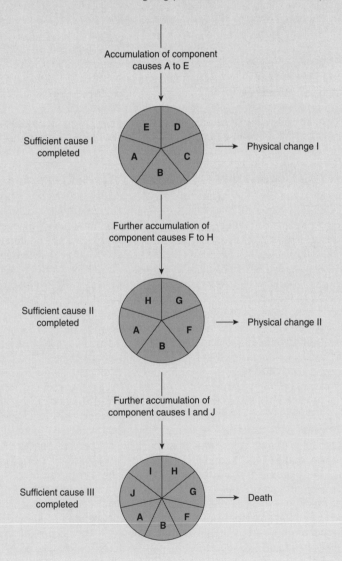

(Continued)

(Continued)

A cause is defined by Rothman as an event or a state of nature that initiates or permits a sequence of events, which results in an effect. A cause is considered 'sufficient' if it inevitably produces the effect. However, most causes of relevance in medicine are not sufficient but are merely 'components' of a sufficient cause. A component cause thus reflects what is commonly called a risk factor. The principle is that a specific combination of component causes must be present before a sufficient cause is assembled, resulting in an 'effect' or physical change (see figure first circle).

A particular effect can be caused by different combinations of component causes. Each combination of component causes then constitutes a different sufficient cause. For example, the combination of hypertension, smoking, hypercholesterolaemia, sedentary lifestyle and family predisposition is a sufficient cause of atherosclerosis. Another sufficient cause, however, might be the combination of hypertension, hypercholesterolaemia, stress, inflammation and family predisposition. These different sufficient causes of atherosclerosis have some components in common – hypertension and family predisposition – but have other components that are different. On the other hand, sometimes the same component cause may contribute to different sufficient causes, resulting in different effects. When this happens, it is found that different diseases share the same risk factors. For example, smoking is a component cause not only of atherosclerosis but also of lung cancer. It is the specific combination with other component causes that determines which effect becomes manifest.

When a component cause is present, some of the other component causes that are necessary to complete a sufficient cause may be lacking. However, over time the missing component causes can develop, and the completion of a sufficient cause will then result in a physical change. It is this gradual accumulation of component causes over a lifetime that provides a model to understand the physical changes that occur with ageing. The more component causes that have accumulated during life, the more sufficient causes will be completed, and the more effects (physical changes) seen (see figure). Since there may often be an element of chance in the occurrence of specific component causes, this model helps us to understand the diversity of the physical manifestations of ageing, even though the body may be susceptible to the same set of component causes being triggered.

Death from old age can be explained by similar reasoning. Death is an effect that has several sufficient causes. Since their pathophysiology is complex, each of the sufficient causes of death consists of a large number of component causes. At puberty, when mortality risk is lowest, only a few component causes are present. With increasing age, more component causes will have accumulated. The sufficient causes that together constitute the different potential causes of death are built up step by step throughout life. Every new component cause increases the chance that one of the sufficient causes is completed. This model, which has some formal similarity with the ideas of reliability engineering in the mechanical sciences, explains the increased mortality risk in advanced age that is the hallmark of ageing.

Some older people are characterised by frailty, with a high risk of becoming dependent or of dying. People who are frail have a reduced reserve capacity because many physiological functions decline with increasing age. In this situation, one single factor can trigger a cascade of events leading to a deterioration of physical functions and eventually death. For example, if an older person becomes bedridden due to a femoral fracture, the disease course may

(Continued)

(Continued)

subsequently be complicated by a urinary tract infection and a delirium, followed by, pressure ulcers, septicaemia and finally by death. The cascade of adverse events occurs easily because a frail older person may have numerous almost-complete sufficient causes, with several of these almost-complete sufficient causes having missing components in common. In these circumstances, the development of a new component cause may complete a number of sufficient causes, so that several events occur together. Furthermore, the first sufficient cause to be completed may initiate an event that is itself a component cause of another almost-complete sufficient cause. Thus a run of events may follow each other in a kind of 'domino-effect' process.

In a clinical context, it often makes sense to try to draw a distinction between normal ageing and disease, since this may have implications for treatment. However, if our aim is to understand the mechanisms responsible for age-related conditions, such a distinction can obscure what is really going on. The majority of chronic, degenerative conditions, such as dementia, osteoporosis and osteoarthritis, involve the progressive accumulation of specific types of cellular and molecular lesions. Since the ageing process, as we have seen, is caused by the general accumulation of such lesions, there may be much greater overlap between the causative pathways leading to normal ageing and age-related diseases than has hitherto been recognised. In the case of osteoporosis, for example, progressive bone loss from the late twenties onwards is the norm. Whether an individual reaches a critically low bone density, making him or her highly susceptible to fracture, is governed by how much bone mass there was to start with and by the individual's rate of bone loss. The process that leads eventually to osteoporosis is thus entirely 'normal', but what distinguishes whether or not this process results in an overtly pathological outcome is a range of moderating factors. In the case of Alzheimer's disease, most people above age 70 have extensive cortical amyloid plaques and neurofibrillary tangles (the so-called 'hallmarks' of classic Alzheimer's disease) even though they may show no evidence of major cognitive decline (Esiri *et al.*, 2001). In this instance, what determines whether or not the diagnosis of Alzheimer's disease is called for may be not so much the presence of lesions as which specific targets are affected.

Mechanisms of cellular damage

Ageing is highly complex, involving multiple mechanisms at different levels. Much recent evidence suggests that an important theme linking several different kinds of damage is the action of reactive oxygen species (ROS; also known as 'free radicals') which are produced as by-products of the body's essential use of oxygen to produce cellular energy (Martin *et al.*, 1996; von Zglinicki *et al.*, 2001). Of particular significance are the contributions of ROS-induced damage to cellular

DNA through (i) damage to the chromosomal DNA of the cell nucleus resulting in impaired gene function, (ii) damage to telomeres – the protective DNA structures that appear to 'cap' the ends of chromosomes (analogous to the plastic tips of shoelaces), and (iii) damage to the DNA that exists within the cell's energy-generating organelles, the mitochondria, resulting in impaired energy production.

Damage to DNA is particularly likely to play a role in the lifelong accumulation of molecular damage within cells, since damage to DNA can readily result in permanent alteration of the cell's DNA sequence. Cells are subject to mutation all the time, both through errors that may become fixed when cells divide and as a result of ROS-induced damage which can occur at any time. Numerous studies have reported age-related increases in somatic mutation and other forms of DNA damage, and suggested that an important determinant DNA of the rate of ageing at the cell and molecular level is the capacity for DNA repair (Promislow, 1994; Burkle *et al.*, 2002).

Although DNA damage may take many forms, it is estimated that oxidative damage is among the most important, accounting for large numbers of oxidative hits per cell per day. A key player in the immediate cellular response to ROS-induced DNA damage is the enzyme poly(ADP-ribose) polymerase (PARP). Grube and Bürkle (1992) discovered a strong, positive correlation of PARP activity with the species lifespan, cells from long-lived species having higher levels of PARP activity than cells from short-lived species. In a similar vein, it was found that human centenarians, who have often maintained remarkably good general health, have a significantly greater poly(ADP-ribosyl)ation capacity than the general population (Muiras *et al.*, 1998).

Short telomeres

In many human somatic tissues a decline in cellular division capacity with age appears to be linked to the fact that the telomeres, which protect the ends of chromosomes, get progressively shorter as cells divide (Kim *et al.*, 2002). This is due to the absence of the enzyme telomerase, which is normally expressed only in germ cells (in testis and ovary) and in certain adult stem cells. Some have suggested that in dividing somatic cells telomeres act as an intrinsic 'division counter', perhaps to protect us against runaway cell division as happens in cancer. The price of this counting is 'collateral' damage as cells that are critical for the maintenance of the body are also discarded and thus contribute to ageing (Campisi, 1997). While the loss of telomeric DNA is often attributed mainly to the so-called 'end-replication' problem – the inability of the normal DNA copying machinery to copy right to the very end of the strand in the absence of telomerase – it has been found that stress, especially oxidative stress, has an even bigger effect on the rate of telomere loss (von Zglinicki, 2002). Telomere shortening is greatly accelerated (or slowed) in cells with increased (or reduced) levels of stress. The clinical relevance of understanding telomere maintenance and its interaction with stress is considerable. A growing body of evidence suggests that telomere length is linked with ageing and mortality (Cawthon *et al.*, 2003). Not only do telomeres shorten with normal ageing in several tissues (e.g. lymphocytes, vascular endothelial cells, kidney, liver), but also their reduction is more marked in certain disease states. For example, there appears to be a higher incidence of vascular dementia in people with prematurely short telomeres (von Zglinicki *et al.*, 2000). Viewed together with the observation that oxidative stress accelerates telomere loss, the intriguing possibility arises that prematurely short telomeres *in vivo* are an indicator of previous exposure to stress and may therefore serve as a prognostic indicator for disease conditions in which oxidative stress plays a causative role (von Zglinicki, 2002). More than intriguing is the preliminary evidence that other forms of stress may chip away the ends of chromosomes also. Women with the highest levels of perceived psychological stress have shorter telomeres on average (Epel *et al.*, 2004).

An important connection between oxidative stress and ageing is suggested by the accumulation of mitochondrial DNA (mtDNA) deletions and point mutations with age (Wallace, 1992). Mitochondria are intracellular organelles, each carrying its own small DNA genome, which are responsible for generating cellular energy. As a by-product of energy generation, mitochondria are also the major source of ROS within the cell, and they are therefore both responsible for, and a major target of, oxidative stress. Any age-related increase in mutation of mtDNA is likely to contribute to a progressive decline in the cell and tissue capacity for energy production. Age-related increases in frequency of cytochrome c oxidase (COX)-deficient cells have been reported in human muscle (Müller-Höcker, 1989; Müller-Höcker *et al.*, 1993; Brierley *et al.*, 1998), brain (Cottrell *et al.*, 2000) and gut (Taylor *et al.*, 2003) associated with increased frequency of mutated mtDNA.

Protein damage

So far, we have concentrated on damage to DNA. However, damage can also affect any of the macromolecules that make up the cell, as well as those that form extracellular structures such as cartilage and bone. In particular, damage to protein molecules occurs to a considerable extent, and accumulation of faulty proteins contributes to important age-related disorders such as cataract, Parkinson's disease and Alzheimer's disease. In some ways, the accumulation of defective proteins is harder to explain than the accumulation of DNA damage, since individual protein molecules are subject to a continual cycle of synthesis and breakdown. Thus, damage to any individual protein molecule should be cleared, as soon as that molecule is degraded. The exceptions occur when the defective protein molecules become resistant to breakdown, for example, because they form aggregates large enough to withstand the normal removal systems. It is the build-up of such aggregates that is commonly linked with cell and tissue pathology.

Metabolism

Of particular significance in terms of metabolic factors influencing ageing rates has been the discovery that insulin signalling pathways appear to have effects on ageing that may be strongly conserved across the species range (Gems and Partridge, 2001). Insulin signalling regulates responses to varying nutrient levels and so the discovery of the major role for these pathways in ageing fits well with the central concept of the disposable soma theory, namely that ageing results from and is controlled by the metabolic allocation of the organism's metabolic resources to maintenance and repair.

One of the clearest examples of how metabolic signalling affects ageing and longevity comes from a study on genes of the insulin signalling pathway in *C. elegans* (Murphy *et al.*, 2003). When threatened with overcrowding, which the larval worm detects by the increasing concentration of a pheromone, it diverts its development from the normal succession of larval moults into a long-lived, dispersal form called the dauer larva (Larsen *et al.*, 1995). Dauers show increased resistance to stress and can survive very much longer than the normal form, reverting to complete their development into adults should more favourable conditions be detected. An insulin/IGF-1-like gene, *daf-2*, heads the gene regulatory pathway that controls the switch into the dauer form, and mutations in *daf-2* produce animals that develop into adults with substantially increased lifespans (Kenyon *et al.*, 1993). The *daf-2* gene product exerts its effects by influencing 'downstream' gene expression, in particular via the actions of another gene belonging to the dauer-formation gene family, *daf-16*, which it inhibits (Kimura *et al.* 1997). It was shown by Murphy *et al.* (2003) that more than 300 genes appeared to have their expression levels altered by *daf-16* regulation. These genes included many that were concerned with regulating key maintenance processes such as resistance to oxidative stress, capacity to clear damaged proteins and capacity to fight off bacterial infections. Thus, it is turning out that on the one hand the essential simplicity of Figure 2.3 is confirmed by the data, while on the other hand there remains a lot of complicated research to be done to unravel the multiple mechanisms of cellular damage and repair.

Hierarchy

By this point, it will be seen that, from a range of studies at the genetic, cellular and molecular levels, both in humans and a variety of other organisms, a picture is clearly emerging of the main elements of the biological science of human ageing (see Figure 2.1). These elements are the relentless role of biochemical *stresses*, such as exposure to ROS, driving a gradual but progressive accumulation of *damage* to cells, tissues and organs. The process is not entirely passive, since the rate of accumulation is strongly resisted by maintenance and repair processes, which are controlled by *genes*. Furthermore, the regulation of these genes may, at least in some organisms, be influenced by metabolic factors, such as responding to levels of nutrition.

This picture is one that readily accommodates the role of at least five major elements contributing to the individuality of the human ageing process: genes, nutrition, lifestyle (e.g. exercise), environment and chance. The recognition of this interplay of factors is likely to be crucial for integrating biological, clinical and social gerontology. For example, environment is often defined by social factors such as housing, transport and income. Poor environments may adversely affect an individual's opportunities to do the optimal things for healthy ageing in terms of nutrition, lifestyle, etc. In particular, a poor environment can reinforce a tendency for the older person to suffer social isolation, which in turn can exacerbate psychological and physical deterioration. On the positive side, the understanding that we now have of the biological science of human ageing supports the idea that the ageing process is much more malleable than has hitherto been recognised. This opens the way to a range of interventions that may improve health in old age and extend quality life.

THE RECENT DEVELOPMENT OF HUMAN LIFE SPAN

In the years to come, addressing the cumulative damage associated with ageing will be one of the biggest challenges faced by industrialised countries (Westendorp, 2006). We are now armed with the biological knowledge about ageing that can help us to make sense of the factors that have driven the recent dramatic increases in human longevity. Since the industrial revolution in the middle of the nineteenth century, average female life expectancy has increased in western societies from about 45 years to currently more than 80 years, corresponding to an increase of 2.3 years per decade (Oeppen and Vaupel, 2002). Life expectancy has also risen for men, although more slowly; over the years the gap between females and males has extended from 2 to 6 years (Oeppen and Vaupel, 2002). The increase in life expectancy since 1850 is a straight line and, despite the estimates of the United Nations, who predicted the rate of increase to plateau (United Nations Secretariat, 2003), there are no data supporting such an expectation. (see Figure 2.4.)

It might have been expected, and was indeed forecast by all of the major national and international agencies, that the increase in lifespan would slow down and eventually reach a plateau as the gains from further reductions in early and middle life mortality became negligible in terms of their potential impact on life expectancy (since mortality in these age ranges was already so low), and as the fixed, ineluctable ageing process made its presence ever more clearly felt. Thus it has taken demographers and policy planners by surprise that, during the final decades of the twentieth century, life expectancy not only did not reach a plateau but to date has shown no sign of slowing its rate of increase at all. This new phase of human ageing is sometimes referred to the 'demographic transition', following upon the heels of the preceding epidemiological transition.

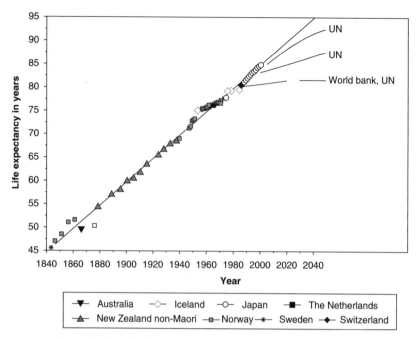

Figure 2.4   Recorded female life expectancy from 1840 to the present

The increase in life expectancy that has occurred during the last two centuries has occurred much faster than can reasonably be explained by any change in genetics, so the answer must be sought in the range of non-genetic factors. Of course the first phase of the increase in life expectancy was driven by the reduction in infectious disease mortality, through sanitation, then antisepsis followed by vaccination and antibiotics. This had a particularly important impact on child mortality, which has the biggest quantitative effect on life expectancy, but its effects on adult mortality should not be ignored. The taming of infectious disease mortality ushered in the epidemiological transition, from a pattern of disease dominated by infection to one dominated by intrinsic, age-related deterioration (Omran, 2001).

Box 2.2   Environmental effects on lifespan: the example of Japan

A unique example showing the impact of improved environmental conditions on lifespan is provided by data from Japan, which experienced an exceptionally rapid increase in life expectancy during the last 50 years. Japanese life expectancy from

(Continued)

(Continued)

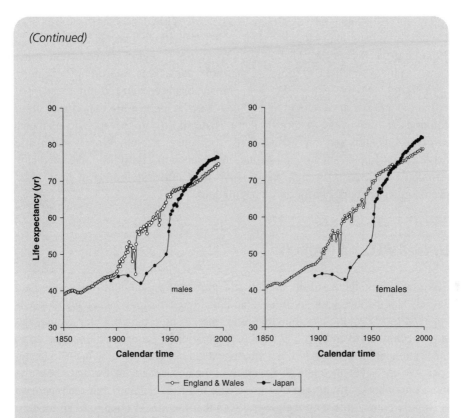

birth did not increase significantly until 1950 but since then has grown to become the longest in the world.

According to the first life tables (1891–98), life expectancy in Japan was 42.8 years for males and 44.3 years for females at the end of the nineteenth century. Life expectancy in Japan remained less than 50 years until after the Second World War. From 1950 to 1952, life expectancy increased by more than two years annually. In 1995, life expectancy at birth was 76.4 years for males and 82.9 years for females. The graphs illustrate the increase in life expectancy in Japan over calendar time for males and females. For comparison, life expectancy for males in England and Wales is also presented. In 1850, life expectancy in England and Wales was 39.2 years for males and 41.2 years for females. Life expectancy for males has been above 50 years since 1909 and for females since 1902. In 1995, life expectancy in the UK at birth was 74.2 years for males and 79.5 years for females.

The rapid increases in life expectancy in Japan and the UK reveal the epidemiologic transition that has taken place in all developed countries, with high child mortality and deaths from extrinsic causes at any age being largely replaced by mortality caused by age-associated degenerative disorders. This notion is reinforced by the observation that the mean age at death for British aristocratic women remained around 45 years until the first decades of the eighteenth century. Thereafter life span steadily increased to a mean of 68 years for women born in 1850. The epidemiologic transition among the British aristocracy thus began some 150 years earlier than in the general population.

The curve for Japan provides a key to what drives life expectancy (see Box 2.2). There is no other country that has seen such a dramatic increase in lifespan. From 1900 until the Second World War, life expectancy in Japan lagged behind other countries by as much as 30 years. At that time, Japan was an economically poor, agricultural society. Since the war, Japan has experienced unprecedented economic and social development and now has the highest life expectancy of all countries in the world. Although there is debate as to the specific elements involved, wealth and an affluent environment correlate closely with life expectancy. Improvements in sanitation, education, nutrition and medicine afforded by increased wealth are positive indicators for long-term health and decreased early mortality for entire populations.

LONGER WELL OR POORLY?

The continuing increases in human life expectancy, although surprising, are entirely compatible with the understanding of the biology of ageing that has emerged from evolutionary thinking. Since there is no programme for ageing, and since ageing is driven by the gradual accumulation of faults, anything that slows the accumulation of faults will potentially extend not only lifespan but also health span. We are as yet uncertain about which of the non-genetic factors have been the more important in driving the recent increase in life expectancy, but such increase is entirely compatible with the general idea that the kinder conditions of modern life may be allowing the current cohorts of older people to have reached old age with less accumulated damage.

The increase in average lifespan observed in all developed countries is accompanied by an incremental burden of age-associated diseases. The expectation is that scientific advances will prevent disease from occurring or, if disease does strike, will protect us from permanent damage. Over the last 20 years, the United Kingdom has gained about four years in both female and male life expectancy, but only two years in female healthy life expectancy (House of Lords Science and Technology Committee, 2005). The overall increase is far greater than that for healthy living, and this contradicts recent thinking. In 1980, Fries published the concept of compression of mortality and morbidity, based on survival curves (Fries, 1980). Juxtaposing curves from 1900 and 1980, it appeared that the curve became rectangular with increasing survival to higher age (see Box 2.3). Projecting the same curve forward in time, it was expected to become ever more rectangular, to a point where individuals all survive to a similar age. Mortality would be compressed into a shorter period; individuals born around the same time would die over the same 5- to 15-year period instead of being threatened over the lifetime. And, as Fries concluded, since there is no mortality without disease, compression of mortality also implied compression of morbidity; individual suffering prior to death would also be limited to those 5–15 years.

Box 2.3   On compression of morbidity and mortality

The continuing increase in life expectancy has prompted many to make predictions about the future length of the period during which we suffer from disease and disability towards the end of life. Underlying much of the thinking to date has been an expectation that progress in medical knowledge will lead to prevention or postponement of disease, independently of the underlying process of intrinsic biological ageing. This optimism led Fries (1980) to introduce the concept of 'compression of morbidity', often linked to the progressive tendency towards rectangularisation of the survival curve (see the figure).

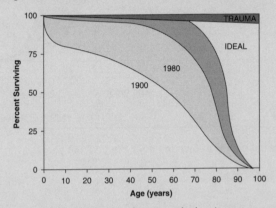

The concept has wide appeal on the grounds that it captures what many see as the objective of research on biomedical aspects of ageing, namely, 'to add life to years, not years to life'. The reverse possibility – that lifespan will continue to increase but that healthspan will not – is seen by most as a highly unlikely and undesirable outcome.

The idea of compression of morbidity does not, however, stand up well to scrutiny in the light of our understanding of the biology of ageing. The difficulty with this concept is that it assumed a fixed maximum human lifespan. It became clear in the 1980s that this was not the case. The concept also failed to consider the effects on survival during the extreme environmental change that occurred during the 80 years between datasets, therefore assuming that survival was independent of environmental factors.

It should also be noted that compression of morbidity and rectangularisation of the survival curve are not the same thing at all. If individuals continue to die at variable ages, due to a variety of innate and acquired characteristics, the survival curve will not become any more rectangular, even if for each individual morbidity is compressed into ever shorter periods. As for compression of morbidity, the idea that diseases can be further postponed within a fixed biological lifespan is increasingly less plausible, now that we know that ageing itself is almost certainly not programmed and at a time when we are seeing continuing increase in life expectancy driven primarily by the increased health, vitality and longevity of older people. New biological understanding of ageing tells us that the length of life is intrinsically much more malleable than was thought previously. Of course, this malleability also extends to the underlying component causes of ageing process (see Box 2.1), so whether in future our healthspan will increase faster or slower than lifespan is largely unknown.

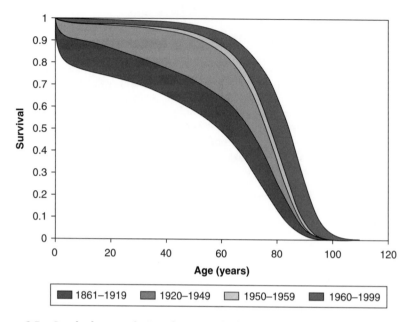

Figure 2.5   Survival curves in Sweden over the last 140 years

When we examine age at death in Sweden over the last 140 years, we notice a steep increase over the last 40–50 years (Wilmoth *et al.*, 2000). Examination of trends in the improvement of survival show that the tendency of the survival curve to become rectangular existed only for the period between 1860 and 1950. From then on, there was a parallel shift of the curve to the right (Yashin *et al.*, 2002) (see Figure 2.5).

Using the same data sets, Wilmoth *et al.* (2000) were able to further calculate that the rise of the maximum age at death in Sweden from the 1860s to the 1990s was due primarily to reductions in mortality at older ages. Of the total increase, 72.5% is attributable to decreased mortality above the age of 70. The increasing size of successive birth cohorts and decreased mortality below age 70 account for the balance. It is known that a reduction in old-age mortality has been a primary factor behind population ageing and the proliferation of centenarians during recent decades. It was also shown that mortality decline above age 70 has also been the main cause of a gradual increase in maximum achieved lifespan over more than a century. Only a minor part of this increase is due to the larger size of recent cohorts, defined either as numbers of children born each year or numbers of survivors to old age. It appears that, although the maximum age has increased more slowly than the average, the entire distribution of age at death has been shifting upward for more than a century in industrialised countries.

The right shift of the survival curves and analyses of changes in mortality patterns from the last half century line up with the basic idea that there is no biological limit to life. Therefore, compression of mortality and morbidity are not valid either. It may even be, since we still suffer from disease in middle age, that there is actually a decompression of morbidity, as the trend in the UK suggests. Analysis of death registries in the Netherlands corroborated the UK findings. A right shift in survival curves occurred from the 1950s onwards (Statistics Netherlands, 2004). Over the last decade in the Netherlands, comparing 1989 to 2000, there was an increase of two years in average life expectancy accompanied by an increase in the number of years with disease, hence decompression of morbidity. Under current conditions, we are going to live longer with more years spent in poor health (Perenboom *et al.*, 2002). Despite this depressing forecast we are increasingly able to overcome the complications of disease, explaining that the years without functional limitations or disability is still on the increase.

ORIGINAL GENES IN A NEW ENVIRONMENT

Currently, we have a fairly solid understanding of the evolutionary mechanisms that make us age and also allow us to survive in such disparate environments as Greenland and the Sahara. Darwinian fitness constantly shapes the genome to better adapt the organism to its habitat. Our mounting lifespan is determined by genes that were originally selected for survival in an adverse environment and are now expressed under completely new affluent environmental conditions. This may result in different, sometimes opposing, biological effects. Given the surprising patterns revealed by human longevity over the last 200 years, it is perhaps unwise to speculate too much about what might yet occur in the future. Nevertheless, it is important, not least for policy planning purposes, to look at what the biology tells us might occur.

The first point to make is that populations continue to adapt. Although we might suppose that natural selection is no longer operative in human societies, where many inherited problems such as short-sightedness have no discernible effect on reproductive success, we should not lose sight of the enormous changes that have taken place in our life history and the messages that might be contained therein. We indicated earlier how the current evolutionary understanding of ageing is founded on the idea of trade-offs, particularly between fertility and survival. Recently, we sought evidence in human populations that the kind of trade-offs that have been so clearly revealed in animal populations might apply in our species too (see Box 2.4). We found strong evidence that this is so and that a genetic predisposition towards above-average longevity may be associated with a genetic predisposition towards below-average fertility, and vice versa.

Box 2.4   Life history trade-offs among British aristocratic women

When human life history data are analysed to identify trade-offs between investments in reproductive success and in body maintenance, one should take into account not only genetic factors but also the socio-economic conditions that affect both the preferred family size and the probability of attaining long life. The detailed records of births, marriages and deaths of British aristocratic families, which have been kept over the centuries, provide an unique resource which we have used to study life history trade-offs in a population that is reasonably homogeneous with respect to its socio-economic characteristics and in which social deprivation has not unduly interfered with the prospects for reaching old age and thereby revealing an individual's intrinsic capacity for longevity (Westendorp and Kirkwood, 1998).

Table 2.1   Number of progeny and age at first childbirth dependent on the age at death of married aristocratic women.

Age at death (yr)	Number	Proportion childless	Number of progeny		Age at first childbirth (yr)	
			Mean	(95% CI)	Mean	(95% CI)
<20	42	0.66	0.45	(0.29–0.69)	19.1	(15.9–22.5)
21–30	176	0.39	1.35	(0.86–2.11)	20.5	(19.4–21.6)
31–40	218	0.26	2.05	(1.33–3.18)	23.2	(22.3–24.2)
41–50	210	0.31	2.01	(1.30–3.11)	23.9	(22.9–24.9)
51–60	299	0.28	2.40	(1.56–3.71)	24.6	(23.8–25.4)
61–70	337	0.33	2.36	(1.53–3.63)	23.8	(23.0–24.6)
71–80	322	0.31	2.64	(1.71–4.07)	24.6	(23.8–25.3)
81–90	247	0.45	2.08	(1.35–3.24)	25.1	(24.1–26.1)
>90	57	0.49	1.80	(1.12–2.90)	27.0	(24.8–29.2)

Point estimates and 95% confidence intervals (95% CI) are adjusted for the trends over calendar time using Poisson regression (number of progeny) and linear regression (age at first childbirth) respectively.

We have also found evidence of a possible mechanistic basis for such a trade-off, in that women with an innate, pro-inflammatory immune system are likely to have greater difficulty conceiving a child but may be better protected against fatal infectious disease (Westendorp et al., 2001). This concept may explain why British aristocrats who lived longer were less likely to reproduce (Table 2.1). Their innate pro-inflammatory immune system favoured resistance to infection. At the same time, it prevented pregnancy from proceeding, a 'trade-off' that is more pronounced under poor environmental conditions. It also explains why a genotype associated with impaired fertility persisted in spite of its obvious disadvantage with respect to evolutionary fitness. Selection for resistance to infection was traded against selection for fertility, resulting in a compromise that was optimal for the fitness of the species in the particular environment.

From an ageing perspective, old age is associated with systemic chronic inflammation and has been found to be related to mortality risk from all causes in older persons (Bruunsgaard *et al.*, 2001). Age-related diseases such as Alzheimer's disease, atherosclerosis, diabetes mellitus, sarcopenia and osteoporosis are initiated or worsened by systemic inflammation, suggesting the critical importance of unregulated systemic inflammation in old age (Bruunsgaard *et al.*, 2001; Brod, 2000; Pawelec *et al.*, 2002). Accordingly, pro-inflammatory cytokines are believed to play a predominant role in age-related diseases especially now in affluent societies where the majority of the population survives up to old age. In line with this, genetic variations located within the promoter regions of these pro- and anti-inflammatory cytokines have been shown to influence the susceptibility to age-related diseases by increasing gene transcription and therefore cytokine production (Pawelec *et al.*, 2002; Bidwell *et al.*, 1999; van den Biggelaar *et al.*, 2004).

It is easy enough to see that during an era when infectious disease was the dominant cause of mortality, such a pro-inflammatory host immune system might have made evolutionary sense. The set point of the response, balancing resistance to infection on the one hand and successful pregnancy on the other, is genetically controlled and is likely a result of Darwinian selection in the environment we live (Westendorp, 2004). It is also clear that the effective removal in developed countries of the threat of fatal infectious disease within just a few generations may have tipped the evolutionary balance. Nowadays individuals with an anti-inflammatory host response are likely to escape death from infection, and genetic variations determining increased production of the anti-inflammatory cytokine IL-10 or decreased production of the pro-inflammatory cytokine TNF-α have been shown to be associated with healthy ageing, suggesting a role for the control of the pro-inflammatory mode in older age (Lio *et al.*, 2003). Whether and how fast such a change might result in altered frequency within the population of genes affecting human longevity are interesting questions to ask.

FUTURE PERSPECTIVE

Of course, an immediate practical challenge that many developed countries must confront is the threat to health and future longevity that comes from a lifestyle of affluence, characterised by excessive food and sedentary lifestyle. This threat is not distinct from the challenge of understanding the biology of ageing. Poor nutrition and lack of physical exercise exacerbate the accumulation of cellular and molecular damage through biochemical and physiological pathways that we already understand reasonably well. A child raised on a diet with excessive saturated fat and sugar, who takes insufficient exercise, is not only more likely to suffer diseases such as diabetes and atherosclerosis; he or she is also likely to age faster as well.

An open issue in ageing research is the extent to which responses to the environment during development can influence variability in lifespan in animals, and the health profile of older humans. Both affluence and adversity in human societies have profound impacts on survivorship curves, and some of this effect may be traceable to effects *in utero* or in infancy. Data from human observational studies suggest that a pregnant woman's diet affects not only the health of her children but also that of her grandchildren (Barker, 2002). The idea, known as the 'Barker hypothesis', links caloric restriction in very early life to disruptions of glucose–insulin metabolism in later life and has attracted much attention, as well as some controversy, in medical circles.

One crucial mechanism by which animals can respond in an adaptive manner to adverse conditions – for example in nutrition or infection – during development is *phenotypic plasticity*, which describes the ability of a genotype to express different phenotypes in response to different environments. However, it is only rarely considered by evolutionary biologists working on phenotypic plasticity, or by bio-gerontologists studying model organisms such as *C. elegans* or *Drosophila*. Recently, we started a discussion of adaptive plasticity in animals, asking what such a phenomenon may reveal that is relevant to the rate of ageing in animals and in man, and gathering the evidence that environmentally mediated events taking place very early in life may determine the biological status of an individual at the end of life (Brakefield *et al.*, 2005).

The biological mechanisms underlying this heritable, epigenetic information have yet to be understood. The findings, however, corroborate with findings concerning the regulation of lifespan in ants and honeybees. Secretion of larvae juvenile hormone (corresponding to thyroid hormones in humans) is food-dependent. Should it be stimulated at a critical time in development, the larvae develop into diploid queens with a prolonged lifespan. In the absence of this food-triggered hormonal signal, the same larvae will develop into haploid workers with a short lifespan (Keller and Genoud, 1997). This signalling by the environment to invest particular attributes in the new organism is a clear example of early environmental programming. Applied in humans, and given our much longer average lifespan relative to ants and honey bees, depending on early environmental programming of food, a life history of 100 years could only be an average. There is enormous potential plasticity in our life history, but we have not yet identified the signals controlling it.

THE KNOWLEDGE SHADOW

Upon further improvement of our environmental conditions, with continuous increase of average life expectancy and no biologically determined limit, the question becomes one of disease-related morbidity. How do we optimise an increasingly ageing population's health such that we don't simply spend more years in misery before we die? The answer lies in a thorough understanding of the ageing process and how available interventions may be applied to protect and preserve health.

Of immediate concern for health of the ever-increasing numbers of older people is our constrained knowledge domain. The bulk of medical research has been invested in early development, adulthood and middle age. Scientific and medical advances in the last century targeted prevention and control of diseases that threatened survival through the 'prime' years, and these represented enormous contributions to the quality of life we now enjoy in youth and middle age. While this was happening, however, we were not investing in our understanding of the natural consequence of this – i.e. a growing elderly and ageing population. Using population data from 'developed' countries, approximately 80–90% of deaths now occur after the age of 75. The problem is that disease, morbidity and deaths at this age are actually occurring in a 'knowledge shadow'.

CONCLUSIONS

Ageing is under environmental and genetic control but it is not programmed nor is it inevitable. As evolutionary pressures for early survival and reproduction decrease, more metabolic resources can be invested in soma maintenance and repair, increasing both average life expectancy and maximum lifespan. Ageing is best explained as the balance between investments in fitness and investments in body maintenance: if investment in body maintenance is not optimal, ageing occurs. Increasing our understanding of the ageing process and applying available interventions will greatly enhance a healthy ageing.

FURTHER READING

Kirkwood, T. B. L. (2005) Understanding the odd science of ageing. *Cell* **120**, 437–447.

Oeppen, J. and Vaupel, J. W. (2002) Demography: broken limits to life expectancy. *Science* **296**, 1029–1031.

Westendorp, R. G. (2006) What is healthy aging in the 21st century? *American Journal of Clinical Nutrition* **83** (suppl.), S404–409.

3

Psychological ageing

Alfons Marcoen, Peter G.
Coleman and Ann O'Hanlon

INTRODUCTION

The phenomenon of human ageing has many faces. Physical ageing is the most
visible face. We encounter it in our mirror image and in bodily experiences as
decreasing velocity, early tiredness and unwanted sleepiness by day, sleeplessness at
night, lack of energy, and occasionally waves of indefinite pain. Genome-based
physical ageing and its impact on changes in motor, perceptual, cognitive and emotional functioning, is a given; it befalls us. Human ageing is also a socio-cultural phenomenon. The eloquent comments and gazes, the compassionate questions and
well-intended considerations of other people around us may reflect, even more
vividly than the real mirror, our physical and functional ageing. Indeed, we age in
the context of complex networks of personal relations in micro-systems as the family
and groups of friends, and in the ever-widening circles of social systems as neighbourhoods, towns and countries, which directly or indirectly affect our lives through
views (images, prejudices and stereotypes), rules, legislation and policies. Society
and culture co-construct human ageing for better and worse. We proceed through a
succession of emerging roles, deeply patterned upon the (changing) views of the
society and culture we live in. We become intimate partners, parents and grandparents, junior and senior professionals, poor or well-to-do retirees, patients (not) enjoying excellent social security and health provisions, and eventually, (very) old dying
persons. Through views and regulations about ageing and old age socio-cultural

ageing is put upon us. However, human ageing is not only a biological given and a societal destiny; it is also a personal task. To a certain extent we are able to shape our own ageing into a positive experience even in front of irreversible decline. By using adequate strategies of adaptation we generally succeed in maintaining, restoring and enhancing a relatively high level of subjective well-being.

In view of the above-described multifaceted nature of human ageing, it makes sense to distinguish normal, pathological and optimal ageing with regard to different biomedical, psychological, cognitive and social functions as well as the way of living and the adaptive style of the individual (Rowe and Kahn, 1987). From a biomedical point of view, 'normal ageing' does mean to be able to live in healthiness and good physical condition as far into advanced old age as the majority of the ageing people in the community do. Normal ageing obviously consists of genome-based decline in different physical, psychological and cognitive functions and systems. What appears as normal functioning and normal conduct in old age also depends on the criteria used in the community. These criteria may change together with views in the society about normality. *Pathological ageing* implies – apart from the effects of normal ageing processes – the symptoms and decline effects of diseases that normally are not age-linked. Pathologically ageing persons do not live as long as other older people in the community and their quality of life is below the average. *Optimal ageing* is an ageing process characterised by physical and psychological functioning on a level above the average of ageing people in general. Personal and environmental conditions may have led to a successful ageing trajectory in a minority of older people in a given community. 'Successfully ageing' individuals live longer in good health with minimal cognitive impairments; they are socially well integrated and mainly in an excellent state of well-being.

Scientific questions on psychological ageing are rooted in the daily experiences of individual adults facing (non) age-related changes in themselves and others, and societies facing ageing populations. Systematic investigations produce more or less generalised knowledge about the *what?* and the *why?* of psychological ageing. Indeed, three basic questions guide psycho-gerontological research:

- What age-related and non-age-related psychological changes are taking place in middle adult-hood and old age?
- Why and how are these changes emerging?
- What is the differential meaning of these changes?

The first question aims at a *description* of age-related psychological changes in the second half of life. Research generates a kind of normative image of the psychological ageing trajectory. The second question focuses on the *explanation* of these changes. Research detects personal and environmental factors that determine decline and stability in different dimensions of psychological functioning. The third question aims at a critical *interpretation* of the complex of generalised findings in the context of the lives of ageing individuals, and in how old age is thought of and dealt with in the community. Systematically gathered knowledge is mostly probabilistic in nature. Relations and causal links found in the analytic phase of empirical investigations have to be validated through its application in the context of the understanding and shaping of ageing trajectories in particular individuals in different societal contexts. Then the circle is round. Scientific knowledge contributes to the elucidation and enrichment of the lives of ageing individuals and the attitudes and policies toward older people in society.

In the present brief overview of some of the main research topics and theoretical insights in the domain of psycho-gerontology, we focus on the dynamics of development and ageing, different research perspectives, main domains of study and, finally, the challenge of the fourth age.

DYNAMICS OF DEVELOPMENT AND AGEING

The three basic questions on psychological ageing are equally valid for the phenomenon of psychological development. Indeed, both ageing and development consist of psychological *changes* that shape the life course of the person. These changes interact. Leaving behind the starting point of one's life that is still full of in-determination and potential, in a lifelong process of development, necessarily implies approaching the end of life in an equally lifelong process of ageing and eventually dying. The view that development and ageing are co-occurring processes of change is increasingly recognized in theory and research on psychological changes in adulthood and old age. Views on the growth–decline and gain–loss dynamic in development and ageing across the whole life course, theories on the adaptive potential of older people, clearly illustrate the entanglement of psychological development and ageing.

Gains and losses

Aware of positive and negative psychological changes across the whole life course, theorists attempted to integrate development and ageing. Schroots (Schroots, 2002; Birren and Schroots, 1984) introduced the concept of ontogenetic psychology. He labelled the processes of development and ageing (on the levels of biological, psychological and social organisation, respectively) as:

- growth and senescing
- maturing and geronting
- adulting and eldering.

The concepts of adulting and eldering actually refer to the lifelong processes of socialisation in, respectively, childhood and then late adulthood and old age. Maturing is defined as attaining levels of self-regulation and independence in childhood that characterise the functioning of adult organisms, whereas geronting refers to adapting and optimizing these levels in adulthood (Schroots, 2002). The ageing processes of eldering and geronting are not inherently negative. They occur only against the background of the effects of the age-related biological processes of senescing. In the first stages of life, development prevails with processes of ageing in the background; in late adulthood processes of ageing prevail while development remains latent.

Innovative views on the relationship between psychological development and psychological ageing in the lifespan perspective originate from the work of Baltes and his colleagues. They challenged the traditional conception of development 'that emphasises a general and universal development of an entity geared toward a higher level of functioning which, in addition, incorporates most if not all previously developed capacities' (Baltes *et al.*, 1998, p. 1044) and broadened the concept by considering development in a dynamic gain/loss perspective.

Lifespan researchers discovered that behavioural change processes can differ a lot in terms of onset, duration, termination and directionality. Many developmental trajectories are possible. Baltes *et al.* (1998) therefore reformulated development as *selective age-related change in adaptive capacity* (p. 1044). Development contains processes of selection and selective adaptation or optimisation. People do not develop all possible human attributes, and do not adapt to all possible contextual conditions. From the beginning, individuals, with their unique genetically based dispositions, try to adapt successfully to the unique contexts they find themselves in, and start creating their personal worlds in which they learn to function as optimally as possible. Without denying the relevance of the traditional growth-oriented conception for certain age-related psychological changes, this view embraces the diversity of lifespan developmental trajectories. Inherent to this conception is the insight that development is always associated with *gains and losses* (Baltes, 1979, 1987; Baltes *et al.*, 1998). Selective adaptation necessarily implies the stimulation and growth of certain human attributes at the expense of investment of energy in the development of other attributes. So, losses and gains co-exist. Baltes *et al.* (1998) also distinguish three central sets of adaptive tasks:

- *growth* (behaviours aimed at reaching higher levels of functioning or adaptive capacity)
- *maintenance/recovery* (resilience – behaviours aimed at maintaining levels of functioning in the face of challenge, or returning to previous levels after a loss)
- *regulation of loss* (behaviours that organise adequate functioning at lower levels when maintenance or recovery is no longer possible).

These functions of development occur in all phases of the life course. Growth is especially prominent in the early phases of life, whereas resilience and regulation of loss become increasingly important in adulthood and old age.

Adaptation in ageing

Age-related growth and decline of adaptive capacity occur across the whole life course. Although older people eventually loose their physical capacity to survive, psychologically they may be able to adapt themselves to difficult and challenging life circumstances. Indeed, older people by and large impress by their ability to master negative emotions and present a positive face to the world. They display much higher levels of well-being than might be expected, and generally find ways to maintain their needs for competence, control and quality of life. Older adults use different strategies to adapt successfully to the challenges and disadvantages that can occur in later life.

Baltes' model of development as change in adaptive capacity (e.g. Baltes and Baltes, 1990a; Baltes *et al.*, 1998; Freund and Baltes, 1998) provides a prototype strategy of both adaptation and successful ageing through the use of the three above-mentioned strategies: selection, optimisation and compensation (SOC).

Selection refers to the adaptive task of focusing on those domains that are of high priority to the individual, and which suit his or her skills and situation. In this context individuals are encouraged to select only the most rewarding interests and commitments, and ones that can be performed without great effort. However, an individual may make the wrong choice, and focus on activities that do not optimize his or her sense of identity, meaning or even pleasure. For this reason, selection should be a consequence of both subjective preferences and objective judgements. Selection is further defined in terms of elective selection (regulative processes that are involved in selection from a pool of alternative developmental pathways) and loss-based selection (response to a decline of resources; defined in terms of a downward shift to less important goals) (Freund and Baltes, 1998, p. 531). The process of selection implies a continual narrowing in the range of alternative options open to the individual. Although this narrowing of options may occur throughout the life course, including childhood, it is likely to be more salient into old age given the pressure of increasing constraints on the self as a consequence of decreases in ability and energy, and the declining effectiveness of the culture in supporting older adults (Baltes, 1997). By reducing activities to high-efficacy domains, the activities can be as enjoyable as before they were reduced in number (Baltes and Carstensen, 1996). The process of selection is initiated by the anticipation of change and restriction in functioning brought on by age. Strategies of selection can be *re*-active as well as *pro*-active.

Optimisation refers to strategies, by the individual or society, to modify the environment to create more favourable or desired outcomes for the self and to meet continual challenges and changes being experienced. Optimisation strategies can occur at physical, psychological and social levels.

When some capacities are reduced, strategies of compensation involve the use of alternative means to reach given goals and keep performance at desired levels. Compensation has been defined as the progress through which a 'gap or mismatch between currently accessible skills and environmental demands is reduced or closed' (Dixon and Bäckman, 1995, p. iv). Facilitating effective strategies of managing losses and overcoming problems is important in order to facilitate greater autonomy and well-being for adults entering their later years.

Research on SOC strategies, with recently developed short measures (Freund and Baltes, 2002; Wiese *et al.*, 2000), indicates that use of these strategies is related to better health, successful ageing and improved relationships. The fact that there is such diversity among people in terms of their health, their attitudes and their coping strategies indicates that much more research is needed examining possible facilitators or barriers to use of SOC strategies (e.g. stress, family relationships, psychosocial well-being). For instance there is strong evidence that adults' goals, beliefs and expectations can have a strong influence on later behaviour and health (see research on the placebo effect, self-fulfilling prophecies), and that individuals can suffer much negative affect before surrendering goals. Therefore, research exploring the possible role of current and past experiences in shaping current strategies of goal selection could be very valuable. A separate line of research could examine the health and social consequences of SOC strategies for different groups of adults, such as those from different age cohorts and social or occupational groups. The latter could be especially important given a possible link between the use of SOC strategies and the availability of social, educational or economic resources.

Brandtstädter and colleagues (Brandtstädter and Greve, 1994; Brandtstädter and Rothermund, 1994) presented a theory of *assimilation and accommodation* to describe and to explain how old persons succeed in maintaining a positive self-concept and outlook on life. Indeed, underpinning their theory is the assumption that later life has many biological, social and psychological challenges and losses that pose 'considerable strain on the individual's construction of self and personal continuity' (Brandtstädter and Greve, 1994).

Assimilation refers to strategies by which the individual actively attempts to change the environment in ways congruent with his or her own goals and expectations. Strategies of assimilation can include behavioural changes that enable individuals to continue functioning at higher levels and engage in their preferred activities. For these reasons, examples of assimilation strategies can include strategies of selection, optimisation and compensation as described above. However, Brandtstädter argues that processes of accommodation are needed when threats or losses with age become too demanding and too difficult to maintain. Accommodative coping refers to strategies of readjusting goals or aspirations downwards in the light of constraints and limitations within the environment or the self, for example as a result of physical ill-health or reduction in mobility. Examples of accommodative strategies include reappraisal of experiences or the attribution of positive meaning to new goals and experiences, and the making of self-enhancing comparisons (Brandtstädter and Greve, 1994).

Underpinning strategies of both assimilation and accommodation are immunising processes:. These are mechanisms that can influence the process of receiving information relevant to the self, such as beliefs about the self, the availability of alternative interpretations, or the rejection (or euphemistic interpretation) of self-threatening evidence. Further distinctions within immunisation processes can be made between processes of encoding and interpreting evidence in ways that reduce or deny its relevance for the self (i.e. data-orientated immunisation) and the reshaping or reorganisation of items of evidence so that these are excluded from its range of application (i.e. concept-orientated immunisation). The latter form of immunisation tends to occur when data-orientated immunisation strategies are not available.

Brandtstädter's theory has much theoretical and applied value. It challenges pessimistic views of later life (Rabbitt, 1999a) to portray the reality of later life as a time of both positive and more challenging experiences. Furthermore, contrary to expectations about older people as being passive and helpless, the theory highlights the active role that older people play in influencing and managing their own lives. This perspective reflects recent thinking in social psychology where researchers have moved away from a static and fixed model of the self and towards an understanding of the self as an 'active ... multidimensional, multifaceted dynamic structure that is systematically impacted in all aspects of social information processing' (Markus and Wurf, 1987, p. 301).

Empirical research exploring these strategies is still scarce. In a study involving patients with chronic pain, aged 18–68 years, Schmitz et al. (1996) found that accommodative coping (i.e. adjusting personal goals) attenuated the negative impact of the pain experience on well-being, and helped maintain a positive life perspective. However, there are limitations to Brandtstädter's theory that warrant more research. Inherent in his theory is the notion of flexibility in adjusting goals and expectations, yet we have little information about the mechanisms and personal demands involved in these processes. People can have very optimistic (even unrealistic) expectations and goals that they find difficult to lower; at the other end of a continuum, people can continue to be demotivated over long periods of time by a lack of goals and challenges.

Therefore, adjusting goals in line with the context and environment individuals find themselves in is a complex process and one that needs more research. Further research is also needed to examine the appropriateness of accommodative strategies in different contexts, such as among adults of differing health status, or adults of different economic groups. This research could shed light on instances in which resistance rather than accommodation might be a more appropriate response.

Another relevant framework for the conceptualisation of the strategies of adaptation used by older people is the theory of control and its model of developmental optimisation in primary and secondary control (Heckhausen and Schulz, 1995; Schultz and Heckhausen, 1996; Heckhausen, 1999). This theory is based on the assumption of the existence of a fundamental motivation for primary control, producing effects in the environment contingent on one's own behaviour. The concept of secondary control refers to the person's internal world and maintaining resources needed to be able to exert primary control. Individuals vary in their ability to regulate their control strategies, which impacts on their mental health and affective well-being (Heckhausen et al., 2001). Assimilation is similar to primary control in that it refers to active efforts on the part of the person to influence the situation. However, the primary function of the former is consistency of goals, and hence sense of identity, over time, rather than control over the environment.

Future studies need to find ways to interlink these and other theoretical approaches by elucidating the similarities and interrelations between the different central theoretical concepts.

RESEARCH PERSPECTIVES

The study of psychological ageing may focus on both the ageing individual as the agent of his/her life course, and the psychological functions and personality attributes that constitute the individual person. Person-centred psycho-gerontological research aims at a well documented generalised narrative about changes in behaviour and experiences in ageing persons. The description of the generalised ageing person is based on the more or less systematic observation and interpretation of many lives in progress. The result is a kind of normative, sometimes rather ideal, pattern of age-related changes in the person as a whole. Function-centred psycho-gerontological research focuses on ontogenetic changes in different psychological functions and personality characteristics.

Besides the person–function distinction, different perspectives frame the study of psychological ageing and development. Each perspective has its aims, benefits and advantages. Research from different perspectives provides building blocks of knowledge for a comprehensive view on the psychology of the ageing person-in-context.

A general perspective

Research may aim at a general description of changes in different psychological functions and attributes that together constitute the complex system of the ageing person. Determinants of ageing sensorial and cognitive functions are studied mainly in experimental settings and/or with psychometrically sound tasks and self-report instruments. In the last decades a lot of attention has been given to the multidimensionality of the phenomena of memory and intelligence. The distinction between registers of memory (sensorial, short-term memory and long-term memory), processes (decoding, encoding and retrieval) and different types of memory (e.g. semantic and episodic) constitutes a conceptual network or heuristic model to structure the domain of memory ageing research. The distinction between fluid and crystallised intelligence (Horn and Cattell, 1976; Horn, 1982), and its integration in the distinction between the mechanics of intelligence and the pragmatics of intelligence (Baltes, 1987; Baltes, 1993), furthered research on cognitive ageing considerably. Developmental trajectories of each of the different dimensions of cognitive functioning or intelligence have been studied. This research yielded a differentiated picture of a person's ageing mental capabilities, and validated the day-to-day observations of enduring adaptability of older people far into old age. In the same vein, age-related changes in personality attributes such as traits and well-being components have been investigated. Investigators in these and other domains of function- or attribute-centred research abstract from the specific individuals in whom the phenomena they study are observed. In a similar way, researchers who focus on the whole person (e.g. Erikson, 1963) abstract from inter-individual differences when they try to describe the generalised individual's journey in late adulthood.

Psycho-gerontological research from a general perspective mainly generates normative knowledge about the trajectories of psychological functions and attributes. Although other perspectives are rooted in criticism on research from a general perspective, the knowledge that research from this perspective generates will always deliver indispensable building blocks for more comprehensive approaches of ageing individuals in research and practice.

A DIFFERENTIAL PERSPECTIVE

A differential perspective may guide the function-centred as well as the person-centred research on psychological ageing. General trends in the age-related changes (e.g. in intelligence, memory and other psychological attributes) may mask the existence of different trajectories related to individual characteristics (e.g. gender, education) and contextual characteristics (e.g. culture) of the people studied. The differential perspective became especially relevant in the person-centred approach (Thomae, 1975). In the 1960s and 1970s, several investigations yielded typologies that made the uniqueness of trajectories and patterns of ageing in individuals more visible (e.g. Havighurst, 1968; Maas and Kuypers, 1974; Reichard et al., 1962; Thomae, 1970; 1976; 1983). These pictures complemented, on the one hand, the description of the generalised ageing person, and transcended, on the other hand, the compilation of biographies. However, the difficulty of assigning every participant to a well-defined category of ageing style or pattern, based on a restricted set of criteria, remained.

The need for a differential approach of psychological ageing also emerged during the last decades from the emancipation movements of women, minority groups and non-western nations. Theorists detected gender bias not only in Erikson's lifespan theory (Franz and White, 1985), but also in such more recent content-less models of successful ageing as provided by Baltes (Labouvie-Vief, 2003). The significance of social class, ethnicity and culture as sources of differences in psychological ageing is now increasingly recognised and accordingly dealt with in research (Dittmann-Kohli, 2001).

An ecological perspective

In the ecological study of development and ageing the focus is on changes in individuals embedded in a socio-physical environment conceptualised in terms of nested systems (see Chapter 10). Bronfenbrenner (1979) distinguished micro-, meso-, exo- and macro-systems to indicate the ever widening circles of environmental influences in which age-related behavioural and experiential changes occur. Bronfenbrenner's initial model developed into a bioecological model of psychological development in which the terms 'proximal process' (the interaction between the person and the immediate and more remote environmental contexts), 'person', 'context' and 'time' are the core concepts (Bronfenbrenner and Crouter,

1983; Bronfenbrenner and Morris, 1998). It has a lot of potential to inspire psycho- gerontological research.

In the study of the evolving interactions between individuals and their environment, researchers may primarily focus either on behaviour and behavioural development, or on the influencing environmental contexts. The latter is the case in the so-called environmental gerontology that in the past four decades 'focused on the description, explanation, and modification or optimisation of the relation between older people and their socio-spatial surroundings' (Wahl and Weisman, 2003, p. 616) (see Chapter 10). Socio-spatial environments studied ranged from micro- to macro-environmental systems, such as private homes, residential homes and specialised care settings, neighbourhoods, social policy and rural–urban differences (Wahl and Weisman, 2003). Lawton (1989a) distinguished three basic functions of the residential environment in terms of maintenance, stimulation and support. The constancy and predictability of the environment provide the basis for the maintenance of functional status, self-concept and well-being of the residents. The function of stimulation implies the challenge and optimisation of the adaptation potential of older people. The function of support consists of the environment's potential to compensate for irreversible losses of competence.

Based on the distinction between these three functions and three main topics of environmental gerontology research (private home environments, planned environments, and residential decisions), Wahl and colleagues (Wahl, 2001; Wahl and Weisman, 2003) reviewed the literature. They reaffirmed the worthiness of research from an ecological perspective, but at the same time appealed for theoretical and empirical innovations in the domain. Wahl's overview confirms the general assumption that older people are strongly attached to their own home environment and prefer to stay in their familiar environment as long as possible, even when their health is failing. Physical and social characteristics of neighbourhoods and communities in interaction with personality, family and other variables, at different ecological levels, shape the older person's outdoor activities and mobility. The maintenance of the person–environment fit in old age may be considered as a main developmental task that mobilises different types of coping strategies ranging from thoroughly adjusting the physical features of the home environment to restricting activities in the unchanged environment. The inter-individual variability between older people in how they achieve an appropriate person–environment fit is pronounced, but determining factors remain to be explored.

Depending on a variety of factors, older persons moving into a nursing home mostly succeed in the adaptation to the institutional setting, and learn to feel at home. Evidence of the therapeutic effects of skilled care units, especially on dementing residents, seems mixed. Research has clearly indicated that certain characteristics of the socio-physical environment of a residential setting can stimulate aged residents to more social contact, activity and autonomy, and reduce problem behaviours in demented residents. Physical and programme features of an institutional environment can support residents in compensating for their losses in cognitive and behavioural functioning (Wahl, 2001, p. 224).

An interventionist perspective

A lot of research in gerontology is primarily focused on interventions aimed at the optimisation of psychological ageing in terms of the maintenance or improvement of functional status in different domains of life. Behavioural intervention research began to appear in the 1970s. Cognitive training and care environment improvement were objectives of many small- and large-scale intervention studies (Willis, 2001). Actually, intervention research is a kind of experimental research in a near-to-real or real-life context. It is characterised by behavioural or socio-physical environmental manipulations. Willis refers to different types of designs. These are, depending on the comparisons that are made with the experimental group, to detect the effectiveness of the intervention (e.g. designs with a no-treatment control group, a non-specific comparison group, and a component control condition), and the comparison of interventions. For instance, in an intervention study with a placebo or non-specific comparison group, Willis *et al.* (1983) compared cognitive training on attention and flexibility outcomes to the levels of performance of two other groups. One was a social contact group that met for an equivalent number of hours focusing on social support and friendship, the other was a no-treatment control group. The treatment group's performance on the target ability measures was significantly above that of the social contact group, which did not differ from the no-treatment group.

Ideally, intervention research should be 'translational' research. This means that insights from theory and basic research are used to guide intervention programmes that in their turn are systematically tested with regard to their effectiveness. These programmes may aim at the improvement of the person–environment fit, the enhancement of the adaptation capability of the individual and/or the creation of stimulating and inspiring (caring) environments. Basic behavioural research is supposed to yield findings that can be translated into 'outcomes that will benefit older people, enhance their quality of life and productivity, and reduce their care needs' (Pillemer *et al.*, 2003, p. 20). For instance, the Roybal Centers on Applied Gerontology of the National Institute on Aging in the USA are typically established to bridge the gap between basic gerontological research and the implementation of effective interventions in specific domains such as mobility and driving, social integration and exercise adherence in older adults. In the model that guides their projects, theory and basic research deliver the necessary knowledge building blocks for the design of interventions, the carefully measured results of which may lead to the improvement of future intervention designs and even the adaptation of basic theories. This is the ultimate goal of intervention studies rooted in sound social and psychological theory and basic research findings. In the field of cognitive ageing, considerable efforts have been made to approach the ideal of intervention research rooted in basic theories and research findings (Willis, 2001). In other fields, however, the reality still lags far behind this ideal. Indeed, interventions primarily focusing on the achievement of a desired outcome (a change in behaviour) may be typically a-theoretical, and therefore do not yield an understanding of the processes or mechanisms underlying the change in behaviour. With regard to caregiver intervention studies, Pillemer *et al.* (2003) refer to this anomaly and the difficulty of attributing intervention outcomes to a specific cause if – which is frequently the case – interventions are multidimensional. A strong theoretical or conceptual framework for interventions may include research-based hypotheses about what is supposed to actually determine the aimed for behavioural change.

In sum, both theory and practice in the domain of psychological ageing may benefit from intervention research firmly rooted in theory and basic research findings.

MAIN DOMAINS OF RESEARCH

The domain of psychological ageing research is actually a fabric of rather loosely linked theories and empirical investigations on age-related changes of different psychological functions and attributes in late adulthood and old age. Cognitive ageing continues to dominate the study of the psychology of ageing. In recent years notable advances have been made in other previously neglected fields, particularly within the interrelated areas of emotion, motivation and personality. Though much of the work in these fields remains at the exploratory stage, it holds the potential of a major contribution to ageing studies. We shall consider each of these three research areas in turn, after we discuss cognitive ageing (see also Chapter 12).

Cognitive ageing

Development and ageing of memory and psychometric intelligence in late adulthood and old age were the focus of numerous investigations. This was also the domain in which the above-mentioned innovative views on the basic processes of development and ageing were first tested out (Baltes *et al.*, 1998).

Subjective beliefs
Older people seldom report cognitive growth. On the contrary, memory complaints, doubts about one's abilities to adapt to new technologies, and the expectation of further decline are only a few examples of the perceived association between ageing and cognitive decline. Age-related changes in cognitive functioning are generally investigated in a perspective of losses rather than gains. Recently, attempts are made to at least consider the possibility that the execution of some cognitive tasks or everyday cognitive activities may improve or remain on the same level in old age (Dixon, 2000). What follows is a very brief overview of what is known about age-related cognitive changes.

Decline in cognitive functions and intelligence
Cognitive ageing research revealed that practically no form of (non-automated) cognition is fully resistant to the negative impact of ageing. Age-related, but differential, decline in the various types of memory, several other kinds of cognitive

functioning and intelligence is well documented. Normally ageing adults typically have difficulties in recalling names or remembering details about where and when something happened. They experience fewer problems with recognition tasks and explaining word meanings (Salthouse, 1991a). The overall concept of memory may not be considered as a monolithic entity. Cognitive psychologists proposed different types of memory in order to better understand the observations they made on memory deficits in adults affected by ageing or brain damage.

Procedural memory implies so-called implicit memory processes, well-learned, automatic mental processes that lay at the basis of a lot of motor and cognitive skills, such as driving a car, counting and reading. These processes are not affected by ageing. The perceptual representational system or the sensory memory is also not affected by age. As far as sensory systems play a role in memory through holding unprocessed sense information for a very brief period, no age-related decline is observed. This does not mean that sensory losses are not affecting higher-order cognitive processes (see later).

Waugh and Norman (1965) introduced the term 'primary memory' to refer to the capacity to keep in mind a bit of information over a very short period. All other acts of the retrieval of information from memory they called 'secondary memory'. Primary memory corresponds to what some called short-term memory. The time span of storage of information in primary memory may be very short as is mostly the case in experiments where it refers to the fragment of information that is still consciously present after the presentation of several other stimuli. In other approaches, short-term memory refers to memory for recent events over a few hours or days. However, primary memory is clearly related to another type of short-term memory, called 'working memory' (Baddeley and Hitch, 1974). The latter term indicates the dynamics of manipulation, storage and transformation of held information over a short period. As the term suggests, in the working memory the incoming formation is worked upon in order to adequately select and store the information necessary to maintain the ongoing higher-order cognitive processes. There is no manifest age-related decrement in primary memory, but large age decrements seem to exist in working memory.

'Episodic memory' is the ability to recollect events that a person has experienced. It results from several stages of processing, among which the first is the encoding of information, and the final is the retrieval of stored information. Older people may have difficulties in both these stages. There is a lot of evidence of an age-related decline of the ability of free recall of, for example, previously presented words, sentences or pictures in an experimental setting, or names of people recently met, or issues in the newspaper read the day before. Older people also tend to forget contextual details of events of everyday experiences and therefore, for example, tell the same story to the same person a number of times. This type of memory performance declines with age from the thirties and forties and remains a source of embarrassment and frustration to many older people.

'Semantic memory' refers to the store of decontextualised knowledge, such as general knowledge and vocabulary. Age-related decrements in semantic memory functioning are rather minimal from young adulthood to the mid-seventies. However, in some aspects of semantic memory decrements exist especially in advanced old age. Increasing word-finding and name-retrieving difficulties are well-known examples of this downward trend.

In sum, there seems to be no extensive age-related decline in procedural, sensory and primary memory, and in most aspects of semantic memory, but significant decline with age in working and episodic memory, and in some aspects of semantic memory. In very old age no memory form escapes completely from age-related decline.

Age-related changes, from early to late adulthood, have been observed in psychometric intelligence also. The magnitude of the age-related impairment varies across different aspects of intelligence. Psychologists distinguish between fluid and crystallised intelligence (Horn, 1982; Horn and Cattell, 1976). Fluid intelligence consists of relatively culture-free types of information processing such as pattern recognition, spatial orientation, memory, reasoning and abstraction. Crystallised intelligence refers to a largely culture- and education-related knowledge that involves general knowledge, vocabulary and application of knowledge. Baltes (1993) introduced the terms *mechanics* and *pragmatics* of intelligence to discern two types of cognitive abilities. The first form of intelligence, which is dependent on the hardwiring (neurophysiology) of the mind, consists of basic cognitive processing of information abilities (cognition as cognition). The second type of intelligence consists of culturally determined factual knowledge, and patterns of thinking and problem-solving, resulting in uncountable types of culturally valued expertise. Age-related decline in fluid abilities or the mechanics of intelligence is well documented. Performances based on crystallised intelligence or pragmatics remain stable in the adult years far into young old age, but finally join fluid abilities and the mechanics of intelligence in their downward course.

In search of an explanation of age-related changes in memory and other (encompassing) aspects of cognition, researchers frequently pointed to slowing of perceptual speed Salthouse (1991a, 1996), reduced working memory capacity (Light, 2000), inhibition deficit (Hasher and Zacks, 1988; Park, 2000; Rogers, 2000), reduced attention capacity (Light, 2000), and more recently, changes in sensory functioning (Baltes and Lindenberger, 1997). From these potential sources of the age-related decline in the performance of memory tasks and psychometric tests of fluid intelligence, especially, processing speed and primary working memory emerged as important predictors of age-related differences in performance. Recently, evidence has been presented that apart from these two sources, measures of sensory and sensorimotor function are also capable of mediating age-cognition relationships (Lindenberger and Baltes, 1994). These observations led Baltes and Lindenberger (1997) to posit a common-cause hypothesis. Performances on sensory measures as well as cognitive measures may be taken as indicators of a general age-related decline in a common factor. This factor must be sought in the functioning of the brain. What this actually means remains an open question.

A gains perspective on cognitive ageing: post-formal thinking and wisdom
In the overall picture of cognitive ageing, references to losses predominate. Research on the positive gain of wisdom, for instance, has been described as one of the 'least studied' (Sternberg, 1990, p. ix) and 'long neglected' (Birren and Fisher, 1990, p. 317) of all psychological constructs. The scarcity of research in this area is due to a more immediate concern to identify and offset deficits and declines. Nevertheless, recently, researchers have sought to define and measure cognitive gains in later adulthood.

Dixon (2000) explored the concepts and mechanisms of gains in cognitive ageing. He distinguished three main views on gains in the context of cognitive losses in old age: gains as gains, gains as losses of a lesser magnitude, and gains as a function of losses. The first are real gains contrasting with the general background of loss in cognitive abilities. Gains of the second type are rather through use of adequate coping mechanisms to alleviate losses. Personally experienced cognitive losses are made bearable by taking into consideration that they appeared later than expected, are not universal, of a level less than expected, and not debilitating everyday skills. The third sort of gains are apparent gains 'that are linked to specific or general losses, that are occasioned by losses, or that compensate for losses' (Dixon, 2000, p. 30). The two explicitly loss-based types of gains in old age have been made visible in theory and research on coping, resilience and compensation in late adulthood. Genuine age-related gains in the cognitive domain have been studied by neo-Piagetians and by lifespan psychologists focusing on wisdom.

Originally, Piagetians supposed that the fourth stage of cognitive development, namely formal operational thinking, normally reached in late adolescence, was the final one. However, some scholars hypothesised a continued growth in thinking and reasoning with advancing age, and started searching for a post-formal stage of cognitive development (Commons *et al.*, 1984, Commons *et al.*, 1990). The key question of this search is whether there exists a kind of rationality that is qualitatively higher than formal operations. Sinnott (1998) introduced a theory of relativistic post-formal thought. Guided by the Piagetian inspired question about what adaptive intelligence is like at different points in development, she and other scholars went into the realm of thinking and reasoning of mature adults in the second half of life. A person who can use formal operational thought can *think about thinking* and can use hypothetical–deductive reasoning in his or her confrontation with a multifaceted reality. However, this is not the highest level of thinking. A next step in the hierarchy of sophistication of thinking operations is possible. Sinnott (1998, p. 24) defines the essence of post-formal thoughts as 'the ability to order several systems of formal operations, or systems of truth'. According to Sinnott (pp. 24–25):

> [This way of thinking] requires a degree of necessary subjectivity to make a commitment to one logical truth system and to act within that one system. It is relativistic in the sense that several truth systems do exist describing the reality of the same event, and they appear to be logically equivalent. … It is also non-relativistic in that the knower ultimately does make a serious commitment to one truth system only. That truth system then goes on to become

true for the knower, since the knower's committed action makes it so. The knower finally sees that… all knowing involves a region of uncertainty in which, somewhere, truth lies. All knowledge and all logic are incomplete; knowing is partly a matter of choice.

Post-formal thought may be considered as both a special form of intelligence (clearly related to crystallised intelligence and the pragmatics of intelligence) and an expression of wisdom.

Research on wisdom has many theoretical and applied benefits reasons, not least its association with a range of positive attributes and experiences including greater autonomy and psychological mindedness (Wink and Helson, 1997), better psychological health (Erikson *et al.*, 1986; Wink and Helson, 1997) and greater success in dealing with life's challenges (Kramer, 2000). The judgements made in wise decisions can facilitate a more harmonious world.

Yet defining wisdom is not easy and there is much debate about its associated components. Early research examined the characteristics people associate with wisdom or wise people. In one such study, Holliday and Chandler (1986) asked 150 participants (age range 22–86 years) to generate descriptors of wise people, as well as shrewd, perceptive, intelligent, spiritual and foolish people. They found that wisdom was defined in terms of learning from experience, being open-minded and knowledgeable, being of an older age, and having the ability to consider different perspectives. Additional components identified to date include greater awareness and empathy with others, and greater insight into human experiences and human potentials. The occurrence of wisdom is also believed to necessitate an awareness of conflict and ambiguity (Sternberg, 2001), greater use of humour (Taranto, 1989), greater openness to experiences (Wink and Helson, 1997; Staudinger *et al.*, 1997) and the ability to successfully regulate emotions (Kramer, 1990). Synthesising a set of provocative chapters on the nature, origins and development of wisdom (Sternberg 1990), Birren and Fisher (1990, pp. 331–332) concluded that:

[The authors] view wisdom as an emergent property of an individual's inward and external response to life experiences. A wise person has learned to balance the opposing valences of the three aspects of behaviour: cognition, affect, and volition. A wise person weighs the knowns and unknowns, resists overwhelming emotion while maintaining interest, and carefully chooses when and where to take action.

This description echoes Sinnott's and other authors' views on post-formal thought.

The above characteristics might suggest that wisdom occurs only rarely. This was disputed by Randall and Kenyon (2001), who used biographical interviews to explore wisdom as being more broadly and regularly manifested in the lives of 'ordinary' people. The dimensions of wisdom they delineated include cognitive, practical/experimental, interpersonal, ethical/moral and spiritual/mystical. In documenting 'narrative wisdom', they argue that wisdom can be discovered in all our lives, by exploring the lives we have lived, the challenges that have been addressed and the choices that were made.

One of the most dominant and influential recent theories on wisdom is that of Baltes and colleagues (Baltes *et al.*, 1992, 1995; Dittmann-Kohli, 1984; Baltes and

Staudinger, 2000). Wisdom relates to the pragmatic features of the mind, including culturally acquired information and knowledge, and is likely to increase with age and experience at least into the seventh or eight decade of life. In their empirical work, Baltes *et al.* (1995) hypothesised five criteria necessary for this pragmatic acquisition of a knowledge-based state of wisdom:

- (1) factual knowledge (2) procedural knowledge
- (3) lifespan contextualism
- (4) value relativism (5) the recognition and management of uncertainty.

They hypothesised a developmental shift in the onset and development of these five criteria, with the acquisition of (factual and procedural) knowledge occurring first, while the three process criteria develop later alongside greater experience of life and of others.

An alternative way for researchers to define and examine wisdom is not in terms of knowledge, but in terms of reflexivity and affect alongside the cognitive components of wisdom (see Kramer, 1990). While the cognitive components of wisdom necessitate knowledge particularly about intrapersonal and interpersonal experiences, reflective practices can be central to the process of knowledge accumulation. It is only by engaging in reflective thinking and by looking at experiences and phenomena from different perspectives that the cognitive and knowledge-based aspects of wisdom can occur. Through a process of reflexivity, people are more likely to see reality without the occurrence of distortions, and increase the probability of gaining true insight about people and experiences.

The development of questionnaires (Ardelt, 2003; Webster, 2003) and interview instruments (Montgomery *et al.*, 2002) for the measurement of wisdom now enables researchers to carry out empirical research with groups of individuals. Such studies could address a range of questions, including uncertainties about the antecedents of wisdom or the consequences of wisdom on health, quality of life or quality of relationships with others.

Emotions and ageing

Psycho-gerontology, like psychology in general, has not given anything like equivalent attention to emotional compared with cognitive functioning. This reflects in part a western bias towards defining humans in terms of their thinking and reasoning abilities. Feelings tend to be regarded as part of the lower animal order, often looked down upon as vestiges of patterns of action that once were useful in our evolution but are no longer so. Yet in fact it is the partnership of our emotions with our rational faculties that distinguishes us as higher animate beings. It has taken a different, more respectful, attitude to emotions, stimulated especially by the work of ethologists, to realise that they are centrally important in human and animal behaviour. Emotions are our way of responding to situations where we are not sure how we should respond. Humans, as well as animals, are not automata. They often find themselves in situations where they lack appropriate patterns of behaviour, when they are not fully adapted to an environment that has changed, or when no habit or instinct fits a situation. Emotions are important at such junctures because they prompt us towards certain types of action when perhaps we should do something but lack already established modes of action (Oatley and Jenkins, 1996).

Psychologists who work in this field employ the concepts of 'primary' and 'secondary' emotions. The primary emotion systems are born with us and relate to action systems that are triggered by events we experience in relation to our goals: thus, happiness at the achievement of goals, sadness at their loss, anger at frustration of a plan to reach a goal, and anxiety because of a conflict between goals, including the important goal of self-preservation. Secondary emotions, such as embarrassment, guilt and pride, arise early in life as children develop complex forms of representation of the world around and of an inner world of mental states shared with others.

In striking contrast to the general picture of decline which the study of cognitive ageing presents, older people by and large impress by their ability to master their negative emotions and present a positive face to the world. Many commentators start from the so-called 'paradox' of late-life well-being (Westerhof et al., 2003). Whereas ill-health, disability, bereavement, loss of expectations and the many other social disadvantages that often characterise late life are associated with diminished morale and life satisfaction at younger stages of life, older individuals display much higher levels of well-being than one might expect on the grounds of these general associations alone. Clearly people as they age acquire a certain emotional resilience, ways of coping with loss that younger people in general lack. As will be stressed again further on, it is important not to over-generalise these differences; not all older people display equivalent levels of resilience.

Investigations of emotions by means of self-report assessments have indicated a systematic decline in negative emotions with age while positive emotions appear to remain fairly constant (Charles et al., 2001; Dittmann-Kohli et al., 2001; Labouvie-Vief and Medler, 2002). Older people are less likely to use immature defences, are better able to control emotions, and show generally less reactivity and lower arousal. Socio-emotional selectivity theory developed by Carstensen and colleagues (Carstensen et al., 1999; Carstensen et al., 2003) explains this bias towards positive images in terms of older individuals' greater emphasis on maintaining the positives in their lives in the light of their limited time expectation. As a result they are less interested in the more time-demanding task of identifying and removing threats in the future which may never materialise for them.

However, this generalisation is dependent on the context. Where older people are dealing with familiar situations and can rely on well-rehearsed solutions to emotional problems they appear less reactive than younger people; but where they are dealing with novel and demanding situations older people may experience greater levels of disturbance (Labouvie-Vief, 2005). Consistent with socio-emotional selectivity theory, they also function better in situations that are personally relevant to them (Rahhal et al., 2002). Thus older people's continued positive emotional functioning may depend on control of demands put upon them by the environment (Labouvie-Vief and Marquez Gonzales, 2004).

Research in this area often seems to assume that adjustment is always desirable. The notion of individual adjustment implies a harmony between an inner state and an outer condition. A perfectly adjusted organism would be silent, wrote Freud. But some conditions are intolerable and deserve protest rather than acquiescence. Gerontology has been diminished by an over-emphasis on individual subjective well-being as the primary outcome variable to be studied. The contribution older people make and the example they set to the rest of society are certainly as important. In neglecting 'virtue', gerontology has followed trends in contemporary society (MacIntyre, 1984). The role of prophet, for example, is not necessarily a comfortable or pleasant one. It is interesting that Labouvie-Vief (2005), in her review of the field of ageing and the emotions, acknowledged that maintenance of positivity is not always a sign of 'good' emotional development. It may indicate an inability to secure an overall objective representation of reality. This is at least as important a goal as maintaining positive affect.

Motivation and ageing

Theories of developmental changes in motivation in adulthood have typically emphasized two basic needs, variously worded (Bakan, 1966; Bode, 2003):

- 'agency', 'power' or 'mastery'
- 'communion', 'intimacy' or 'belonging'.

Often these are seen to be at odds with one another, and one of the themes of the psycho-dynamic literature on ageing from Jung (1972) onwards has been the possibility for their integration and reconciliation in later life (see especially Henry, 1988).

These developments are often depicted as having a gendered character, with older men learning to display more 'feminine' motivations and older women more 'masculine' motivations. Greater relatedness can compensate for men's loss of competence, whereas women's often late-won independence is something they may safeguard strongly. The resultant greater androgynous character of later life is claimed to be advantageous to both men and women. Although the evidence for such theories in modern societies as opposed to traditional societies (Gutmann, 1987) is slight – a recent representative Dutch study found no decrease in gender differences with age (Westerhof and Bode, 2006) – they continue to have appeal to those searching for greater purpose and meaning in the experience of ageing.

New impetus has recently been given to research on ageing and motivation by Deci and Ryan's (2000) examination of the concept of psychological need, and their specification of competence, relatedness and autonomy as three needs essential to goal-related activity. Their fundamental postulate is that 'humans are active, growth-oriented organisms who are naturally inclined toward integration of their psychic elements into a unified sense of self and integration of themselves into larger social structures' (Deci and Ryan, 2000, p. 229). Although Deci and Ryan give relatively few illustrations from the field of ageing, it is clear that their approach has much to offer to understand older people's behaviour. Some researchers have already begun to apply this theory in studies on institutional care. For example, O'Connor and Vallerand (1994) have focused on the concept of autonomy, which is subtly but significantly different from the concept of control, also an important concept in health psychology. Whereas the literature on locus of control and learned helplessness focuses on the perception of contingency between the person's own behaviours and observable outcomes, autonomy or self-determination refers to the experience of freedom in initiating one's behaviour. Control does not ensure autonomy, and autonomy does not ensure control. It is choice which is central to autonomy. Deci and Ryan (2000) describe four types of behaviour that vary along a continuum of autonomy or self-determination. Using these distinctions O'Connor and Vallerand (1994) have developed a measure of elderly motivational style applicable to the domains of life relevant to the lives of older people.

In a study of intermediate-care nursing homes in Montreal, the older people were assessed on the needs for self-determination, and the homes were independently classified on the basis of information they supplied on the degree of self-determination provided. As one would expect, residents in high self-determination nursing homes tended to score higher on self-determined motivation. But more interesting was the finding of interaction effects with motivational styles. There was a tendency for low self-determined motivation individuals to report better psychological adjustment in low self-determination nursing homes, and for high self-determination motivation individuals to report better psychological adjustment in high self-determination nursing homes.

This is a good example of the so-called 'person–environment congruence' theory of ageing (Lawton, 1980). One cannot expect all elderly nursing home residents to benefit from high levels of autonomy. But O'Connor and Vallerand (1994) suggest the interesting hypothesis that long-term adjustment is better served by an environment that provides opportunities for autonomy that are always slightly greater than one's initial level of self-determined motivation. In a further test of 'person–environment congruence' in institutional settings, O'Connor and Rigby (1996) carried out an intriguing study on 'baby talk' in nursing homes, again independently recording the elderly residents' need for succourance and the behaviour shown by staff . Significant interactions were again evident, suggesting the harmful effect of receiving baby talk on self-esteem for those who perceived it negatively. Thus Deci and Ryan's concept of relatedness also has to be seen in the context of a person's history. What can be perceived as 'warmth' by one person may be seen by another as being 'talked down to' by another, thus undermining feelings of competence.

Some of the best examples of work on motivation in institutional settings in Europe are provided by the late Margret Baltes' programme of research in German nursing homes (Baltes and Carstensen, 1996). She has shown how it is necessary to counteract professional carers' 'preference' for older people who give up self-control and thus become more easy to manage. Moreover, a pattern-of-dependency script operates in institutions, whereby dependent behaviour is most likely to result in staff providing social contact and attention. These are usually highly valued by most residents and, in learning theory terms, function as 'rewards'. Baltes *et al.* (1994) have developed training programmes that have proved effective in reversing these patterns. It is important to note that, in a large representative sample from East and West Germany, older men and women expressed fear of becoming dependent and losing their ability for independent living with advancing old age (Bode, 2003; Dittmann-Kohli, 1995a; Dittmann-Kohli and Westerhof, 2000).

Personality and ageing

The studies just referred to are clear examples of the importance of individual differences in the study of ageing. However, the question whether personality itself changes with age has remained a difficult one to resolve. Answers to this question also depend on how personality is defined. One way of resolving the paradoxes in the literature on this subject is to think of the realm of personality in terms of two types of variable:

- those that remain relatively stable throughout adulthood (typically referred to as personality traits)
- those that develop and change (including attitudes to the self and to the world around, values, beliefs, goals and reference systems).

Unfortunately most research has not taken both aspects of personality into account.

There is now a well established consensus that the 'big five' traits of neuroticism, extraversion, openness to experience, agreeableness and conscientiousness are consistent across age groups, cultures and measurement instruments as dimensions of personality on which individuals differ (John, 1990; Costa and McCrae, 1997). The structural invariance of the measurement techniques means that one can confidently assert the relative stability of these personality traits with age (Staudinger, 2005). Individuals retain the same profile relative to one another. There is consistent evidence for relatively small mean changes with ageing. Neuroticism appears to decrease across adulthood (Mroczek and Spiro, 2003), although it may show some increase in very late life (Small *et al.*, 2003), as also does openness to experience and extraversion (McCrae *et al.*, 2000; Field and Millsap, 1991). Agreeableness and conscientiousness, by contrast, increase (Haan *et al.*, 1986; Helson and Kwan, 2000). Longitudinal evidence of similar changes has led McCrae, Costa and others to speculate whether this developmental pattern may have been selected for by evolution (McCrae *et al.*, 2000).

McAdams (1995) makes a useful distinction between three levels of knowledge of personality. The first level comprises the traits that are independent of context, but are so broad that they give only limited knowledge of the person. McAdams refers to personality traits as the 'psychology of the stranger'. By contrast, when one knows a person better one moves to the second level of understanding their motives, values, attitudes and skills, including ways of coping, all of which McAdams groups under the term 'personal concerns'. But particularly in the modern world even this type of information is insufficient for in-depth awareness of the person. Some additional understanding is needed of the inner story of the self, how people make sense of their lives, how they integrate their past, present and future, and their various characteristics, so as to experience their life as having unity, purpose and meaning. Not everyone succeeds in this integration but this is what McAdams means by 'identity', using the term first coined in this way by Erikson (1963).

Some of the most interesting work on age changes at the second level has been done on ways of coping. Already in the 1980s there was evidence of systematic change with age towards greater control of the emotions and less use of problem-solving. Using the methods developed by Lazarus, the pioneer American researcher on stress and coping (Lazarus, 1966; Lazarus and DeLongis, 1983), Folkman *et al.* (1987) reported that these differences in styles of coping remained even when controlled for the different areas of stress experienced by older and younger people. For example, older people report more stresses having to do with environmental and social issues and less with family, friends and finance. The one exception was the health area where older people appear to be more proactive than younger people (Leventhal *et al.*, 1992), perhaps because of their greater experience of the difficulties caused by neglecting a health problem.

More recently, Labouvie-Vief has conducted interesting work on individual differences in two self-regulation modes, affect-optimization and affect-differentiation (Labouvie-Vief, 2005; Labouvie-Vief and Marquez Gonzales, 2004). In the former condition negative feelings are minimized, there is no exploration of feelings, and unpleasant facts tend to be ignored; in the latter, by contrast, emotions are analysed, ambiguities are accepted and there is much less repression of negativity. Affect-optimization increases linearly with age whereas affect-differentiation shows a curvilinear pattern of growth and decline peaking in late middle age. Labouvie-Vief employs Werner's (1957) categories to distinguish those high in both qualities ('integrated'), low in both ('dysregulated'), high in the former and low in the latter ('self-protective'; hi/lo), and low in the former and high in the latter ('complex'). Whereas 'self-protective' people place less emphasis on personal growth and more on environmental mastery, 'complex' persons magnify negative affect. Labouvie-Vief has produced evidence that 'self-protection' increases from mid-life onwards while the numbers showing 'complex' characteristics decline. This appears to be a promising line of research for understanding individual differences in late-life coping, and perhaps also for identifying interventions to promote more effective coping.

Recent work on personality and ageing which really does focus on the individual person is scarce. Between the world wars there was an active tradition of case-study analysis carried out by well-known psychologists such as Murray and Allport, but its value was overlooked in the postwar enthusiasm for quantitative methods. Those who have tried to recover this tradition (e.g. Runyan, 1984; Bromley, 1986; McAdams and West, 1997; Fishman, 1999) have emphasised that disciplined study can be carried out and testable generalisations formulated on data collected on individual lives. Coleman has pointed to the particular applicability of case-study research to the study of adaptation in later life (Coleman, 1999, 2002) and has argued for its inclusion alongside quantitative surveys within longitudinal studies of ageing.

STAGES OF AGEING: THE CHALLENGE OF THE FOURTH AGE

A neglected field of study

As the study of ageing has developed, psychologists as well as sociologists have wanted to make distinctions between stages of ageing, often attempting to use chronological age markers, to distinguish the young-old from the old-old and more recently even the oldest old (Poon *et al.*, 2005). The use of the term 'third age' for the first period of ageing characterised by individual control and freedom of action (Laslett, 1989) has inevitably led to a contrasting conceptualisation of the 'fourth age' as a time of increasing disability, frailty and constriction of opportunity.

Advanced old age has been a neglected field of study. The opportunities of the third age, of continued employment and expansion of activity arouse more interest than managing more appropriately declining involvement while maintaining commitment in the face of death. Psychological theory for this period of life has only recently developed sufficiently for it to be considered in its own right (Coleman and O'Hanlon, 2004). This reflects what Baltes (1997) has described as a cultural lag. Human development is insufficiently supported in its last stages. Baltes' metaphor is that of an ill-designed building whose vulnerabilities become more manifest after a certain time. 'Neither biological nor cultural evolution has had sufficient opportunity to evolve a full and optimizing scaffolding (architecture) for the later phases of life' (Baltes, 1997, p. 367). The result is that – paradoxically – 'historically speaking, old age is young'. A major investment of resources, social, material and technical, as well as improved psychological and spiritual understanding is required to support human development and adaptability in its last stages.

Perhaps such support will never be sufficient, because the processes of human development and ageing are fundamentally incomplete. As people through history have lamented, the advantages of age do not fully compensate for the losses of youthful vigour. The discrepancies between human wishes and human potentials widen, so that eventually death is a blessing, a release from decay. This is a theme of stories in many cultures. But the fact that we shall eventually encounter failure in our attempts to maintain quality of life in old age does not mean that we should not seek to promote human development *in extremis*.

It is important to recognise that frailty rather than disability is the distinguishing mark of this stage of life. Disability is not necessarily a progressive characteristic of people's lives. Many of those who suffer severe injury when young and become disabled as a consequence can hope to live full lives within the limits set by their disability. Moreover, disability does not necessarily imply need for care or supervision. The concept of 'frailty' has appeared with increasing frequency in the gerontological literature in recent years (Campbell and Buchner, 1997; Strawbridge *et al.*, 1998; Hamerman, 1999). Although harder to define than disability, it is more useful to the study of late life in that it encompasses 'a combination of deficits or conditions that arise with increasing age and contribute to making the elderly person more vulnerable to changes in the surroundings and to stress' (Nourhashemi *et al.*, 2001, p. M448).

Lack of attention to advanced old age has led to an imbalance in ageing theories. A major focus of recent developmental literature on ageing has been on the concept of 'successful ageing' (Rowe and Kahn, 1998). But one consequence of this has been to stigmatise further the very old. The nature of the criteria employed in this discourse, including avoidance of disease and disability, preservation of higher mental function, and active engagement with life, means that sooner or later many people fail the test. Positive meanings need to be found for this last stage of life not only for the sake of the old themselves but also because failure to do so casts a shadow over the preceding stages of life.

A further reason for the neglect of late life by psychologists is that it is a stage of life that is difficult to study using standard quantitative methods. Longitudinal studies of ageing have typically given an over-optimistic view of the later stages of life because of selective drop-out. Those willing to respond to long schedules in their late eighties and nineties tend to be the fit old, those with high self-esteem and low depression ratings, who perceive much continuity with their earlier life styles and activities. More representative studies of this age group typically employ more qualitative interview and observation but as a consequence have limited generalisability.

Psychological theorising about late life

The first major theoretical developments in the psychology of late life came with studies of institutional care in the USA in the 1960s and 1970s (see, e.g., Lieberman and Tobin, 1983). For many years the study of the developmental psychology of advanced old age was the study of institutionalised elderly people.

Robert Atchley's review chapter on 'the influence of aging or frailty on perceptions and expressions of the self' (Atchley, 1991) was an important indicator that the psychological differences between the various stages of ageing were being taken seriously by gerontologists. He distinguished carefully between the experience of ageing and that of frailty, and showed how the latter raised challenges which were much harder to deal with. Atchley reviewed the literature on the self and ageing and articulated a theoretical position in which the experiences of normal ageing influenced the self in many ways, mostly for good, until the onset of frailty. Older people had generally developed an effective stable set of processes for managing the self, as well as more robust self-concepts. But the onset of frailty posed more serious challenges to self-esteem.

Older people do not become, by virtue of their age, expert at dealing with problems resulting from disability and frailty. These include interrupted continuity in way of life, more need for more extreme coping methods, reduced capacity to use defences such as selective interaction, difficulty in identifying new possible selves, depersonalisation of the social environment, changes in reference groups, and rusty skills in using feedback from others to fashion new self-conceptions. In fact the very stability and long continuity of the self that have been achieved and preserved through adulthood make adjustment more difficult now that *real* change is required.

Self-esteem shows decline in later life, but the trajectory is very different from that, for example, of cognitive functions such as memory. Global self-esteem, in western populations at least, tends to show two periods of marked decline during the course of the lifespan, during adolescence and during late life (Brown, 1998; Ranzijn *et al.*, 1998; Robins *et al.*, 2002). In between self-esteem consolidates, so that those in their sixties often show peak levels of self-esteem (Dittmann-Kohli, 1990). In fact, of all psychological variables, self-esteem is the one on which differences between the young-old and the old-old are maximised. This supports the distinction that Atchley draws between the influences of ageing and of frailty on the self. But care needs to be taken in interpreting late life decline in self-esteem. Not every very old person shows such decline, and, as Robins *et al.* (2002) acknowledge, the decline may mean simply a more modest, balanced and ultimately truthful view of the self.

The Berlin Ageing Study provides the most detailed recent evidence on a large range of psychological indicators into advanced old age. By means of profile analysis, Smith and Baltes (1997) compared very old Berliners (85 years and over) with younger old people (65 to 84 years) on intellectual functioning, self and personality characteristics, and social relationships. Proportionately many more of the over-85s (75%) belonged to cluster groups with less desirable profiles (with high scores of one or more of neuroticism, loneliness, external control, and cognitive impairment) than did the younger group (31%). It is of particular interest that two of the apparently most dysfunctional cluster groups reported average levels of well-being. These included predominantly very old people who were markedly cognitively impaired and either had perceptions of high external control (i.e. believing that the actions of other people determined what happened to them) or high social aloneness (i.e. perceiving themselves as neither belonging to a social group nor having other people to rely on). These findings suggest caution in assuming that the undoubted social, physical and cognitive losses of late life inevitably result in lowered states of well-being.

Nor is advanced age necessarily associated with increased depression. The results of several studies (Blazer *et al.*, 1991; Halpert and Zimmerman, 1986; Haynie *et al.*, 2001; Smith and Baltes, 1999) support the view that very old people adapt to disability, and that they are in fact less depressed and anxious than one might expect when one takes the greater prevalence of disability and loss into account.

These findings strongly suggest that there is a developmental process of adaptation at work, underlying the emergence of this resiliency, which allows the very old to accept loss more easily (see also Brandtstädter and Greve, 1994; Staudinger *et al.*, 1995; Aldwin *et al.*, 1996). This is not to say that all very old people achieve a high level of serenity. Variation is the most evident fact about ageing through until death.

Late life in institutional and community care settings

Early studies into the psychology of late life were carried out in the USA, in the only form of institution existing there, the nursing home. There was rising social concern about quality of life in these institutions (Vladeck, 1980). Indeed, regimes were clinical, physical care poor, and mortality rates high. The research in these homes focused in particular on maintenance of the self (Lieberman and Tobin, 1983) and the influence of subjective control (Langer, 1983, 1989). Institutionalised older people provided a readily available and captive set of participants with whom ingenious psychological studies could be carried out.

In a set of detailed studies, Lieberman and Tobin (1983) examined how older people in the United States adapted to the stress of relocation to nursing homes. The studies demonstrated the remarkable stability of self image that many older people maintained across these transitions, but this was often achieved by changing the basis on which the self was constructed. Rather than relying on incidents from their current interpersonal interactions to confirm their image of self, people in these situations of loss and change also gave many examples from their past lives as well as reiterating general statements of conviction about themselves and their lives. They even seemed prepared to forego present reality altogether and use evidence based on wishes and distortions to maintain self-consistency. In a quite different context, Kaufman (1987) has also illustrated how older people transform present experience in ways that conform to important themes of their lives. It is the theme, for example, of being the loved mother of a united family that provides the persistent sense of meaning even when the reality fails to match.

In other ways, though, very old people appeared to show a truer awareness, particularly of their own feelings. Destructive and antisocial feelings were admitted without the embarrassment and defensive explanations that might have been elicited earlier in life. According to Tobin (1991), this was because even previously unwelcome motives can be useful for self-definition in the face of the losses of old age. They affirm who one is and has been. The studies of relocation to institutions show that it is the older people who are prepared to be more assertive and combative in defining their own interests who survive longer.

In a separate set of studies on US institutional care, Langer and Rodin (Langer and Rodin, 1976; Rodin and Langer, 1977; Rodin *et al.*, 1985) highlighted the importance of the experience of being in control of daily life. Those residents of nursing homes who felt – truly or falsely did not seem to matter so much – that they had a say over their daily activities fared better emotionally and cognitively than those who felt life was determined for them. The studies involved manipulating variables such as staff instructions and behaviour. Even taking minor responsibilities (e.g. for the care of a plant) was associated with more favourable outcomes. Similar findings have been found by other investigators (Baltes and Baltes, 1986).

Subsequent research has provided a more nuanced view of the contribution of control to well-being (Moos, 1981; Reich and Zautra, 1990). There is an optimum level of subjective control for a particular individual in a particular situation. In most environments we operate below optimum; but exceeding that level can also be counterproductive, provoking anxiety and consequent under-performance. This type of U-shaped performance function can be seen in other areas of psycho-gerontology. For example, studies of social support show limits to the beneficial effects of assistance provided to older people. Social support beyond a certain level may actually exacerbate the noxious impact of stress (Krause, 1995). Older adults may be able to increase their coping skills if they are encouraged to confront stressful situations without the undue involvement of others.

It is also apparent that in high-constraint environments that cannot be changed, older people with an external locus of control appear better adjusted (Felton and Kahana, 1974; Cicirelli, 1987). Also, Smith and Baltes (1997) have shown that high belief in control by others can co-exist with average levels of well-being in cognitively impaired older people. These findings illustrate the value of 'person–environment congruence' theory where well-being is a function of matching between environmental characteristics and a person's needs (Lawton, 1980; Parmelee and Lawton, 1990).

Evidence so far from studies on older people living in their own homes provides a highly contrasting picture. They confirm that some average loss of morale and self-esteem does occur in the eighties and nineties, but there is a wide variation in outcome, and successful coping patterns emerge that are quite distinct from the institutional studies. For example, the San Francisco studies of the over-85s indicate that acceptance of change is normal among the very old, as well as disengagement from potentially bothersome or stressful roles and relationships (Johnson and Barer, 1997). Contrary to findings on the younger old, the oldest old appear to gain benefit from giving up some control. Living in the present, one day at a time, is a favoured mode of life, and new emotional attachments are avoided. The sense of aloneness resulting from multiple bereavements is counterbalanced by the very olds' special status as long-term survivors.

The psychology of dementia

The many disabling consequences arising from mental frailty make dementia the major health problem of later life. It is the most age-related of all the disabling conditions affecting older people; the overall prevalence is increasing. Dementia has now become the major reason for receiving institutional care, and a challenge to the physically frail but mentally intact people cared for in the same environment.

Unfortunately dementia has until recently been a neglected condition, not only in terms of quality of provision but also of research into its nature, cause and treatment. The role of psychologists in dementia has also been limited, until recently almost exclusively focused on developing appropriate cognitive tests for use in its detection. This remains a very important task. However, psychological interest in dementia has recently broadened to include the development and evaluation of different types of therapeutic intervention. Perhaps most important of all recent developments has been psychologists' contribution to understanding what it means to be demented (Woods, 2001).

With greater publicity and openness about dementia, there is now much greater curiosity about the condition. This has extended to the sufferer's own experience of becoming and being demented. Also, family caregivers' accounts have become important material for books and popular films as well (Bayley, 1998). Considerable imagination is required to appreciate the impact of crumbling powers of memory and identification upon the individual's feelings of security. A lifespan developmental approach can be valuable in understanding an individual's behaviour and the cues to which he or she responds as a consequence of habits established earlier in life. There is also the possibility that a study of psychological factors, motivational and affective as well as cognitive, will eventually contribute in significant ways to a total picture of the aetiology and process of dementing illnesses.

Much has been contributed by European psychologists to this new wave of thinking about dementia. In particular, Tom Kitwood began already in the 1980s to argue for a radical rethinking of our understanding of dementia, to give more attention to internal psychological factors, such as personal reactions to the stress of finding oneself mentally frail, as well as external social circumstances, including the quality of family care (Kitwood and Bredin, 1992; Kitwood, 1997). He drew attention not only to the role of personality in affecting behavioural symptoms in dementia alongside neurological impairment, but also to factors in individual biography, social psychology, and physical health (Kitwood, 1993). Personality, of course, may also influence the rate of mental impairment in later life by its influence on styles of life, including mental exercise, which may protect against dementia.

An understanding of emotional reactions appears to be the key to quality dementia care. Emotions remain intact longer and it is through emotions that demented people can continue to make contact. A very important principle, therefore, that should guide dementia care is respect for emotions. Their very presence is a sign of continuing vitality. Both their expression and the type of responses they elicit from care staff have been used to develop systems of monitoring quality of dementia care within institutions, such as 'dementia care mapping' (Kitwood, 1997; Brooker et al., 1998).

New ideas are entering the psychological study of dementia. One interesting development is the application of attachment theory, originating in studies of child deprivation but now applied to issues throughout the lifespan. Attachment theory (Bowlby, 1973, Bowlby, 1980, Bowlby, 1982; Ainsworth, 1989) emphasises the importance of relationships and affective bonds with others for emotional development throughout life. Ageing, and even more so dementia, are the time of the greatest loss of established relationships. Miesen, (1992) has suggested that the experience of becoming demented is rather like entering Ainsworth's Strange Situation (Ainsworth et al., 1978). Behaviours such as crying, clinging and calling out represent attachment behaviours in older people with dementia. The constant request and searching for parents, which becomes more common as the illness progresses, can be seen partly as a reflection of the greater clarity of the more distant past, but more helpfully as a search for security and comfort in an increasingly uncertain world, a response to feeling 'unsafe'.

CONCLUSIONS: A LIFESPAN PERSPECTIVE FROM CHILDHOOD TO OLD AGE

This brief overview of theories and research in the field of psycho-gerontology is necessarily selective and incomplete. We focused on the psychology of the ageing – but still developing – individual facing gains and losses, experiencing cognitive, emotional, motivational and personality changes, but nevertheless, generally, able to maintain a positive self-concept and outlook on life far into advanced old age. By considering the fourth age we intended to do justice to the fact that inevitable frailty in the last phase of life mobilises all human strengths of the older people themselves, and the caregiving potential of their social and cultural environment.

The growing awareness in developmental psychology of the interconnectedness of development and ageing has led researchers to explore neighbouring developmental disciplines in search for adequate descriptions and explanations of their observations. An excellent example of the benefits of scholars crossing borders between the domains of child development, adult development and psycho-gerontology is the increasing number of studies on attachment and attachment-related topics in old age (Bradley and Cafferty, 2001; Magai and Consedine, 2004; for an overview, see Shaver and Mikulciner, 2004). Strong and secure emotional bonds with parents in infancy and with other preferred individuals throughout the life course should have great protective potential (Bowlby, 1973, 1980, 1982). Internal working models of attachment, in childhood and adulthood, have been classified as secure–autonomous, preoccupied, dismissing–avoidant, and disorganized–disoriented (Ainsworth et al., 1978; George et al., 1985). The correlates and effects of the strength and the patterns of attachment in adulthood are studied in the framework of two research traditions, the nuclear family and the peer/romantic partner tradition (Simpson and Rholes, 1998). The first tradition typically sticks to the use of the Adult Attachment Interview procedure (George et al., 1985) or theoretically founded further elaborated versions (Crittenden, 1995, 1997, 2002). The second tradition mainly uses categorically based self-report measures (Hazan and Shaver, 1987). For psycho-gerontological research in an attachment perspective, the consideration of the caregiving system that is 'an integral component and direct outgrowth of the attachment system' (Berman and Sperling, 1994, p. 9) is especially relevant. The proximity-seeking/proximity-providing ratio that characterises the early child–parent attachment/caregiving relationship generally becomes increasingly reciprocal and is eventually reversed (in the adult child's care of parents); it is also transferred to other adult attachment relationships with, for example, spouses and friends. Attachment representations, be they generalised or attachment-figure specific, and stable or reorganised over the years, and the strength of the actual secure attachment, have been studied in connection with a variety of individual and relationship characteristics in ageing people and their partners, adult children and caregivers. Patterns of attachment or attachment-related state-of-mind characteristics are affecting, for example:

- the way of coping with war memories in veterans (Hautamäki and Coleman, 2001)
- adults' evaluation of their own ageing and future old age (O'Hanlon and Coleman, 2004)
- the responses adult daughters seem to trigger in their mothers with dementia in a separation–reunion scenario (Steele *et al.*, 2004)
- how adult children provide care to their elderly parents (Mahieu, 2004; Marcoen, 2005)
- the capacity of spouses of persons with dementia to regulate proximity and distance, and the reactions of the people with dementia themselves (Ingebretsen and Solem, 1998)
- well-being among older adults (Wensauer and Grossmann, 1995).

The application of attachment theory to the description and explanation of change and stability of behaviours and experiences in older adults and their most significant others will greatly contribute to furthering the establishment of a real lifespan developmental psychology. The plea for considering continuing links between child psychology and the psychology of ageing echoes a comparable call in social gerontology for 'linking the two ends of life' through the establishment of a 'new social studies of old people and old age' (Settersten, 2005). In the domain of psycho-gerontology, the availability of several different interview and self-report measures of the many aspects of attachment (patterns, constituting dimensions, strength) will undoubtedly continue to stimulate attachment research. However, it is to be hoped that the relevance of the research questions will prevail over the accessibility of instruments, in the conceptualisation of the research. Indeed, proliferation of the term *attachment* and the diversity of existing instruments suggests an urgent need for the development of a taxonomy of attachment definitions and measures.

FURTHER READING

Baltes, P. B. and Baltes, M. M. (eds) (1990) *Successful Aging: Perspectives from the Behavioral Sciences.* New York: Cambridge University Press.

Birren, J. E. and Schaie, K. W. (eds) (2006) *Handbook of the Psychology of Aging*, 6th edn. San Amsterdam: Elsevier Academic Press.

Coleman, P. G. and O'Hanlon, A. (2004) *Ageing and Development: Theories and Research.* London: Arnold.

4

Social theory and social ageing

Chris Phillipson and Jan Baars

INTRODUCTION

The purpose of this chapter is to address relationships and connections between ageing populations and social structures, with a particular focus on arguments and theories in social gerontology as developed over the past 50 years. Some clarification of terms and concepts is necessary before highlighting the main areas to be reviewed in the chapter. The approach developed will draw upon social scientific perspectives applied to understanding ageing as a social, economic and cultural construction. The concern of social science, as applied to the study of ageing, is to examine the processes associated with growing old and how these are interpreted by different groups of women and men. This may be contrasted with social policy and government interests, where ageing is invariably viewed as a 'problem' to be solved through certain forms of social regulation and public intervention. The social science perspective also emphasises a broad definition of the relationship between 'age' and 'society'. Rather than 'old age' as such, interest is typically focused on ageing within the context of the 'life course', the latter signifying the movement of individuals through time and through socially defined transitions such as adolescence, mid-life and retirement (Daatland and Biggs, 2006; Hagestad and Dannefer, 2001).

Social science also emphasizes the impact of change as cohorts of people are born, grow older, die, and are replaced by oncoming cohorts. Riley *et al.* (1999, p. 333) point to the way in which this leads to differences between cohorts:

Because society changes, members of different cohorts (i.e. born at different times) age in different ways [authors' emphasis]. Over their lives, from birth to death, people move through structures that are continually altered with the course of history; thus, the lives of those who are growing old today cannot be the same as the lives of those who grew old in the past or of those who will grow old in the future.

The approach adopted in this chapter also works from the basic assumption that ageing can only be understood within the context of social environments – the two must be seen as working together in complex ways that shape the individual's journey through the life course. This point has been elaborated by Dannefer (1999) in his review of approaches to understanding the relationship between the individual organism and the surrounding environment. The first he describes as the parallel or dichotomous approach where the organism is viewed as being born into a pre-given environment; its success based on its capabilities to survive to reproduction in that environment. The second perspective focuses on how discrete organisms and discrete environments influence each other in a range of interactions (Dannefer, 1999, p. 69):

This approach can be called interactive or dialectical because it centres on the dynamics between an actual individual and the immediate environment. The individual is shaped to varying degrees by its exchanges with the environment, and these exchanges also affect the environment itself … In the parallel model, individual and environment are largely pre-structured entities that engage in a matching game (a game in which natural selection plays a central role); in the dialectical model, individual and environment are not fixed entities to be 'matched', but are continuously being reconstituted in everyday interaction.

The distinction made by Dannefer is helpful in thinking about the relationship between the phenomena of 'ageing' on the one side, and 'society' on the other. The two should not be seen as independent entities, forming around specific areas – such as the family, or welfare provision – but essentially operating in isolation from one another. Rather, ageing should be viewed as constructed through social institutions that provide the basis of what means to be 'young', 'middle aged' or 'old' (Schaie and Achenbaum, 1993). Equally, grouping people within these classifications also changes society in important ways – both its image of itself ('young' or 'old') and in the range and type of institutions which it develops (Estes *et al.*, 2003; Featherstone and Wernick, 1995).

The rest of this chapter explores the ties between ageing and society and the different ways these have been constructed through the application of social theory. A number of reviews are already available on this topic, notably those from Marshall (1996), Bengston and Schaie (1999) and Biggs *et al.* (2003), these building upon earlier work from Marshall (1986), Passuth and Bengtson (1988) and Hendricks and Hendricks (1986). The purposes of this review are:

- to provide a context for understanding the development of social theory within gerontology
- to re-assess the main areas of development over the past 50 years
- to highlight debates that have emerged over the past five years, particularly in the field of critical gerontology.

EARLY THEORIES OF SOCIAL AGEING

European and North American perspectives on ageing can be generalized as following three main phases over the past half-century:

- ageing approached as an individual and social problem (roughly from the late-1940s to 1960s)
- ageing treated as an economic and employment issue (1970s to 1980s)
- ageing constructed as a global issue and concern (1990s and continuing).

These phases reflect different ways in which the relationship between ageing populations and social institutions have evolved, with accompanying shifts in theoretical perspectives about the relationship between the ageing individual and social and economic institutions.

The period after the Second World War was characterized by an extensive debate within western societies about the impact of demographic change (Amann, 1984; International Association of Gerontology, 1954; Thane, 2000). The background to this was growing awareness of the significance of long-term population trends, combined with economic pressures following a period of sustained global conflict (Judt, 2005). Ageing became identified as a new social problem to be addressed through the development or consolidation of pension systems and more generally through the building of the welfare state (Lowe, 1993; Walker, 1999b). The creation of public pensions and the accompanying retirement condition accelerated retirement at fixed ages (these varying across western countries). This was subsequently theorised (Townsend, 1981; Walker, 1980) as fostering a climate of 'structured dependency', this arising from problems associated with loss of employment, low income, and health and social services which were seen to stigmatise older people.

The period of the 1940s and 1950s was also one in which social gerontology developed what Amann (1984, p. 7) refers to as its 'historical identity'. Essentially this was driven by the emergence of research institutes and surveys of older people-in the USA and in many European countries (Achenbaum, 1995; Katz, 1996). The context for this work was the perception, in demographic, economic and medical research, that old age represented a major problem that would demand new initiatives in areas such as employment, income support and health and social care. For social scientists, the dominant theoretical framework at the time (drawn from the USA) was the structural–functionalist paradigm as developed by Parsons (1951) and others. This theoretical model was itself complementary to the equally influential biomedical perspective on ageing, both contributing to the construction of later life as a medical and social problem (Estes and Binney, 1989).

The social problems perspective generated two main theoretical models, one focusing on attempts to maintain older people as 'active' individuals within society, the other justifying their withdrawal from mainstream social roles (Biggs, 2006). Cavan et al. (1949) and Havighurst and Albrecht (1953) addressed the former by arguing that the individual's self concept was directly linked to participation in social roles. To maintain morale in old age, substitutes would need to be found in situations where roles were lost or reduced, for example as a result of retirement or widowhood.

Lynott and Lynott (1996) suggest that this approach was pre-theoretical in the sense that it was never codified into a formal set of testable propositions. Essentially, it reflected a set of assumptions about appropriate behaviour in later life, these subsequently reproduced in research findings. They argue (p. 750) that:

> From Cavan to Havighurst, among others in this period, researchers were writing about age-ing as an individual social problem. The implicit sentiments of the researchers dealing with individual membership in the social order, embracing the moral obligation of self-realization through hard work, reveals, in the data, its mirror image. What these researchers discover to be the nature of ageing – individual and life satisfaction in readjustment – has its source in the implicit 'theory' of the nature of growing old. Their work and data reproduce the vision. What is characteristic of this period [i.e. the 1950s] is that there is little or no clue that these researchers are aware of this connection.

The relationship between activity and life satisfaction was pursued in a variety of ways during the 1950s and into the 1960s (see, e.g., Cavan, 1963), but for a time the theoretical debate was taken over by the publication in 1961 of Cumming and Henry's *Growing Old: The Process of Disengagment*. As with activity theory, this perspective drew inspiration from the functionalist paradigm, focusing on the way in which social institutions promote disengagement, for the benefit of the individual and the social system. The disengagement hypothesis suggests that old age is a period in which the ageing individual and society engage in a process of mutual separation (e.g. retirement and disengagement from the workforce). A key assumption made in this approach is that 'ego energy' declines with age and that, as the ageing process develops, individuals become increasingly self-absorbed and less responsive to normative controls. It is further argued that disengagement or withdrawal from social relationships will lead to the individual maintaining higher morale in old age – higher, that is, than if he or she attempted to keep involved in a range of social affairs and activities. Thus, disengagement is viewed as both a natural and desirable outcome, one leading to a stronger sense of psychological well-being. Finally, this feature of ageing is suggested to be a universal phenome-non, associated with ageing in all cultures.

The disengagement hypothesis quickly attracted criticism from within and without gerontology, with a notable contribution from Hochschild (1975) who highlighted what she saw as the 'escape clause' contained within the theory. Thus, included in the data were a significant proportion of older people who had *not* withdrawn from society to any noticeable degree. However, this group was treated by the researchers as either 'unsuccessful' adjusters to old age, 'off-time' disen-gagers, or members of a 'biological or psychological elite'. Hochschild (1975) also pointed to the way in which the authors conflated a variety of changes in later life, obscuring as a result the contribution that different processes – social, psycholog-ical and physical – might make to the experience of growing old.

Later commentaries focused on the value of the model in developing theoret-ical debates around social and psychological dimensions of ageing. Daatland (2002) and Lynott and Lynott (1996) suggest that its real significance was making social gerontology aware of the importance of theory, and in presenting a systematic approach to linking individual ageing to the social system. The process of critique also generated new theoretical perspectives including modernization theory (Cowgill and Holmes, 1972), exchange theory (Dowd, 1975), life-course perspectives (Neugarten and Hagestad, 1976) and age stratification theory (Riley et al., 1972). Although challenging many core assumptions of the disengagement model, these theories furthered the debate about the experience of growing old, applying in the process central concepts from within the social sciences (Lynott and Lynott, 1996).

In the European context, however, use of the disengagement hypothesis as an explicit tool for organising empirical studies was relatively limited. Activity theory was probably more influential during the 1950s and 1960s, though the research literature (mainly American) was probably less well-known. More significant was the use of role theory to interpret empirical findings, with Townsend's (1957) observations about the impact of retirement on working-class men a notable example. Activity and disengagement theory were, however, important (and certainly influential) in reinforcing a central message of the social problem perspective, namely, that growing old represented a significant degree of discontinuity from prior life events and experiences. Physical and mental changes were seen to bring processes of decline and mental inflexibility. At the same time, the pace of economic and cultural change was viewed as limiting the value of older people's contribution to the social system – views that Townsend (1986) was to summarise as a form of 'acquiescent functionalism' and which featured prominently in the modernization theory as propounded by Cowgill and Holmes (1972).

Equally characteristic of the social problem perspective, however, was the absence of any consideration of the impact of social structure in determining the lives of older people. Marshall (1986, p. 12) highlighted this point where he noted the emphasis of studies in the 1950s and 1960s on the 'adjustment of the individual to the society'. He went on to observe that:

> Whether measured by degree of social integration or more psychological variables such as morale and life satisfaction, the adjustment of the ageing individual became the dependent variable of choice for hundreds of investigations [during this period]. No equivalent measure of conceptualization of the 'adjustment' of the society to the individual ever gained prominence in the research armamentarium of gerontology. Even disengagement theory, which did attempt to provide a theory linking the individual and societal levels of analysis, in practice stimulated research focused on individual ageing people and their adjustment to society. Social change or the social dynamics surrounding disengagement have rarely been addressed in this theoretical tradition.

The next phase of theorising begins to address a number of the above issues, notably in attempts to engage with age and its relationship with social structure, and later with studies of the relationship between individual biographies and historical events as they influence movement through the life course (Elder, 1974). More generally, we find a rejection from the 1970s onwards of attempts to build general theories of ageing or changes covering all points of the life course (Clausen, 1972). John (1984, p. 92) summarised this position with the view that:

To the extent that one can characterize theoretical developments in social gerontology, the trend has been away from a search for a special as well as a universal theory of ageing. It is wise to abandon these endeavours since any effort along these lines will remain fruitless as long as material and ideal conditions vary from country to country.

THEORISING LATER LIFE: THE MIDDLE PHASE

The period from the 1970s through to the 1980s represents a complex series of changes in the position of older people. There is a gradual shift – uneven in timing across Europe and the USA – away from presenting older people as a social problem, beset by problems of loneliness following forced retirement and unwanted leisure. This point was highlighted by Shanas (1971, p. 114) in her critique of disengagement theory:

> The evidence that retired people from various countries say that they miss nothing about their work or that they miss primarily the income, the diverse ways in which retirement is accepted in various countries and by different individuals, the fact that industrial workers in many countries are asking for earlier retirement ages, should serve to alert us that there is not necessarily a decrease in social activity or engagement with retirement.

Retirement and in particular the growth of early retirement were in fact to become key issues during the 1970s and 1980s. On the one hand, a new generation of studies was generating more positive views about retirement (Atchley, 1976). Such perspectives (in part influenced by the growth of retirement communities in the USA) had begun to emphasise the active lifestyles that could be associated with retirement (especially for middle-class retirees in possession of occupational pensions). On the other hand, the crisis of employment affecting economies from the early 1970s encouraged the growth of earlier retirement across most European countries (see Chapter 8). Employment after age 65 was virtually eradicated. Workers (men especially) aged 60 and above (55 in countries such as Holland and France) found themselves targeted for special schemes of 'job release' (e.g. in the UK) or pre-retirement benefits (as in Denmark and Germany). The development of earlier retirement was significant in opening up new areas around which theories of social ageing were developed. Walker (1999b) makes the point:

> [Earlier retirement] reconstructed old age from a simple age-related status with a lower entry point into a much broader category that stretches from age 50 to death. This has necessitated the widespread functional separation of the third (50–74) and fourth (75+) ages, the young-old and old-old, a distinction that first appeared in France in the 1960s.

Changes to the social and economic context, together with the steady retreat of functionalism, created space for fresh perspectives on ageing. From the late 1960s onwards, new theories were introduced into gerontology, drawn from diverse sources including symbolic interactionism, revisions to existing approaches (such as activity and role theory), psychological models such as socio-emotional selectivity theory, theories of the life course, early political economy models, and the adoption of cohort perspectives (Baltes and Baltes, 1990; Carstensen, 1991; Estes, 1979; Marshall, 1986; Marshall and Tindall, 1978; Passuth and Bengtson, 1988). Increasingly, attempts were being made to move beyond an individual-level focus with attempts to link together macro- and micro-sociological perspectives (Riley, 1987).

This shift in theorising reflected broader currents within the social sciences, with the questioning of dominant functionalist models (see especially Gouldner, 1970) and the rise of phenomenological and Marxist perspectives (Giddens, 1984). Dawe (1970), in a much cited article, drew an important distinction between what he termed the 'first' and 'second' sociologies. The former were best illustrated by functionalist perspectives that gave priority to the social system over the individual and viewed social norms as not just regulative but also constitutive of the self. In the second sociology, in contrast, society is seen 'as the creation of its members; the production of their construction of meaning, and of the action and relationships through which they attempt to impose that meaning on their historical situations' (Dawe, 1970, p. 260). Ryff (1986, p. 45) viewed the latter as part of a significant shift in sociology, with a 'reaction against oversocialized views of the individual that saw the person as merely internalizing values and norms of society and following stable, socially prescribed roles'.

In the case of theory in gerontology, there was no simple shift from one type of sociology to another. The first major theoretical perspective in this phase – *age stratification theory* – drew strongly on the functionalist tradition but at the same time provided a link to future theorising with its emphasis on birth cohorts and life-course perspectives. Crucially, as a theoretical model, it took the debate beyond individual adjustment towards issues focusing on the influence of social structure. Age stratification builds on the role and influence of social structure on the process of individual ageing and the stratification of age in society (Riley and Riley, 1994; Riley, 1998). Members of different cohorts are viewed as comprising 'age strata' (i.e. children, middle-aged adults, older people), among whom differences may be counted not simply in age but also in respect of the historical experiences to which they have been exposed (Riley, 1987).

Two important arguments follow from this type of approach. The first is that age is an important mechanism for *regulating* behaviour through the life course, determining as a result access to positions of power and life chances more generally. Second, birth cohorts themselves play an influential role in the process of social change (Riley, 1987).

Passuth and Bengston (1996) see the importance of the age stratification approach in terms of the way in which it placed social gerontological theorising within mainstream sociology. They further argue (p.17):

> [The] model emphasizes that there are significant variations in older people depending on the characteristics of their birth cohort; this suggests the need for a more explicit analysis of historical and social factors in ageing. [Moreover] age stratification's emphasis on the relations of cohorts within the age structure of society offers a useful analytic framework for distinguishing between developmental changes and cohort age differences.

But the limitations of the theory were also important, with three issues identified in the literature:

- the way that it exaggerates the role of age status in the distribution of economic and social rewards
- the lack of attention to differences within birth cohorts
- the retention of functionalist assumptions regarding consensus in determining the structure and operation of social systems and institutions (Passuth and Bengtson, 1996).

More generally, critics were to seize upon its continued emphasis on an 'over-socialised' (Wrong, 1961) model of human agency. Dowd (1987) noted, for example, the failure of the age stratification approach to theorise about how cohort membership influenced attitudes or personality, its silence on issues relating to power and social class, and its failure to grant any degree of autonomy to the individual. These limitations were further exposed with the rise of Marxist and conflict perspectives within gerontology (Estes, 1979) and the steady influence of interpretative models drawing upon ethnomethodology, phenomenology and symbolic interactionism (Ryff, 1986).

Age stratification did, however, leave one major (and lasting) legacy to gerontology, with many of its basic propositions anticipating later work coming within the orbit of the life-course perspective (Marshall, 1996). Here ageing individuals and cohorts are viewed in terms of one phase of the entire lifetime, influenced by historical, social, economic and environmental factors that occur at earlier ages (Elder, 1974; George, 1993; Neugarten and Hagestad, 1976). In the work of George (1990) and others, life-course theory bridges macro–micro levels of analysis by considering the relationships among social structure, social processes and social psychological states. Passuth and Bengston (1996, p. 17) suggest that key elements of the approach are that: '(1) ageing occurs from birth to death (thereby distinguishing this theory from those that focus exclusively on the elderly); (2) ageing involves social, psychological and biological processes; and (3) ageing experiences are shaped by cohort-historical factors'.

The above argument emphasises the influences of birth cohorts both on the construction of the life course and on the experience of ageing itself. Instead of generalising, for instance, about the characteristics of 70-year-olds, we can see that 70-year-olds who were born in 1890 are in many ways different from 70-year-olds who were born in 1930. In other words, cross-sectional data cannot be relied upon to construct or predict life-course patterns. This discovery of cohort differences in ageing helped to undermine the idea that ageing could be a universal, biologically driven process which would work in much the same way in all times and all places. Against this, ageing appeared to vary according to different social, cultural and historical contexts.

Marshall (1996, p. 22) summarised the advantages and disadvantages of the life course approach as follows:

[Its value lies] in its explicit attempt to view the individual biography within the context of society, and to take a historical perspective on both the individual and society … What the perspective does not do (and this might reflect the normative, structural–functionalist strain in its intellectual heritage) is focus on the dynamics of social structural change itself … It is better suited as a theoretical model of ageing than as a model of the social structure in which ageing takes place. Moreover, like age stratification theory, its focus on intercohort comparisons over the life course has at times deflected attention away from within-cohort contrast or differentiation.

AGEING AS A SOCIAL CONSTRUCTION

Moving into the 1980s, the legacy of functionalism (as expressed in age stratification and life-course perspectives) was increasingly challenged by influences drawn from Marxism, feminism and interpretive traditions within sociology and social psychology. The difference between this period over previous ones is that no single theory (such as functionalism) was especially dominant, although political economy (subsequently critical gerontology) assumed major significance during the 1980s and 1990s (Estes *et al.*, 2003). The precursor of critical gerontology can be seen in a number of approaches grouped under the heading of the 'social construction of ageing', an important theme developed in research from the late-1970s onwards (Estes *et al.*, 2003; Gubrium, 1986; Phillipson, 1982). In an early formulation of this approach, Estes (1979, p. 1) begins with the proposition that:

The major problems faced by the elderly in the United States are, in large measure, ones that are socially constructed as a result of our conceptions of ageing and the aged. What is done for and about the elderly, as well as what we know about them, including knowledge gained from research, are products of our conceptions of ageing. In an important sense, then, the major problems faced by the elderly are the ones we create for them.

Similarly, national and global crises are socially constructed in relation to: (a) the capacity and power of strategically located agents and interests to define 'the problem' and to press their views into public consciousness and law; and (b) the objective facts of the situation (Estes, 1979). The constructionist perspective posits that 'facts' are highly contested and are not determinative alone of how problems are defined and treated in society.

The processes of social construction are seen to occur at all levels – the macro- and micro-levels as well as the meso-level of organisations that operate between the micro and the macro. The state and economy (macro-level) influence the experience and condition of ageing, while individuals also actively construct their worlds through personal interactions (micro-level) and through organisational and institutional structures and processes (meso-level) that constitute their daily social worlds and society.

At the micro- and meso-level, a major focus is understanding the constructions of personal meaning in the lives of older people and the settings in which these meanings emerge and evolve. Jaber Gubrium (1986, 1993), for example, focused on the issue of Alzheimer's disease, examining the way in which the meaning of the illness is derived and communicated. He uses the example of support groups for people with Alzheimer's to show the way in which these can provide a basis for speaking about and interpreting the caregiving experience. For Gubrium, the 'local cultures' of residential settings, day centres and support groups provide important contexts for working through and assigning meanings to particular experiences. In this approach, language is seen to play a crucial role in the construction of reality. Lynott and Lynott (1996, p. 754) summarise this approach as follows:

> Instead of asking how things like age cohorts, life stages, or system needs organise and determine one's experience, [the question asked instead is] how persons (professional and lay alike) make use of age-related explanations and justifications in their treatment and inter-action with one another … Facts virtually come to life in their assertion, invocation, realisa-tion and utility. From this point of view, language is not just a vehicle for symbolically representing realities; its usage, in the practical realities of everyday life, is concretely pro-ductive of the realities.

Estes (1981) took the view that the social construction of reality approach, building upon the original theories of Berger and Luckmann (1966) and the labelling theory perspective of Becker (1963) and Matza (1969), offered several insights for gerontology (p. 400):

> The experience of old age is dependent in large part upon how others react to the aged; that is social context and cultural meanings are important. Meanings are crucial in influenc-ing how growing old is experienced by the ageing in any given society; these meanings are shaped through interaction of the aged with the individuals, organizations, and institutions that comprise the social context. Social context, however, incorporates not only situational events and interactional opportunities but also structural constraints that limit the range of possible interaction and the degree of understanding, reinforcing certain lines of action while barring others.

By the end of the 1980s, some of the themes associated with the social construction approach had coalesced into the idea of a 'critical gerontology', building first on work in political economy but subsequently extending to research in the humanities. At the same time, earlier theoretical approaches such as life-course perspectives continued to develop, notably with the development of the 'cumulative advantage and disadvantage' (CAD) model (Dannefer, 2003a). The context for this work will now be briefly sketched before more detailed consideration is given to these later approaches.

CRITICAL GERONTOLOGY AND SOCIAL INEQUALITY

From the 1980s onwards, perceptions of ageing populations as representing a threat to western economies became widespread (Estes and Phillipson, 2002; World Bank, 1994). With this came the steady erosion of those sections of the welfare state targeted at older people, notably in relation to areas such as expenditure on pensions and social security. At the same time, the extension of retirement – underpinned by earlier withdrawal from work on the one side and improved health (in developed countries at least) on the other side – also came under scrutiny. Increasingly, western governments were urging older people – 'baby-boomers' in particular – to remain in the workforce for as long as possible (Phillipson and Smith, 2005). This was accompanied by anxieties about what was viewed as the burden represented by public pensions and the financial pressures likely to be faced by succeeding generations (Vincent, 2003a). Increasingly, the debate about demography moved from national to global contexts, with influential International Governmental Organisations (IGOs) such as the World Bank, the International Monetary Fund and the World Trade Organization, contributing to what was termed the 'crisis construction and crisis management of old age' (Estes *et al.*, 2001).

Critical gerontology followed two main paths in response to these changes. The first documented the roots of inequality in old age whereas the second explored issues of meaning and the nature of subjectivity in later life. Dannefer (2006, p. 103) identifies these trends as the structural and hermeneutic dimensions contained within critical theory:

> The first [deals] with issues of political economy and distributive justice – of material inequality, its consequences, and the processes that sustain it; the second with human wholeness – with the relationship of consciousness and the symbolic apparatus to the material conditions of life and at the socio-cultural level.

Research around social inequality was reflected in an extension of the life-course model (Dannefer, 2003b) and in political economy perspectives on ageing (Baars *et al.,* 2006). The former was reflected in the development of the cumulative advantage and disadvantage (CAD) model through the work of researchers such as Dannefer (2003a, 2006), Crystal and O'Shea (2002) and O'Rand (1996). This approach focuses on growing old as a collective process of intra-cohort stratification, as social processes allow the accumulation of advantages over the life course for some but the accretion of disadvantages for others. The specific contribution of studies of ageing and the life course to a further clarification of problems of social inequality is that they have been able to show how inequalities have the tendency to become more pronounced during the process of ageing. In the CAD paradigm the popular expression 'the rich get richer, the poor get poorer' translates into a more precise meaning that refers to the systemic organisation and differentiation of ageing processes. Based on research from this paradigm it becomes possible to analyse the problems of social inequality and ageing more precisely than before. Instead of portraying older people as poor and dependent on insufficient old age pensions, or claiming that the 'baby-boom' generation will be much better off or relying on misleading averages, the approach is to identify problematic life-course trajectories that widen inequalities from mid-life onwards (see further Evandrou and Falkingham, 2006). Anticipations of the CAD paradigm can be found in neo-Marxist class analysis (Estes, 1979; Walker, 1981) and theories of status maintenance (Henretta and Campbell, 1976) as well as aspects of continuity theory (Atchley, 1989).

Crystal (2006) has argued that, although early advantages and disadvantages such as parental status and formal education, have long and persisting influences, it is the resources and events characteristic of the mid-life period that have a direct bearing upon later-life economic and health status. He observes here that (p. 207):

> By midlife, as well, the relationship between the economic and health domains becomes more apparent. The cumulative consequences of differences in socio-economic status on health are often long-term in nature; they become more marked in midlife after decades of exposure to differential stresses and risks. Disparities are generated through multiple pathways, including socio-economic differences in risky health behaviours; differences in access to health care ...; and differences in occupational stress and occupationally based coping resources.

Issues of inequality have also been a preoccupation of the political economy approach within critical gerontology (Baars *et al.*, 2006; Estes *et al.*, 2003; Phillipson, 1998; Vincent, 1995). Early work in this area focused on the various elements contributing to what Townsend (1981, 1986) referred to as the 'structured dependency' of later life, this viewed as a product of forced exclusion from the labour market, passive forms of community care, and the impact of poverty (see also Estes, 1979). This initial focus on dependency broadened out in two main ways during the 1980s and 1990s, first in relation to research on social inequality, and second in studies on the role of the state in the production of dependency. Social class became a major concern in respect of the former, this reflecting the influence of Marxism within the political economy model (Katz, 2003; Walker and Foster, 2006). In parallel with the CAD approach to intra-cohort stratification, political economy theorists took the view that older people were as deeply divided along class (and other social fault lines) as younger and middle-aged adults. Walker (1996) contrasted this approach with functionalist theories that tended to view age as erasing class and status differentials. He argued that (p. 33):

> There is no doubt that the process of retirement, not ageing, does superimpose reduced socio-economic status on a majority of older people ... but even so retirement has a differential impact on older people, depending on their prior socio-economic status. For example, there is unequal access to occupational pensions. Women and other groups with incomplete employment records are particularly disadvantaged ...There are also inequalities between generations of older people, arising from their unequal access to improved private and occupational pension provision.

Political economy also emphasised the importance of other social divisions affecting the period of old age, notably those associated with gender (Estes, 2006) and ethnicity (Dressel, 1988). Minkler (1999, p. 1) suggested that these were best viewed as 'interlocking systems of inequality' which determine the experience of growing old and which illustrate the construction of ageing on multiple levels. Minkler (1999, pp. 1–2) went on to conclude:

> Critical gerontology in the tradition of political economy ... offers a rich and multiperspectival framework within which to view and better understand old age as a 'problem' for societies 'characterised by major inequalities in the distribution of power and property' (Kart, 1987, p. 79). As such, it provides a much needed supplement to the study of the biological

and psychological aspects of ageing, which, for all their contributions, reveal little about the social construction of aging in a broad socio-political context.

An additional concern of political economy, again reflecting the Marxist legacy, was attention to the role of the state as representing a site of class struggle and for managing the affairs of dominant class interests (O'Connor, 1973). The study of the state was viewed as central to understanding old age and the life chances of older people since it had the power to (a) allocate and distribute scarce resources to ensure survival and growth of the economy, (b) mediate the different segments and classes of society, and (c) ameliorate social conditions that could threaten the existing order. Estes (1999), one of the few researchers in gerontology to give detailed consideration to the operation of the state, argued that a key task for political economy was to analyse: 'the aged and state policy intrinsic parts of the broader phenomenon of crisis construction and management in advanced capitalism and [to] consider … how the aged and [policies toward older people] are used in this process' (p. 23).

Another important element within critical gerontology is the development of cultural and humanistic gerontology, sometimes referred to as moral economy or more broadly *cultural gerontology* (Andersson, 2003; Cole *et al.*, 1992). This approach built on the concern articulated by Marshall and Tindale (1978, p. 65) about the way in which social gerontology 'neglects human concerns' in favour of the study of pre-structured attitudes and quantifiable performance characteristics that are easy to measure. This approach has gained popularity as the classical theoretical opposition of structure versus agency and culture versus structure has given way to an appreciation of the interplay and 'recursive' relationships of culture, structure and agency (Estes, 1999; Giddens, 1991). Cultural gerontology provides a reformulation of the unidirectional causality implied in the classical 'base–superstructure' model of Marxism, with an intensified focus on questions of meaning and experience.

Humanistic gerontology adds still another dimension to critical dimensions to ageing, by seeking both to critique existing theories and to construct new positive models of ageing based upon research by historians, ethicists and other social scientists (Cole *et al.*, 1993). Moody (1993) identifies several goals for this perspective within gerontology, including:

- developing theories that emphasise and reveal the subjective and interpretive dimensions of ageing
- developing a commitment to praxis and social change
- producing emancipatory knowledge.

Estes *et al.* (2003, p. 22) conclude:

> Consistent with and complementary to both the political economy and feminist theories, this approach draws upon the concepts and relations of power, social action and social meanings as they pertain to ageing. At its core, this approach is concerned with the absence of meaning affecting older people, and the sense of doubt and uncertainty that is thought to permeate and influence their day-to-day lives and social relations.

AGEING AND GLOBALISATION

For much of the period from the 1970s through to the 1990s, critical perspectives in gerontology focused upon national concerns about policies and provision for older people. Scholars worked within the boundaries of the nation state in developing perspectives around issues such as dependency and inequality in later life. A significant change at the end of the century, reflecting developments within core disciplines such as politics and sociology, has been the link between critical gerontology and broader questions arising from the pressures and upheavals associated with living in a global world (Held *et al.*, 1999; Hutton and Giddens, 2000).

In general terms, globalization has produced a distinctive stage in the history of ageing, with tensions between nation state-based policies concerning demographic change and those formulated by global actors and institutions. Social ageing can no longer be viewed solely as a national problem or issue but one that affects individuals, groups and communities across the globe. Local and national interpretations of ageing had substance where nation states (at least in the developed world) claimed some control over the construction of welfare policies. They also carried force where social policies were being designed with the aim or aspiration of leveling inequalities, and where citizenship was still predominantly a national issue. The changes affecting all of these areas, largely set in motion by different aspects of globalisation, is likely to generate significant implications for theoretical work in the field of gerontology (O'Rand, 2000).

In the first place, a global perspective raises issues about the construction of the life course as typically understood within social gerontology. Dannefer (2003b, p. 649) makes the point that:

> Quite different patterns are found in the 'Majority World' – the poorer and less developed countries where most of the people inhabiting the earth live … If the life course area is to encompass the full range of human diversity and human possibility, these diverse patterns cannot be ignored. Many 'alternative' life course configurations are also strongly institutionalized. Such established patterns can be observed in spite of the high population turnover of countries that have not undergone the demographic transition – witnessing powerfully to the fact that the life course is indeed a social institution that transcends, and yet encases, the biographies of individuals. In some cases, such patterns are well entrenched, and are clearly older than the 'three boxes' of the 'modern' life course with which the term institutionalization has often been equated.

The challenge for studies in ageing lies in acknowledging the way in which the life course may, as a result of the above processes, assume a 'nonlinear' shape, with features of so-called 'normal ageing' occurring earlier or later in life depending upon a particular sequence of biographical events (Hoerder, 2001). By extension, an additional issue concerns greater variability in respect of images and definitions of ageing. In the context of accelerated movement of populations, interlaced with powerful global networks, ideas about the meaning of old age, when old age begins, and normative behaviors for later life, will demonstrate greater variation within any one society than has historically been the case (Phillipson and Ahmed, 2006).

A second issue is that globalisation – both through the spread of worldwide communications and via the power of global organisations – has elevated ageing to an issue that transcends individual societies or states. Gerontology, for much of the twentieth century, was preoccupied with issues affecting older people in advanced capitalist societies (Dannefer, 2003b). Indeed, theories such as disengagement and modernisation theory took the view that the western model of ageing would ultimately be diffused across all cultures of the world (Fennell *et al.*, 1988). Globalisation has provided a fundamental challenge to vestiges of this approach. Global interests may indeed continue to be subject to US hegemony and/or western imperialism in various guises, but globalisation also illustrates the emergence of new social and political forms at international, national, regional and local levels (Held and McGrew, 2002). Cerny and Evans (2004. p. 63) make this point in the following way:

> The central paradox of globalization, the displacement of a crucial range of economic, social and political activities from the national arena to a cross-cutting global/transnational/domestic structured field of action, is that rather than creating one economy or one polity, it also divides, fragments and polarizes. Convergence and divergence are two sides of the same process. Globalization remains a discourse of contestation that reflects national and regional antagonisms and struggles.

But the globalisation of communications has introduced a further dimension into the understanding of demographic change. Thompson (2000, p. 212) has explored the processes involved in the appropriation of globalised media products as follows:

> I want to suggest that the appropriation of globalized symbolic materials involves what I shall describe as the *accentuation of symbolic distancing from the spatial–temporal contexts of everyday life* [author's emphasis]. The appropriation of symbolic materials enables individuals to take some distance from the conditions of their day-to-day lives – not literally but symbolically, imaginatively, vicariously. Individuals are able to gain some conception, however partial, of ways of life and life conditions that differ significantly from their own. They are able to gain some conception of regions of the world which are far removed from their own locales.

The process described by Thompson is transforming ageing in a variety of ways. Global communications sharpened awareness in the 1990s of the suffering of older people in zones of conflict, notably in the former Eastern Bloc countries and in sub-Saharan Africa (Lloyd-Sherlock, 2004). But from another perspective it also generated ideas about the new lifestyles that might be possible to develop in middle and older age. Older people in developed countries became aware of the possibilities of travel and migration and the potential benefits of global tourism. Bauman observes that 'spiritually at least we are all travelers' (1998, p. 78). Into the twenty-first century this has been put into practice by a minority of wealthier retirees, even though many of their contemporaries remained tied to localities experiencing the costs associated with global change (Scharf *et al.*, 2002). Such examples confirm the way in which globalisation has been radical in its transformation of ageing – with, to paraphrase Beck (1992), few social groups or societies immune to its effects. Further work in this area is likely to be a key aspect of theoretical work in gerontology over the next decade (Phillipson, 2006a).

CONCLUSIONS

Looking ahead over the next decade, what are the likely challenges affecting social theory as applied to gerontology? A continuing challenge will be to mainstream social theory as a valid and significant activity within the study of ageing. On the one side, it is possible to look back upon some 60 years of theorising – from theories of social adjustment in old age in the 1940s (Pollack, 1948) to theories of globalisation and ageing at the beginning of the twenty-first century (Estes *et al.*, 2003). Theory continues to be used, to paraphrase Craib (1984), to try and make sense both of the issues that confront older people in their daily lives, and the choices and dilemmas for society in resolving their questions and concerns. But the status and value of theory needs to be constantly reaffirmed against pressures to restrict the study of social ageing either to the evaluation of public policies or to the enumeration of the conditions associated with being an older person. Hagestad and Dannefer (2001) view this as part of what they present as a 'persistent tendency towards microfication in social sciences approaches to ageing'. They argue that (p. 4):

> Microfication refers to a trend in the substantive issues and analytic foci, what we might call the ontology of social research in aging. Increasingly, attention has been concentrated on psycho-social characteristics of individuals in micro interactions, to the neglect of the macro level. Apart from the population characteristics, macro level phenomena of central interest to social scientists, such as social institutions, cohesion and conflict, norms and values, have slipped out of focus.

A major challenge for the foreseeable future will be to continue to evolve macro-level theories that make sense of the increasing complexity of the links between ageing on the one side and social structures on the other side. Indeed, it is precisely the intricacy of these relationships that demand coherent social theories to be developed, these continuing to acknowledge ageing both as a lived, individual experience as well as one constructed through social, cultural and economic relationships. For this to take place, however, important changes will need to be made to the way in which theory develops within gerontology. Daatland (2002, p. 7) highlights what he sees as the 'relative isolation of gerontology from basic disciplines like psychology and sociology – or for that matter, like economics, anthropology, and history'. One outcome of this has been – especially in the case of Europe – the limited range of theory drawn into gerontology, much of it lagging behind developments in the major social science disciplines. In some respects, this has begun to change with the wide range of influences drawn upon by critical gerontology – from the humanities, feminism, critical theory, and mainstream sociology (notably via the work of Beck and Giddens). But much social gerontology remains distinctly a-theoretical in approach, continuing to use theory as an *implicit* rather than *explicit* medium for testing ideas and hypothesis.

Producing coherent theory in gerontology may also require greater attention to some of the disadvantages as well as the advantages of the interdisciplinary form of the gerontological enterprise. The idea of interdisciplinarity is viewed as a major feature of studies of ageing, with researchers pointing to the virtues of crossing boundaries both within the social sciences and across to the natural sciences and humanities. This has led to some significant developments in theoretical work – for example in ideas about successful ageing (Baltes and Baltes, 1990) and in the evolution of critical gerontology (Moody, 1988). On the other hand, the problems attached to interdisciplinary working should also be noted. Daatland (2002), for example, refers to the problem of gerontology being 'trapped in the cage of interdisciplinarity', noting that (p. 8):

> Most established disciplines and universities resist such an effort, which, while it may be an advantage when you want to solve practical problems, may be a drawback when you develop theories. Theories are more or less by their nature discipline specific; in fact they may even refer to sub-disciplines within each discipline.

The solution to this problem will not be to abandon interdisciplinary research, which has in any event great virtues in fields such as ageing. Rather it must be to engage in such work from the standpoint of greater confidence about disciplinary-specific theoretical standpoints. Thus gerontological work in geography, psychology and sociology, to take three examples, must achieve closer integration with mainstream developments within those disciplines. This must be viewed as a precondition both for developing both new types of theory as well as creating more effective forms of interdisciplinary activity.

Despite the obstacles identified above, much has been achieved in the 60-year span of theorising about the experience of individual and social ageing. The immediate future for older people poses new risks and insecurities in the context of financial insecurities and instabilities across a global stage. These also provide a fresh justification – if one were needed – for theories to address both the changes in the way individuals experience later life and alterations in the social relations which underpin growing old. Achieving a secure identity given the risks associated with late modernity will be a major task for older people in the future. Sociological and social psychological theories must continue to evolve to assist understanding about how individuals and social institutions respond to this challenge.

FURTHER READING

Baars, J., Dannefer, D., Phillipson, C. and Walker, A. (eds) (2006) *Globalization and Inequality*. Amityville, NY: Baywood Publishing.

Estes, C. L., Alford, R. R., Binney, E. A., Bradsher, J. E., Close, L. *et al.* (2001) *Social Policy and Aging: A Critical Perspective*. Thousand Oaks, CA: Sage.

5

Researching ageing

Christina Victor, Gerben J. Westerhof
and John Bond

INTRODUCTION

Gerontology, the study of ageing, is a challenging, rich and diverse area of scientific enquiry. As this book illustrates, this is characterised by the involvement of a diversity of scientific disciplines drawn from the behavioural, natural and social sciences and one that concerns a range of professional and lay publics. Gerontology poses a plethora of research questions and draws upon a range of diverse methods and theories. Gerontology is characterised by its multidisciplinary approach (see for example the contrasting approaches highlighted by Chapters 2–4) but increasingly by its interdisciplinary approach (see for example Chapters 9, 10 and 11). Consequently the breadth of topics requires the synthesis and integration of research data derived from a wide range of methodological and theoretical traditions in order to understand complex phenomena such as the causes of ageing or cognitive decline; experiences of ageing such as loneliness, vitality or quality of life; and the analysis of public policy such as policy on age discrimination or provision of pensions.

Gerontological knowledge therefore takes many forms, is always in a state of evolution and what counts as gerontological knowledge changes over time, although many ideas and theories remain relatively enduring. From different perspectives in gerontology the nature of gerontological knowledge remains contested. For some, research facts provide a realist or positivist interpretation of the natural and social world. For others, all facts are socially constructed and mediated through the eyes of scientists and the public alike. How scientific facts are viewed influences the kinds of research questions asked and the methods and research designs employed by gerontologists. And the kind and extent of knowledge about ageing and old age is influenced by the types of question that are asked and the methods used to answer them.

The diversity of research methods employed in the study of ageing should come as no surprise given the range of different perspectives and theoretical positions already identified in this book. Just as gerontologists view ageing from different perspectives, accept different theoretical assumptions and ask different questions, they also use different methods. There is a strong relationship between perspective and method in that 'methods and theory are inextricably connected' (Smith, 1975, p. 27). However, this is often not obvious when theory is left inexplicit or is non-existent as has been often the case in gerontology (Biggs *et al.*, 2003; Settersten and Dobransky, 2000). 'Methods' here means not merely whether to use interviews or observations when collecting data but more fundamentally whether to study causes or function, whether to describe or explain, whether to determine the meaning of phenomena or examine the relationship between different concepts or variables, or whether to involve users or consumers in the research process.

Although there are a wide range of texts that describe social and behavioural science methods, there exist few that are specific to the study of ageing. There are two useful texts devoted to methods used in social gerontology (Jamieson and Victor, 2002; Peace, 1990) that provide further details about some of the major methodological issues involved in studying ageing and supplement some of the points made in this chapter. The focus of this chapter, however, is on the key issues related to the study of ageing and late life at both the macro (societal) and micro (individual) levels.

STUDYING AGEING AND OLD AGE

Gerontology is primarily concerned with identifying, investigating and understanding the ageing experience and the effects of 'ageing' or the effect of age. Within social gerontology there has been an enduring tradition examining the experience of later life that has been maintained by a strong humanitarian and theoretical perspective that views old age as a social problem (see Chapter 4). Such studies provide little insight into the process of ageing: rather they provide an often detailed description of the characteristics of older people at particular points in history that are usually contextually and culturally specific. The designs of studies are usually cross-sectional rather than longitudinal, often characterised by the integration of social surveys with more qualitative approaches such as case studies or in-depth interviews. This approach has been well represented in the ESRC Growing Older Programme in the UK (Walker, 2005).

There is also a strong body of work that investigates ageing. Here there is a different emphasis, rather than classifying, describing or understanding the social world of the group of interest, the aim is to identify, describe and ultimately explain the processes of ageing. Here the emphasis may be on the processes of ageing both at the individual level as in psychological studies of cognitive decline (see Chapter 12) or healthy ageing (see Chapter 2) and at the societal level as in accounts of the development of social protection in Europe (see Chapter 7). Study designs here are often longitudinal following the same cohorts of individuals over time or use time-lag designs comparing different individuals of the same age at different points in time. Both quantitative and qualitative methods have been used in the collection of data.

An emerging policy-oriented body of work concerns the evaluation of interventions in gerontology. This is particularly ubiquitous in the health arena, such as the evaluation of dementia services, but also in other aspects of societal intervention such as the built environment (in terms of both accommodation and neighbourhood design) or the implementation of public policy. Study designs here can be experimental or quasi-experimental with different forms of allocation to the intervention and control setting, or contextual with importance placed on evaluation, adaptation and understanding of meaning. Again both quantitative and qualitative methods of data collection have been employed.

An important distinction here is between research designs and methods (de Vaus, 2001), although these terms are often confusingly used interchangeably. Research design is concerned with how the structure of the enquiry is organised in order to ensure the capture of appropriate evidence to support the investigation of the study questions. In contrast, research methods are concerned with the way that data are collected and analysed, and the implementation of different data-collection techniques such as psychological tests, structured interviews or ethnographic fieldwork.

The rest of this chapter is organised around three main sections. First, different designs in gerontological research are presented, highlighting the purpose of cross-sectional, longitudinal, time-lag, sequential and experimental designs. The next section focuses on different methods and techniques in gerontological research through a review of different types of studies including laboratory, population, evaluation, qualitative and historical studies and the emergence of mixed-methods studies. The final section deals with questions of quality in gerontological research through an investigation of issues concerning study participants, quality in data capture, qualitative research and triangulation.

DESIGNS IN GERONTOLOGICAL RESEARCH

Age, cohort, and period effects

As testified in the other chapters of this book, individuals of *varied ages* differ in a wide range of biological, psychological and sociological aspects of their functioning. Studying such age differences offers the gerontologist a unique set of methodological challenges. The simple observation that more older than younger people have grey hair may well be represented in the media and elsewhere as both demonstrating the (negative) effects of ageing and determining the onset of 'old age' (see also Chapter 11). However, the simple observation that something is more common amongst older than younger people does not automatically mean that we may attribute the cause of this difference to ageing or the passing of time. As individuals grow older they may change physically, socially and psychologically and it is these changes that may be conceptualised as the process of ageing. For such changes to be defined as ageing they must fulfil several criteria. They must be universal (i.e. they should happen to everyone regardless of time or place), and hence they would be evident in populations living in different parts of the world. They also should not be pathological or related to disease states found only in particular individuals. Third, ageing differences should not result from hazardous lifestyles such as smoking or excessive use of alcohol or from other environmental exposures such as mobile phone use or living near to a particular hazard such as a chemical waste dump. Last, they should not be amenable to 'reversal' (Strehler, 1962). Using these four criteria, dementia clearly does not fulfil the criteria for an 'age effect' because, for example, it is a disease that is not universal.

What makes gerontology especially challenging is that there may be alternative explanations for age differences. Whereas age effects reflect the influence of individual, biographical or developmental time, age differences may also be a result of *historical time*. Historical time may result in either cohort or period effects.

Cohort effects refer to influences of historical time that are specific for a group of people born within a specific time; i.e. a birth cohort. Ideas about the influences of historical time upon populations may be traced back to Mannheim (1952) who argued that a cohort would develop a common identity and social consciousness as manifested in a 'generation consciousness' as a result of historical events and changes taking place during the years of entry into adulthood. The generation of 'baby-boomers' is an exemplar of this concept. They were born after the Second World War, had their formative years in the late 1960s and early 1970s and who are now entering old age. However, one should be aware that there is considerable variation within cohorts in their experience of the same historical event. For example, the long-term effects of the Great Depression in the 1930s differ in terms of social class, gender and actual experiences of hardships during this period (Elder, 1982).

Alternatively, historical time may result in *period effects*. The notion that specific and self-limited historical events, such as war or depression or radical social change, can effect the entire population is the source of this third explanatory framework for the observation of ageing differences. Period effects relate to historical time and its influence upon entire populations, rather than a single cohort. This suggests that certain historical processes and events may stimulate changed attitudes or behaviours throughout the whole of society and not just in a single age group. As the groups affected by this event die out the period effect may appear to be an age or birth cohort effect. Food rationing during the Second World War in Britain is a good example of a period effect, as is the London smog of the 1950s, although this was geographically limited in extent.

Thus when presented with an observed difference in, for example, cognitive impairment or the performance of activities of daily living between people of different ages, the gerontologist has to consider whether this observation is due to age, cohort or period effects. Although these three explanatory perspectives are discussed separately there is obviously the potential for interaction and overlap; and this complicates the study of gerontology still further and makes the search for simple solutions and explanations for complex phenomena highly unlikely. Recognition of the importance of these differing frameworks is important not only for the interpretation of research findings but also for the choice of research designs used. Different research designs are commonly used in gerontological research, each with its own advantages and problems.

Studying old age

When studying old age the simplest of all designs would be to study a group of older people at a certain point in time, say people in their sixties in 2005. This design refers to the study of old age and later life, rather than the study of ageing as discussed earlier in this chapter. Worldwide there is an extensive body of research that has concentrated upon enumerating the many and varied characteristics of older people. This provides an often detailed description of the key characteristics of older people at a particular time point in particular settings and in particular cultures. The data are often characterised by the integration of careful survey data and case studies or interviews. It is typified by such studies as those on living arrangements of older people, presented in Chapter 10. Some studies focus on particular contexts in which older individuals are growing old, such as the studies on social interactions in daycare centres or nursing homes discussed in Chapter 11. Often such studies are commissioned to provide an evidence base for social policy, for example in planning healthcare arrangements. Whereas it is impossible to disentangle age, cohort and period in such studies, they are usually not used to study ageing as a process. Rather, they provide information on a particular group in our society. They are also suitable to address diversity in later life, by comparing men and women, social classes or ethnic groups.

Studying ageing

Cross-sectional design

The first design used to study ageing rather than old age is referred to as a *cross-sectional design*. At a certain point in historical time, say 2005, a cross-section of the population is used to compare people of different ages, like people in their thirties, forties, fifties, sixties, seventies and eighties (see Box 5.1). The key feature of a cross-sectional study is that it takes place at a single point in time and that we obtain a 'structured' set of data that enables systematic comparisons to be made between individuals or groups. Hence the same data are collected from multiple cases.

Box 5.1   Designs used in studying ageing

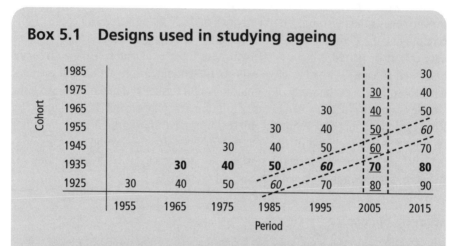

- A cross-sectional design (underlined) compares different age groups at a certain point in time, but confounds age and cohort effects
- A longitudinal design (bold) compares the same individuals at different ages, but confounds age and period effects
- Time-lag designs (italics) compares the individuals of the same age at different point in time, but confound cohort and period effects

The fundamental assumption underpinning the cross-sectional approach to the study of ageing is that observing people of different ages at a single point in time is the same as observing a single age group over time. This assumption is questionable because people of different ages at the same point in time vary along dimensions other than age, such as social class, gender or ethnic minority status. Variations in these factors, rather than age per se, may 'explain' the observed apparent age-related differences.

Furthermore this approach does not offer any insights into, for example, how many of the older people with a longstanding limiting illness also had this when they were younger. There is thus no 'time' dimension to this type of design and we are reliant upon existing differences rather than looking at changes. Whereas the period effect is held constant in this design, the design confounds ageing and cohort effects. It remains unclear whether age groups differ as a result of ageing processes or as a result of different historical experiences experienced earlier in life.

Longitudinal design
A second design is the *longitudinal design*. A longitudinal research design is the theoretically most appropriate approach for the study of ageing as it involves

following the same group of people over a period that may range from a few months to an entire lifetime, depending upon the topic under investigation. As in a cross-sectional design, individuals of different ages are compared, but as they are individuals from the same birth cohort, age and cohort are not confounded. Whilst longitudinal studies are often associated with large-scale, long-term, statistically sophisticated data, such approaches are also used in qualitative settings. Hence the longitudinal or prospective design can be used in a variety of settings and is, perhaps, a more versatile research approach than it is often given credit for.

Intuitively, longitudinal studies are conceptualised as prospective. However, there are examples of retrospective designs where asking participants to recall previous experiences and circumstances collects the 'time and change' dimensions. There are also examples of 'historical' longitudinal studies in which the discovery of a set of historical records can prompt the follow-up of participants many years later. It was studies of this nature that led to the recognition of the importance of the fetal environment for health status in mid and later life (Barker, 2004).

Longitudinal designs have conceptual limitations. The observation of differences in outcome variables, such as cognitive function over time, may indeed be the result of ageing. However, observed differences do not reflect effects such as variations in the environment in which the measures were taken or the increased familiarity of the study participants with the measurement regimen. For example, longitudinal study participants may perform better on a psychological test when it is conducted in a familiar environment such as their home in comparison to when it is undertaken in a research laboratory or medical school. As longitudinal studies involve the repeated administration of tests and questionnaires, it is possible that participants may become familiar with the tests or remember their previous responses. It is also possible, in theory at least, that participation in a longitudinal study will alter the behaviour of participants and thereby compromise the main outcome variables.

Longitudinal studies also cannot disentangle the ageing and period effects. Period effects may not only complicate the interpretation of age changes observed in longitudinal studies (Wadsworth, 2002). The prospective and enduring study period of many longitudinal studies means that secular change, the current state of scientific knowledge and the socio-political environment may influence the questions posed and measures collected. Furthermore, longitudinal designs are costly pursuits and need a stable research environment, in particular when they last across a lifetime.

Time-lag design

A third design compares individuals of the same age at different points in time, for example 60-year-olds in 1985, 1995 and 2005. This design is called a time-lag design. As in the cross-sectional design, different people are compared. The ageing effect is held constant, but the design confounds cohort and period effects. An example is the labour force participation rates in particular age groups which are presented in the figures of Chapter 8.

Sequential design

In order to be able to accurately distinguish age, cohort and period effects, Schaie (1967) proposed a sequential design. A sequential design involves a sequence of studies and combines cross-sectional, longitudinal and/or time-lag designs. In its fullest expansion, a sequential design involves starting with a 'simple' cross-sectional study of two (or more) age groups measured at the same time point. These initial subjects are then re-tested at a later time point to provide longitudinal information on these cohort groups. At the second time point two (or more) new cohorts are recruited. All groups are longitudinally followed-up at later points in time and new cohorts are added at every measurement. This cycle continues for as long as the study lasts. Using this sophisticated type of design the researcher can interrogate the data to evaluate the differing contributions to age, cohort and period effects.

Using the example of cognitive function we could investigate the influence of age and cohort upon our outcome dependent variable, such as processing speed. A cohort sequential analysis involves comparing two longitudinal studies, one between 1985 and 1995, the other between 1995 and 2005. One can compare changes in processing speed between ages 60 and 70 in a group born in 1925, with changes between 60 and 70 found in a cohort born a decade later. It thus gives information about the robustness of intrinsic ageing processes. A time sequential analysis involves comparing two cross-sectional studies of people in their sixties and seventies in 1995 and 2005. Again, the comparison provides information on the robustness of ageing effects. Combining both sequences allows examining changes in cognitive function in all groups between 1985, 1995 and 2005. This is clearly a much more complex and sophisticated way to look at the process of ageing but achieved at a cost of a much more complex research design which is expensive to set up, maintain and analyse.

Other study designs

Experimental design

Within gerontological research, experimental designs appear in a number of different contexts. They are widely used in the laboratory with animals or human participants to investigate the biological, clinical or psychological 'basic science' aspects of ageing. For example they are used in the development of biomarkers in bio-gerontology (see Chapter 2) and for understanding cognitive decline in psychology (see Chapter 12). Experimental designs in the form of randomised controlled trials and case–control studies are used in clinical research to determine the efficacy or effectiveness of therapeutic interventions for older people (e.g. drug therapies or complex service interventions such as schemes for early hospital discharge). They are also used in policy research in 'whole' populations or 'community' settings to determine the effectiveness or efficiency of social or environmental interventions such as the provision of free public transport for older people. The common components of all experimental designs is the comparison between experimental and control groups and the use of some kind of random allocation between groups. Experimental designs are longitudinal with prospective assessment of outcomes. Used within the positivist paradigm, outcomes and specific hypotheses are defined *a priori*. Some common experimental designs are shown in Box 5.2.

Box 5.2 Experimental designs

- *Randomised controlled design* (in bio-medical research referred to as the randomised controlled trial [RCT]) in which study participants are randomised to an experimental or control arm.
- *Cluster randomised design* in which groups of study participants (e.g. people living in the same area) are randomised to an experimental or control arm.
- *Controlled or quasi-experimental design* in which study participants are allocated in a non-random way (e.g. even/odd street number) to an experimental or control arm.
- *Matched-pairs design* in which study participants are selected non-randomly to receive an intervention (e.g. all people using a particular public service) and compared with a matched control from the general population, and paired comparisons are made.
- *Before-and-after design* in which study participants are used as their own control.
- *Historical controlled design* in which data are collected after an intervention from a non-random selected group and compared to similar data in some other non-random selected group, and unpaired comparisons are made.

Case-study designs

Case-study designs are used to explore single entities in contexts that have clear boundaries. These might be people (e.g. life histories), organisations (e.g. residential units), events (e.g. a pensioner's political demonstration), processes (e.g. retirement) or programmes (e.g. the provision of free public transport to older people). Case-study designs can employ quantitative, qualitative or mixed methods (Yin, 1984) but they are all characterised by a bounded phenomenon that is clarified in terms of the questions asked, the data sources used, the settings and people involved and the theoretical perspective of the researcher.

Participatory designs

Recognition of the oppressive and exploitative nature of the relationship between the researcher and his or her subjects has been a catalyst for the development of more emancipatory methods in social science that change the social relations of research production (Oliver, 1992). There has been an increasing trend in gerontological research to increase the involvement of older people in the research process (Peace, 2002). Participation or involvement in research has been characterised to reflect the different levels of empowerment of participants (Boote *et al.*, 2002) (see Box 5.3).

Box 5.3   Levels of 'consumer' participation in research

- *Consultation* may involve the researcher asking 'consumers' about their views and using these views to influence decision-making regarding research. This is akin to the traditional role of participants in research as passive suppliers of information.
- *Collaboration* involves an on-going partnership between researchers and 'consumers' in the research process most frequently as members of advisory committees for projects.
- *Participation* may involve 'consumers' in aspects of research design, fieldwork and dissemination.
- *Consumer-controlled research* involves consumers designing, undertaking and disseminating results of a research project. Researchers may only be involved at the request of consumers themselves; or consumer groups commission research of interest to them.

A specific example of participatory designs is action research which has been used widely in community development projects as a way of combining the production of knowledge with the process of changing practice. Action research is problem-oriented with research, action and evaluation being linked as one continuous process in a cyclical research design: planning, observing and reflecting back into the next planning cycle. Participants are involved at all stages with results and their interpretation shared between researchers and participants (Hart and Bond, 1995).

Historical designs

Historical designs allow the investigation of the interrelationship between ageing, time and social change. At the individual level, life-history and biographical research using the biographical method (see later) examine the processes of individual and social change as perceived by the individual, who is encouraged to look backwards in time and reflect on his or her life and evaluate key transitions and changes. By comparing life-history patterns the experience of ageing over time can be presented. Life-history research is used in different contexts to answer a variety of research questions, such as individual or group biographies (Humphrey, 1993), step families (Bornat, 2002) and housing histories (Holland, 2001).

METHODS

There is no simple way of categorising different methods in gerontological research. A simple dichotomy that is often used is the quantitative/qualitative distinction. In general, quantitative and qualitative methods are grounded in different epistemologies. Studies that are grounded in positivist or post-positivist paradigms generally use quantitative methods and study designs while those grounded in a broadly interactionist or constructionist paradigm generally use qualitative methods and designs. The distinction is not clear-cut and increasingly confused by the emergence of mixed-methods studies and the adoption by positivists and post-positivists of some elements of qualitative method and the adoption by interactionists and constructionists of some elements of quantitative method. It is far too easy to see quantitative and qualitative approaches as opposing and in conflict. Rather they represent different ways of investigating ageing processes and the social worlds of older people and are appropriately viewed as complementary and representing different perspectives. The common link between these different approaches to methods is the role of systematic enquiry in methods and adherence to issues of quality.

Quantitative methods

Population surveys and experiments both use quantitative methods employing a range of statistical methods in analysis of data and share an epistemology based on deductive method – a process by which 'valid' conclusions can be logically deduced from 'valid' premises. Experimental designs are generally used for explanatory purposes, but survey designs have been used for both descriptive purposes (e.g. for studying later life) and explanatory purposes (e.g. for studying ageing). Research designs that involve human participants use language – through self-completed questionnaires or structured interviews – and observation as the dominant methods of data capture. A typical survey will capture data from a random sample of participants (e.g. people aged 65 years or over) drawn from a specified population (e.g. countries of the European Union) such that the sample may be used to estimate characteristics and understandings for the total population. A predefined set of questions will be asked of all participants through a variety of different mediums:

- brief self-completed questionnaires that can be in the style of paper-and-pencil tests, interactive computer tests and web-based forms and questionnaires
- longer structured interviews comprising fixed-choice and open-ended response categories for individual questions and tests that can be administered using traditional pencil-and-paper recording, telephone interviews or computer-assisted interviewing.

An example of the latter is the German Aging Survey, an interdisciplinary study on the life circumstances in relation to well-being and meaning in life among the present and future generations of German older people (Dittmann-Kohli et al., 2001; Kohli and Kunemund, 2000).

Surveys involving observation have been less widely used in gerontology, but for research concerning the context of everyday life – such as intergenerational use of public space – it has been an appropriate method (Holland et al., 2006). Observation within a survey framework involves systematically recording the occurrence of predetermined defined events, behaviour or interactions. So a survey of public space would not only count the number of older people using predefined space but might record certain categories of activity that older people engage in and the number and type of interactions they have with others using the space. Sampling strategies might involve not only the sampling of spaces to observe but also the sampling of observation periods and events or interactions. In experimental studies, similar data-collection methods might be used but the experimental design is likely to demand a different strategy for the selection of participants (see above).

Secondary analysis

Secondary analysis – the analysis and interpretation of data initially collected for other purposes (Victor, 2002) – is most commonly associated with quantitative methods but potentially can be performed for qualitative data. A fruitful source of data for British gerontologists has been data collected routinely in regular surveys from the UK Office of National Statistics and the UK Economic and Social Research Council (ESRC) national data archive service (www.data-archive.ac.uk; www.esds.ac.uk/qualidata). Similar data services exist in other European countries (e.g. www.dans.knaw.nl for the Netherlands and www.gesis.org for Germany). In particular, the General Household Survey, which was designed as a general 'social barometer' of living conditions in the UK, has been used, for example, in the investigation of gender variations (Arber and Ginn, 1991) and neighbouring (Perren et al., 2004) in later life. Similarly the British Household Panel Survey has been used to investigate changes in living arrangements in later life (Hirst, 2001).

Secondary analysis of data sets clearly provides added value to the original study and provides a cost-effective method for answering specific policy or research questions or for testing specific hypotheses. However, the study population and the concepts and variables measured are not always appropriate for the objectives of the secondary analysis and may lead to an incomplete answer to the study question.

Qualitative methods

Qualitative methods are more heterogeneous than quantitative methods but in general they share an epistemology grounded in inductive logic – a process by which the truth of a proposition is made more probable by accumulations of confirming evidence. It cannot ever be ultimately valid because there is always the possibility of unconfirming evidence. In qualitative research there is therefore an emphasis of seeking negative 'cases' in order to challenge the proposition – a process described as analytical induction (Robinson, 1951).

Quantitative approaches are well suited for describing the nature and characteristics of older populations or enumerating the processes of ageing, but they rarely offer insight or understanding of such issues as the meaning of ageing or the lived experience of older people. They also assume a cultural and social homogeneity that few populations in Europe meet. Hence the importance of qualitative approaches in ageing research where the emphasis is on the analysis of the other's perspective through words, actions, concepts and meanings. The common element of qualitative methods is to represent reality as seen by the study participants rather than imposing on the study the reality of the researcher. What follows is an overview of the major qualitative approaches in gerontological research.

Ethnography

In gerontology the ethnographic tradition is reflected in studies of residential communities and institutions (Ballinger and Payne, 2002; Hazan, 1980; Hertogh *et al.*, 2004; Li and Orleans, 2002; Schröder-Butterfill, 2004). Ethnographies have been used in the elicitation of cultural knowledge, detailed investigation of patterns of social interaction and holistic analysis of institutions (Hammersley and Atkinson, 1983). Ethnographies draw on a range of sources of information, most often through the process of participant observation. Participant observation involves the ethnographer participating in the day-to-day lives of individuals or organisations over an extended period during which the ethnographer watches what happens, listens to what is said and asks questions about what is observed. In addition the researcher may access other sources of information such as documents or official records. Data capture has been greatly assisted through the use of digital technology – audio and video recording. Ethnographers take an empathetic perspective – they take the perspective of the other in order to understand how participants view their social world. Important to the ethnographer's role is the active and constant reflection on all aspects of the research process; he or she should always try to maintain a sceptical approach to the data, particularly the interpretations provided by study participants.

Qualitative interviews

In qualitative research the commonest form of data are from interviews. Both face-to-face and focus group interviews have been widely used in gerontological studies. In contrast to the highly structured and 'researcher programmed' nature of the structured interview as used in surveys and experiments, qualitative interviews are much less pre-determined. A distinction between structured interviews used in surveys and experiments and the different types of qualitative interview described below is the use of language. In quantitative research, language is treated as relatively unproblematic, but for qualitative research language is central to understandings of method. It is through language that individuals make sense of their world when thinking, reading, listening and speaking. It is through the interpretation of language that an understanding of others' perspectives can be achieved, and it is through language that these understandings are represented to others.

Face-to-face qualitative interviews have been described as 'conversations with a purpose' in which the researcher aims to obtain the different perspectives, feelings and perceptions of study participants. They take many heterogeneous forms and a range of terms have been used to describe them. In decreasing order of structure and standardisation and in increasing order of participant control, the main types are: semi-structured, focused or in-depth, non-directive or active, and narrative or biographical (see Box 5.4).

Box 5.4   Types of interviews in gerontological research

- In quantitative research, *structured interviews* use highly standardised formats. Every question is asked in the same way and in the same order and answers recorded into pre-defined closed response categories. Interviewers are provided with clear instructions for structured probing for responses. See for example Oppenheim (1992).
- In quantitative research, *semi-structured interviews* are structured interviews with few closed response categories or without response categories. In qualitative research the interviewers would have greater freedom in the ordering of questions and in the probing for responses.
- In qualitative research, *focused in-depth interviews* are researcher-led. The interview would be structured around a topic guide in which suggested questions may be provided as an *aide-mémoire*. The interviewer would have freedom in the ordering of the questions and in the probing for responses.
- In qualitative research, *non-directive or active interviews* (Holstein and Gubrium, 1995) take a more empathetic perspective and allow the study participant to engage equally in the interaction. Interviews are active occasions in which meanings are produced. Although the researcher will have her own agenda she will be a sympathetic listener and facilitate participant-led discussion. In non-directive interviews the interview guide will be less structured and unlikely to provide pre-defined questions.
- In qualitative research involving *narrative or biographical interviews* (Atkinson, 2002; Rosenthal, 2004) the interviewer asks the study participant to tell everything about a specific issue such as his or her experience of using public transport. A more biographical approach would place the research issue within a biographical frame such as the experience of living with arthritis. In narrative styles of interviewing, after the initial narrative question the participant is encouraged through non-verbal cues to provide a main narration or story in the style of a self-structured biography while the interviewer actively listens. Only after this has been completed will the interviewer ask 'internal narrative questions' following from topics mentioned by participants and subsequently 'external narrative questions' questions that introduce new topics.

The choice of interview method will reflect the perspective of the researcher, the nature of the topic being investigated and the overall purpose of the research. In ethnographies all types of interviewers could be employed in 'formal' interview sessions or in 'informal' conversations; but because of the researcher's agenda, particularly where there is an evaluative focus, they are likely to be either in-depth focus interviews or non-directive and active. In studies where participants' understandings of self or identity are the focus, such as studies that investigate the lived experience of older people, the active interview is likely to be employed (Holstein and Gubrium, 2000). In oral history, narrative or biographical interviews are preferred (Bornat, 2002).

Focus group interviews (Kitzinger, 1994) are structured discussions around a focused issue or topic such as, at the macro level, changes to the built environment of local communities or the structure of public services, or at the micro level the use of the dayroom in a residential home. The common elements of all focus group interviews is the bringing together of a group of people to discuss a specific issue under the moderation of a researcher. It is generally seen as good research practice for the discussion to be independently observed by a separate member of the research team who remains a non-participant in the discussion. But focus group interviews will differ widely in practice. Diversity in the method reflecting the nature of the topic and participants involved will influence the level of structure and degree of researcher involvement or control. Homogeneous groups might need relatively little intervention from the moderator, but groups comprising a number of different constituencies – for example older people, their carers and formal professionals – may need greater intervention and direction by the researcher. The moderator's role is to facilitate the discussion but, as with face-to-face interviews, the level of control by the researcher will depend on the perspective of the researcher, the nature of the topic being investigated and the overall purpose of the research.

Documentary sources

Documents are a fruitful source of data and theoretical ideas as part of ethnographies or as separate studies. All documents provide an historical account, even if it is about the relatively recent past (even in the previous year), and are therefore important data sources for historical studies. A classic historical study in gerontology was the use of parish birth registers to examine family structures in England in the sixteenth and seventeenth centuries (Laslett, 1977), and documents provide an ideal way for investigating changes in attitudes to ageing and older people (Thane, 2000). Documentary sources go beyond textual materials such as diaries, personal letters, newspapers, novels or memoirs to include representations of ageing such as paintings, photographs and film (Blaikie, 1999; Blaikie and Hepworth, 1997). All documents are locally and temporally located, but also their interpretation will depend on the lens through which the analyst is looking (Blaikie, 2002).

Gerontologists using quantitative methods would be likely to analyse textual documents using content analysis (Weber, 1990). A set of categories is established and the number of instances in each category is counted, such as the number of instances that the phrase 'senior moment' is used in newspaper articles (Bonnesen and Burgess, 2004). But in qualitative research a small number of texts and documents would be examined with the purpose of understanding the participants' categories to see how these are used – for example, how the print news media 'frames' stories on genetics and medicine (Petersen, 2001). As with other forms of qualitative research the lens used by the analyst will depend on theoretical orientation.

Qualitative analysis

As with quantitative analysis there is no one method of qualitative analysis. Again theoretical perspective is an important influence that locates the interpretations of

a study in the broader historical, political and social context. However, there are three common processes in qualitative analysis: developing an organising system, segmenting the data and making connections. To do this a careful reading of the data is required – not only the formal transcripts of interviews or documents but also the reflective field notes or memos (Strauss and Corbin, 1990) of the researcher – in order to gain familiarity. Analytical approaches range from those that give voice to the participants to represent their individual subjective experience to theoretical analysis that takes little account of subjective experience. In between these two extremes is the use of participants' accounts to draw out meanings, to reflect on the complexity of participants' life-worlds, and to make sense of and represent the underlying structures of this complexity. Three analytical approaches have commonly been used in gerontological research:

- thematic content analysis
- the constant-comparative method (often referred to as grounded theory) (Glaser and Strauss, 1967; Strauss, 1987)
- framework analysis (Ritchie and Spencer, 1994).

Mixed methods

Gerontological research is a rich site for the use of mixed methods. The interdisciplinary approach encourages methodological as well as theoretical pluralism. Yet it is only relatively recently that mixed methods have become widely accepted in the broader social and behavioural science community with the emergence of an epistemology that supports the integration of quantitative and qualitative methods. Two perspectives have emerged.

- First is the pragmatic perspective in which the nature of the research question posed has supremacy over the method that is used or the paradigm that underpins the method (Tashakkori and Teddlie, 2003). A pragmatic perspective is supportive of applied social and behavioural research and therefore well suited to applied gerontological research, for example in the evaluation of services for older people.
- The second perspective is rooted in critical theory with the objective of producing through research a democratic and just society. From this perspective the choice of method will be determined by ideology.

Emancipatory designs and methods such as action research and the involvement of users or stakeholders in the research process are also conducive to a mixed-methods approach (Murphy *et al.*, 1998).

The use of a mixed-methods approach raises a series of questions (Cresswell, 2003):

- What is the sequence of quantitative and qualitative data collection?
- What priority will be given to quantitative and qualitative data collection and analysis?
- At what stage will data and findings be integrated?
- Will an overall theoretical perspective be used?

Depending on the answers to these questions, six major approaches to implementing mixed methods in gerontological research can be highlighted (see Box 5.5).

Box 5.5 Strategies for mixed-methods research

- In *sequential–explanatory strategies,* priority would be given to the quantitative data with analysis of the qualitative data assisting the interpretation of the results of the quantitative study. An example of this is a study of the quality of life of older people (Gabriel and Bowling, 2004).
- In *sequential–exploratory strategies,* qualitative phases of the study are used to inform the development of data collection methods for the quantitative phase. An example of this is the development of a measurement tool of quality of life for older people (Grewal *et al.,* 2005).
- In *sequential–transformative strategies,* there is a strong theoretical perspective guiding the research. No method has priority and the findings are integrated at the interpretation stage. An example of this is a study of loneliness in later life (Victor *et al.,* 2004).
- In *concurrent–triangulation strategies,* findings from both the quantitative and qualitative phases are used to cross-validate the findings from each phase which are integrated at the interpretation stage. An example of this is a study of the dimensions of cognitive evaluations in research on life satisfaction (Westerhof *et al.,* 2001a).
- In *concurrent–nested strategies,* one method has priority and the less dominant method is nested within the main method. This frequently happens in evaluative studies using an experimental design with nested qualitative study such as in the evaluation of residential accommodation for older people (Bond *et al.,* 1989; Bowling *et al.,* 1991).
- In *concurrent–transformative strategies,* there is a strong theoretical perspective guiding the study which may be triangulated or nested.

QUALITY IN RESEARCH

Gerontology strives to identify evidence concerning ageing and old age. Even when an appropriate design and method is chosen, there may still be problems with regard to the evidence provided by studies.

- The first type of problem concerns the study population: who is being studied and how representative the older people involved in the research are of the general population of older people. The main question here concerns the generalisability or external validity of the research.
- The second type of problem concerns the processes of data collection. Instruments, whether they are psychological tests, standardized questionnaires, interview questions or observation protocols, may be flawed in some sense or another. The concepts of internal validity and reliability are generally used to describe the quality of the instruments used.

When describing errors it is important to distinguish between random errors and systematic errors. *Random errors* are generally less easy to avoid, but they are less harmful to the evidence base generated in gerontological research as they occur randomly across study groups. *Systematic errors* are much more dangerous, because they affect some parts of the data more than others do. Systematic errors are also called 'bias'. This may lead to erroneous results and the subsequent mis-interpretation of findings. In the end, bias may generate inaccurate and incorrect knowledge about ageing and later life. Researchers can minimise the potential for bias by careful research design and the maintenance of high quality in terms of the instruments they use and the methods by which these are realised, such as in-depth interviews or surveys. There is also a more subtle type of bias, which may impinge upon gerontology (and other aspects of social science). This relates to prejudice in the posing of research questions, design and methods used to answer the research question or interpretation of the findings, because of the ideological orientation of either the researcher or the funding body (or both).

Issues concerning study participants

The first main area where bias may be introduced is in the definition, identifica-tion, selection and response of the study population. When studying older people or ageing, the process of recruiting participants in a research project consists of several steps, each of which may be amenable to errors: the definition of the study population, the selection of a sample, and the response of people selected for par-ticipation in a study.

Definition of the study population

The first question one has to ask is which age group(s) one wants to study. Unfortunately, there is no scientific criterion that enables one to determine age boundaries. As will be argued in Chapter 11, age boundaries are a matter of social construction, and not only of scientific definitions. In earlier gerontological studies the age of 65 was often used as the landmark to define when old age began. Nowadays, studies often use the age of 55 to define old age, in part related to the ear-lier retirement age (see Chapter 7) – though this may change – and researchers often distinguish between the 'third' and 'fourth' ages (Laslett, 1987) (see Chapter 13).

In determining the participants to be included in one's research, it is important to remain aware of the diversity within old age and to avoid the systematic exclu-sion from studies of people from minority communities or hard-to-reach popula-tions. Studies may be designed to provide information about ageing amongst the general population or 'special' populations. The definition of the study population is therefore an important first step in designing a study. In order to avoid bias, it is important to be explicit about what age groups and which sub-groups of older people to study. As long as these definitions are accurate and the study findings not generalised beyond the study population, bias can be easily avoided. Problems arise when inferences are generalised from the specific to the general.

Sampling

It is neither always possible, nor necessary, to include an entire target population to answer a specific research question, and unless it is a very small target population, sampling will be necessary and efficient. There are a number of sampling strategies or designs (see Box 5.6) and the one selected for any given study will depend on the research question, study design and methods, and the characteristics of the target population. There are different modes of selection for different designs. In survey and experimental designs random or probability sampling is preferred. In qualitative studies purposeful sampling is used. But random sampling is used in qualitative research and purposeful sampling in some quantitative research designs.

Box 5.6   Sampling strategies

- *Probabilistic random sampling* strategies involve the random selection of participants from a defined sampling frame representing the target population. Stratified random sampling and cluster sampling are strategies to improve the efficiency of data capture and representativeness of sub-groups.
- *Purposive sampling* strategies involve the researcher selecting participants on the basis of predetermined criteria to generate a sample that is believed to be representative. Within the differing strategies included within the general domain of purposive sampling it is evident that the researcher may introduce bias in the way that the sample is generated by excluding/including particular sub-groups of older people.
- *Quota sampling* is a form of purposive sampling whereby the researcher selects participants according to a predefined algorithm and is an approach widely used in market research. Prior to the start of the study the researchers establish the profile of the sample that they wish to achieve such as ten individuals aged 65–69, ten aged 70–74 etc., usually according to the distribution of these characteristics within the general population. Having established the profile the researcher then looks for individuals who match these characteristics. Clearly there is the potential for bias in several ways including both the initial sample specification and the identification of specific individuals to participate.
- *Convenience or volunteer samples* are, as the name suggests, based upon those who 'volunteer' to participate by, for example, responding to an advertisement or people who are readily available. Such samples should always be treated with caution as 'volunteers' are usually inherently different from the general population because of experiences, such as family members having experienced breast cancer, or motivation, e.g. being paid to participate.
- *Snowball samples* involve the researchers identifying a small number of participants who possess the pre-specified characteristics, such as older people who have been recently bereaved or never-married men, and then use these participants to identify others from the same group who might be willing to participate. This type of approach is often used with 'hard to reach' groups such as prostitutes or homeless people but it is a technique which has applicability beyond its use with those on the fringes of society or who indulge in 'deviant' behaviours.

The simple idea behind random sampling is to select from the target population a group of study participants who are representative of that population. Ideally such samples are drawn from a sampling frame that represents the total population such as municipal population registers or telephone listings. This approach is problematic when no reliable potential sampling frame is available, for example for older people from ethnic minority groups. Available sampling frames are also a source of bias, for example when particular households do not have a telephone. Samples of older people drawn from lists of clubs or organisations usually over-represent the healthy, while studies using sampling frames derived from service users will over-represent the chronically ill. Observations based upon such samples must not be inferred as being attributable to all older people but may only be used to extrapolate to the population that the sampling frame represents.

Non-random samples including purposeful sampling, quota sampling, convenience sampling and snowball sampling should not be used to provide a representative description of the target population. These study designs have other purposes. Psychological quantitative studies, for example, may be interested in the relationship between variables and not in their frequency within a population. For these studies it is necessary to recruit a diversity of participants to ensure sufficient variation in the variables of focus. Similarly studies using qualitative methods to establish or further theory require diversity and contrasts in the participants sampled.

Response rates and sample attrition

Even if one has the possibility to draw a random sample from an adequate sampling frame, this is not a guarantee that the study results in unbiased population estimates. A major aspect that can compromise the scientific robustness of ageing research is that of response rates and sample attrition. *Response rate* refers to the percentage of people who are invited to participate in a study and who actually agree to do so. *Sample attrition* refers to the loss to follow-up in longitudinal research. Large sample sizes are often a necessity in longitudinal research, because sample attrition can reduce the numbers included within the study drastically (Wadsworth, 2002).

Non-response may result from a number of reasons. Some people are not reached, even when researchers repeatedly try to contact them. Others might refuse to participate: some have no interest in the subject matter of the study, others distrust the organisation conducting the study, and still others find no time or feel too frail to participate. If there is a low uptake of the invitation to participate this can also compromise the robustness of any results. This is particularly true when there is confounding factor between the subject matter and reasons to refuse participation. For example, in studying political interest among older people, estimates will be biased when older people who have no interest or even distrust in politics refuse to participate.

The problem of non-response might not only result in systematic errors when trying to obtain population estimates, comparisons between groups may also be biased when different groups refuse for different reasons. In the first wave of the German Ageing Survey (Dittmann-Kohli *et al.*, 2001), it was found that response rates were higher for younger groups: 62, 56 and 40% in the respective age groups (40–54, 55–69 and 70–85 years). Furthermore, older people refused for different reasons than younger people. Older people refused in particular more often because of illness and impairments (20.6% of those between 70 and 85 years versus only 2.6% of those between 40 and 54 years).

It is therefore not correct to assume that those who do not participate in research possess characteristics identical to those who do respond. Non-responders may well be an unrepresentative component of the sample. Consequently the measured results may be subject to bias. Researchers need to try to establish whether a low response rate has introduced bias, and if so in which direction, and develop analytical strategies to take this into account. Besides maintaining contact protocols containing information on reasons for non-response and possibly some characteristics of the non-responders (e.g. gender and region of living), the researcher can estimate the degree of bias in the results brought about by non-response if he or she knows something of the characteristics of the non-responders. We can go some way to determining the representativeness of our samples by drawing comparisons with already established population distributions. For example, Victor *et al.* (2005), in their national study of loneliness, compared the population they surveyed with that derived from analysis of the 2001 Census and General Household Survey. For most studies the extent and direction of bias is unknown and we are unable to take this into account in either analysis or interpretation of data and results. In all cases it is necessary to provide some standard information on the sample (about age, gender, health, institutionalization, marital status, education, migration) and to discuss the findings in relation to these sample characteristics.

Longitudinal research involves repeated contact with, and the tracing of, sample members often over lengthy time periods; for example the 1946 birth cohort (Wadsworth *et al.*, 1992) has been followed for almost 50 years. This is expensive, labour-intensive and time-consuming. Taking part in such a study requires a high level of commitment and support from the researchers involved in the project and from the study participants. Sample attrition occurs in longitudinal studies for a number of reasons, including: (a) deaths of study participants, (b) withdrawal of participants for health or other reasons, (c) moving house/area/type of residence, and (d) non-response. For example, in a study of people aged 85 years and over, sample attrition greatly reduced the size of the population studied (Bowling and Grundy, 1997). Of the 900 people aged 85 initially selected, 630 (70%) participated. At follow-up, three years later, 441 of them participated again (70%). This means that the final results are based upon data from 441 of the original sample of 900: 49% of those originally approached. Loss due to follow-up may render participants no longer representative of the original sample if there is a systematic pattern to those who no longer participate such as the poorest, frailest or fittest. However, this is usually less problematic as previous data from the first wave can be used to determine the nature and extent of sample attrition and allow correcting for this in the analysis by weighting procedures. Good follow-up rates can never compensate for low initial response rates. Hence when considering the veracity of evidence from longitudinal studies we need to consider both the response to the initial invitation to participate and subsequent follow-up rates.

To conclude, issues concerning the definition of the study population, the sampling procedures, and the non-response are important in determining the quality of a gerontological study. Researchers should be explicit about these issues and provide data on the actual composition of the participant group involved in the study. They should be cautious in generalising the findings of a study to a larger population. In determining the quality of a study, the way participants are found should be judged in relation to the questions a researcher wants to have answered.

Issues concerning data collection

The development of measures to record complex phenomena such as loneliness, quality of life or cognitive impairment is a complex process. The technical terms to describe the quality of measurement instruments are 'internal validity' and 'reliability'.

- *Internal validity* concerns the question whether instruments are robust in that they actually measure the specified construct.
- *Reliability* concerns the question whether instruments consistently measure this construct, for example when measuring the same attribute more than once (test–retest reliability).

Hence when evaluating the utility of, in particular, quantitative measures and scales for use with older people we need to consider issues of both reliability and validity. This obviously involves the examination of the reported processes by which such measures have been developed. We also need to examine wider notions of the appropriateness of the measures. This can involve an examination of whom the measure was developed with. Some measures were not developed for older people. An important question is therefore whether instruments developed for other age groups are valid and reliable for older people.

Interpretation of questions

A number of problems might be encountered here. Ageist content of stimulus material is a first problem to be encountered. Schaie (1988) mentions an item from the educational testing service kit, meant to measure logical reasoning (Ekstrom *et al.*, 1976). Respondents are presented with a series of three words ('youth/beauty/life') and have to give the second word in a second series of words ('age/?/death'). The correct word to be placed on the question mark would be 'ugliness'. Clearly this example has ageist content.

A second problem is that instruments have been designed for research in younger populations and are therefore not suitable for older people. For example, the Individualism–Collectivism scale, an instrument used for cross-cultural research (Hui and Yee, 1994), refers to items (e.g. 'I would not share my ideas and newly acquired knowledge with my parents') that reflect choices related to transitions in young adulthood and to the influence of important others which may be of less relevance to older people. Such an instrument clearly needs to be adapted to the life contexts of older people before it can be used among them.

A third problem refers to the different ways of attributing meaning to a question by people of different ages. Brugman and Heymans (1994) give the following example from a test on syllogistic reasoning: 'Downstairs there are three rooms: the kitchen, the dining room and the living room. The living room is at the front side of the house, whereas the kitchen and the dining room face the garden at the back-side of the house. The traffic noise is particularly disturbing in the front rooms. Mother is cooking a meal in the kitchen and grandfather reads his newspaper in the living room. The children are at school and will return only later in the after-noon. Who is most disturbed by the traffic noise?' According to syllogistic rea-soning, the grandfather is most disturbed, as he is in the room with most noise. This is also the answer younger adults tend to give. Older people mark the mother as being most disturbed, using a practical kind of reasoning: if the noise is loud in the living room, the grandfather couldn't read his newspaper. So he must be deaf and not annoyed by the traffic noise.

Similar problems are encountered when instruments are adopted from a differ-ent cultural context. For example, the widely used health status measure, the SF-36, was developed within a US population but had to be culturally adapted in Britain even though the English language is common to the two cultures. For example, the questions in the scale concerned with 'work', which was meant to be an encompassing notion of activity, was misunderstood by respondents to mean paid employment (Hayes *et al.*, 1995).

With the increase in older people who have migrated from other cultures to Europe, the cultural sensitivity of instruments becomes all the more important. Smits *et al.* (2005) have studied the presence of bias in instruments for diagnosing depression in older Turkish and Moroccan labour migrants in the Netherlands. Mental health problems are a subject of shame for the participants and their fami-lies. Posing questions on the topic is therefore experienced as a taboo. The inter-view situation was strange and awkward and it was often difficult to get answers from the women, as husbands were seen as responsible for contacts with the exter-nal world such as in the interview. The often long and abstract questions were not always understood well and some topics were too sensitive to get appropriate answers.

A last issue concerning the interpretation of questions by older adults concerns the relevance of items used in cognitive impairment screening tools such as iden-tification of key historical events for succeeding generations of elders for whom these may have little relevance. This is also of relevance when conducting a lon-glasting longitudinal study, where instruments in earlier phases of the research might not be suitable in later phases of the research.

To avoid such problems in the interpretation of measurement instruments, gerontologists – particularly in North America – have developed instruments that are particularly suited for research with older people. Examples of such instru-ments are the Geriatric Depression Scale, the Philadelphia Geriatric Centre Morale

Scale, and the Life Satisfaction Index. As gerontological research has become embedded more in lifespan psychology and life-course sociology, the development and use of such instruments for particular age groups has become less widespread, as they are not suited for comparisons between age groups. But even if instruments are well suited for the older population, in terms of non-ageist content, being attuned to the living conditions of older people, and lack of interpretation problems, it remains necessary to establish their reliability and validity for an older population.

Bias in answering questions

A last question about measurement concerns bias in answering questions. In this case, bias refers to the systematic errors inherent in formulating responses to questions. An extensive overview of these issues is given in the volume edited by Schwarz, Park, Knäuper and Sudman (1999). Participants in research have to fulfil certain tasks such as to comprehend a question and to recall or compute a judgement. During the different phases of fulfilling these tasks, respondents might be influenced by task characteristics, such as preceding questions or the formulation of answer alternatives, interviewer characteristics such as the age of an interviewer, as well as by their own characteristics such as susceptibility to social desirability. Each of these characteristics may result in a biased response.

The issue becomes even more important when such biases differ between age groups. There has not been much research concerning this question, but (Knäuper, 1998) gives a summary. Older people may make less use of contextual information than younger people which may result in systematic age-related differences in question interpretation. Older people tend to focus on interpreting the meaning of value labels rather than on numerical values assigned to them, a finding that may be related to their more limited cognitive resources in combining information (see also Chapter 3). Older people are also more likely to offer a 'don't know' answer. Some studies also found that older people are more susceptible to social desirability. These kinds of age difference in formulating answers to questions can have an effect on the substantial conclusions we draw about differences between age groups.

QUALITY IN QUALITATIVE RESEARCH

The above discussion of quality in data collection is focused mostly on the use of quantitative measurement instruments. They have the advantage that statistical procedures can be used to evaluate the reliability and validity of the instruments. In qualitative research like interviews or observations the quality criteria are less amenable to objective assessments. Nevertheless, quality is an important issue in this kind of research, too.

In fact, what many quantitative researchers describe as bias is part and parcel of the research interests of qualitative researchers (Westerhof, 1994). Quantitative researchers argue that an instrument is reliable and valid only when respondents attribute the same meaning to them. By contrast, and as we have seen above, qualitative interviews strive to bring different meanings to the fore and thereby create an insight into the life-worlds of older people. The most important quality issue in qualitative research relates to the tension between individual meanings and the theoretical interpretations of researchers. This is found during the process of data collection as well as during the process of data analysis.

As in quantitative research, qualitative researchers acknowledge that the way they pose questions and the way they interact with older people may influence the answers and behaviours of the latter. It is considered important to try not to impose one's own frame of reference on the participants in the study. Conversational techniques are generally used to avoid this, like giving summaries of what the participant has said to check for understanding.

Some researchers argue that it is impossible to find the only true representation of the life-world of the study participants. Rather, they interpret the interview as a social construction, and therefore as a result of the interaction between a researcher and a participant. They argue that it is important to try to understand how one's own preconceptions, whether originating in everyday life or in a scientific theory, are related to the research topic. For example, what conception of ageing and old age has the researcher conducting an interview, and how do they influence the interview process? In other words, they introduce a moment of reflexivity on how their data are brought forward in their research (Bourdieu, 1992).

Everyday and theoretical preconceptions may also intrude in the process of the analysis and interpretation of data. Qualitative research generally results in a number of highly idiosyncratic findings. In order to make these amenable for further analysis, researchers may want to categorise the data. Alternatively they may look for typologies of people or situations or at least make comparisons between them. All these kinds of analysis result in a more or less systematic description of the data as well as a reduction of them to the most important analytical dimensions. Ideally, the result of the analysis fits or gives rise to theoretical explanations, while at the same time being well-grounded in the original data. Often, this asks for an iterative process of switching back and forth between data and theory. This process is again related to issues of quality.

To counteract the subjectivity of the process, researchers may not do it on their own, but in groups. Some researchers also discuss their analyses with the participants in the research. Researchers using more formalised coding systems may calculate the inter-coder reliability using standard statistical methods such as *kappa* (Cohen, 1960). In any case, it is important to give readers and reviewers of the research the possibility to understand what has happened with the raw data to produce the results. This asks for the process of analysis to be well-documented, to explain what kind of decisions were made for what kind of reasons, to ground the analytic dimensions in the empirical data and provide examples (Elliot *et al.*, 1999; Henwood and Pidgeon, 1992). Ideally, another researcher would be able to come to the same conclusions when using the same kinds of procedure.

Besides providing this kind of more technical insight, reflexivity is once again important with regard to the quality of research (Elliot *et al.*, 1999; Henwood and Pidgeon, 1992). Qualitative researchers should disclose their own (theoretical) assumptions to allow readers to interpret the analysis and consider possible alternative interpretations. It is only by being reflective that a researcher makes it possible for others to discuss and criticise the study and to come to a better understanding of the life-world of older people.

TRIANGULATION

The study of ageing and later life is clearly not confined to the provinces of a single academic discipline nor does it involve a single methodological approach. Given the multidisciplinary nature of research questions and methods used, researchers are often faced with the challenge of having to integrate and synthesise different forms of data to provide a coherent response to their research questions. Integrating data collected 'between different methods' provides breadth of perspective and offers a mechanism for testing the reliability and validity of the findings; i.e. whether the same themes and issues emerge across a variety of different sources (Fielding and Fielding, 1986; Kellaher *et al.*, 1990). There is no one approach to the triangulation of data as the use of mixed methods in Box 5.5 also illustrates.

As an example of the approach we can illustrate the ideas of Rossman and Wilson (1985) of corroboration, elaboration and initiation. *Corroboration* is an analytical approach whereby the researcher examines, for example, quantitative and qualitative data on complaints about discharge planning and care transfers for evidence of convergence: the findings from one approach being confirmed (or refuted) by those obtained by the other methods. *Elaboration* refers to depth of understanding of a particular problem with quantitative and qualitative data being used to inform each other, for example patient interview data being used to expand and develop a delayed transfer category generated from the case note review. *Initiation* focuses upon instances where findings from the different data sets diverge in order to generate ideas for further analysis or suggest areas for further research.

CONCLUSIONS

As a multidisciplinary field, gerontological research can be categorised in a number of different ways. However, a single research project, such as a study of loneliness and isolation in old age, may contain elements of each type of research. What is important for the critical (in the sense of being reflective) student of gerontology is that each different approach to research generates different types of information about old age/ageing which develops our state of knowledge about our chosen field of interest.

Reflecting on this process is essential. The production of knowledge about old age and ageing takes place within a specific social, political and cultural context. Hence the humanitarian political economy tradition in British social research results in a huge body of research about the 'problems' of old age and rather less attention being paid to the 'non-problematic' aspects of ageing. Furthermore, in this example, policy-makers/researchers and not older people define the problems. Hence when considering the state of knowledge about a specific aspect of ageing or older people, such as the provision of 'informal' care or the need for chiropody services, we need to consider the implicit assumptions, ideological positions and potential biases resultant from the social context within which the research has taken place. What we don't know or have never researched may tell us as much as documenting what we do know.

Another important issue is whether any findings can be attributed to pure age effects. However, within the field of social gerontology age effects are extremely difficult to identify with any certainty. We have seen that the combination of age effects with period and cohort effects as explanatory factors serves to underpin the difficulties facing the gerontologist. One should look critically at any evidence that claims to prove that X or Y is the result of, or is caused by, ageing. To date there has been insufficient cross-national, cross-cultural and historical research for us to determine whether any of the observed age-related changes are indeed intrinsic age effects. Furthermore, it is extremely important to remain aware of the large diversity among older adults. Diversity exists by social categories like gender, ethnicity or social class, but also by dimensions like pathological, normal or successful aging in psychological, social or physical domains of functioning.

In designing specific research studies the gerontologist must use appropriate research designs, measurement techniques and samples in order that he or she may unambiguously investigate a specific research question. Without being unnecessarily prescriptive, gerontologists need to consider a series of questions before embarking upon their research. These questions include the following:

- *How much is already known about the subject?* Areas where there is already an extensive body of knowledge enable the researcher to build on previous research by replicating methodologies to enable comparability. Such studies may be very highly specific. More exploratory, groundbreaking research is more broadly focused and may use in-depth exploratory methods. Additionally we need to consider if there are already data in existence that we could use to answer the question by undertaking secondary data analysis.
- *What type of research is being planned?* Is this applied research which is linked to a particular policy initiative or is it knowledge or theory generating? Applied research is often 'quick and dirty' and is usually much more constraining in terms of time than other types of research which can limit its complexity.
- *What is the nature of the research question?* This includes a number of issues. First is the study concerned with enumeration and empirical matters (e.g. looking at the relationship between numbers of doctors and mortality) or is it concerned with understanding the social meanings and behaviours (such as why older people who experience ageism present with ageist attitudes). It is usual to undertake qualitative studies when the research is focused upon the meanings attributed to social factors or when understanding behaviours, whereas quantitative studies are usually concerned with counting the distribution of specific events and outcomes.

These two approaches should not be seen as mutually exclusive but as complimentary and both may be used in the same project. A second consideration concerns the focus of our research. Are we concerned with older people as a distinct social category or group, or with the processes of ageing? For the former, cross-sectional research is adequate but for the latter a longitudinal design may be required. Again both types of study design can be used in quantitative and qualitative contexts.

- *How should we collect the data?* This question relates to the nature of the research question discussed above. Depending upon the specific question there is a number of different ways of collecting data: observation, experiments, interviews, review of health/social care records. Again a variety of different data collection techniques may be used in a single project. Triangulation of data from a variety of sources can help reveal the complexity of many issues assessing whether findings conflict or add depth.

The precise research design to be employed depends upon the question that the researcher wishes to answer. The gerontologist must be aware of the limitations imposed by the type of sample population achieved and the measurement techniques employed and strive for high quality in research. Erroneous generalisations and extrapolations should not be made from inappropriate study populations. Perhaps one reason why old age is viewed in such a negative way by society is that many early research studies were based upon samples drawn from institutions, thereby giving a highly biased picture of the nature of old age.

As gerontologists we have a responsibility to see that research is properly designed, conducted and interpreted so that we do not contribute to the validation of the myths and stereotypes of later life. Yet, at the same time, this laudable aim must be balanced by the obligation to report the results of research truthfully and completely however much they represent a challenge to cherished ideologies.

FURTHER READING

Jamieson, A. and Victor, C. R. (2002) *Researching Ageing and Later Life: The Practice of Social Gerontology.* Buckingham: Open University Press.
Peace, S. (1990) *Researching Social Gerontology: Concepts, Methods and Issues.* London: Sage.

6

Health and dependency in later life

John Bond and Gregorio
Rodriguez Cabrero

INTRODUCTION

An enduring stereotype of human ageing is one of inevitable ill-health and mental and physical incapacity leading to disability and dependency. It underpins ageism (Bytheway, 1995) and reflects personal constructions of normal ageing (Bond *et al.*, 2004; Bond and Corner, 2004). In this chapter we explore concepts of health and illness, disability and dependency. We examine the reality of health and dependency in later life from the perspective of older people and compare the provision of formal and informal support within different European societies. The chapter has two broad themes. We describe first the nature of health disability and dependency in European societies. A final section provides a general overview of healthcare systems within Europe.

We start by highlighting the importance of the way that health and ageing are represented in European cultures. We consider the health beliefs of older adults and their beliefs about ageing. An important idea is the way that beliefs about health and ageing are entwined and the impact that this relationship has on the nature of ageism. Our review of health and dependency in later life then focuses on the nature of disability and the contrasting discourses of the 'medical' and 'social' models of disability. We review the World Health Organization's (WHO) model of functioning and disability (World Health Organization, 2001). We then examine different uses of the concept of dependency with a particular focus on physical and psychological dependency. Using data from the Office for Official Publications of the European Communities, we provide an overview of the experience of health, disability or dependency in selected European countries.

In the remainder of the chapter we describe the evolution of health and social care systems in Europe and highlight recent key reforms and the political debates challenging the way that healthcare and social care policy is developing in the context of ageing societies. We provide a typology of different health and social care systems in Europe and examine the competing paradigms for the development of healthcare and social care systems: privatisation and the pressure for increasing individual responsibility on the one hand, and ideas of collective responsibility represented within the traditional social protection systems of the original six member states of the European Economic Community on the other.

REPRESENTATIONS OF HEALTH AND AGEING

In different societies and within those societies, both health and ageing are defined from a range of perspectives and seen through a variety of lenses. Images of health and ageing provide symbolic representations of such perspectives using oral and written language and other mediums such as traditional art, photographs or film. Images of the ageing body reflecting disease and disability and the dominant stereotypes of later life readily come to mind. Wrinkles, grey hair, edentulousness and physical or mental frailty are images of the ageing body represented through the media and popular and traditional culture. Although such images are normally self-evident, we should not be misled by the common sense nature of such images since they are only representatives of a particular symbolic order defined within a specific culture or society (Blaikie and Hepworth, 1997).

In biomedical science and the public's perception, both ageing and health are bodily affairs. But the public's explanations of ageing and health and those of biomedical scientists often differ. Within European societies, public explanations are likely to include biomedical explanations since we have all been taught to think, at least in part, in biomedical terms (Blaxter, 1983; Calnan, 1987; Cornwell, 1984). Although we may all accept and take for granted some biomedical knowledge – like the germ theory of disease – it is clear that our explanations of health and ageing are often complex, subtle and sophisticated and based on belief systems and cultural meanings that extend beyond biomedical knowledge.

HEALTH BELIEFS

The beliefs of older people about health and illness, like those of younger people, are both particular to the individual and reflect the dominant ideologies of particular cultures or societies. Individuals act with agency. Agency embodies not only ideas from social action theory (Gerth and Mills, 1948) and explanations of objective human action in terms of intention and rationality (Mead, 1934). Agency is also about individual action, which is passionate and intuitive and distinctly subjective (Lash and Urry, 1986). Individuals' conceptions of health and illness are influenced by a sense of self (Charmaz, 1983) and especially their sense of control over mind and body (Stainton Rogers, 1991). In recognising agency we cannot ignore the role of structure in defining health and illness. Beliefs about health and illness are ideological (Calnan, 1987; Charmaz, 2000; Crawford, 1984). Within Europe and North America the values of capitalism and individualism are mirrored in our conceptualisations about health and illness (Nettleton, 1995). They are imbued with notions of self-discipline, self-denial, self-control and willpower. Health may be seen as a metaphor for generalised well-being (Crawford, 1984).

One approach to the study of health beliefs that bridges individual agency and social structure uses the Durkheimian notion of social representation (Durkheim, 1964). This approach influenced Claudine Herzlich (Herzlich, 1973; Herzlich and Pierret, 1985; Herzlich and Pierret, 1987) in the investigation of how French people make sense of ideas like 'health' and 'illness'. She concluded that people's experiences and conceptions of health and illness can be properly understood only in relation to the cultural context of their lives. Study participants' perceptions of health and illness go well beyond biomedical explanations of health.

From interviews with Parisians and participants from Normandy, Herzlich (1973) concluded that different understandings and explanations for health and illness are not polar opposites of each other but remain discrete conceptions. Study participants distinguished between illness that was produced by ways of life and positive concepts of health that came from within the individual. Health was identified as having three dimensions: 'health in a vacuum', 'reserve of health' and 'equilibrium'.

- *Health in a vacuum* was the term used to describe the idea of health being the simple absence of disease, a lack of awareness of the body or not being concerned about the state of the body.
- *Reserve of health* represents health as an asset or investment rather than a state. Two aspects were characterised: physical robustness or strength that enables one to work and play, and resistance to illness that enable one to defend one against disease or recover from illness.
- *Equilibrium* was used to highlight the notion of positive well being described by study participants to include notions of internal harmony and balance.

The descriptions of illness described by study participants were less clear. They were able to distinguish between four classes of illness: serious illness that may be fatal, chronic conditions, trivial illnesses, and childhood ailments. Interpreting these data, Herzlich (1973) suggests three metaphors that clearly distinguish between three social representations of illness: illness as 'destroyer', illness as 'liberator' and illness as 'occupation'.

- *Illness as destroyer* was an image held by people who were particularly engaged or active in life and for whom illness interfered with their lives by limiting their ability to continue with their daily activities and responsibilities.
- *Illness as liberator* reflects the ability of individuals to be freed from the responsibilities of life and to receive the privileges of sympathy and care from others.

- *Illness as occupation* describes the reaction of individuals who respond to illness as a challenge to overcome. In responding to the challenge of illness all other activities and responsibilities are relegated while the individual concentrates on recovery.

Older people in Aberdeen, Scotland, were found to define health and illness in similar ways (Williams, 1983). Health was perceived *negatively*, as the absence of illness; *functionally*, as the ability to cope with everyday activities; or *positively*, as fitness or well-being. Since, within the modern world, health continues to have a moral dimension, ill-health and moral wrongdoing are interconnected. Health is therefore constructed in terms of willpower, self-discipline and self-control (Blaxter, 1983).

Despite differences in the characteristics of study participants and cultural variation between France and Scotland, Blaxter (1990) has observed that there are several areas of agreement. Four representations of health and illness prevail: freedom from illness, ability to function, fitness, and the idea of health as a reserve. In a survey of health and lifestyles, Blaxter (1990) asked a cross-section of adults for their ideas about health (Table 6.1). Most survey respondents offered multiple concepts of health. Gender and life-course position influenced responses. Younger men tended to describe health in terms of fitness whereas younger women focused on energy, vitality and being able to cope. Survey respondents who were middle-aged emphasised overall physical and psychological well-being. In later life the focus was on function, particularly among older men, although ideas about contentment and happiness were commonplace.

Table 6.1   Representations of health.

Definition	Sample response
Health:	
as not ill	Someone I know who is very healthy is me, because I haven't been to a doctor yet.
despite disease	I am very healthy despite this arthritis.
as a reserve	Both parents are still alive at 90 so he belongs to healthy stock.
as 'the healthy life'	I call her healthy because she goes jogging and doesn't eat fried food
as physical fitness	There's tone to my body, I feel fit.
as energy or vitality	Health is when I feel I can do anything.
as social relationships	You feel as though everyone is your friend, I enjoy life more, and can work, and help other people.
as function	She's 81 and she gets her work done quicker than me, and she does the garden.
as psychosocial well being	Well I think health is when you feel happy.

Source: (Blaxter, 1990, ch. 2)

BELIEFS ABOUT AGEING

The importance of health to older people is widely documented (Bowling, 1995; Farquhar, 1994, 1995). Taken-for-granted common-sense knowledge leads many older people to accept that ill-health is an inevitable part of human ageing (Bond and Corner, 2004). Older people often expect to experience mental and physical symptoms in later life and consequently fail to mention symptoms to their doctors, even when effective treatments exist (Williams, 1990). But not all older people accept physical or mental decline in later life as inevitable. We have all observed biological changes associated with ageing such as the emergence of wrinkles, the balding of heads and the greying of hair. And we will have also observed differences in the rate of ageing among our close friends and relatives. But whether we attribute ill-health to our own experience of ageing will depend on the culture, time and place in which we live and our own personality (Bond and Corner, 2004). Corner (1999) found that study participants who were 'dominated' or 'oppressed' were more likely to attribute 'old age' to many of the medical conditions for which they were being treated. They had a sense of fatalism about their conditions, and a belief that 'it was just old age'. But for the 'empowered', a sense of control gave them a different perspective on health and ageing, one that recognised the association between ill-health and old age and one that challenged its inevitability. However this was a minority view and the majority continued to describe ageing using negative stereotypes reflecting our ageist culture.

AGEISM

Our modern European consumer culture admires youth and the beauty, energy, grace, moral fortitude and optimism of youthful bodies. In contrast, ageing bodies represent ugliness, degeneration and moral failure. These negative stereotypes of older people go beyond images of the ageing body to incorporate moral interpretations of physical decline in the 'normal ageing' body to describe behavioural and attitudinal aspects. Older people are perceived as senile, rigid in thought and manner, and old-fashioned in morality and skills (Butler, 1987). In everyday life we use metaphors such as 'crinkly', 'crumbly' and 'gaga' to describe older people. It is the systematic negative stereotyping of older people on the basis of age and the associated prejudice and discrimination against older people that defines ageism in contemporary European society.

The institutionalisation of ageism in later life is reinforced by the legal, political, educational, and health and welfare structures of many European societies. Ageism is internalised in the attitudes of individuals toward older people, which are reinforced by these same structures in society. Older people are equally ageist. The language used by older participants in Corner's (1999) study was principally negative, reflecting that used by the media and popular culture. Participants described the problems of old age for society and the 'burden' of the ageing population. Participants were concerned with becoming a 'burden' themselves and the dominant stereotype they presented was of later life being one of ill-health and dependency.

One feature of ageism in European societies is the rationing of health services on the basis of age. Health economists have long argued that the demand for healthcare in a modern industrial society will always outstrip supply and therefore that rationing will always be necessary (Maynard, 1993). Rationing of healthcare services is achieved explicitly using market mechanisms such as price in European states in which privatised medicine predominates. Where socialised medicine survives, implicit rationing is achieved by doctors using 'clinical freedom' and explicitly through the control of resources and the use of waiting lists (Bowling, 1999; Dudley and Burns, 1992; Evans, 1991; Henwood, 1990; Jennett, 1995; Pettersen, 1995; The Lancet, 1991; Wicclair, 1993).

DISABILITY

The difficulty with the term 'disability' is that it is a complicated multidimensional concept experienced and characterised from a variety of different perspectives: people with disabilities living in a range of social contexts, their significant others such as partners and family members, and members of formal institutions and professions such as doctors, teachers and social workers. Disability has political, social and psychological dimensions. Consequences of disability are social exclusion and oppression (Oliver, 1996), stigmatisation of 'spoiled identities' (Goffman, 1968) and issues of self-identity and self-esteem.

In understanding disability, the dominant discourse has been the dialectic between the 'medical model' and 'social model'. For the 'medical model', disability is a personal issue that is directly caused by disease, trauma or other health problem. It is often seen as a personal tragedy that can sometimes lead to the blaming of the individual for his or her condition and the labelling of people with disabilities as 'victims' or 'sufferers' (Oliver, 1996). These processes are part of the medicalisation of disability (Oliver, 1990). The solution for the individual is perceived as medical treatment in order to 'cure' the condition, manage the symptoms and maintain the individual's adjustment to the disability and subsequent behaviour change. Thus the development of biomedical science and medical interventions is seen as the main political response to disability.

In contrast, for the 'social model', disability is not an attribute of the individual; rather it is constructed by society through social interaction within the context of the political, social and physical environment. The personal responses of individuals to disability and its consequences are central to a social model. They cannot be understood as merely a reaction to the condition or as a response to the oppression by the social structure (Foucault, 1973). An understanding of disability has to be located within a framework that takes account of the life histories of people with disability and their informal caregivers, their material circumstances, the meaning disability has for the individual, and the struggle to be included as citizens of their societies. The solution requires social action to change the physical environment as well as attitudes to people with disabilities. Disability has political and societal solutions rather than simply medical ones.

Within this dialectical discourse there are a number of models of disability (Altman, 2001). From a medical or public policy perspective, disability remains a useful concept for summarising the impact of disease and biological ageing on older people. The approach has been to consider the outcomes of disease and ageing processes using the World Health Organization's classification of impairment, disability and handicap (World Health Organization, 1980) and its more recent presentation the International Classification of Functioning and Disability (ICIDH-2) (World Health Organization, 2001). The recent version moves away from the idea that disability is a consequence of disease or ageing – the medical model – to focus on the components of health. It goes some way to accommodating the traditional criticisms of the medical model of health, disability and ageing and addressing some of the concerns expressed by people with disabilities by embracing the social model.

The WHO model of functioning and disability is shown in Figure 6.1. The centre of this model is human activity and interactions with agency (health condition, body function and structures and social participation) and structure or context (environmental and personal factors).

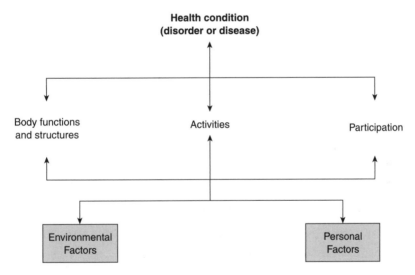

Figure 6.1   World Health Organization model of functioning and disability

Source: WHO (2001)

The individual components of the model are defined in Box 6.1. Human activity has traditionally been operationalised in medical and social research in terms of activities of daily living (ADLs) in order to measure levels of disability. This approach usually focuses on physical function but increasingly is also used to reflect the impact of cognitive function. The strength of the WHO model is the recognition that ADLs are context-specific, being influenced by either environmental (or social) and personal (or psychological) factors. However, it is noteworthy that in the implementation of the model into a measurement tool only body structure and activity have been developed. These are grounded in the existing measures of impairment and ADLs. Measures of participation, and environmental and personal factors, were not developed as part of the new model when it was accepted by the World Health Assembly in 2001. The successful development of methods for describing and measuring these aspects of the model is essential if the credibility of ICIDH-2 as a social model is to be accepted. At present it remains very much a medical model.

Box 6.1   Components of international classification of functioning, disability and health (ICF)

In the context of health:

- Body functions are the physiological functions of body systems (including psychological functions).
- Body structures are anatomical parts of the body such as organs, limbs and their components.
- Impairments are problems in body function or structure such as a loss of a limb or reduction in use of any body structure.
- Activity is the execution of a task or action by an individual including activities of daily living and other activities of everyday life such as work and leisure activities.
- Participation is involvement in a life situation.
- Activity limitations are difficulties an individual may have in executing activities.
- Participation restrictions are problems an individual may experience in involvement in life situations.
- Environmental factors make up the physical, social and attitudinal environment in which people live and conduct their lives.
- Personal factors are social and psychological attributes including gender, ethnicity, age, class, fitness, lifestyle habits and personal coping styles.

Source: WHO (2001), www.who.int/classifications/icf/en/, accessed: 16 August 2004.

What types of indicators of participation would make this an acceptable social model? And what are the environmental and personal factors that would need to be addressed? Participation denotes an individual's degree of involvement – the lived experience of people in different social contexts. Individual contexts are influenced by the physical and social environment as well as personal factors experienced across the life-course. The variety of lived experiences and associated social contexts makes participation a difficult concept to measure. One way to understand what participation means for people with disability – and particularly older people with disability – is to investigate the barriers to participation. Goffman in his essay on the total institution (Goffman, 1961) characterised life as being divided into three key elements: work, leisure and family. To these we might add community in terms of involvement in political, voluntary and religious organisations.

Older people, and particularly older people with disability, are increasingly excluded from the world of work (see Chapter 8) because of statutory retirement policies, attitudes of older people towards paid work and the negative attitudes of employers towards older workers. Yet exclusion from the world of work remains one of the strongest barriers to participation. Ageism and disablism are partly the result of societies' preoccupation with the value of youth who are 'our future' and who generate the wealth. Access to work for many is the source of resources to enable involvement in a range of leisure activities. Yet the most popular activity, watching television, is pursued by all age groups and disability levels. But a key judgement here is whether the tastes of minority groups are catered for by the broadcasters. Leisure activities outside the home remain more problematic for older people with disabilities. Even when finances permit, exclusion from popular leisure pursuits occurs. Physical barriers such as poor wheelchair access to historical monuments and attitudinal barriers such as the stigmatisation of people with dementia or movement disorders in restaurants and other public places are examples of barriers to participation. Similar physical and attitudinal barriers also prevent older people with disabilities from being included in community life, particularly political and voluntary organisations, although increasingly the involvement of the 'user' or 'consumer' in organisations focusing on their needs and concerns is occurring; see, for example, the involvement of people with disabilities in the UK National Health Service (Department of Health, 2001). Participation in family life remains a positive experience for many older people with disabilities who have remaining 'family'. However, age segregation is playing an increasing role in the social life of older people. A recent study in the Netherlands identified a clear deficit of young adults in the networks of older people, with the extent of the deficit increasing with age. This study also found that the overwhelming proportion of the younger network members identified by older people were family and kin (Uhlenberg and de Jong Gierveld, 2004).

Of course social exclusion, the exclusion from participation and involvement in all aspects of social life, is not just the lived experience of people with disabilities. Other social groups, usually minority groups, also experience exclusion. Throughout European history, religious minorities, minorities from different faiths, have been excluded and oppressed by the majority faiths. People from different ethnic and cultural backgrounds, lower socio-economic groups and women have all experienced oppression and social exclusion. Being a member of an oppressed social group is an additional barrier for people with disability to full participation in European societies. The experience of 'intersectionality' (Hulko, 2002) – being oppressed on a number of these dimensions among older people or people with disability – increases their social exclusion from everyday life.

DEPENDENCY

Many of the negative stereotypes of later life are brought together in the single word 'dependency'. Ageism is manifested in the way we define dependency in old age. The images of later life highlighted by Butler (1987) in his analysis of ageism are often used metaphorically in comparison with childhood (Hockey and James, 1993). Rather like Shakespeare in the oft-quoted verse of the seven stages of man (and woman) in *As You Like It*, 'deep' old age (sometimes referred to as the fourth age) is seen as the coming of the second childhood. The use of metaphors of childhood provides implicit frames of reference for everyday social interaction and encourages infantilisation and practices of infantilisation – the treatment of older people as if they were children. Thus implicitly the use of the term dependency is infantilising of older people.

Yet the term 'dependency' is institutionalised in public policy through its use in describing the economic indicators known as dependency ratios. A key issue for policymakers is the maintenance of economic growth. One of the perceived barriers to economic growth is the absolute decline in the proportion of the population who are economically active. In economic models the idea is overly simple: the greater the proportion of the population who are economically active the smaller the proportion of the resources that need to be diverted to the economically inactive (the dependent population). Thus for policymakers concerned with national, European and world economies, any decline in the proportion of people economically active or the ageing of the population inevitably means that older people will be an increasing economic burden. In contrast, children, the other main dependency group, are seen as the future. This is also an argument that has often been used in the support of rationing health services for older people (Callahan, 1987). Given the hegemony of economic policy the fallacy of this argument is often overlooked.

Dependency ratios

Formally, dependency ratios are a measure of the relative sizes of the economically active (often defined as those in paid employment) and the economically inactive (all those not in paid employment including children, unpaid homemakers, people in full-time education or skills training and the majority of older people). Three ratios are routinely calculated: total dependency ratio, gerontic dependency ratio and neontic dependency ratio. The ratios are calculated by dividing the number of dependent people (older people or children) by the number of people of working age. The actual statistics calculated will vary because of the use of different age cut-offs over time and between different countries, but the general trends are relatively robust as economic indicators.

As was noted in Chapter 1, different European societies are ageing at dissimilar rates because of different demographic population profiles. These differences are reflected in the dependency ratios in each country. Data for selected European Union countries (Figure 6.2) show that the gerontic dependency ratio (number of people aged 65 or over expressed as a percentage of the number of people aged 15–64) is projected to rise in all EU states by 2050. The ratio is projected to double from some 24% in 2000 to 49% in 2050 among the EU-15 states. There are striking differences across European countries, with the highest ratios of some 60% in 2050 projected for Italy and Spain.

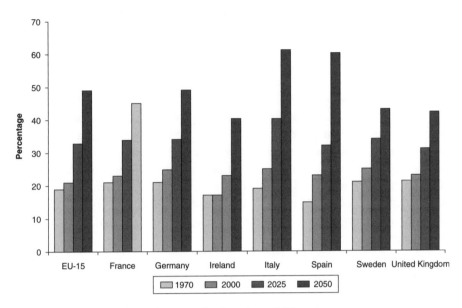

Figure 6.2   Old-age dependency ratios in selected EU states (population aged 65 or over as percentage of population aged 15 to 64)

Source: Eurostat, central scenario (2004d)

It would be very easy to become alarmist about these changing dependency ratios (Katz, 1992). They provide food for thought in relation to pensions policy (see Chapter 7), but it is often assumed that the ageing of the population and associated shifts in the dependency ratios will damage European economies through increased consumption of health and welfare services (Clark and Spengler, 1980; quoted in Bond, 1992). Not only does this use of dependency ratios reinforce ageism but it ignores the invisible contributions that older people make to the European economy in their personal consumption and productivity. Assumptions about the use of health and welfare services are based on historical data and take no account of changing patterns of morbidity and mortality in later life (see Chapter 2). Similarly assumptions about labour force participation of women and older people are subject to change.

Types of dependency

A number of writers have voiced concern about the way the term 'dependency' is used. Wilkin and colleagues (Wilkin, 1987; Wilkin and Thompson, 1989) have reviewed the meaning of dependency as reflected in different usages and identified two broad approaches to classification. First, it can be classified in terms of activities of daily living for which an individual is dependent on others; and second, in terms of the causes of dependency. Walker (1982), in the development of the concept of structured dependency (Townsend, 1981; Walker, 1981), has also highlighted a number of uses of the term. His concept of life-cycle dependency mirrors at the individual level the dependency ratio and is the concept of dependency at the centre of Hockey and James' (1993) analysis of ageing along the life-course. Walker (1982) also highlights political and economic dependency. Political dependency relates to loss of personhood and citizenship with the curtailment or restriction of individual autonomy and empowerment. Economic dependency is the dependence of individuals on financial support from families and informal social networks and the State. Central to this chapter, however, is the concept of physical or psychological dependency (Wilkin, 1987). Chronic ill-health, disability and mental or physical frailty are all dependency-creating attributes and the majority of people who are physically or psychologically dependent are also likely to experience economic and political dependency. An important issue here will be how different actors perceive the older person's physical and mental state and how it is subsequently defined.

Physical and psychological dependency

At the centre of many ideas about dependency is the idea that it is part of a social relationship. Physical and psychological dependency therefore refers to an individual's physical and social needs that result from illness, impairment or disability and, importantly, the individual's reliance on others for assistance in meeting these recognised personal care and health needs. But reliance on others is not necessarily all one way in a social relationship. For example, caregivers of dependent individuals may experience fulfilment as a result of their caregiving actions. Reciprocity therefore remains an important element in understanding dependency that will lead to a discussion of interdependency in later life. But first let us explore further aspects of physical and psychological dependency.

An innovative idea developed by Isaacs and Neville (1976), which has survived the course of time for the purpose of service planning at the population level, is one that tries to identify categories of personal need and determine the reliance that individuals have on others. The central concept here is 'interval need' defined by the time interval that an individual can be left before his or her needs should be met. The simple classification distinguished personal and health needs as 'long', 'short' or 'critical'. A more complex classification has been used for population planning purposes (Bond and Carstairs, 1982). Individuals' needs are classified according to their health status, in particular their level of physical or mental disability. The original classification identified four categories: independent, long-interval dependency, short-interval dependency, and critical-interval dependency. People who are independent may have medical conditions but experience little or no functional incapacity. An individual's functional capacity may be affected by physical illness (e.g. arthritis) or mental illness (e.g. dementia) or more likely a combination of physical and mental illnesses. But functional capacity will also be affected by environmental and social factors such as the quality of the built environment (see Chapter 10), the presence of a strong social support network (see Chapter 9) as well as personal and psychological factors (see Chapter 3). Therefore people defined as long-interval dependent may have needs like shopping or cleaning that can be met by someone else at no specific time and not necessarily on a daily basis. Those defined as short-interval dependent may have needs such as showering, bathing or washing which need to be met at specific times of the day and at least once a day. Different social and cultural perspectives will mean that these are not uniform categories but defined by each individual. However, in population studies it is pragmatic to ignore such diversity. People who are critical-interval dependent have needs that are unpredictable, such as assistance with toileting or supervision because of cognitive impairment; they probably require 24-hour supervision. Again individual needs will vary, perhaps because of different perspectives of risk. Table 6.2 illustrates interval needs for different functional incapacities.

Table 6.2   Categories of physical or psychological dependency.

Dependency categories	mobility	Personal Care	House Care	Continence	Mental Health
Independent	Able to do all mobility activities	Able to do all personal care activities	Able to do all house care activities	Continent	No mental health problems
Long Interval	Difficulty walking on level surface outside. Unable to travel by bus	Difficulty with: • dressing • washing hands or face Unable to: • wash hair • bath or shower	Difficulty with: • light housework • preparing/ cooking a meal Unable to: • heavy do shopping • wash clothes • iron clothes	Incontinent of urine only	Mild memory impairment or mild depression or anxiety
Short interval	Unable to walk on a level surface outside	Unable to: • put on shoes • dress • wash hands or face	Unable to: • light do housework • prepare or cook a meal • make bed	Not continent of faeces	May have mild disorder
Critical interval	Unable to: • get out of chair • walk	Unable to • use toilet		Incontinent of urine and/or faeces	Severe memory problem, depression or anxiety

Source: Bond J and Carstairs V (1982), Fig. 5.

EXPERIENCING HEALTH, DISABILITY OR DEPENDENCY

Health and the capacity to remain independent are important aspects of older people's lives. Ill-health and incapacity are often the first topics in conversations involving older people. When meeting each other, older people almost inevitably enquire about the other's health. A negative response will often be followed by a detailed description of the signs and symptoms of any maladies, and hospital experiences can be reported with great enthusiasm. Yet it is important to remind ourselves that not all older people experience poor health, disability or physical or psychological dependency. Of course, ill-health and disability can be a major source of pain and suffering to many older people and lead to loss of independence and autonomy, self-esteem and dignity, mobility, and social interaction and participation in everyday life. But the diversity of experience in later life is now widely recognised at a policy level (Joint Taskforce on Older People, 2000) and there is recognition of substantial evidence to support this picture in national and European data.

Even in countries like the United Kingdom where there is a long tradition of collecting health statistics about the population, these remain notoriously difficult to use to describe the experience of health in the older population. Traditionally, epidemiologists have used both mortality and morbidity data. Because of the high prevalence of co-morbidity in later life, both mortality and morbidity statistics may mask what is really going on. By co-morbidity is meant the presence of more than one disease or chronic illness; for example many older people will live with arthritis and heart disease. Survey researchers have therefore developed self-report techniques for assessing health status and incapacity. Yet successive surveys of older people in Europe and North America consistently find that older people rate their health as good while morbidity data suggest that their health is poor. Self-report data may not reflect absolute levels of morbidity, but rather the expectations of older people about their health at their age in life. However, self-ratings of health have been, time after time, reliable predictors of survival and mortality (Idler and Benyamini, 1997). In response, one approach has been to focus on measurement of disability and incapacity, although again these often rely on self-reports. Such measures have their limitations. Many studies suggest that older people's evaluations do not necessarily equate with those of other family members or formal assessments by health professionals. They also are often culturally specific and therefore biased against ethnic minority groups (Blakemore and Boneham, 1994) within European societies.

From the European Community Household Panel 1998 we can get a general picture of the level of ill-health and incapacity among older people (OPOCE, 2003). Unlike the data from individual national surveys, the questions used to map self-perceived health are comparable in both question wording and the number of categories allowed for participants' responses. Figure 6.3 shows for selected European countries the percentage of people in different age groups who rated their health as either good or very good and shows that health status declines with age. Figure 6.4 summarises this information for all fifteen EU states and shows that women are less satisfied than men with their health in all age groups. The

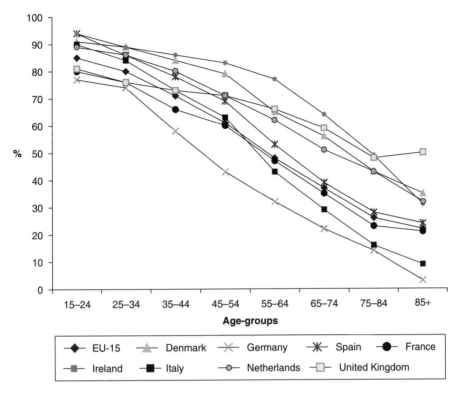

Figure 6.3 Self-perceived health by age in selected EU states

Source: ECHP UDB Eurostat (2003)

slight increase in the percentage of men aged 85 or over satisfied with their health status probably reflects a survival effect or sampling error.

Using data from different national surveys like the General Household Survey in the UK, Figure 6.5 shows the percentage of the population who report having a chronic condition. We need to treat these data with caution since they use different although similar questions, and much of the variation between countries may be accounted for by the survey methods used and variations in the prevalence of non-responses. The data presented indicate an increase with age in the proportion of men and women in selected countries who report a chronic condition. The decrease in proportion of those reporting among the older age groups may reflect the survival affect, the exclusion from the survey of older people resident in long-term care institutions or different expectations of younger and older people.

Figure 6.6 compares the percentage of the population limited in terms of walking, by age, in different European countries. These data are also drawn from national surveys and the questions asked differ in both wording and response categories and should be interpreted with considerable caution. The data, however, highlight the relationship between the age of men and women and the extent of incapacity among people living at home in the community.

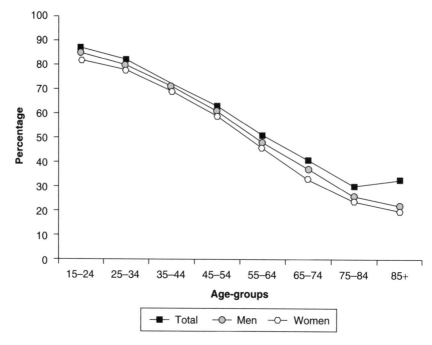

Figure 6.4   Self-perceived health of men and women in EU in 2001

Source: ECHP UDB Eurostat (2003a)

Using data from the European Community Household Panel in 1999, Table 6.3 shows the proportions of people in Europe with disabilities or chronic physical or mental health problems who are in need of support with everyday activities, by age group and severity of impairment. Differences in the ways that different cultures report disability and ill-health means that these data should only be used as a rough guide to the level of physical and psychological dependency among the older population in Europe. In Table 6.3 we have grouped survey respondents into four groups of countries according to geography: the Nordic countries (Denmark, Finland and Sweden), the Continental countries (Austria, Belgium, France, Germany, Luxemburg and the Netherlands), the southern European countries (Greece, Italy, Portugal and Spain) and the UK and Ireland. As we will see below, these geographical groupings also reflect cultural similarities and different models of healthcare and social care systems (see also Chapter 7). The rates of physical and psychological dependency assessed in the survey show a similar profile for three of the country groups; the exception is the Continental countries where rates are significantly higher for both age groups presented.

Increasing incapacity and ill-health with age can also be seen in health service utilisation data. For example, Figure 6.7 shows the average number of consultations with a medical doctor, by selected countries. Some caution is needed in interpreting these data because of the different way data are collected between countries and the small numbers surveyed in the oldest age groups. Use of medical services

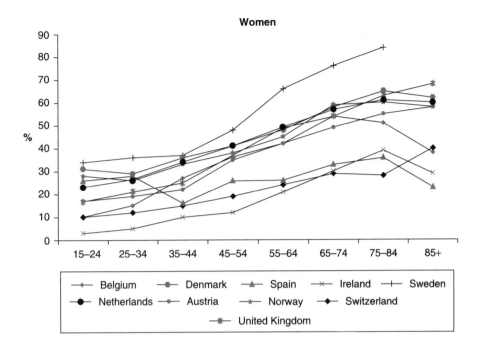

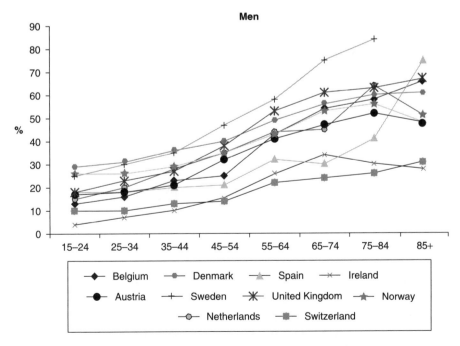

Figure 6.5   Population with chronic conditions by age in selected EU states

Source: European Commission (2003a, Table 2.2)

**Table 6.3   People with disabilities or chronic physical or mental
health problems who are in need of support with everyday
activities by age group and severity of impairment in Europe
(percentages).**

Countries	Age	Group
Nordic countries	*65–79*	*80+*
Severe impairment	14.4	26.4
Moderate impairment	23.7	23.8
Total	**38.1**	**50.2**
Continental countries	*65–79*	*80+*
Severe impairment	20.6	37.9
Moderate impairment	34.7	34.1
Total	**55.3**	**72.0**
South European countries	*65–79*	*80+*
Severe impairment	13.5	27.7
Moderate impairment	19.4	19.5
Total	**32.9**	**47.2**
United Kingdom and Ireland	*65–79*	*80+*
Severe impairment	13.5	34.5
Moderate impairment	21.5	26.6
Total	**35.0**	**61.1**

Source: European Community Household Panel (ECHP) (EUROSTAT, 1999).

increases with age in all the selected countries but there are significant differences
between Norway and Sweden on the one hand and other selected European countries on the other. These differences do not reflect differences in the prevalence of
chronic conditions (see Figure 6.4) and therefore may be the result of the way medical services are organised in different European countries. It is these differences to
which we now turn.

HEALTH AND SOCIAL CARE FOR OLDER PEOPLE IN EUROPE

The needs of older people for healthcare and personal care have traditionally been
met informally by families and their social networks and formally by the state.
Throughout the twentieth century the increasing hegemony of the medical profession and the subsequent medicalisation of health and illness (Freidson, 1975) has
seen the development of formal 'illness' services organised by the state. In contrast, personal social care for older people has traditionally been provided informally by families (predominantly by women) and, until the last half of the
twentieth century, formal personal social care tended to be available for only a

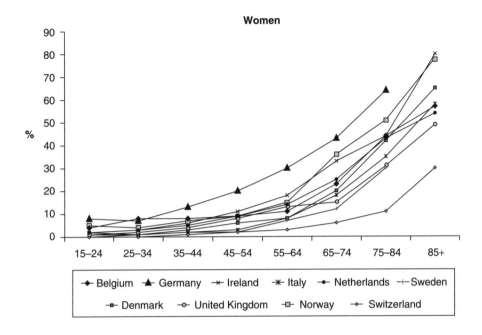

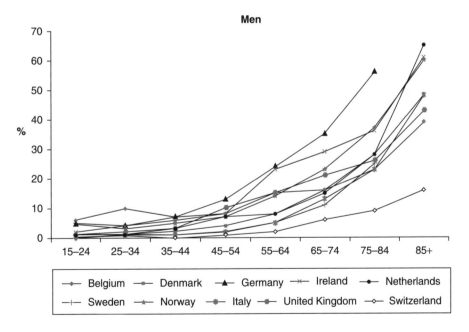

Figure 6.6   Population limited in terms of walking, by age in selected EU states

Source: European Commission (2003a, Table 3.1.1)

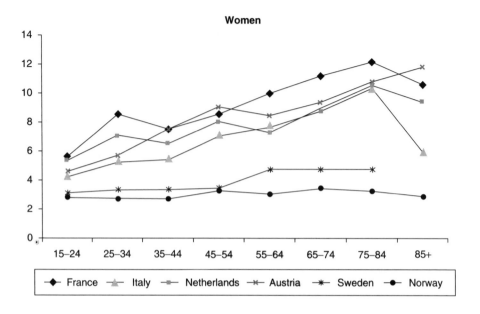

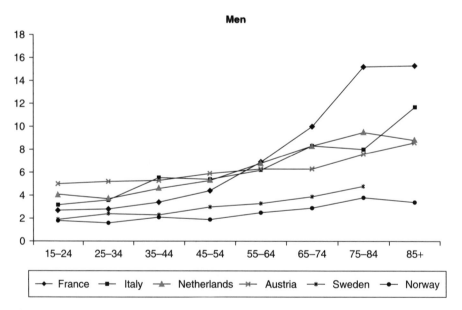

Figure 6.7 Average numbers of consultations with a medical doctor by age in selected EU states

Source: European Commission (2003a, Table 2.8.2)

minority of financially better-off older people. The development of formal social care services for older people in recent decades reflects the changing demography of families, changes in the role of women and changes in the nature of communities. Formal personal social care services have therefore tended to develop

Table 6.4   Gender of informal caregivers and whether the older person is living within or separately from the caregiver's household in Europe.

	Nordic countries (%)	Continental countries (%)	South-European countries (%)	United Kingdom and Ireland (%)
Men	36.4	40.1	24.9	40.6
Women	63.6	59.9	75.1	59.4
Total	**100**	**100**	**100**	**100**
Inside of carer household	23.6	55.5	59.2	30.4
Outside of carer household	73.6	43.6	37.8	65.8
Inside and outside carer household	2.8	0.9	3.0	3.8

Source: European Community Household Panel (ECHP) (EUROSTAT, 1999).

independently of healthcare systems in most European countries. Yet, for older people, perhaps more than those of any other group, the necessity for 'joined-up thinking' between the providers of healthcare and personal social care is increasingly recognised.

The continuing importance of informal caregiving for the provision of personal care is highlighted by data from the European Community Household Panel in 1999 (Table 6.4). Again (as in Table 6.3) the information is presented by four geographical areas, rather than individual countries. The table shows the gender of informal caregivers and whether the older person is living within or separately from the caregiver's household. The proportion of caregivers who are women is higher than the proportion who are men in all 15 countries of the EU in 1999, but in southern European countries women caregivers outnumber male caregivers 3:1. The place of residence of the older person and the caregiver also suggests interesting differences between the groups of countries. Noteworthy is the higher proportion of older people who live in separate households in the Nordic countries, the UK and Ireland. This may reflect the model of healthcare and social care system and something which we turn to below.

The ageing of the population and the development of new effective technologies have led to an increase in resources being spent on healthcare, while the ageing of the population, demographic and social change in families and the increased quality of formal long-term care (including personal social care provided at home) have led to increases in resources demanded for long-term care. Spending on formal long-term care now represents an important proportion of total healthcare and long-term care expenditure as measured by the percentage of gross domestic product (GDP) (Table 6.5). With the continuing ageing of the population (see Chapter 1), irrespective of improvements in disability-free life-years (see Chapter 2), the demand for healthcare and long-term care resources is anticipated to increase during the next fifty years (Schulz *et al.*, 2004).

Table 6.5   Total public expenditure on healthcare and long-term care (percentage of GDP).

Countries	Total health and long-term care	Healthcare	Long-term care
Denmark	8.0	5.1	3.0
Sweden	8.8	6.0	2.8
Finland	6.2	4.6	1.6
Belgium	6.1	5.3	0.8
Austria	5.8	5.1	0.7
France	6.9	6.2	0.7
Holland	7.2	4.7	2.5
Germany		5.7	
Greece		4.8	
Spain		5.0	
Portugal		5.4	
Italy	5.5	4.9	0.6
United Kingdom	6.3	4.6	1.7
Ireland	6.6	5.9	0.7

Source: European Commission and the Council (2003).

The exponential increase in demand for healthcare and long-term care over the last 20 years or so, and the forecast increase, has led to a reconsideration of social protection in many European countries and to the restructuring of the welfare state (Taylor-Gooby, 2001). Underpinning structural changes has been the containment of costs to the state and the introduction of explicit rationing (Bond, 1997), both of which undoubtedly have consequences for the quality and quantity of healthcare and social care for older people. A key instrument of cost containment has been the selective privatisation of healthcare and long-term care, both through the increasing use of non-governmental organisations in the provision of services and the transfer of some of the increasing cost of services on to the individual and the family. Selective privatisation is reflected in the dual nature of healthcare and social care which can be considered in part as a public good and in part as a commodity. As a public good, healthcare and social care are relatively consolidated and a widely legitimated social right of citizens; as a commodity, healthcare and social care reflect the ideology of consumerism contained in many private health schemes. However, despite the ideological drive by most European governments towards increased privatisation and market solutions to the challenge of rising demand and costs, there remains strong public support for the welfare state. Such support may be limiting the extent to which co-payments for health and long-term care are being introduced.

Changes to European healthcare and social care systems

In the evolution of healthcare systems within the European Union we can differentiate two key processes of change:

- within the institutional and organisational framework
- in the policies and programmes.

Table 6.6 shows the characteristics and interrelationships between these two processes.

Table 6.6 Institutional evolution and main health policies in the EU-15 in the last 40 years.

Period of time	Institutional evolution	Main health politics
1960–1970s	Centralisation and bureaucratic delivery system	Universal coverage through general taxes finance
1980s	Decentralisation, provider– purchaser split and quasi-markets	Politics of cost–containment, rationing an efficiency
1990s	Central state as regulator and finance and regions with full competences in planning and management	Quality of services, patients rights and equality programmes
2000s	Coordination between health and personal social services and partnership between authorities and private agencies	Prevention, rehabilitation and programmes for frail elderly people and excluded groups in need Long-term care as new ageing social policy

In terms of the institutional and organisational framework and the provision of health services, four stages can be distinguished. First, during the 1960s and 1970s there was a development of healthcare systems based on greatly centralised organisational models. These systems were bureaucratic and were financed through taxes in the Nordic and Anglo-Saxon countries, and through social security contributions in other continental and southern European countries. Second, during the 1980s, healthcare systems faced a process of decentralisation, with greater power for planning and management awarded to regional and municipal authorities. This facilitated the purchaser–provider split, the separation of the management of services from the funding of services. It provided opportunities for non-governmental organisations (NGOs), particularly in long-term care services, to manage services and led to greater consumer and user involvement. Third, in the 1990s a model for state finance and regulation was consolidated in most European healthcare systems, with further advances in the privatisation of healthcare and long-term care. Territorial and social inequality emerged as an important policy issue reflecting the needs and greater involvement of the user. Finally in the first decade of the twenty-first century priority is being given to models that place an emphasis on internal and external coordination between private and public providers on the one hand and healthcare and social care systems on the other hand.

In terms of healthcare policies and programmes, the 1960s and 1970s supported policies of universal coverage. Rates of coverage varied enormously between

Table 6.7   European models of healthcare and social care systems

	Anglo-Saxon	*Continental*	*Nordic*	*Mediterranean*	*Eastern Europe*
Right to social protection of the dependent	Mixed right: universal in healthcare and assistant in personal social services	Universal right with two levels: contributive and non-contributive	Universal right in health and in long-term care	Mixed right: universal in healthcare; in social services contributive limited assistance	Universal right limited in healthcare and residual assistance in social services
Financing	Taxes and co-payment for those exceeding an assistance income level	Social security contributions, taxes and co-payments	Taxes and some co-payments	Taxes, contributions and co-payments for those exceeding an assistance income level	Taxes and co-payments
Type of social benefit	Services and monetary and assistance	Services and monetary assistance with a universal ceiling	Universal social and health services	Monetary help and secondary assistance type services	Residual services and some monetary assistance
Responsibility for organisation and management	Municipal	Social Security, Regions and Municipalities	Municipal	Regional and Municipal	Municipal
Provision of services according to importance	Companies, NGOs and municipalities	NGOs and companies residual role for municipalities	Municipalities and recently companies	Municipalities, NGOs and increasingly companies	NGOs and municipalities
Policy of support for informal care	Support limited to the carer/ family and high individual responsibility	Broad support for the carer/ family which has ultimate responsibility	Supports and replaces the family	Residual support for the carer/ family	Very residual support for the carer/family

different European countries as did the financing mechanisms. To compare two different cases: the British NHS has been a universal system since its inception in 1948 and has been financed through general taxation. In contrast, the Spanish health system achieved universal coverage only in 1990 (in 1978 it covered 89% of the population) and changed its financing from social security contributions to general taxation in that year. During the 1980s, in central and northern Europe in countries with right-of-centre governments, the emphasis of healthcare policies was on cost containment and the extension of co-payments by users, although older citizens often continued to receive services free at the point of delivery irrespective of their ability to pay. The countries in southern Europe with left-of-centre governments continued to subscribe to policies that allowed the universalisation of healthcare. However, during the first few years of the 1990s cost containment policies became part of the political agenda throughout member states of the European Union. The 1990s were characterised on the whole by the development of healthcare programmes that emphasised quality, the importance of user rights and the extension of community-based services for frail and older people. These changes occurred first in northern and central Europe and later in Spain and Portugal. At the beginning of the twenty-first century, greater emphasis is being placed on prevention and rehabilitation. Recent European debates continue to focus on the types of institutional and organisational reforms that can guarantee the following criteria: access for all, healthcare and social care quality, and the financial viability of systems (European Commission and the Council, 2003).

How have these changes affected the position of older people? Three points can be made:

- Universal coverage is now available throughout the EU states for older people, although there still remains evidence of age discrimination in the rationing of healthcare and social care resources.
- In some member states there remains a scarcity of resources and services for older people with severe mental health problems or chronic illness.
- Older people often need greater personal care or support than is available within the current healthcare and social care systems (Pacolet *et al.*, 2000).

Types of healthcare and social care systems in Europe

Although the changes that influenced the development of European healthcare and social care systems were similar throughout the second half of the twentieth century, there are still very real differences in the nature of systems. Each system will reflect the underlying values and ideologies of different societies as well as their historical, economic political and social development. Different systems will also generate their own vision of the reality of ageing, reflecting also cultural stereotypes of ageing and the historical, cultural and professional backgrounds of professionals working with older people.

A useful heuristic device for the analysis of systems is to construct a typology of healthcare and social care systems based on economic, ideological and institutional characteristics (Esping-Andersen, 1990). Of course, no typology is definitively right. (For example, a slightly different typology is used by Naegele and Walker in Chapter 7 when discussing social protection systems for income and poverty in later life.) Equally it is unlikely that any pure type will exist in reality. There are no pure types, but rather hybrid forms such that each country's healthcare and social care systems are a mixture of market, family and civil society (Arts and Gelissen, 2002). In constructing our typology we have considered healthcare and social care systems on two levels:

- as a set of social protection institutions and practices that tend to be maintained and reproduced over time
- as processes for social and institutional innovation that reflect the pressure of demographic change, changes in government, new social aspirations and new economic, political and social ideologies on the role of health in developed countries.

In considering the European Union of 25 countries in 2005, we can identify five contrasting models named in accordance with their geographical dimension: Anglo-Saxon, Continental, Nordic, Mediterranean and East European (Table 6.7).

The Anglo-Saxon model

If we look at the paradigmatic case of the United Kingdom, we see a universal healthcare system financed through taxation and with extensive citizens' support. In contrast, the social care system is means-tested (except in Scotland where a devolved government supports the public funding of long-term care) and personal care remains the responsibility of the individual and family and social support networks. During the 50 years of the welfare state in the UK the principles enunciated by the Beveridge Report (Beveridge, 1942) have remained broadly the same. Changes in policy have, however, been a distinctive feature of the last 25 years with successive governments responding to the increasing demand for healthcare from an ageing population with increasing expectations (partly fuelled by these changes in policy). It was the Thatcher administrations of the 1980s that led welfare reforms throughout Europe with the introduction of cost-containment measures and market-oriented reforms such as the purchaser–provider split (currently known as the commissioner–provider split) and the development of an internal market and increasing access to the private market in healthcare. When New Labour were elected in 1997 there was some suggestion that the pro-market vision would decline with greater collaboration between the agents involved being facilitated by changes in policy (Le Grand *et al.*, 1998). In 2006, the developing policies support additional public funding and so continue the pro-market theme of the 1980s and 1990s. Recommendations by the Royal Commission on Long-Term Care (1999) for a universal service free at the point of delivery for the care component of long-term care (with the exception of Scotland) was not adopted by the government in 2002. The established division between healthcare and social care systems in the UK therefore remains.

The Continental model

The Continental care system founded on Bismarkian principles is typical for most countries in central Europe (Austria, Belgium, France, Germany, Luxemburg and the Netherlands). It has been based on the combination of healthcare systems financed by social security contributions and private healthcare provision (NGOs including insurance companies, religious and other not-for-profit organisations and commercial healthcare companies) and a social security system managed by large NGOs for people without resources. There is a central role for the family, and in some countries such as Germany children have a legal responsibility to support their parents in later life.

From the early 1990s there have been significant changes in the policies in countries having the Continental model. The healthcare systems have begun to be financed mainly through taxation but have introduced charges as part of their cost-containment policies. Changes in family structure and the role of women have led to the development of protection policies for personal care or long-term care as an extension of statutory social insurance: first in Austria (1993), then in Germany (1995), Luxemburg (1999) and France (2002). In the case of Belgium, Flanders has created a long-term healthcare system. In the Netherlands the healthcare system has been extended to cover new social health needs. The new system does not replace the statutory responsibilities of families to support older people, but rather compensates for social changes in family structure and roles.

The Nordic model

The Nordic model (Denmark, Finland, Norway and Sweden) is based on the principle of citizenship, which guarantees free universal healthcare and personal social services financed through general taxation. Social care users pay partial contributions according to their levels of income. Over the years the Nordic countries have progressively extended the healthcare and social care system to accommodate the changing needs of an ageing population. However, they have not been unaffected by the increasing demand and the associated increased costs and have responded by introducing market-oriented approaches to the management of the services. User charges are increasingly being used to dampen demand.

The Mediterranean model

The Mediterranean or southern European model (Greece, Italy, Portugal and Spain) is characterised by its recent development compared with the established models of central and northern Europe. Healthcare systems financed from taxation that led to the guarantee of universal healthcare for the entire population did not emerge until the late 1980s and early 1990s. Private provision of healthcare still remains widely available, but the new healthcare systems lack resources and the capacity to respond to the ageing population. Consequently specialist health services for older people remain relatively under-developed.

Within the Mediterranean model the social care system is poorly developed. The family and social support networks provide the majority of personal care, and residential long-term care is provided by religious organisations. However, increased recognition of the changing roles of women and the changing family structures has led some countries (particularly Italy and Spain) to develop rudimentary social care services in support of families.

As in other European countries, privatisation of providers and other market-oriented policies have been used in response to increasing demand for healthcare and social care from their populations. Private healthcare and user charges remain an important feature of the financing of services. Although the state guarantees financing and regulation of services, the actual planning and management has been decentralised to regional and local authorities. In response to the increased demand from families for social care support and the poorly developed public social care system, the private sector in social care has expanded markedly. Yet there remains continuing debate around the need to develop publicly funded universal healthcare and social care systems that meet the long-term care needs of the ageing population in the light of changes to family structure and roles.

The model of transition in eastern Europe

To describe social protection systems in the countries of eastern Europe implies an exercise of unavoidable simplification given the diversity between the countries involved (Czech Republic, Hungary, Latvia, Lithuania, Poland, Slovakia and Slovenia). However, we can highlight some of their more general characteristics.

The healthcare systems of these former members of the Soviet bloc have evolved since 1990 from centralised to decentralised systems. There has been decentralisation of both purchasers and providers and partial privatisation of both purchasers and providers. In general they are national or regional systems more or less independent from central government and based mainly on Bismarkian principles. The healthcare systems are hospital dominated and primary care as we understand it in other European countries is poorly developed. They have mixed low-level funding that affects the reality of any universal cover and greatly challenges the quality of services provided. Yet healthcare reforms in these countries have, to date, continued to support the principle of universal availability of health services to the population. But these reforms have not removed the uncertainty of financing arrangements. Being part of the European Union since 2004 might favour convergence with other European healthcare systems in the coming years (Threlfall, 2003).

For eastern European countries, community-based social care services are virtually non-existent and represent a very new policy direction with much of the social care provision being traditional state-controlled residential institutions. The future development of social care systems is likely to rely on NGOs, particularly religious and other not-for-profit organisations.

CONCLUSIONS

For public policy the ageing of the population in Europe is seen as a major challenge. For some commentators it is a disaster waiting to happen (Clark and Spengler, 1980, quoted in Bond, 1992; Hertzman and Hayes, 1985; Thane, 1988), while others interpret demography more soberly within its historical, political and social context (Katz, 1992; Laslett, 1996; Mullan, 2000; Robertson, 1991; Robertson, 1997). As we have seen in Chapter 1, there is no doubt that the population of Europe is ageing and that for many countries the rate of ageing is something that no human society has experienced before. Of course it is not the increase in the absolute numbers of older people that is taxing the minds of politicians and policymakers but the relative proportion represented in the increasing gerontic dependency ratio discussed above. Based on these data, the prevailing belief is that an increasing ageing population inevitably means increasing demands on the resources of society particularly for healthcare and social care services and the funding of pensions. Whether the assumptions underlying these beliefs are correct is not really the point. It would appear that healthcare costs are increasing across Europe. But there are other explanations for rising costs, not least of these being the successful scientific activity of bioscientists and clinicians and the economic activity of pharmaceutical and healthcare companies. The challenge can easily be reconfigured as: how do we continue to provide cost-effective healthcare and social care for our ageing population within an equitable and moral framework rather than blaming older people for one of the triumphs of human advancement?

How will healthcare and social care systems evolve in the EU and, in particular, how will they evolve for the benefit of older people in the coming years? It is probably an understatement to say that the answer to these questions is complex! On the one hand the different models will tend to maintain their institutional traditions, values and methods of care. On the other hand, the more-or-less common demographic (ageing), institutional (decentralisation, belonging to Europe), economic (cost containment, mixed healthcare system management) and ideological (demand for quality care) problems and experiences will tend to favour a certain kind of asymmetric convergence regarding the vision and development of the functions of the healthcare and social care systems in general and, in particular, regarding the care of older people.

FURTHER READING

Bond, J. and Corner, L. (2004) *Quality of Life and Older People*. Buckingham: Open University Press.

Charmaz, K. (1983) Loss of self: a fundamental form of suffering in the chronically ill. *Sociology of Health and Illness* 5(2), 168–195.

Hockey, J. and James, A. (1993) *Growing Up and Growing Old: Ageing and Dependency in the Life Course*. London: Sage.

7

Social protection: incomes, poverty and the reform of pension systems

Gerhard Naegele and Alan Walker

INTRODUCTION

This chapter concentrates on older people's material circumstances and the role of pension systems in providing incomes in old age. Our focus is primarily on the member states of the European Union (EU) and, due to the lack of data available on the ten new member states that joined the EU on 1 May 2004, in practice this means the 15 countries that comprised the EU prior to that date. First of all we provide a typology of the different approaches to social policy, or 'welfare regimes', in the EU and how those impact on older people. Then we focus on the evidence about the material circumstances of older people in different EU countries, drawing on comparative data concerning poverty. Finally we review the recent reforms that have taken place in the EU's pension systems and provide a major case study of Germany, because of the immense importance of the Bismarckian system as a model for other countries both in southern Europe

(Ferrera, 1996; Rhodes 1997) and in parts of East Asia (Walker and Wong, 2005). That is followed by a comparative review of proposals to reform the UK pension system.

A TYPOLOGY OF EUROPEAN WELFARE REGIMES

While all of the world's major public welfare systems – 'major' in terms of their level of expenditure and extent of state responsibility – are clustered in western Europe, there is no single model of provision that is dominant, even within the EU, although there are common European values that underpin the welfare systems (Schulte, 1997, p. 61). Thus, before examining the different EU old age pension and income security systems and how they perform it is essential, by way of background, to understand the corresponding social policy or welfare regime within which they are embedded.

In comparative international welfare research over the past two decades, repeated attempts have been made to develop a comprehensive typology of welfare regimes for the western European countries. While recognising the limitations of such endeavours – particularly that all typologies tend to over-generalise and over-simplify and the fact that the western European ones have been criticised for being gender-blind (Lewis, 1992) and ethnocentric (Walker and Wong, 2005) – even the most basic versions do capture key elements of the socio-political, legal and organisational features of different countries' approaches to the provision of welfare, including pensions, and the regulation of labour (Esping-Andersen, 1990). Following Leibfried (1990), we can distinguish four types of welfare regimes:

- the 'social–democratic' welfare regime, which is typified by the Scandinavian countries
- the 'liberal' welfare regime, which is typified by the UK and Ireland (as well as Australia and the USA)
- the 'corporatist–conservative' welfare regime, which is found in most of the continental European countries
- the 'rudimentary' welfare regime, which is found in the southern European countries as they are still building up their welfare systems particularly in the health care and social care fields (see also Chapter 6).

These four welfare regimes are described in Box 7.1.

Box 7.1   Types of welfare regime in Europe

- The *social-democratic model* can be characterised as 'universalistic' and in general aims at reducing social inequality on different levels. Social security is defined as a civil right and all citizens in principle are entitled to the same tax-financed social security benefits and services. These are usually provided at a high level compared with other regimes and are mainly financed by taxation.
- Opposite to this, the *liberal welfare regime* primarily emphasises the roles of both the free market as well as the family. The market is considered to be the main arena for the distribution of resources and social security benefits are modest and social rights are rather limited. Consequently, welfare benefits often are means-tested and/or are usually paid at a rather low level. One of the consequences is that, in this type of regime, the necessity of family support is widespread.
- The *corporatist-conservative welfare regime*, which is represented by Austria, France, Germany and the Benelux countries, has been shaped by the church with a strong emphasis on traditions – such as the family and the pre-existing class and status structure. In these countries social insurance forms the core of the social security system and is thus predominantly linked to paid employment. In other words, following the Bismarckian principle: the level of social security benefits (including pensions) is strongly influenced by a person's occupational status.
- The so-called *rudimentary welfare regime* covers Greece, Italy, Portugal and Spain and our preference is to label them 'Southern' ones. In these countries social security is only partially developed compared with the other regimes and legal entitlements are relatively weak. In these countries it is assumed that traditional, non-state based stakeholders in the provision of welfare, like families and churches, play an important role. In the process of building their welfare systems the four Southern European countries have implemented a dual approach: on the one hand a social security system based on occupational status, influenced by the Bismarckian approach, and, on the other, a national health system aiming at universal coverage (Ferrera, 1996) (see Chapter 6). At present, however, they remain dualist in welfare terms by giving generous protection to those in secure employment (including some of the highest pension levels in the EU) but excluding entirely or partially those in the insecure or informal sectors of the economy. A similar dualism is evident in their health services (Rhodes 1997).

Often a simple contrast is made between the Beveridge and Bismarckian approaches particularly to public pension provision – with the former favouring a universal minimum floor and the latter an occupationally linked pension level. However, this distinction is complicated in Europe, first by the Scandinavian countries which followed Beveridge's universalism but rejected his minimalism, second by the addition of earnings-related pensions to the UK system, and third by the emergence of hybrid systems such as the southern European ones.

There are no classifications, as yet, of the welfare regimes of the ten new EU member states. The majority were ex-Soviet satellites and, therefore, for more than 40 years had state-dominated systems. The collapse of the totalitarian

Table 7.1   How should pensions be provided?

	Mainly public[a]		Mainly employers[b]		Mainly private arrangements[c]		Don't know[d]	
	1992	1999	1992	1999	1992	1999	1992	1999
Austria	–	52.5	–	23.1	–	15.8	–	8.7
Belgium	58.5	63.7	19.7	16.2	11.8	10.7	10.1	9.4
Denmark	56.2	51.5	28.2	24.8	11.0	18.1	4.6	5.5
Finland	–	26.9	–	54.2	–	8.5	–	10.4
France	51.1	44.5	26.8	30.0	14.4	15.0	7.7	10.5
Germany	37.9	40.3	48.4	40.5	6.7	9.7	7.0	9.5
Greece	60.8	61.4	13.3	13.5	7.9	5.0	18.0	20.1
Ireland	45.2	49.2	25.3	23.4	9.7	13.6	19.8	13.8
Italy	51.9	40.5	23.9	22.8	9.1	17.7	15.1	19.0
Luxembourg	55.1	51.6	20.2	20.5	11.9	14.6	12.8	13.3
Netherlands	32.1	36.6	35.1	29.2	20.4	23.2	12.4	11.1
Portugal	75.6	66.4	8.7	12.7	8.2	5.4	7.2	15.6
Spain	62.9	61.4	14.2	13.5	5.9	5.0	17.1	20.1
Sweden	–	52.6	–	23.3	–	12.9	–	11.2
UK	47.9	38.6	30.9	30.7	12.8	19.5	8.3	11.1
EU–12 (1992)/ 15 (1999)	48.9	44.7	29.8	28.8	10.6	13.7	10.8	12.8

[a]Mainly by public authorities, financed from contributions or taxes.
[b]Mainly by employers, financed from their own and their employees' contributions.
[c]Mainly by private arrangements between individual workers and pension companies.
[d]Includes no answer.
Source: Walker (1999a, p. 14).

political systems had a profound impact on the welfare provision of many of them: deep economic recessions coupled with the election of neo-liberal governments practising monetarist economics. Examples of the resulting policy changes include the removal of universalism, the reduction in standards of insurance schemes including the de-indexation of pensions, and the spread of social assistance (Ferge, 1997). In addition, the loan conditions set by the International Monetary Fund and World Bank included heavy pressure to privatise the state pension systems and follow the Chilean model or one of the other South American ones (World Bank, 1994).

Table 7.1 shows that as far as the general public of the EU-15 is concerned there is a strong preference for public or occupational pensions. The 1992 Eurobarometer survey asked how pensions should be provided and paid for (Walker, 1993) and a majority of citizens in eight out of the then twelve EC member states said they should be provided mainly by public authorities and financed from taxed contributions. The only significant deviations were Germany, presumably because of the occupational focus of its system (see later) and the Netherlands, which has a large private sector. Ireland and the UK were not far from having a majority favouring public provision. When the question was repeated in 1999 there was hardly any change in the overall proportions but some noticeable shifts in opinion within countries. The continuing public belief in social solidarity and resistance to the privatisation of risk is remarkable given the general drift of policy against this position (see later).

POVERTY IN THE EU MEMBER STATES

Currently there is no uniform European welfare state model. Each welfare regime is characterised by a combination of different forms of social security and by different types of financing and there are considerable variations within them. One consequence is that the approach to organising the relationship between the state, the market and the family has a strong influence on the level of both income security and poverty as well as quality of life in economic terms. This is particularly the case for older people: Esping-Anderson (1990) has shown that the percentage of older people living with their children is much higher under the liberal regime than under the social democratic regime.

If we take poverty as a measuring stick to evaluate the efficiency of different welfare regimes, we first of all have to ask how it is conceptualised and measured. Within the EU member states usually a relative poverty concept is used. This is mirrored firstly in the *definition of poverty* which has been developed within the framework of the first European Anti-Poverty Programme in 1975 and which is still in force today. According to this definition, 'those individuals or families are poor, whose financial means are so poor that they are excluded from the way of living which is regarded as the acceptable minimum in the country they live' (European Commission, 1983, p. 498). According to this definition, and one of the consequences of the relative concept, is that, the poor in Scandinavian countries can afford a higher level of consumption than poor people in the Mediterranean countries.

The second indicator of the relative poverty concept used in the EU is how poverty is measured. Here income data are usually used to define (income) poverty in relation to the general level of income in the country concerned. Poor households are conventionally defined as those whose income falls below some fraction of average household income, very often 50% or 60% of the median. Nowadays, OECD and Eurostat classify as poor all those below 60% of the national median. Using this measure, in 2001, 15% of the EU population (EU-15) can be classified as poor. However, there are significant country differences. Income poverty ranges from 10% in Sweden up to 20% in Greece or Portugal and 21% in Ireland (Figure 7.1). In fact, we can distinguish between three groups, which mirror the different welfare regimes in the EU. Within the old EU-15 the highest poverty rates are found in the UK, Ireland, Greece and Portugal, the lowest in the Scandinavian countries, while the central EU member states range in the middle.

When looking at the ten new EU members – Cyprus, Czech Republic, Estonia, Hungary, Latvia, Lithuania, Malta, Poland, Slovenia and Slovakia – recently published poverty estimates by Eurostat show a total poverty rate (60% of the median) of 13%, with a range from 8% (Czech Republic) to 10% (Hungary), 17% (Lithuania) and 18% (Estonia) (Figure 7.2).

However, compared to the EU-15, the general level of income in the new member states is significantly lower or, conversely, the level of poverty is significantly higher than in the EU-15. In 2000, for example, on average the gross

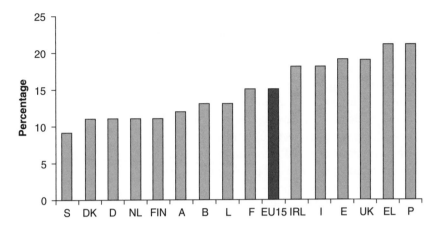

Figure 7.1   Poverty rates in the EU-15 in 2001 (60% of the national median income)

Source: Eurostat (2004a)

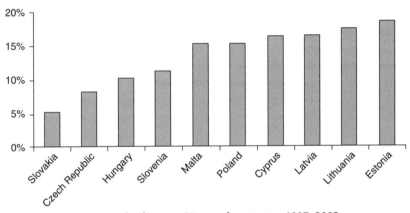

Figure 7.2   Poverty rates in the new EU member states, 1997–2003 (60% of the national median income)

Source: Eurostat NewCronos (2004b)

domestic product (GDP) per person was less than half of the EU-15 average, based on a comparison between the standards of purchasing power (European Commission, 2003b). The latter is mainly an illustration of the low income level inherited from the state-socialist period (Bradbury and Jäntti, 1999).

However there are again significant country differences, measured in terms of GDP per head as a percentage of the EU average: Estonia 38%, Poland 39%, Hungary 52% and Cyprus 83%.

POVERTY AND ECONOMIC INEQUALITY IN OLD AGE

With regard to poverty in old age in the EU-15, we can observe that in those countries representing the corporistic–conservative welfare regime – like

Germany, France, the Netherlands, Belgium and Austria – the poverty risk declines with rising age. In these countries in the past a shift has taken place in the risk of poverty away from the older generation and in the direction of young one-person households and households with two and more children. However, this is not true for the countries representing the liberal and the southern regimes. Particularly in Ireland, Greece and Portugal the rates of poverty among the older generation are far above the average (Figure 7.1 and Table 7.2). In the Mediterranean countries this particularly is true for the rural areas.

Poverty in old age is still a continuing problem in the EU but only among a significant minority of older people. Within the economically vulnerable groups of older people we still can identify the following well-known structural divisions (Walker and Maltby, 1997).

- The incidence of poverty is highest among older women, particularly widows.
- There are generational/cohort differences, especially a higher poverty risk among the very old.
- Income inequalities in old age to a large degree mirror income inequalities coupled with the former working life and thereby reflect still widespread socio-economic differences according to former employment status.
- Currently, in some EU member states a new type of old age income inequality is gaining rising importance: low income and even poverty within the group of older labour migrants.
- This for example is particularly true for Germany and mirrors the double effect of both lifelong low earnings of the so-called 'guest-workers' as well as disadvantages in the qualifying conditions for both the statutory pension schemes and the company pension schemes (Bäcker et al., 2006).

Nonetheless, across the EU-15 poverty in old age is still a minority problem; while poverty among young families with children and, above all, among mostly female single parents is a rising problem in many EU states. This recent development has been illustrated by the distinction between the 'old poor' (older people) and the 'new poor' (families with children and single parents) (Walker and Maltby, 1997). The alarming increase of the 'new' poverty reflects on the one hand the economic consequences of increasing unemployment across Europe, but, on the other hand, it demonstrates severe deficiencies in the social security provision for a significantly rising number of people who do not follow a 'normal' biography both in the working and family life-courses (Naegele et al., 2003). This is particularly true for single parents in Germany in the case of divorce or separation which primarily affects women. Consequently German researchers increasingly speak of both a 'feminisation' as well as of 'infantilisation' of poverty. Similarly UK researchers have previously referred to the 'feminisation' of poverty (Glendinning and Millar, 2002), although recently it has been pointed out that the feminisation of old age itself is in decline (Arber and Ginn, 2004).

Looking at the living standards of older people across Europe it is obvious that, in the majority of EU states, they have been rising in recent years. This is partly a direct result of positive action by governments such as France, Italy and the UK (Walker and Maltby, 1997). This relative affluence is mirrored in the

Table 7.2 **Persistent risk of poverty by broad age group and gender in 2001 (percentages).**

		B	DK	D	EL	E	F	IRL	I	L	NL	A	P	FIN	S	UK	EU15[a]
Total		7	6	6	14	10	9	13	13	9	5	7	15	6	–	10	9
0–15 years		6	3	7	10	16	10	15	18	13	9	7	22	1	–	16	12
16–64 years	Total	5	4	6	11	9	7	10	12	8	5	5	11	5	–	7	8
	Women	6	3	6	12	10	7	10	13	8	5	5	10	5	–	8	8
	Men	4	4	6	10	9	7	9	11	9	5	4	12	4	–	5	7
65 years & over	Total	17	18	7	26	11	14	31	10	5	0	18	24	16	–	15	12
	Women	17	19	9	28	10	15	40	12	6	1	24	25	21	–	17	14
	Men	17	17	5	24	11	13	19	8	5	0	10	22	7	–	12	10

[a]The EU-15 average is calculated as a population-weighted average of the available national values.
Source: Commission of the European Communities (2003, p. 12).

mainly positive subjective perceptions of living standards among older people (Walker, 1993). A recent comparative study of five EU countries, including Germany and the UK, reiterates this positive picture of satisfaction with their standards of living (Walker 2004). We will return in the final section to the question of whether or not this positive picture will continue.

RECENT CHANGES TO OLD AGE INCOME SECURITY SYSTEMS IN THE EU

The differences in the living standards of older people in the EU to a large degree mirror structural differences in access to, and performance of, the different old age income security systems. However, there are significant differences with regard to structures, benefits and expenditures.

Throughout Europe the public pension system is the main source of income for older people. This places the state in a special relationship with older people and emphasises the vital importance of public policy in determining the living standards of this group of people (Walker and Maltby, 1997). In most countries of the EU there are two tiers of pensions: the basic statutory pension schemes and the supplementary or complementary ones, which are mainly occupational ones like the company pension schemes in Germany. However, there is considerable variation *between countries* in the qualifying conditions for receipt of a pension and in the formulas used to calculate the earnings-related basic pension with a voluntary occupational one (Schmidt, 2002). Very often they result in gender inequalities in incomes among older people mainly due to both the occupational disadvantages of women in the labour market at earlier states in their lifecourses and inadequate compensation made for the effects of motherhood and other caring activities (Walker and Maltby, 1997).

In many cases gender inequalities reflect well-known socio-economic old age income inequalities coupled with the effects of former employment status. The latter is definitely the case in those countries like Austria, France and Germany where the traditional Bismarckian social security principle is dominant and where pensions are linked to the amount and the duration of contribution payments according to the former working life income and status. Consequently those people with a short working life or low earnings within working life have a higher poverty risk in old age, and vice versa. This particularly affects women and, currently in some European countries, older migrants.

These gender inequalities are less marked in those countries with a social–democratic welfare regime, which have a universal flat rate pension that is paid as a right of citizenship and is not coupled with a social insurance contribution record. But all EU member states with a basic pension scheme also provide supplementary pension schemes, which as a rule are like the traditional Bismarckian model in being linked to one's former employment record. Thus, occupational income inequalities being translated into pension differences is also characteristic of this second type of scheme. In practice there are no 'pure' basic pension schemes but a mixture of both, for example in Denmark, Finland, Sweden and the Netherlands.

Recently in most EU states governments have introduced reforms to their public pension systems. Mainly due to the foreseeable demographic changes and in order to reduce pressure on the financial sustainability of their public pension schemes, most states have, to a varying extent, begun to restructure their old age income security systems in order to make them 'economically and demographically stable'. Although there is not a uniform strategy, a kind of a diversification-policy can be observed, which includes changes in the following directions:

- the qualifying conditions
- the basis of financing
- the procedure of financing
- the mixture of pensions (Hinrichs, 2000; Hicks, 2001; Schmidt, 2002)
- changes in the retirement policy (see next section).

Undoubtedly, the most significant change, politically and socially, in pension policy in the EU-15 concerns the attempt to establish an old age income security system that is based not only on one prime pension source but on a combination of different types of pension and which, at the same time, guarantees a mixture of different financing sources. The different options for types of pensions and financing sources are shown in Box 7.2.

Box 7.2   Types of pensions and financing sources

- Public pension schemes that are financed by both taxation or by social transfers These are mainly either social security pension schemes (Bismarckian type) or basic pension schemes (Beveridge type)
- Occupational/company schemes with a variety of financing schemes (usually providing 'defined benefit' pensions where the pension is a proportion of earnings).
- Private pension schemes, financed by capital funds invested in stocks and shares (e.g. in Sweden and Germany), usually based on 'defined contributions', where the pension level is not certain
- Private savings

Public pension schemes are often referred to as the first pillar of retirement income, occupational schemes as the second and private pensions and savings as the third. The fourth pillar is employment (Reday-Mulvey, 2005).

On analysing the recent pension policies practised in the EU-15 countries, three ways of adapting the country-specific pension systems can be distinguished (Hicks, 2001):

- cutting the level of pensions, for example by both reducing second-tier public pensions or the highest level as the basis for the calculation of pensions (e.g. in Italy, Finland, the UK and Portugal) as well as reducing the frequency or degree of pension uprating (e.g. Germany and Finland)
- the introduction of (additional) private pension schemes that either introduce or raise existing elements of capital-stock-financing in order to bring the total pension system on to on a broader footing – this is true for example in Germany, Sweden and the UK
- adaptation of the qualifying conditions for pensions in order to change the ratio between contributions and the level of benefits, usually to make full eligibility harder to achieve.

In this direction we may distinguish the following pathways:

- raising the legal retirement age (e.g. Belgium, Germany, Portugal and the UK)
- reducing pensions for those who still retire early (e.g. Sweden, Germany)
- raising the number of years and/or periods of contributions necessary to be entitled for public pensions (e.g. Finland, France, Italy)
- establishing more actuarial 'fairness' in terms of differences in the level of pension between those with longer and those with shorter periods of contribution payments (this is true for most of the national pension reforms in the EU)
- reducing remaining incentives for early retirement outside the pension schemes, such as via disability, unemployment and tax benefits (e.g. Denmark, Finland, Germany and the Netherlands).

On the face of it, the slight decline in the proportion of pension expenditure to GDP between 1993 and 2002 (12.9% to 12.6% for the EU-15) was a sign that these policies were effective. However, in only Belgium, Finland and the Netherlands was this decrease unambiguously related to policy changes. In the other countries that saw a significant decrease in the share of pension expenditure to GDP, the main causes were high economic growth (Ireland, Luxembourg) and a declining share of the population aged 65 and over relative to the total population (Sweden). In France, Denmark, Spain, Italy, Austria and the UK, the share of pension expenditure to GDP remained fairly constant between 1993 and 2002 as a result of the combination of two contradictory influences: on the one hand the number of beneficiaries increased but, on the other, policy changes contained the knock-on rise in spending. The continuous increase in the share of pension expenditure to GDP in Germany over this period was mainly the result of low economic growth. Meanwhile in Portugal and Greece a similar increase was due, in the former, to policies extending eligibility and raising the minimum pension and, in the latter, to rapid ageing (the fastest in the EU-15 between 1993 and 2002) which resulted in an increased number of pension beneficiaries (European Commission, 2005).

PENSION POLICY CHANGES IN GERMANY

Before examining the differences in pension policy between Germany and the UK we will give a rough outline of the German pension system.

Box 7.3   Germany's old-age income security system

First pillar – mandatory

- Means-tested basic pension scheme (since 2002)
- Statutory pension insurance scheme for all private sector employees (*Gesetzliche Rentenversicherung*) and civil servants (*Beamtenversorgung*)
- Old-age income security systems for the self-employed

Second pillar – voluntary

- Private company schemes (occupational pension schemes) and specific (public) occupational pension schemes

Third pillar – voluntary

- Completely on a private basis (e.g. life insurance policies, interests on savings)
- Officially promoted and certificated private provisions (*since 2002: Riester-Rente*)

The German old age income security system is a three-pillar model (Box 7.3). The first pillar includes the so-called 'regular (rule) systems' (*Regelsysteme*) which provide the old age income security for:

- all employees in the private sector (statutory pension insurance scheme for all employees (*Gesetzliche Rentenversicherung: GRV*)
- civil servants (*Beamtenversorgung*)
- the self-employed.

The third category currently consists of nearly 70 different schemes including those for craftsmen, farmers and artists. Out of these three 'regular systems' the statutory pension insurance scheme (GRV) is the most significant. Currently, it includes more than 80% of the whole German population. More than 30 million people are insured, which amounts to more than 50% of the total German workforce. Currently more than 24 million pensions are being paid. In addition, since 2002, a means-tested basic pension (*Bedarfsorientierte Grundsicherung*) has been introduced payable to those older people who otherwise are not entitled to benefits from the social assistance schemes. The political aim is to prevent older people with pension entitlements below the poverty line from being dependent on social assistance.

The second pillar includes private company (occupational) pension schemes which can be found in many (mainly big) companies. Until recently private company pension schemes used to be a voluntary fringe benefit, but in 2001 the '*Altersvermögensgesetz*' introduced a right for employees to build up an entitlement to private company pensions by using parts of the earned income and transferring it into such entitlements. This has led to an increase in the spread of entitlements to occupational pension schemes. Currently about 80% of German companies are included accounting for more than 60% of all employees working in the private sector. However, these schemes are still less common in the new länder. Furthermore, women are clearly under-represented. Currently, about a third of German pensioners receive occupational pensions. In addition, due to their voluntary status in the past, private company (occupational) schemes as a rule are primarily paid to longstanding, mainly male employees and/or to those in higher income categories – which creates an additional financial bonus for those pensioners who already receive high pensions from the statutory pension schemes.

Compared to this, in the public sector, all employees (non-civil servants) are entitled to specific (public) occupational pensions schemes which – regarding their benefits – are similar to those from the old age pension schemes for civil servants. In addition social differences in the distribution of pensions are not known in the public sector.

The third pillar includes different forms of private provision for old age income security, such as life insurance policies and interest on savings. Usually, their benefits are paid in addition to those coming from the first and second pillars. In all, this kind of additional income is widespread. For example, it is estimated that more than 60% of German private households have a life insurance policy. However, the overall distribution of private provision shows distinctive social differences within the entire population: they are clearly over-represented in both the higher income and the higher occupational categories. Also, former East German seniors, on average, have less access to private provision than former West German ones. However, the third pillar is going to become significantly more important in the future for the entire population because, since 2002, as part of the recent German pension reform, the so-called 'Riester Rente' has been introduced, which is regarded as a supplement to the statutory pension schemes (see later).

The current German pension reform policy started back in the early 1990s and is still in process, most recently with the *Rentenversicherungs-Nachhaltigkeitsgesetz* (2004) and the *Alterseinkünftegesetz* (2005). The two goals of the different steps of adapting the systems to overarching demographic and economic challenges are, according to official statements of all federal governments over the last 15 years, reducing the rise in the contribution rates for the statutory pension insurance scheme for all employees and reducing the pension level to ensure its sustainability. These aims have to be seen against the background of overarching socio-political goals, of which the most important are:

- adjustment of the social security systems which are based on the social insurance principle and financed by the pay-as-you-go (PAYG) method in response to demographic challenges
- reducing the financial burdens of long-term unemployment and early exit
- moderating the increase of labour costs in order to favour the international competitiveness of Germany's economy and to promote the readiness of companies to offer jobs.

The German pension reform policy is characterised by the following main measures of adjustment:

- modifying the formula for calculating the pensions by introducing a factor that aims at balancing the relationship between the number of contributors on the one hand and the number of pension recipients on the other hand (as a result German workers need to prolong the period of paying contributions in order to receive a sufficient pension level)
- introducing taxation of high pensions and other forms of old age income sources such as interest or rent
- lowering the basis for contribution payments for the unemployed and the long-term sick
- removing periods of qualification for pension entitlements without contributions by the persons concerned (e.g. periods of education and training)
- cutting and reducing certain social compensations when it comes to calculate the pensions
- modifying the adjustment of pensions
- creating incentives in order to inspire companies to introduce or enlarge company pension schemes and workers to join them
- introduction of partial retirement schemes
- raising of the statutory retirement ages
- introducing actuarial cuts in pensions for those still retiring early.

The current German pension policy is not only typified by reducing the level or even cutting social benefits for pensioners. At the same time some financial improvements have been introduced, particularly for mothers, disabled workers and older and/or disabled people being dependent on the social welfare system due to too small pensions. For example, in 2002, for the first time in Germany, a basic means-tested pension system (*Bedarfsorientierte Gundsicherung*) was introduced which puts an end to being on supplementary benefit due to a low income in old age. As mentioned earlier, the *Altersvermögensgesetz* in 2001 led to an enlargement in the entitlement to occupational pension schemes and will in future lead to an increase in the significance of the so-called 'second pillar'.

With respect to possible consequences for (further) income discrepancies in old age, two key elements of current German pension policy have to be mentioned. First announced in 1992 and finally confirmed in 2002, the retirement age was raised to 65. However, early retirement is still possible at 60/63 but with greater financial loss for the individual concerned. If people want (or are forced) to retire early, they have to accept a financial loss throughout the whole period of retirement resulting from an actuarial cut of 0.3% of the pension for every month of early exit. In other words, retiring at the age of 60 now means that a pension reduction amounting to 18% must be taken into account. The second key element of the pension reforms is the introduction of a supplementary private pension scheme that aims at raising the pension level to 67–68% of earnings by 2030.

The core of German pension policy is the introduction of a private pillar of old age income by the Supplementary Private Pensions Act (*Altersvermögensergän-zungsgesetz*) which came into force on 1 January 2002. Its prime intention is to compensate for the pension reductions arising from the planned decrease of the pension rate. In other words, its major aim is to replace the cuts and losses in the public pension schemes, due to the pension reforms, by a new type of private old age income but supported by financial incentives provided through public finances.

The goal of the *Altersvermögensergänzungsgesetz* is to encourage people, especially those with small incomes and families with children, to build up a private or occupational pension on a voluntary basis. Incentives are given either by tax relief or by direct financial allowances to those who would not benefit from possible tax relief. A total of just under 10 billion euros is being set aside in the final phase in 2008 to encourage investment in a private or occupational pension. The Supplementary Private Pensions Act is aimed at all those people who pay compulsory contributions to the statutory old age pension scheme. However, the provisions are going to be extended to include civil servants and public service employees.

Types of investment that may be subsidised include occupational old age pensions in the form of direct insurance and pension funds, privately funded pension provisions in the form of pension insurance schemes, and funds and bank saving schemes. Funds and bank saving schemes must be accompanied by payout plans. Existing contracts and residential property may, under certain conditions, also be eligible for subsidies. Private old age pension products must fulfil specific requirements in order to comply with the state criteria for financial incentives: investments have to be made before the age of 60 or before a partial disability or old age pension is payable under the statutory old age pension scheme; investments cannot be used to secure a loan; and the type of investment must guarantee payment of a fixed or incremental monthly allowance for the rest of the investor's life.

The pension scheme is made up of a person's own contributions and state allowances which are either tax reliefs or direct allowances. A certain minimum personal contribution, which varies with the marital status and the number of children, is necessary to get the allowances. To simplify the arrangements, eligible people pay their own contributions only and apply to have the state allowances credited by the relevant Inland Revenue Office directly into the contract. The amount of the allowance depends on marital status and the number of children as well. For people with higher incomes, it may be more advantageous to apply for tax relief, whereas for people on lower incomes direct state allowances might be more advantageous. The allowance is made up of a basic allowance (for an adult person) and a children's allowance. The Inland Revenue Office will automatically weigh up the relative advantages of the two options.

The new private old age pension products will be introduced step-by-step. The expenditure on pensions (personal contributions plus allowances) started at a level of 1% of the social security contribution ceiling for the statutory old age pension scheme for waged and salaried employees in 2002 and will climb to 4% in 2008. It is permitted to save less, but the allowances are cut correspondingly. The federal government believes that the personal contributions will be compensated for by the promised stability of the contributions to the statutory old age pension schemes.

PENSION POLICY CHANGES IN THE UK

The United Kingdom's pension system still reflects the pattern established in the late 1940s by Beveridge (1942): a flat-rate national insurance pension based on the individuals' contributions while in employment, coupled with either an occupational pension, individual savings, both, or neither. Despite the growth of occupational (organisation-based) pensions from the 1950s to the 1980s, the addition of the State Earnings-Related Pension Scheme (SERPS) in 1975 (which was due to reach full maturity in 1998), and the energetic official encouragement of private personal pensions in the 1980s and 1990s, the basic state pension is the main source of income for the majority of UK pensioners. Moreover it has been set at a level below the social assistance level for pensioners for most of the past 50 years, so to attain the minimum (poverty) income level it is necessary to claim a means-tested benefit (currently called the Pension Credit). Up to one million older people do not claim this benefit and therefore they live below the official poverty line. These deficiencies of the UK's pension system, along with the decoupling of upratings from earnings in 1980, explain why the poverty rate among British pensioners is twice as high as that of German ones (Table 7.3). The key elements of the UK system are shown in Box 7.4.

Box 7.4   The basic elements of the British pension system

First pillar – mandatory

- Basic state pension

Second pillar – mandatory

- State second pension (DB)
- *or* final-salary occupational pension (DB)
- *or* money purchase occupational pension (DC)
- *or* personal pension – eg. stakeholder pension (DC)

Third pillar – voluntary

- Personal pension
- *or* additional voluntary contributions (DC)

Although, as we have shown, there is not a single path of pension reform in the EU, Germany may be regarded as a typical case in that it combines the three main characteristics of the recent changes: the introduction of private pension

Table 7.3 At-risk-of-poverty rate for individuals aged 16 years and over by age group and gender in 2001 (percentages).

		B	DK	D	EL	E	F	IRL	I	L	NL	A	P	FIN	S	UK	EU15[a]
Total	Total	14	11	11	21	18	15	20	18	11	10	12	18	13	10	15	15
	Women	15	12	12	22	19	16	22	19	11	10	15	19	15	11	18	16
	Men	12	11	9	19	16	14	18	17	11	10	9	18	10	9	13	13
16 – 64 years	Total	10	8	10	17	16	14	16	18	12	11	9	16	10	11	13	14
	Women	12	9	11	18	18	14	16	19	12	11	10	15	11	10	15	14
	Men	9	8	9	16	15	13	15	18	12	11	8	17	10	11	11	13
16 – 24 years	Total	12	21	16	19	20	21	12	25	20	22	11	18	23	18	20	19
	Women	12	24	15	21	21	21	15	25	17	21	14	15	28	20	21	20
	Men	11	18	17	18	19	21	10	25	22	24	7	21	19	16	18	19
25 – 49 years	Total	10	7	9	14	15	12	17	18	11	10	8	15	7	7	12	12
	Women	11	7	11	15	16	13	18	19	11	10	9	15	7	7	14	14
	Men	8	7	7	14	14	11	17	17	10	10	7	15	8	8	10	11
50 – 64 years	Total	12	5	10	21	17	13	16	16	9	7	9	16	9	5	11	12
	Women	13	5	9	22	18	13	14	16	10	7	11	16	10	5	12	13
	Men	10	5	10	19	15	12	18	15	9	6	8	15	7	5	10	12
65 years and over	Total	26	24	12	33	22	19	44	17	7	4	24	30	23	16	24	19
	Women	26	25	14	35	24	21	51	19	8	3	30	31	31	20	28	21
	Men	24	23	9	30	20	17	35	16	7	5	14	28	12	10	19	16

[a]The EU-15 average is calculated as a population-weighted average of the available national values.
Source: Commission of the European Communities (2003, p. 12).

schemes on a voluntary basis, raising retirement ages, and imposing actuarial cuts in pensions in cases of early retirement. Encouraging the spread of responsibility for pensions from the first pillar to the third pillar is the policy advocated by the World Bank (1994) and one which was pioneered in the EU by the UK. In fact the UK's first pension reforms pre-dated those of most other EU countries by a decade. In global policy terms, the UK was more in tune with the USA and Japan, countries that started pension reform in 1988 and 1986, respectively. But the UK's first and second tier public pensions were already low in comparative EU terms and there was no suggestion of an impending pension crisis. In fact in the 1980s the OECD advised the UK that there was no need to take any action on its pension system until 2010 at the earliest, partly because of the relatively low cost of pensions and partly because the UK's population aged earlier than those of most other EU countries.

What happened in the UK in the 1980s is an extraordinary chapter in the annals of pension reform. In its desire to reduce public expenditure and shift future pension funding from the state to the private sector, the Thatcher administrations de-indexed from wages the first pillar pension (in 1980), cut in half the second pillar, the SERPS (in 1986), and encouraged (by tax relief) the substitution of private defined contribution schemes for the state's guaranteed or defined benefit one. As responsibility for pensions was passed from the public to the poorly regulated private sector without adequate safeguards, there was a major scandal of the mis-selling of pensions by over-zealous agents and insurance companies. It is estimated that some three million people were mis-sold private pensions when they would have been better off staying in the state scheme.

In comparison with the mostly measured and incremental pensions reforms conducted in most EU member states, the UK's was an ideologically driven policy which used crisis of ageing rhetoric and which stifled public debate (Walker, 1990). Thus there was virtually no open discussion about the advantages of PAYG as a method of financing pensions, nor of the disadvantages of privately funded schemes, even in the wake of the mis-selling scandal.

What usually occurs are the assertions that PAYG is unsustainable and that the privately funded approach is best. However, the transfer from PAYG to pre-funding does *nothing* to alter the cost of pensions to society and, arguably, it increases the cost to individuals because of the higher administrative burden associated with private pensions. The pensions and other incomes of retired people in any society must be paid from the economic product of the working population, regardless of whether or not the mode of pension financing is PAYG or pre-funding (Barr, 2000). Nor should it be assumed, as it frequently is, that saving to prepare for demographic ageing is the prerogative of the private sector, as the recent examples of Belgium and France demonstrate and, beyond the EU, Canada. Nor is there any evidence that *public* pre-funding is inferior to the private market (Augusztinovics, 2002). The fundamental question for public debate is this: what are the objectives of the pension system? For example, is it to pool risks and to redistribute resources within and between generations or, alternatively, to raise national savings and to strengthen capital markets? Different answers will lead to different institutional structures. The problem is that they have been confused: risk pooling and redistribution could remain the province of the public first pillar with private savings and capital markets being mainly a matter for the second and third pillars. This requires a comprehensive pension policy linking all three pillars and a constructive and open public debate in which both current and future pensioners can have their say.

This debate has been absent in the UK, although the final report of the Pensions Commission set up by the government to review the UK's private pension and long-term savings regime, published in November 2005, provides a large part of the focus required (see later). The reforms to the UK's pension system introduced so far by two Labour governments since 1997 have not challenged either the basic structure of the system or its main deficiencies. SERPS has been replaced by the State Second Pension (S2P) which is aimed at those with relatively modest earnings. The government attempted to encourage the private sector to introduce low-cost personal pensions, called 'stakeholder pensions', for those on low earnings; but providers have proved highly resistant to the 1% ceiling on administration charges and so the scheme has not taken off (except as investment vehicles for some relatively wealthy people!). The role of means testing has been enhanced by the replacement, in 1999, of income support by the Minimum Income Guarantee (MIG) which was later linked to earnings (unlike the basic pension). In 2004, the MIG became Pension Credit and the official estimate is that a maximum of three million out of the eligible four million pensioners are expected to claim this means-tested benefit by 2006. The recent closure of many company pension schemes (estimates suggest that as many as half of them have either closed completely or have been closed to new members) has been attributed to the introduction of a tax on pension fund surpluses in 2001 but there is no evidence to prove or disprove this claim.

The fact that pensions policy was high on the UK's political agenda in the late 1990s and early 2000s is demonstrated by a series of official reports on various aspects of this topic which were paralleled by analyses from a wide range of non-governmental organisations such as the Pensions Policy Institute, the Association of British Insurers, the National Association of Pension Funds, the Confederation of British Industry, the Trades Union Congress and a plethora of academic commentaries. The most authoritative of these were produced by the Pensions Commission. The Commission's first report considered the challenges and choices facing pensions policy (Pensions Commission, 2004) and the second one made recommendations for creating a new pensions settlement (Pensions Commission, 2005). While recognising the impossibility of summarising adequately the two voluminous Pensions Commission reports, their main conclusions were that, on the one hand, the current system of privately funded pensions combined with the state system will become increasingly inadequate and unequal and, on the other, that the problems afflicting the UK's pension system are not solvable through changes to the state system alone nor by incremental measures to encourage voluntary provision. In particular the Commission noted that private provision is 'in serious and probably irreversible decline' (Pensions Commission, 2005, p. 2).

The Commission's proposed reforms centre on three main areas.

- A new national pension savings scheme should be introduced in which all employees not covered by other adequate pension arrangements would be enrolled *automatically* (but with the right to opt out). Matching employer contributions would also be compulsory. The aim of this scheme would be to establish a 'base load' of earnings replacement.
- The state system should become less means-tested and fairer to women. Rather than opting for the single unified state pension, a simplification called for by many diverse commentators in this field, the Commission proposed a two-tier approach with the S2P evolving gradually into a flat-rate system with, over the long term, the basic state pension being re-linked to earnings.
- To offset some of the costs of these proposed reforms, while acknowledging the need for an increase in pension expenditure as a proportion of GDP from now until 2050, the Commission proposed gradual increases in the state pension age, in line with average life expectancy, to 69 by 2050. The Commission's report sets out a number of measures to assist the extension of working life.

Finally, the Pensions Commission (2005, p. 19) also defined its model of the role of the state in pension provision: *ensuring* a minimum income level via a compulsory system; *strongly encouraging* a base load of earnings replacement through auto-enrolment and compulsory employer contributions; *enabling* additional savings at low cost; and *facilitating* purely voluntary pension-saving via tax relief. There are distinct echoes of the World Bank (1994) in this model and it represents a significant shift from the active role of the state in the promotion of private pensions witnessed in the UK in the 1980s and early 1990s.

Although there is little that is genuinely new in the Pensions Commission's recommendations, its reports do provide the most exhaustive and authoritative official analysis of the UK's pension system for many years. Also, its collation and detailed examination of the various proposals for reform means that it is likely to be the reference point for pensions policy debates for decades to come. The Commission undoubtedly swam with the national tide of informed opinion which sees the current system as being in crisis and, therefore, in need of radical reform, although it has not been as radical as many would want. If enacted, the Commission's recommendations would create a more unified pension system, which is fairer to women, and which would look more like those of some of its European neighbours. Indeed the Commission looked closely at pensions systems and reforms in some other countries (though not exclusively European), including Australia and Sweden, and drew from them two major ideas of possible relevance to the UK:

- the potential to reduce costs via a system of nationally administered individual accounts
- the application of automatic enrolment to pensions savings schemes.

What the Commission did not do, presumably because it was not asked to do so, was to examine ways to relieve poverty and low incomes among *existing* pensioners, many of whom will not see any benefit from the enactment of its recommendations. Even if they are fully enforced there would still be around 40% of pensioners having to undergo means-testing by 2020. Furthermore the Commission did not examine in detail the role of tax expenditures in subsidising private pension provision: what should be the limit of Exchequer reliefs aimed at enabling and facilitating voluntary savings?

The government's response to the Pensions Commission's recommendations was published in the spring of 2006 (Department for Work and Pensions, 2006). The White Paper has adopted many of the Commission's recommendations in broad terms. Key proposals included:

- raising the retirement age to 68 by 2050
- restoring the link between average earnings and the basic state pension from 2012 'subject to affordability'
- a compulsory savings scheme (with opt-out option) to which employees, employers and the government will contribute.

However, the government will consult as to whether to run a state national savings scheme as recommended by the Pensions Commission or one of a range of schemes run by the pensions industry.

HARMONISATION OF EUROPEAN PENSION SYSTEMS

The variation in pension systems in the EU has been noted already and social protection is governed by the subsidiarity rule. However, recently a process has started that will inevitably lead to greater correspondence between and, possibly, harmonisation of pension systems. In terms of securing the future for old age in Europe this development is of the utmost significance.

The European Council in Gothenborg endorsed three broad principles for securing the long-term sustainability of pension systems:

- safeguarding the capacity of systems to meet their social objectives (adequacy)
- maintaining their financial sustainability (financial sustainability)
- meeting changing societal needs (modernisation).

The Councils in Stockholm and Gothenborg called for the application of the open method of coordination to the area of pension policy and this was agreed at the Laeken Council, as were the eleven common objectives for Community pensions policies (Box 7.5). Having agreed common objectives, the open coordination reporting process should lead to a greater alignment between the different systems.

Box 7.5   Common objectives for European pensions policies

Adequacy

- The need to prevent poverty and social exclusion among older people
- The maintenance of living standards after retirement
- Promotion of solidarity within and between generations

Financial sustainability

- Achieving a high level of employment
- Incentives for the participation of older workers
- Reform of pension systems to support sustainable public finances
- Achieving a fair balance between the active and retired populations
- Reviewing the management and regulatory framework for funded pension-schemes

Modernisation

- Making pension systems compatible with modern labour markets in terms of mobility, flexibility and security
- Taking account of the changing role of women in society
- Greater transparency and adaptability in pension systems

It remains to be seen whether or not this harmonisation takes place and whether it means the maintenance of the EU's public pension systems as the cornerstone of socio-economic security in old age. We have noted already the challenge that the new member states in eastern Europe represent to the predominantly public pension systems of the old EU-15. The accession reports from these countries reveal European Commission approval for the privatisation of pensions, if this has been carried through, and if not, encouragement to do so (Ferge, 2001). As far as the general public is concerned there is a high level of recognition, if not acceptance, of the trend towards the privatisation of pensions. As Table 7.4 shows, when the general public were asked whether they thought that, in the future, most pensions would be funded by private arrangements with the state less involved, some two-thirds of the EU-15 said yes. This majority may be contrasted with the minority in Table 7.1 who believe that pensions should be privatised.

CONCLUSIONS

The three main forms of pension policy reform implemented in the EU-15 (introducing private pension schemes on a voluntary basis, raising the retirement

Table 7.4   In the future, will most pensions be funded by private arrangements with the state less involved? (1999 percentages).

	Yes	No	Don't know*
Austria	61.7	13.1	25.2
Belgium	53.6	20.6	25.7
Denmark	82.8	8.9	8.3
Finland	65.5	20.1	14.4
France	67.2	15.8	17.0
Germany	59.1	22.4	18.5
Greece	42.0	28.5	29.5
Ireland	50.3	14.7	35.1
Italy	57.8	14.3	27.9
Luxembourg	53.2	25.8	21.0
Netherlands	77.0	11.6	11.4
Portugal	35.1	18.7	46.2
Spain	37.3	20.9	41.8
Sweden	80.5	8.2	11.3
UK	80.5	7.3	12.3
EU-15	61.4	16.4	22.1

*Includes no answer.
Source: Walker (1999a p.17).

ages, and actuarial cuts in the cases of early retirement) tend to create new income risks in old age and, consequently, perpetuate and even deepen social inequalities in terms of income, social security and quality of life in old age. This also applies to the rising number of workers with gaps in their working life, for example due to family reasons, care obligations or long-term unemployment (Naegele *et al.*, 2003) – those who cannot rely on full compensation for the corresponding income or social security losses. This will lead to a further widening of income disparities in old age beyond the well-known country differences.

In the case of Germany, two major risks of the current pension policy are obvious and are already proven empirically. First, because the supplementary private pension schemes (*Riester Rente*) work on a voluntary basis, economically underprivileged, unemployed and other disadvantaged groups are very often excluded because they are not able to afford their contributions or do not know about the new benefits. Furthermore it's doubtful whether creating incentives for occupational pension schemes will have a compensatory effect, because they will continue to discriminate against low wage earners (Bäcker, 2004).

Second, raising the retirement age and introducing actuarial cuts for early retirement, amounts to a special provision for healthy or well-qualified workers who have a chance to stay longer in paid work. These people are likely to be already vested with a higher level of economic security in old age due to their more favourable status in their working life. Workers who have to leave the work force early – for example due to poor health, unemployment, unfavourable working conditions or because they are working in jobs that cannot be done in older age – have to accept severe financial losses due to the actuarial cuts. This risk primarily affects workers with a low occupational status, and one of the consequences is a further rise in social inequality in old age in financial terms.

The German pension policy reforms aim to reduce the level of the public old age income security schemes and, at the same time, fill the gap with a new type of private scheme. The question is whether only a *partial substitution* of the statutory old age income security system by new forms of capital-funded private provision is envisaged, or whether a full *replacement* is the final political goal. The latter reflects the interests not only of German employers' associations but also Germany's financial world.

However, this change of paradigm is linked with a series of problematic economic and distributional effects. First of all, privatisation of old age income security in Germany creates a severe social risk for those who in general do not fulfil important prerequisites for a satisfactory and sufficient individual pension level – the most significant of which are high income, a long working career and an appropriate mental preparedness for private provision. The result will be a significant rise in social exclusion, because at the same time the formula for calculating pensions has been changed by removing elements of social compensation. The consequence will be further deepening of income inequalities in old age (Bundesministerium für Familie, Senioren, Frauen und Jugend, 2006).

Second, one of the core assumptions generally stated in favour of capital-funded old age income security systems – that they are generally less threatened by demographic changes – is not true. For example, liquidising stock capital in order to serve as old age income for growing number of pensioners assumes an increasing number of younger people to buy the capital stock, which is demographically impossible (Schmähl, 2000). As a result a devaluation of the stock capital is highly likely. Also, future cohorts of older people who can no longer rely on a sufficient public pension level are likely to run into additional financial risks and, therefore, are confronted with a further deepening of social inequalities compared to the current cohorts of older people in Germany.

In the case of the UK, its pension system is widely regarded as being in crisis; indeed the consensus about this is remarkable for its coverage of the political left and right. Only the present Labour government and a few commentators appear not to be part of the consensus. Almost everyone else agrees that the basic pension is too low and that pension policy is too reliant on means-testing. Perhaps most surprisingly there is also wide agreement about the key role of the universal basic pension in the policy response to this crisis. Beyond that important point there is no consensus on the way forward. A key issue for future pensioners in the UK, especially women, is whether private pre-funded or direct contribution schemes will continue to occupy a major role and, therefore, contribute to widening inequalities in old age. As we have shown, German policymakers have chosen to follow a very similar path to the UK, despite its demonstrably negative consequences for retirement income and social equality, so this issue will be no less resonant for future German pensioners. Moreover the accession of ten new member states to the EU on 1 May 2004 means that this issue is as relevant for the EU as a whole as it is for Germany and the UK.

FURTHER READING

Barr, N. (2000) *Reforming Pensions: Myths, Truths and Policy Choices.* Washington, DC: International Monetary Fund.

Pensions Commission (2005) *A New Pensions Settlement for the Twenty-first Century.* London: Stationery Office.

Walker, A. and Maltby, T. (1997) *Ageing Europe.* Buckingham: Open University Press.

8

Work and retirement

Harald Künemund and
Franz Kolland

INTRODUCTION

Retirement is a relatively new social phenomenon. Formal retirement programmes may be traced back to the late seventeenth century – the first pension systems became effective in the military and church sectors (Ehmer, 1990), but these were exceptional. Until the development of public welfare schemes in the second half of the twentieth century, older people seldom had a chance to retire from work, and in most cases that meant being dependent on family support or individual savings, namely children, or the farm. The development of retirement as a separate period of life, however, is mainly a result of social security systems that provide adequate income for older people, allowing for withdrawal from the labour force. It was only in the second half of the twentieth century that retirement became such a general phenomenon, but nowadays it is a key part of the modern life-course and widely taken for granted. This development can be characterised as a part of a broader historical process of the 'institutionalisation of the life-course' (Kohli, 1986) – the evolution of a chronologically standardised sequence of life phases and life events with corresponding biographical perspectives, arranged according to the labour force needs of the economies of industrialised societies.

   While today sociologists discuss different welfare regimes and their impact on life-course, as well as consequences of changes in the welfare institutions, the early research and theory on retirement focused on the advantages and disadvantages of retirement for both the individual and society. Does retirement mean social exclusion or late freedom? When does the experience of retirement promote a sense of well-being?

To understand the retirement experience of older people it is necessary to agree on a definition of 'retirement'. Apart from the sociological perspective of understanding retirement as a mass phenomenon with certain economic consequences for society as a whole, the transition to retirement is often considered as a status passage or *rites de passage* (Van Gennep *et al.*, 1960), a withdrawal from active working life due to old age. However, a small minority of older people stay active in the labour force. But it is not easy to define 'active working life': does it include only gainful employment or also a certain degree of integration into the job market? The lower the degree of gainful employment, the more fluid is the boundary between gainful work and retirement, and the less we can speak of a specific event.

From an institutional perspective we may assume that retirement relates directly to the receiving of pensions or similar social security benefits, independent from actual or previous participation in working life. An advantage of such a definition of retirement is the fact that it can be attached to the age boundaries of the pension or social security system. A disadvantage is that it reinforces institutionalised ageism (see Chapter 4). The average age for being entitled to receive old age pension is very similar in most of the OECD countries. For two-thirds of these countries it is the age of 65, although it varies from a minimum of 60 to a maximum of 67. However, the average age of actual retirement is usually three to five years lower than the 'official' age. Only in Japan is the actual age five years above the official age, and in Korea seven years. In consequence, using administrative definitions does not match the experience of individuals very well.

Furthermore, in most OECD countries receiving an old age pension is connected to a certain period of gainful employment, so that such a definition excludes social groups that have not achieved any – or not sufficient – claims for an old age pension (see Chapter 7). Some researchers have therefore tried to avoid these problems by leaving it up to the participants of their surveys to define themselves as being retired or not (Savishinsky, 2000). The disadvantage of this approach is the fact that the definition of retirement is not the same for everyone. People who are still working may consider themselves retired if they receive an old age pension from previous employment. Others, who stopped paid employment many years ago, for example, to care for children or elderly relatives, would not consider themselves retired. Studies of workers and retirees and based on such a definition will therefore possibly compare apples with oranges. With a growing range of lifestyles and activities in later life, such an approach becomes more and more complex to interpret.

But in any case, on the individual level we have the necessity of distinguishing between retirement as a process, for example of planning and adaptation, from retirement as a period of life lasting for many years. If, for example, our interest is focused on the prerequisites, pathways and outcomes of the transition to retirement, it will be useful to understand retirement as an event that may or may not have occurred at a given age. If the economic and social well-being of older people in general is the focus of interest, it will be more appropriate to understand retirement as a period of life, with boundaries to be defined by theory.

THE HISTORY OF RETIREMENT

The origin of public social security for older people goes back to Bismarck's system of social insurance for workers' insurance in Germany in 1889. The main goals of public policy in this period were to provide for income security in old age as a reaction to increasing pauperism in the industrialisation process – industrial workers typically had no farms or savings. Furthermore, in the light of revolutionary tendencies in Europe, it was assumed that the expectation of a pension would create a conservative citizen (Kohli, 1986). However, the pensionable age was high – only one-third of men reached the age of 70 – and the amounts paid did not allow for a complete retirement. This changed in the second half of the twentieth century. The period after the Second World War was one of full employment, and public pensions were regarded as an appropriate way of spreading the costs of retirement as well as assisting industry through rejuvenating the workforce (Graebner, 1980). The proportion of people reaching retirement age increased, and the significance of paid work after retirement decreased dramatically (Phillipson, 1998). Old age came to be uniquely associated with retirement.

Today, most European countries face a demographic change where people – on average – live longer than ever before in history (see Chapter 1 & 2). In conjunction with decreasing birth rates this leads both to an increase in the number of older people and an increase in their proportion of the population, the so called 'ageing of societies' (see Chapter 6). Since the early 1970s this change has been accompanied by decreasing labour force participation rates of older people, the trend to early retirement (Kohli *et al.*, 1991): it is not only that people live longer but they also retire earlier. Figure 8.1 shows this development of the labour participation rates over the last 30 years for men aged 65 and older in the EU and selected European countries.

The labour force participation rate of men aged 65 and older in the EU dropped from 15.2% in 1972 to 5.6% in 2002. Some countries had even lower rates in 2002 (e.g. Spain with 2.2% and France with 1.8%), others fairly high rates (Norway with 15.6% and Sweden with 14.7%). But on average, most countries show a pattern of a decline since the early 1970s that now appears to have ended. The picture is nearly the same for women, although even less women are active in the labour force compared to men (Figure 8.2). However, for both men and women gainful work is seldom a part of later life.

The trend to early retirement becomes more evident when looking at the labour force participation of the population aged 60 to 64. In this younger age group, the

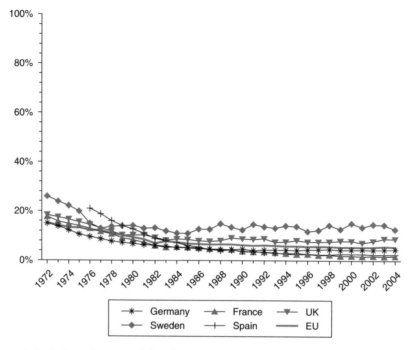

Figure 8.1   Labour force participation rates: men aged 65 or over by country

The labour force participation rate is defined as the ratio of the labour force and the population of an age group. Although several changes of the calculation bases and differences between countries lead to additional variation, the general pattern is well represented in these figures.

Sources: mainly www.oecd.org. Data for UK before 1984 were taken from OECD (1990); for Sweden between 1976 and 1986 from Jacobs *et al.* (1991)

labour force participation rate of men in the EU fell from 61% in 1972 to 36.8% in 2002 (Figure 8.3). The trend to early exit is strongest in France and Germany but is generally visible in all countries.

Again it appears that the trend has come to an end, and in many countries the labour force participation rates of this age group have even been increasing since the mid-1990s. But from Figure 8.3 it becomes obvious that the age of 65 – in many of these countries the 'regular' retirement age for men – is not the usual age of exit from work in the EU. More than 60% of the men aged 60–64 are not participating in the labour force. Early exit from work as well as early retirement seem to have become a mass phenomenon in Europe.

For women of this age group the pattern is quite different: the labour force participation rates are relatively stable over time, with the majority of women being outside the labour market (Figure 8.4). Again, the rates have been increasing during the last few years, and especially in Sweden and Norway the rates are fairly high (above 50% in 2002).

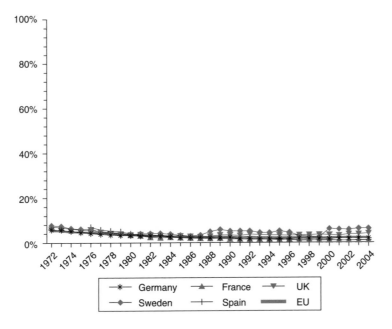

Figure 8.2   Labour force participation rates: women aged 65 or over by country

Source: as Figure 8.1

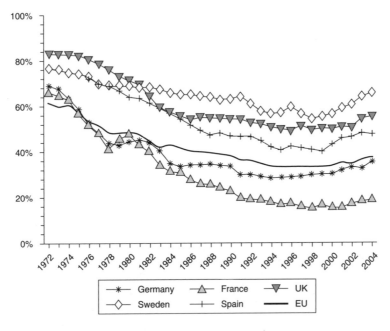

Figure 8.3   Labour force participation rates: men aged 60–64 by country

Source: as Figure 8.1

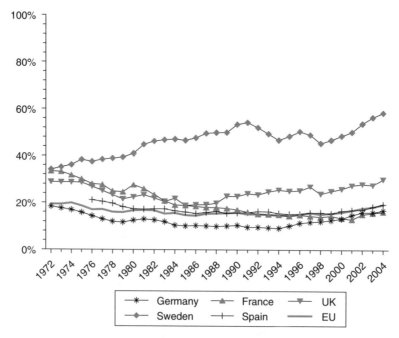

Figure 8.4   Labour force participation rates: women aged 60–64 by country

Source: as Figure 8.1

For several reasons, labour force participation rates underestimate the trend to early exit from work. For instance, these rates include unemployed people although many of them will not return to gainful work. In Germany, firm-based pre-retirement schemes have often made use of the unemployment insurance (with unemployment benefits often being 'topped up by the firm') (Jacobs *et al.*, 1991, p. 198), and unemployment may be a precondition to special early retirement schemes. It follows that the proportion of older people active in the labour force is even lower in most of these countries. But the general trend is obvious: retirement has become a period that is individually expanded due to both increasing life expectancy and decreasing age of exit from gainful work. Retirement is therefore not a 'remaining time' that is gone through only by a small social group but an independent phase of life of considerable duration (Kohli, 1986).

This development is not only a financial challenge to the pension and health-care systems (see Chapters 6 and 7). In comparison to earlier generations, older people today are – on average – better educated, healthier and financially better off, and these trends should hold for the next decades. The resources available for activity and productivity in later life are increasing. Traditional passive roles expected by older people are increasingly less adequate and counterproductive.

Providing meaningful activities for older people will therefore become an increasing challenge for European societies (Riley *et al.*, 1994).

In addition, the ageing of the population is a challenge to the organisation of work in general with the ageing of the workforce. The proportion of older workers in the labour market will increase significantly in future years, while at the same time lower birth rates may cause a reduction of the total labour supply. It is also for these reasons that the retirement age as well as the integration of older people in the labour force needs to be adjusted and, hence, working conditions as well as working abilities need to be improved.

Many European countries have taken up the challenge and have promoted research (Walker, 1997) and measures to enable older workers to further participate in gainful work, for example training of older workers (Clemens, 2003). The Finnish National Programme on Ageing Workers (Ministry of Social Affairs and Health, 2002) has already led to an increase in the labour force participation rate of older people, while at the same time long-term unemployment among older workers has been reduced. However, whether similar programmes in other countries – like the 'New Deal 50 plus' and 'Age positive' in the UK – will have long-term success is an open question (Taylor, 2002). The answer depends largely on the development of the labour market – the demand for older workers.

THEORETICAL APPROACHES

During the last decades, the reasons for retiring from gainful employment and the consequences connected with it – both for the individual and for society in general – have been an important topic in social gerontology. During the 1950s and 1960s, retirement was considered the cause of problems not so much for its financial implications for society but by virtue of its social and psychological significance. Many authors considered old age to be a 'roleless role' (Burgess, 1960; Rosow, 1974). According to the early theories of activity, ageing goes along with a loss of social functions which have to be replaced by taking over new roles to achieve a successful adaptation to retirement (Cavan *et al.*, 1949): older adults live longer and adapt to old age in a more satisfying way if they keep up the level of activity appropriate to their middle years and if they replace abandoned activities with new ones. The loss of gainful employment in old age was viewed critically, particularly because leisure activities are only partly substituting the work role – for example with respect to the social position that is attached to different occupations – and many of the 'leisure' activities had no significance for one's life (Lehr, 1988). At the beginning of the 1960s, Havighurst (1961) even asked the question whether satisfied ageing is possible at all outside the economic world.

At this time (early 1960s) disengagement theory emerged as a significant influence on our understanding of later life. Disengagement theory (Cumming and Henry, 1961), building on functionalist theory (Parsons, 1951), proposed that as people approach old age, they gradually withdraw from those social roles that previously had been important to them – especially work roles – and that this disengagement had positive outcomes for both the individual and the society. From a labour force perspective, disengagement theory proposed that the withdrawal of older members of society from the workforce facilitated its rejuvenation, thus ensuring the continuation of new approaches, ideas and energies into the workplace. For the individual, an increased life satisfaction would be the result of the process of disengagement – to be freed from the roles of an occupation and to pursue other roles not necessarily aligned to economic activity.

The empirical evidence, however, was mixed. Both the activity and the disengagement theories were confirmed and rejected, sometimes even using the same data. Early research failed to support the activity theory, possibly because activities were considered one-dimensional and time spent for engagement in 'activity' was the only variable studied, for example in terms of role diversity. Other studies separated activity into physical, social and solitary domains owing to the different psychosocial processes that are involved when older people engage in these different types of activity. However, only those activities that are psychologically relevant seem to result in satisfaction with life. But aside from difficulties of measuring life satisfaction and activity, a major problem is to identify cause and effect. For example, satisfaction with life may be conceptualised as a result of activity, but social activity may also be conceptualised as the result of satisfaction with life, or both may be correlated with, for example, health – factors that also may be the result of some activities (or disengagement from others).

Today, this puzzle is partly disentangled by the assumption of differential ageing and compensatory disengagement in psycho-gerontology. The disengagement theory also failed to be valid as a general description and explanation, although for some individuals disengagement and life satisfaction were found to be positively correlated. A more differentiated approach assumes partial or selective disengagement in some activities while allowing maintenance of engagement in other activities (Lehr, 1972, p. 223). A similar argument is used in the theory of selective optimisation with compensation (Baltes and Baltes, 1990; Carstensen, 1991): an adaptation to age-specific losses by selecting specific activities and social relations. A rather complete disengagement, on the other hand, is stated by the theory of gero-transcendence (Tornstam, 1989) – at least for a late stage of ageing (cf. also the model of Erikson, 1982). This theory posits the capacity to leave roles as needed with greater peace and acceptance in later life.

In social gerontology, continuity evolved as an important concept to solve the puzzle of activity and disengagement. The continuity theory (Atchley, 1989) assumes that humans tend to maintain the patterns of their former lifestyle, their sense of self-esteem, and their values even after retiring from paid work. Thus, retirement does not necessarily lead to imbalance and desperation. Adaptation to retirement succeeds where continuity in social roles, activities of importance to the individual or personal goals is achieved. Atchley (1971) also suggested that some people within society are not highly orientated towards work and thus may be a model also for others of how contentment could be derived from leisure. Style and values of work seem to influence the style of retirement as shown by continued social activities, social relations, and continuing patterns of interests. Work identity with its role of employment may be kept up, independently from employment being existent or not. However, as far as continuity can be located at the level of personal goals (Robbins *et al.*, 1994), even a change in activity might be an indicator of continuity, which makes empirical investigation of these hypotheses extremely difficult.

As an intellectual contrast to the theoretical dominance of the functionalist view (e.g. disengagement theory), political economy of old age emerged as another important theory in the late 1970s (see Chapter 4). The main point here is the interpretation of the relationship between ageing and economic structure. For example, Estes (1979) investigates in what way the state decides and stipulates to whom financial means shall be allocated. This also concerns retirement and the pension systems. As Phillipson (1982) shows, the experience of retirement is connected to synchronised pay cuts, and forced retiring from employment creates a financially insecure situation for many older people. Today, the state reduces expenses on pensions and increasingly suggests private provisions (see Chapter 7). This policy is legitimated by stereotypically considering older people a 'burden' – which is justified by the statistical concept of the proportion of charges (Phillipson, 1998). In this way the state uses its power to transfer responsibility for social security from the state back to the individual or the family. However, the decisive factors of explanation are not found in social roles, individual activities or coping strategies, but in the structures of society and a social system where only production counts (Estes *et al.*, 1982). The most important argument that can be produced from the theory of political economy is that inequalities in distributing financial means should rather be understood in relation to the distribution of power in society as a whole than by looking at individual differences.

In the 1990s, research on retirement and later life was partly influenced by post-modernism. This perspective on later life and late-life identity focuses on different lifestyles. In post-modernity, personal and social identity is expressed by ways of life that are shaped by the consumer society and numerous activities aside from gainful work. Older people no longer live under the shadow of their former employment, and may increasingly not define themselves in terms of their former work roles. Identity is instead much more expressed by consuming (Gilleard and Higgs, 2000). Employed and non-employed people share the same possibilities of expressing themselves by way of respective patterns of consumption. A change is made from an organised and class-orientated organisation of life towards more individual and more 'private' lifestyles. In this view, the transition from gainful employment to retirement loses its significance, as patterns of consuming are more decisive for one's own identity than gainful employment, and the former do not change basically. Instead, more weight is

placed on human agency and 'self-government that emphasises personal entitlements linked to personal responsibilities' (Gilleard and Higgs, 2000, p. 7). The
view that patterns of consumption help create personal identities is not supported
empirically, however – see Chapter 11. The major difference from the activity
and disengagement theories is that retirement is not viewed as a stressful and
traumatic event, but as an opportunity in which individuals have possibilities of
choice and the opportunity to maintain – or reach – a high quality of life.

However appropriate one regards such a perspective, there are many more
aspects and views on work and retirement that need to be mentioned. In sum,
psychology, sociology and economics emphasised different aspects of the transition to retirement. Roughly outlined, the psychological debate has mainly concentrated on the outcomes for the individual, the adaptation to retirement, the
mechanisms that promote successful or productive ageing, and the relevance of
age stereotypes and prejudices. It has been shown that the process of ageing is
not necessarily associated with a loss of functional capacity and productivity,
and that activity is important to avoid such reductions. Furthermore, the effects
of such reductions 'depend upon the specific constellation of abilities needed in
work tasks and roles' (Dittmann-Kohli and van der Heijden, 1996). The commonly held 'deficit model' of ageing which is made responsible for dismissals
and less training for older workers proved to be wrong. However, although
highly relevant, age stereotypes and age discrimination are only partly an explanation for the trend to early exit outlined above.

The sociology of retirement has mainly focused on the social structure and the
institutional aspects that shape the retirement process, on structural dependency,
societal marginalization, and – most recently – welfare and life-course regimes.
For example, Walker (2000) interprets the development of retirement partly in
terms of an increasing economic dependency of older people and a source of age
discrimination. In such a view, the explanation for the early exit phenomenon
mainly focuses on the 'push' factors of labour markets and firms, and on the
coalition of interests between firms, the older workers, and the state. From a firm
perspective, early exit is an effective way of reducing the workforce or of adjusting the age structure to better suit the market situation. Furthermore, compared
to younger workers, older workers are relatively expensive due to seniority principles, have a higher risk of illness, a higher qualification risk, and better protection against dismissal. Investing in their human capital seems less profitable
since they will retire sooner. From the perspective of the older workers, many
studies have shown that an early exit is highly attractive as long as it is financially acceptable. The unions also emphasise an improvement of the general
quality of life. From the state's perspective, creating specific pathways for early
exit, or letting the other actors use existing institutions such as disability or
unemployment insurance, seems attractive not only in order to fit into the interest coalition of firms, older workers and unions; it has also been a widely
accepted measure to reduce unemployment rates and promote employment of
younger age groups.

While sociologists mainly emphasise 'push' factors, economists have often concentrated on the 'pull' factors that shape the individual decision of the timing of retirement. Incentives for early retirement, for example, were identified in the institutional and legislative rules of the pension systems which have to be changed in order to adjust the retirement age (Gruber and Wise, 2002). Given the expected future financial burden, many countries have taken up such suggestions. Germany, for example, raised her retirement age limits and introduced a reduction in the level of pensions for every year of pre-retirement (see Chapter 7). The current efforts to promote further education ('lifelong learning') and better health by means of improved working conditions, and to combat common prejudices regarding older workers, help to promote labour force participation. But whether such measures of pension reduction are effective with respect to occupation or whether they primarily induce lower pensions depends largely on the broader economic development in conjunction with the other factors relevant to early exit.

Taken together, improvements in social security benefits, the availability of institutionalised early retirement pathways, firm-based early-retirement incentive programmes, broader economic trends, cultural norms, prejudices, and expectations, as well as individual factors like the meaning of work and leisure, the satisfaction with work and working conditions, health situation, family responsibilities, the interaction of choices within couples, and available income – just to name the most relevant factors – are working together in shaping the retirement process. These differences need also to be taken into account in the discussion about retirement and age boundaries. It is also most probably the specific 'mix' of these factors that makes the experience of retirement a story of loss or success – whether the retirement appears as a crisis, as continuity, or as a gain of renewed freedom (cf. the overview in Phillipson, 1990).

PRODUCTIVE ACTIVITIES

Does withdrawal from labour force participation imply non-productivity? Is the transition to retirement paralleled by withdrawal from social participation in general? Are older people free-riding 'on the bright side of the street' (Kolland, 2004), focusing solely on leisure activities, travels and consumer activities? The answers to such questions depend largely on definitions, especially of 'productivity' and 'leisure'. The term 'productive ageing' has recently been used to point out that activity and social engagement play a major role in old age, a fact that seems to be neglected in the discussion of intergenerational equity. There have also been attempts at estimating the value of productive activities in economic terms (Coleman, 1995; Herzog *et al.*, 1989; Herzog and Morgan, 1992; Künemund, 1999). However, the results differ according to how productive activity is defined.

Economic perspectives generally focus on work and activities producing valued goods and services that otherwise would have to be bought in the market –

in the first place paid work, own work and household production. Sociological perspectives add voluntary activities, childcare, personal care and informal help as far as they are of value to others. A broader definition may also take activities into account that help to maintain the ability of an individual to be productive, for example further education. Finally psychological perspectives add activities that help to maintain well-being as well as emotional and motivational aspects of productivity, for example the successful adaptation to age-related losses (Staudinger, 1996). O'Reilly and Caro (1994) provide an excellent overview on definitions of productivity. According to the definition chosen for an analysis, either only a minority of older people is productive, or nearly everyone is productive (and those who are not can hardly be accused of their 'unproductivity' – in most cases we would expect that it is not a voluntary decision to be unproductive in psychological terms).

Using a sociological definition, we find that older people are productive to a remarkable degree. In Germany, for example, older people are seldom active on the labour market (3%), but 16% of the 70- to 85-year-olds had been active in childcare, 8% in personal care, 7% in voluntary activities and 18% in informal help within the last three months. Taken together, 39% of this age group are 'productive' in a way that produces valued goods and services (Künemund, 2000). Furthermore, 39% support their children and grandchildren by substantial intergenerational transfers (Kohli et al., 2000). Summing up the hours of productive activity solely in voluntary activity, child and personal care in the population aged 60–85, we arrive at a projection of nearly 3.5 billion hours of usually unpaid production of valued goods and services a year. The monetary value of these activities – assuming a mean salary per hour of workers in the non-profit sector, such as welfare associations or political parties – was estimated to be equivalent to about 21% of the public pensions in Germany (Künemund, 1999).

From Figure 8.5 it becomes evident that individual opportunities play a major role with respect to age group differences in these activities. Childcare, for example, becomes less relevant in old age also because the grandchildren reach an age where childcare becomes obsolete. Even the difference between East and West Germany reflects mainly the difference in the existence of children. Personal care, on the other hand, declines with age mainly because fewer parents are left. With respect to voluntary activities, disengagement should also play a major role in explaining these differences, but of course there are also age boundaries in this sector.

Similar studies in the USA, however, present very different percentages and values. This is not only due to the much higher labour force participation rate in the United States. For example, more than one-third of people aged 65 or over report voluntary activities, more than 50% informal help (cf. Herzog et al., 1996, p. 327). Coleman (1995) estimated the value of productive activities – care and voluntary activities – to be almost 2% of the gross domestic product of the United States in 1990, or $102 billion. International comparison makes obvious that even the definitions of 'voluntary activity' and 'informal help' differ in these

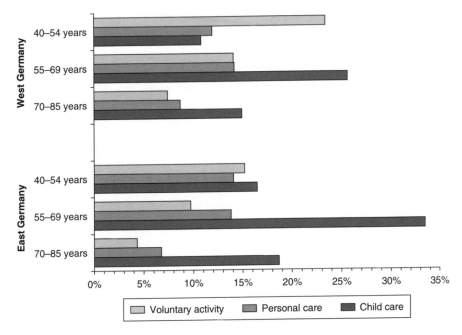

Figure 8.5   Productive activities in the second half of life in Germany

Source: German Survey of Ageing 1996, weighted

countries, and so do the opportunities, necessities and constraints for such activities. Therefore, these values and percentages are hardly comparable. Nevertheless these estimations illustrate fairly well that older people are not merely passive recipients of welfare. Quite the reverse, aside from the economic value, they contribute productively to society in many ways. The psychological aspects include benefits in terms of health, motivation, life satisfaction or meaning of life (see Chapter 13) in addition to the sociological aspects of social integration and cohesion.

However, work and productive activities as defined above are only a small part of everyday life in retirement, and the majority of older people seem not to be involved at all. It is even widely held that retirement is the 'leisure' phase of life, and despite the substantial 'productivity' there also seems to be substantial 'non-productivity'.

LEISURE ACTIVITIES

Leisure in today's understanding of the term is a product of the industrial revolution of the nineteenth century. It came from reorganisation of time beyond gainful employment. In the pre-industrial period, working time and leisure were closely connected. The change of the structure of work and the division of home and workplace brought a polarisation of work time and leisure time and allowed the formation of a leisure area. At the beginning of industrialisation, the small amount of leisure time that was left to workers in the face of a daily work time of more than 12 hours served mostly regeneration and reproduction of work power. Regarding the early nineteenth century, Kelly and Freysinger (2000) illustrate the experience of leisure (in the USA) as follows: 'Sunday was the only time for rest and escape. Further, poverty limited opportunities for expression. As a consequence, drinking to excess was common among workers (p. 35). This also influenced the following work day which often inevitably became a day of leisure time ('blue Monday').

The step-wise reduction of work time and blocks of free time in the form of holidays gave the working population an opportunity to spend leisure time with a variety of possible contents. But the distribution of leisure time is a cyclical rather than a linear process (Lamprecht and Stamm, 1994). For example, leisure time at the weekend grew faster than on work days. In Germany, in 1955 the peak of the working week was reached with about 50 hours (Müller-Schneider, 2001). But not only the high burden of work but also household work left little leisure time. Without today's household appliances, a considerable amount of time and labour was needed for cooking, washing, cleaning or necessary repairs. Leisure was a residual category and served mostly to restore exhausted strength for the next work day.

Nowadays, about one-third of the year is work-free. Working life is shorter, due to later entry into gainful employment, to reduced work time, and to earlier retirement. Leisure became a special time with new collective values. Furthermore, the development of a special leisure industry sector has created new social needs. Leisure is considered as time that may be spent as one likes: for personal development, cultural expression or (self) education. In the course of the modernisation process we may speak of a transition from recreation-orientated leisure time to event-orientated leisure time (Schulze, 1992).

However, at the end of the twentieth century, the idea of a differentiation of the two fields of work and leisure has been questioned. If firms organise programmes where employees take part in outdoor training or if leisure facilities are integrated into the sphere of work, then behind this a re-differentiation of work and leisure is suspected (Lash and Urry, 1994). Another indication of this can be found in corporate volunteering (Schubert et al., 2002), which means that firms induce their employees to civil engagement; i.e. part of paid worktime can be used for charitable activities. Such a development would have consequences for the relationship between gainful employment and retirement.

Taken together, both leisure itself and its meaning are subject to historical change. For example, Stearns' (1977) research on old age in France illustrated the absence of any concept of retirement within the working-class culture. Older people were largely unprepared for retirement and had not really expected to retire. Older peoples' households had very few consumer goods, which are now

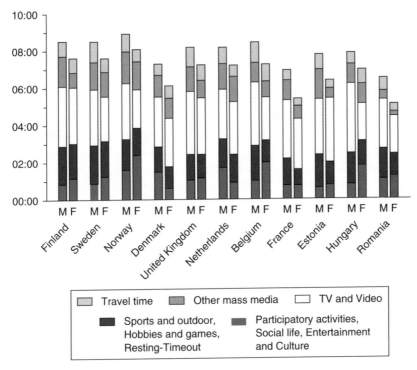

Figure 8.6   Use of time (in hours) by people aged 65 and older, living as a couple, with no children <18

Source: Kolland (2004); EUROSTAT data 'Time use at different stages of life'

taken more or less for granted. Few pensioners had a television or telephone. Leisure was shaped by the daily round of relationships within the family. Alternatively, there were the ubiquitous social clubs for older people which had been established in many towns and cities after the mid-1940s (Dumazedier, 1984; Kolland, 1984). Today the picture is very different from that. Workers anticipate their retirement and develop ideas and plans for it (Ekerdt, 1998). Retirement is considered a well-deserved life phase after many years of hard work. Leisure encompasses a vast range of activities (Phillipson *et al.*, 2001), despite the fact that the most popular leisure activities are sedentary ones – watching TV, for example, is by far the most common activity among older people in nearly all regions of Europe (Walker, 1993). In Germany, watching TV and solving crossword puzzles are the only activities that increase with age (Künemund, 2001).

Figure 8.6 provides a broad overview of time use in Europe based on a EUROSTAT study (2003b). Registered as leisure were television, video recordings and other media sources (radio, music and books), socialising activities (participatory activities, social life, entertainment and culture), travel, sports, hobbies, games and other unspecified (outdoor) activities. Aside from the dominance of media consumption, socialising and cultural activities are usually found to be more frequent among older women, while men spend more time on sports and outdoor activities, hobbies and games, and travel. Here it should be kept in mind that responsibilities of caring might restrict older people's opportunities to participate in leisure activities, especially women (Lechner and Neal, 1999). Nevertheless, the similarity of time use at this level of aggregation might be astonishing, given the recent debates on individualisation and lifestyles, and the diversity of regions and cultures covered in this study. The development of a special leisure market for older people, however, signifies the change from organised and class-orientated leisure to more individualised and private leisure styles. In conjunction with changes in socialisation, education, health and income, it is quite plausible to assume that the patterns of time use of future cohorts of older people will again differ significantly from what we find in present-day cohorts.

LIFE-LONG LEARNING

A large number of researchers – psychologists, sociologists, economists and gerontologists – have argued that further education in later life should become a societal imperative (e.g. Groombridge, 1982; Lehr, 1972). The reasons are manifold: to improve cognitive functioning, the general competence to use modern technologies in everyday life, work-related skills, health, and satisfaction with life, which depend strongly on feelings of autonomy and communication skills that can be enhanced by learning activities. Despite these advantages, the participation rates are extremely low. Attending educational or training courses is a rare phenomenon in later working life, and even more so in old age. Figure 8.7 shows that between 1% (Italy) and 17% (Switzerland) of the population aged 50 and over have attended some type of educational training in the last month. Interestingly the influence of gender is almost insignificant in these countries. Other international studies on the participation of older people in education confirm the conclusion that in most OECD countries no more than 10% of the older people make use of educational training offered (Phillipson, 1998).

The most important factor to explain these participation rates is earlier educational experience: the higher the level of schooling, the higher the likelihood of participating in further education in later life (Sommer et al., 2004). For that reason, educational measures for older people typically tend to increase already existing social inequalities if they are not targeted especially at those with less educational experience. Other important explanatory factors are institutional requirements and health.

It again seems highly plausible to assume that future cohorts of older people will be more frequently engaged in such activities because of better health, biographical experience with learning, and fewer institutional barriers for education

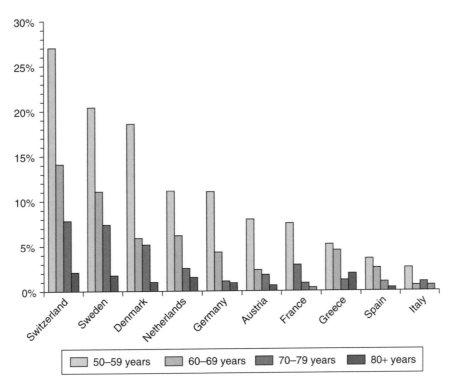

Figure 8.7   Attended an educational or training course in the last month

Source: Survey of health, ageing and retirement in Europe (SHARE), release 1, weighted, own calculations (Börsch-Supan *et al.*, 2005)

in both midlife and old age. But it will be crucial for future development whether society will shape the institutional context in a way that the individual is able to fulfil the requirements, acquire necessary skills and develop them further in a life-long learning process.

CONCLUSIONS

The labour force participation rates of older people in Europe have declined over a long period. The trend to early exit from work may have stopped, with the possibility of a reversal of this trend. The consequences, however, are unclear. Raising retirement age limits and introducing reductions in the level of pensions in case of early retirement, as is the case in Germany, may – as long as these are the only changes – exacerbate existing social inequalities. For example, less well-off ageing workers suffering from health problems would have to work longer or accept lower pensions, while the better-off older workers may compensate with private savings. Or, when the pathway to early retirement via unemployment is closed, less well educated older workers may face longer periods of unemployment and – as a consequence – lower pensions. These effects can be prevented when the demand for older workers increases and their working conditions and working capabilities are improved. Further education, health protection measures, and working time flexibility, then, are probably the most important strategies that have to accompany a raising of the retirement age and the cancellation of incentives for early retirement.

A more general turn-around has also been discussed. For example, Riley and Riley (1992) propose an age-integrated society, where the normal life-course – divided into three parts, namely education, work and retirement – is replaced by parallel activities in these domains in all age groups (or nearly all: we would not expect child work to re-emerge). Unlike our present age-segregated structures, age-integrated structures are those that do not use chronological age as a criterion for entrance, exit or participation. This implies life-long learning as well as earlier 'retirement' phases, for example sabbaticals. Although such a new distribution of work, leisure and training over the life-course is in many respects an interesting model to discuss, the current organisation of work makes such a development highly improbable, if not empowered by social and labour market policy. Especially from a firm's perspective there are many reasons not to take that direction: the higher risk of illness, the transaction cost in reorganising working time and workload, including the necessity to offer career opportunities and therefore succession of positions within firms, just to name a few. And to change the expectations of the individuals, namely to finally reach a retirement phase of life after a long period of dependent occupation, would most likely take a lot of time.

However, members of more recent cohorts are better educated than the previous ones. Education is related to mortality rates and productive activity. Life-long learning will probably counteract the outmoding of skills. Although the empirical evidence is sometimes ambiguous (Crimmins, 1996), a growing number of studies show better health and less inability to work for members of the younger cohorts in their later lives (Crimmins et al., 1996; Manton et al., 1997). These trends may lead to new definitions of retirement.

Finally, we must challenge the current state of research on retirement. Earlier studies show two key limitations. First, most of the studies dealt only with the retirement of men without worrying much about the experiences of women or taking into account the fact that increasingly couples experience two retirements at about the same time. Until now, the change from blue collar work to white collar work has been considered. Still, there have been only few investigations of the effects of the increasing feminisation of the world of work. Second, earlier studies on retirement were mostly cross-sectional studies. But to develop an understanding of why and at what time workers retire from work it is necessary to comprehend the people's experience of work over a longer period. This is possible only by means of longitudinal studies (see Chapter 5) in the course of which the same people are interviewed over longer periods. Based on such empirical research, policy considerations regarding work and retirement in ageing societies may help to further improve quality of life in all age groups.

The possible future developments are manifold. It may be predicted that the nature of employment will change in a way that encourages paid work even at a higher age than is common today (Henretta, 1994). Staying in employment for a longer time will be rewarded, as shown by new legislation in many OECD countries. For example, in Austria a new regulation became valid in 2005, according to which every year of work which is done after the age of 60 – and until the age of 65 – will be rewarded by a pension increase of 1.5%. For older workers there is the prospect of several flexible models of quitting their careers and of more non-professional types of employment to be at hand. Also, the trend towards a fluid transition to retirement may continue. Until the most recent past, retiring from gainful employment typically happened in an abrupt way, it happened in a defined, law-determined interval of age, and in most cases it was once and for all (Arnds and Bonin, 2003). Retirement may lose its character of irreversibility, especially with respect to part-time employment. However, most of these prospects are uncertain to some degree. But in any case, the demographic change will significantly influence institutions and culture (Braungart and Braungart, 1986; Ekerdt, 2004), and – among them – work and retirement.

FURTHER READING

Guillemard, A.-M. (2000): *Aging and the welfare-state crisis*. Newark/London: University of Delaware Press.

Phillipson, C. (2002): *Transitions from Work to Retirement: Developing a New Social Contract*. Bristol: Policy Press.

Taylor, P. (2002): *New Policies for Older Workers*. Bristol: Policy Press.

James, J.P. & Wink, P. (2006): The crown of life: Dynamics of the early post-retirement period. (*Annual Review of Gerontology*, Vol. 26). New York: Springer.

9

Personal relationships in later life

Janet Askham, Dieter Ferring and
Giovanni Lamura

THE NATURE OF PERSONAL RELATIONSHIPS

We have not entitled this chapter 'the family' and older people. Even if people's family or personal lives have always involved a complex range of relationships and behaviours, until recently they have been studied within a fairly rigid set of assumptions about kinship behaviour and the 'institution of the family'. Recent theorising suggests that we no longer *inhabit* an institution of the family, but *construct* it as we experience the changing influences and manifestations of personal relationships. Family is what people feel and perceive it to be, and there is 'less emphasis on what the family is for and more on what families – in all their guises – do' (Smart, 2004; see also Bengtson *et al.*, 2002). Family, or personal, relationships have been shown to have at least some of the following four main characteristics. They are relationships:

- in which intimate communication takes place, a confidante relationship, or one of 'disclosing intimacy', where people gain 'shared detailed knowledge about each other' (Jamieson, 1998)
- in which activities or goods are shared (held or done in common) – this may mean sexual activity, shared home or household goods, shared possession of children, shared leisure activities or other joint enterprises
- which are emotionally laden, with love or affection, trust, loyalty, caring about the other
- in which practical care, personal service to the other, or exchange of resources, takes place.

Clearly these four only suggest an ideal type (even an ideal). They do not necessarily come together even in a close intimate partnership, but at least three out of the four are generally involved in (a) marriage, partnership or cohabitation, (b) friendship, and (c) relationships with parents, siblings, children and grandchildren (whether these are acquired as blood ties, by marriage or by other means). Other kinds of relationship, possessing some of these characteristics, may be useful as points of comparison, for example relationships with professional counsellors or other substitute confidantes, live-in carers or servants, temporary sexual partners, and work-mates.

The institutionalised nature of the family has, until recently, been emphasised, and often described by a set of relationships with accepted, sanctioned and normatively reinforced patterns of behaviour. In particular the nuclear family (a married couple and dependent children) was seen as the most important set of personal relationships, with a belief that the extended family (older parents, siblings and other kin) had declined in importance from a former position when such ties were stronger. There was now an emphasis on the functions of the nuclear family in child-rearing and the support of its adult members, through the inculcation and confirmation of social values and norms, and the preparation and maintenance of a healthy labour force. However, once the notion of a past golden age of the extended family had been effectively demolished, at least for western Europe where historians showed the nuclear family to have been the dominant family form for centuries (Laslett, 1965), the way was open for more attention to be paid to other family relationships. The many ways in which family members supported each other across the generations and within different households has been recognised, including care and support of older people (Phillipson, 2003a).

During the last quarter of the twentieth century across Europe, the notion of the family as an institution also began to lose its hold, as marriages became increasingly varied and vulnerable and newer forms of relationship began to appear (communal living, gay relationships and so on). More emphasis was placed on affection as the root of primary relationships, it being argued by some that marriages broke up because people were unwilling to put up with relationships where love had died. At this time research on intergenerational relationships was also showing that, although obligation was an important part of the motivation of adult children to support elderly parents, it was not an unconditional obligation, reciprocity and affection also being key factors (Finch and Mason, 1993).

More recently still the characteristics of late modernity have led to – and will increasingly lead to – changes in personal relationships as a consequence of growing individuality, the speed of social change, the flexibility of identities, the growth of consumerism and the proliferation of consumer markets. However, the impact on marriage and friendship and other close relationships has not been theorised or tested empirically to any great extent. One of the main sets of ideas comes from Giddens (1991, 1992) who has developed the concept of the 'pure relationship', which he sees as a feature of high modernity, one which involves mutual disclosure, is entered into for its own sake, and continues only 'in so far as it is thought by both parties to deliver enough satisfaction for each individual to stay within it' (Giddens, 1992, p. 58). While it is easy to criticise these ideas – for example, there is plenty of evidence that most personal relationships are not defined by this mutually satisfying intimate conversation (McCarthy et al., 2003), that many are not based on equality but are hierarchical, and that many are maintained long after they cease to be mutually satisfying – nonetheless Giddens gives us one peg on which to hang questions about the personal relationships of older people in Europe today.

The other main peg (though not identified with a particular theorist) is the view that personal relationships have become characterised by the move towards increasingly flexible identities (in themselves linked to consumerism and proliferating markets), so that a relationship – which may be quite superficial – will be sustained only so long as it remains a project that satisfies each individual and his or her consumption needs. This sort of framework opens up the question of what constitutes a personal relationship, divorcing them from traditional views about kin, and encouraging us to examine with no preconceptions the actual personal relationships of older people in their everyday lives. Although it has been cogently argued (Jamieson, 1998) that neither of the latter conceptions (that is, personal ties as pure relationships or as flexible identity projects) is at all strongly supported by the evidence, nonetheless they are beginning to receive suggestions of support and they certainly provide good questions for investigation if we are to understand the developments occurring in personal relationships in Europe today.

Along with these changes has gone an alteration in the way in which we theorise family and personal relationships of older people. From the old model of elderly people disengaged from family functions (Cumming and Henry, 1961), in the 'family-as-institution' era, came an increasing recognition of the reciprocity in support within the 'family-as-caring-relationship', and the use of exchange theory grew. Indeed it continues to be useful, as reciprocity remains an important principle underlying family behaviour even in the context of the 'greater fluidity and instability in personal relationships' (Phillipson, 2003a, p. 63).

Also, more recently has come growing accentuation of the individual construction of ageing and a life-course perspective (see Chapter 3), which have set the background for models emphasising individuals' needs and goals as motors of personal relationship and network construction. The life-course approach also seems a conceptual framework likely to find useful application at both the individual and the institutional levels for understanding and supporting personal relationships in older age (Elder, 1991; Hagestad, 1991; Riley and Riley, 2000) (see Chapter 3). At an institutional level, the life-course approach can support the systematic implementation of measures allowing for smoother communication and individual transitions between life activities, phases and worlds (work–retirement; work–education–leisure; family–community–society; economy– health/social care; religious and/or ethnic groups), which are associated with size, composition and – above all – meaningfulness of personal social networks. Critical gerontology (see Chapter 4) is also useful in helping us understand the social forces – and particularly the powerful force of our socially constructed knowledge – within which individual lives and personal relationships are constructed in late modernity.

PERSONAL RELATIONSHIPS AND DEMOGRAPHIC TRENDS

Discussion of personal relationships at the beginning of the twenty-first century necessitates some reflection of the changing demographic landscape at the beginning of the new millennium. As we saw in Chapters 1 and 2, human longevity continues to extend and in association with changing fertility rates has led to important changes in the demographic profile across Europe. The impact on social relations of the demographic transitions of the last 50 years contrast markedly with the experience of previous generations at the beginning of the twentieth century, when marriage was monopolised by child-rearing, when parents and their children were adults together for very few years, and the experience of being a grandparent was similarly short. Nowadays a couple 'marrying' in their mid-twenties may stay together for over 50 years, having a long-term contract with their adult children and seeing their grandchildren become adults.

The social changes in attitudes toward 'marriage' highlighted above and a change in the patterns of family formation across Europe in recent years reinforces our view of changes in family structure and relations in recent decades. First, there are fewer marriages and more marital breakdowns: in 2002 there were five marriages per 1000 inhabitants in the EU compared with eight in 1970; the proportion of divorces has been estimated at 15% for marriages in 1960, and at around 30% for marriages entered into in 1985. Second, fewer children are born and later in life and there is a rise in births outside marriage. Eurostat (2004c) points out that the proportion of births outside marriage continues to increase, basically reflecting the growing popularity of cohabitation. While 6% of all births in 1970 were births outside marriage, the proportion rose to over 30% in 2002; this trend is most pronounced in Sweden, where more than half (56%) of the children born in 2002 had unmarried parents. Besides births outside marriage, the proportion of lone parenthood (parents living alone with their dependent children) has also considerably increased in the last 20–30 years. Lehmann and Wirtz (2004) report that 4.3 million lone-parent households existed in 2001, and this number accounts for 9% of all households with dependent children in the EU15 (see Chapter 1). Nearly 60% of the lone parents in 2001 lived with one dependent child, about a third with two dependent children, and just over 10% of the lone parents had three or more dependent children. Furthermore, over 90% of all lone parents in the EU in 2001 were women.

Taken together these demographic and social changes have affected the shape of the family, from horizontal to vertical, in the sense that the size of generations has become smaller but the number of living generations has increased. In the Netherlands, research has shown that 55% of older people belong to three-generation families and nearly 20% belong to families of four or more generations (Knipscheer *et al.*, 1995). In Sweden, at the age of 50, half of the population have at least one living parent (Sundström, 1987).

Summing up, one can see dramatic changes both in the temporal span of family life and in family and kinship roles during recent decades. Marriage no longer represents the preferred form of living as a couple, becoming a parent is postponed until middle adulthood, the number of children has decreased, and the grandparent/grandchild relationship extends over a considerably longer period. Furthermore, the genetic links that defined kin relationships are no longer a pre-requisite for the establishment of such relations since other forms of family only partly founded on these biological links have emerged. Diverse forms of the 'patchwork family' composed of partners with children and relatives from for-mer relations describe this trend, and a diversity of new family forms has also come into existence, such as childless married couples (Heaton *et al.*, 1999), or dual-career families (Perry-Jenkins *et al.*, 2000). Special demands and tasks aris-ing from the prolonged temporal frame of family life are described by the 'sand-wich situation' or 'middle generation squeeze' (Brody, 1999), where families have to care both for ageing relatives and for young children; and from the increasing vulnerability of marriage, by grandparents caring for grandchildren after their parents divorce (Cooney and Smith, 1996).

With these changes as our background, this chapter will examine not only the partnerships and friendships of older people, and kin relationships across the generations, but also the personal relationships of older Europeans within the community and wider society. We shall ask about trends in behaviour patterns, the characteristics of relationships, how they vary, and what their benefits and disadvantages are from the perspectives of older people. We shall also examine the links between the personal relationships of older people and the wider insti-tutions within the public sphere: the economy, state and healthcare. For exam-ple, how does the state define and constrain the relationship behaviour of older people; and do the values of consumerism and individualism undermine the rela-tionship commitments of older people? Finally we shall ask what current trends in the personal relationships of older people suggest about their future directions and implications.

NON-KIN PARTNERS AND ASSOCIATES

This section will consider people who live together as partners or live apart as intimates, companions or associates. Our discussion begins with couples as this relationship remains central to the lives and networks of older people. It can be considered within the four models of marriage or personal relationship as *insti-tution*, as a *caring relationship*, as *disclosing intimacy*, and as *identity project*, the first possibly continuing in some shape, but generally overruled in preference for the second, whereas the second now vies with the third and fourth. This shift moves us from, but does not completely make obsolete, the old questions of who does what in the domestic environment in later life, or holds the balance of power, to newer questions of, for example, to what extent the motivation of older people who do not re-partner in later life is based on individualistic values.

We ask first whether we should still be using the older model of marriage as institution for today's partnerships of older people, who perhaps through cultural lag, cultural differences within Europe, or the fact that many of their relationships have endured for a very long time and are therefore less subject to change, have relationships characterised by unequal power, strongly gendered division of domestic labour, and an institutionalised set of assumptions about what such a personal relationship looks like (e.g. heterosexual legal marriage, longstanding, involving living together and with strong legal mutual responsibilities). After examining these issues briefly we shall ask whether there is any evidence to suggest that either disclosing intimacy or individualistic partnerships are increasing among older people. This will lead us on to consideration of looser relationships, such as friendship.

Structures of partnerships

Most older people in all European countries are either legally married and living with a partner only or they are widowed, divorced or separated (but mainly the former) and living alone (Scharf and Wenger, 1995). During the last thirty years or so the proportion of people aged 65 and over who are married has actually increased across Europe, though with these increases being small or negligible in Northern Europe and particularly noticeable in countries such as Italy and Austria (Tomassini *et al.*, 2004). The increasing proportion of older women who have a spouse is very noticeable, though for men it has not changed significantly. This trend – partly reflecting improvements in life expectancy – is related to a levelling-off in some countries, since the mid 1990s, of the proportion of older people living alone. The proportions of older women living alone differ markedly within Europe, remaining high in northern European countries such as Germany, Sweden and the United Kingdom, and being much lower in Italy and Portugal, where it is more common to live with adult children (see Chapter 10). The proportions of older people divorced or separated remain low, though rising in northern Europe.

Thus it looks as though – on these grounds at least - marriage as institution is still relevant. There is, however, some evidence of a growth in cohabitation, divorce, homosexual relationships, or more flexible partnerships. Increasingly older widowed or divorced people are choosing unmarried cohabitation (Chevan, 1996) or to live alone or to live apart together, that is, an arrangement whereby a couple, as intimate friends, retain their own separate homes but occasionally live together (de Jong Gierveld and Peeters, 2003). For example in a Dutch study, among older people who had re-partnered following divorce or widowhood, living apart together (LAT) was as common as remarriage or cohabitation (de Jong Gierveld and Peeters, 2003). Although LAT is a relatively new arrangement and probably more likely in northern than southern Europe for both economic, familial and cultural reasons, surveys did not ask about such relationships until recently and they may have been in existence long before, even if not discussed. Apart from the assumptions that researchers make about what intimate relationships are like, there is also the difficulty of being able to find out about the less conventional modes of behaviour about which people may find it difficult to talk, which they may conceal beneath a conventional exterior, or which are too complicated to explain in a simple survey. Trends such as these suggest that 'in the future older people are likely to experience even greater diversity both in family life and in their living arrangements than previous generations' (Tomassini et al., 2004, p. 32).

The nature of partnerships in later life

Not all marriages are close and intimate; and not all intimate and close relationships are partnerships. We tend to discuss marriage (for people of any age) as though it were synonymous with intimacy. This is dangerous for any age group but perhaps particularly so for older people, who have had more time to develop unique or varied patterns of intimate relationships. So it is wise to be cautious. However, most research on intimate relationships – those relationships which matter most to people – has had to keep the shorthand assumptions about what they are like.

Sadly, the married lives of older people have received little research attention in recent years, and where they have been studied the main themes have been caregiving roles and gender differences – often combined (see Carr, 2004; Davidson, 2001). In division of domestic work, even among younger people there are only very slow changes towards more involvement of men in domestic work (Dex, 2003). A body of research shows a somewhat mixed picture of what happens to domestic labour divisions both on retirement and as people grow older; but much of the cited research is very old and can be criticised on methodological grounds. Recent evidence is limited but suggests that husbands increase their involvement in tasks usually carried out by their wife if they retire before she does (Pina and Bengtson, 1995), but may decrease it again when she retires (Szinovacz, 2000). Again this is probably more likely in northern Europe than southern Europe because of cultural differences. As couples reach late old age and have caring needs, the division of tasks may well become blurred as inabilities dictate who does what. However, the traditional differences in expectations of men and women persist, with older male carers often receiving more assistance from formal services than older female carers (Rose and Bruce, 1995).

There is some evidence that older spouses' communication is less likely to be of the self-disclosing kind than among more recently married people (Mares, 1995). Marital satisfaction changes with age, long thought to improve as children leave home and people retire from, or become less involved in, employment

(Bengtson *et al.*, 1990). Transitions can, however, have both positive and negative effects, with some initial strain particularly when the transition was unsought or unexpected (Szinovacz *et al.*, 2001). However, in general 'burnout' (a sense of physical, mental or emotional exhaustion with the marriage) seems to be low and levels of satisfaction with the marriage high; though we only have evidence from Israel (Kulik, 2002). But older wives seem to have lower marital satisfaction, higher burnout, lower levels of marital adjustment, and to be more likely to be considering separation, than older husbands (Kulik, 2002; Vaillant and Vaillant, 1993), which fits in well with the suggestion that older widows often do not seek, rather than that they cannot find, a replacement marital partner.

Outcomes or benefits

Marriage is generally considered to benefit men more than women (Bograd and Splika, 1996; Cooney and Dunne, 2001). This view has, however, been challenged recently (Simon, 2002), as has the belief that men adapt less easily to widowhood than women, with inconsistent evidence suggesting the importance of examining the specific aspects with which men do or do not cope well (Carr, 2004). Marriage seems to benefit men particularly in relation to health maintenance, domestic tasks and emotional support; and to benefit women in relation to financial support, some traditionally male household tasks and some social activities. Apart from the distress of bereavement, loss of the partner therefore affects them differently. But of course these differences are not gender-specific for everyone, and probably this is increasingly the case: some widows were already financially secure in their own right, some widowers were not dependent on their wives for emotional support. As Carr says, these roles are becoming 'increasingly blurred over the life course and over historical time' (Carr, 2004, p. 222).

Re-partnering in later life is not necessarily the optimum outcome. For example, it seems to disturb the partners' social networks, so that people with new partners – particularly those who live apart together – have fewer weekly contacts with children and siblings than those who do not (de Jong Gierveld and Peeters, 2003). Widowed women living on their own frequently report increased self-confidence and competence and even a preference for not having to cater for anyone else's needs (Carr, 2004; Davidson, 2001). As Carr emphasises, however, it is important to recognise that these outcomes are the consequence of the nature of the preceding marital relationships at a particular historical point; in future, when the conjugal relationships of older people may well look very different, the consequences of widowhood will also be different.

FRIENDS AND ASSOCIATES: PATTERNS OF ASSOCIATION

Not only at younger ages, but also in later life, friendship appears to be becoming a more important part of people's personal lives. Older Europeans tend to have fewer friends as they get older, but this is by no means the case for all. The acquisition and loss of friends is a dynamic process: friends may be lost but they are also replaced (Matthews, 1986). In a longitudinal study of older people in Wales, Jerrome and Wenger (1999, p. 665) found that 'people go on replacing friends until extreme old age'. In fact as one would expect, change is a major feature of friendship patterns in later life. There is not much difference between men and women, any such apparent differences probably being due to marital status, as unmarried people have more friends than the married (Hatch and Bulcroft, 1992). People's future orientations may also help to explain differences; it has been suggested that decline or continuation of friendships with age is due not only to whether or not people experience ill-health or death of previous associates, but also to whether or not they perceive their future as 'expansive or limited' (Lang, 2001).

There are interesting differences within Europe. For example, Britons claim a larger number of friends than kin in their networks (Jerrome and Wenger, 1999), and have more contact with friends than other older Europeans apart from Italians – so this is not a north/south split. At the other end of the spectrum, older Swedes have the lowest contact, with 38% reporting they see a friend less than weekly (Burholt et al., 2003); whereas among Dutch people aged 55–90 only 16% had no-one outside the family in their primary network (Knipscheer et al., 1995) and half said they see friends at least two or three times a week (Burholt et al., 2003). Population density or geographical distances may be implicated as well as cultural factors in understanding these differences.

Older Italians and British also show the highest frequency of daily contacts with neighbours, compared especially to the low levels characterising older Swedes, but – since for older people's social network variation within countries seems to be more relevant than cross-country variation (Wenger, 1997, p. 15) – several other intervening factors affect this kind of relationship more strongly than country of residence (Burholt et al., 2003, pp. 55–70). Among them, a major role is played by living arrangements; (greater levels of non-kinship relationships being reported by older people living with members of a younger generation); working status (employment in older age being associated with lower levels of non-kin relationships); the kind of location of residence (especially among older Austrians and Italians, who have higher levels of non-kin contacts in rural areas); as well as the level of education and of income (those with lower levels showing higher frequency of non-kin contacts).

Characteristics of personal association in later life

Inevitably the term 'friendship' invites consideration of a particular type of relationship. But as people get older the line between friends and neighbours becomes more blurred, as does the distinction between friendships based on similarity of interests and characteristics as opposed to those chosen on grounds of availability and general friendliness; that is, the relationships with people in the community, such as neighbours, and people in intermediate institutions, which lie somewhere between the community and the wider society of impersonal relationships: peer associates with whom people interact through voluntary work, unions, churches, and so on. For example, in their study of very old people in Wales, Jerrome and Wenger (1999) found that most of their friends now lived nearby, and that newer friends often included 'neighbours, district nurses, home helps, doctors and their wives, clergymen and their wives, solicitors and bank managers, younger cousins, nephews and nieces' (p. 671). Because the pool of people similar in age with whom to form friendships decreases as people move into late age, there is also a trend towards friends who are younger.

Friendship in its ideal form has been described as a relationship based on closeness and understanding, but as people age is often shown to involve practical companionship, affection, care work or service rather than self disclosure (Jerrome, 1992). This is supported by more recent research which demonstrates the central role played by friends in later life, who 'emerge clearly in a number of supportive roles, notably among those without children in their networks, and especially among those who are single' (Phillips *et al.*, 2000, p. 849). This latter study which compared life today with that found in three pioneering community studies in England from the 1940s and 1950s (Phillipson *et al.*, 2001) found that friendship had become a more important resource since those days except in the suburban area, where there had been less change. But this increased blurring between friends and neighbours can lead to difficulties. Research on neighbours shows that the balance between preserving ones privacy and being friendly, and between the social control and social support function of neighbours requires great skill (Crow *et al.*, 2002) and if overstepped – as it may very well be if an older person needs practical caring help – is fraught with problems. On the one hand the friendliness of some neighbours and the flexibility of their proximity and informal relationship with the older person makes them ideal practical supporters; but on the other hand, because this is a relationship with no strong normative obligation, any expansion beyond an unclear boundary can cause tension or disaffection (Nocon and Pearson, 2000).

However, neighbours have been shown to play a meaningful role in many older people's everyday lives (Burholt *et al.*, 2003, p. 14), and are often more numerous in their social networks than kin or friends (Wenger, 1997, p. 15). Neighbours seem to provide in general more instrumental support and less emotional support than associates more traditionally defined as friends (Walker, 2004), to be more meaningful for those living alone or with a spouse only (Knipscheer *et al.*, 1995), and to become particularly important with increasing age and infirmity (Lehr, 1994), as well as in cases of migration (Wenger, 1997, p. 16).

Benefits for older people

Most older people appear to be contented with their friend relationships (Jerrome and Wenger, 1999), though there are variations within Europe, mainly showing that countries where contact with friends is higher have higher levels of satisfaction (Burholt *et al.*, 2003). The benefits of friendship are well-rehearsed: friends have been shown to improve psychological well-being in older age, sustaining the sense of self, identity and self-esteem particularly in times of transition such as a move of home, retirement, bereavement; helping to maintain a sense of continuity despite losses; and aiding fulfilment through shared activities (Dykstra, 1995; Rook, 1990; Stevens, 2001). Again the role of older people as agents of their own personal relationships needs to be emphasised. It is not only having supportive friends that is important in later life, but also having control over those relationships, for as Lang (2001) shows, 'relationship regulation contributes to enhanced subjective well-being in later life'. Indeed some have shown evidence that friends may be more important for well-being in old age than relationships with family members (Pinquart and Sorensen, 2000), and this may well be due to the control people can exert over such relationships compared with those of kin.

Concluding remarks

In postmodern Europe, close relationships are changing. For the younger cohorts of older people in the first decade of the twenty-first century, signs of change in their partnerships are beginning to emerge: more second partnerships, more of these not involving re-marriage but cohabitation or 'living apart together'; widows who savour their freedom from marriage; married couples in partnerships which are more equal than they used to be, and who preserve their cherished 'intimacy at a distance' from their adult children. For the older old, although most of them live alone, with partnership a thing of the past and a good deal of reliance on adult children, the dynamism of their relationships with other friends and associates must not be overlooked. There is no strong evidence of rampant individualism or of 'the identity project', and certainly very little in support of the pure relationship and disclosing intimacy. But there are some trends that deserve watching.

RELATIONSHIPS WITH KIN: PARENTS, SIBLINGS, CHILDREN AND GRANDCHILDREN

Family and kinship relations

Parents, siblings, children and grandchildren are terms that describe multiple roles, which everyone may occupy during his or her life and which are not voluntarily chosen. Before considering some of them individually it is useful to examine their place within the social networks of older people.

As indicated by the longitudinal findings of the Berlin Ageing Study (Baltes and Mayer, 1999), two general findings characterise older people within their social networks:

- a reduction in the network size is convincingly reported across the lifespan, becoming most pronounced in old age
- in general, findings show that especially the young old are socially integrated and engaged.

Burholt *et al.* (2003) report a high frequency of contacts between elderly persons and their kin as well as a high satisfaction with family and friendship relations in their European sample. Neyer and Lang (2003) point out that research on personal relationships over the life-course has consistently shown that kin relations, if available, remain relatively important as stable sources for emotional and instrumental support until late in life. These studies also suggest that the most meaningful social events take place within families and kin groups.

In order to elaborate the importance of kin relationships in later life, one may start with the cliché that the majority of older people are parents and have offspring. While the child-rearing tasks of parents during offspring's childhood and adolescence are defined by society, the role and tasks of parents in the 'post-parental' phase of the family life-cycle and in later life lack such a clear societal definition. In their normative model of the family life cycle that is differentiated by developmental tasks, Carter and McGoldrick (1999) describe the responsibilities that arise in the 'post-parental' phase: the renegotiation of the marital system as a dyad; the development of adult relationships with children, the inclusion of 'in-laws' and grandchildren in the family; and dealing with the ageing of parents and grandparents. As we have seen, the structures of relationships are becoming increasingly complex and an additional responsibility is responding to new partnering by older people and their adult children as well as the development of relations with step-children and step-grandchildren (Bornat *et al.*, 1999). The subsequent and last phase within the family life-cycle model comprises the specific tasks and responsibilities of dealing with one's own ageing: the ageing of partner; support and value of the older generation; adaptation to the loss of parents, spouse and supports; preparation for one's own death; as well as life review and integration (Carter and McGoldrick 1999). This model represents a translation of the developmental stages by Erikson (1950) (see Chapter 3), who characterised middle adulthood (40–65 years) by the psychosocial conflict between generativity and stagnation; the first being fostered by having and nurturing children as well as becoming involved with future generations. The conflict between integrity and despair underlies the development in late adulthood (65 years to death) and reflection on, and the acceptance of, one's life represent the *conditio sine qua non* for solving this conflict in a positive way. If the resolution of the respective crises and/or developmental tasks does not succeed, cognitive, social or emotional maladjustment may occur.

The developmental tasks underlying the family life-cycle and the individual in adulthood and age as described mainly reflect the adaptation to losses. The loss of partners, siblings and age-peers is an inevitable experience especially during old age, and although the social network is also open for the integration of new members such as in-laws and grandchildren across the life-span, in general a reduction in the size of social networks has to be expected with growing age (Baltes and Mayer, 1999). Although the loss of persons represents an evident reason for the network reduction, it does not represent a sufficient explanatory factor for the composition of social networks in old age.

Kahn and Antonucci (1980) offered a life-span framework for the study of social relations by introducing the concept of 'social convoys'. According to this approach, social relations surround individuals across the lifespan and the size and composition of these convoys are dynamically shaped in accordance with the specific needs and goals of the individual. A similar position is taken within socio-emotional selectivity theory proposed by Carstensen (1993). The author proposes that older people are highly selective when choosing partners, because their main choice criterion is emotional closeness. This focus on emotional closeness is explained by the limited time perspective in old age, which should lead to a shift in goal hierarchies towards emotionally meaningful goals (Kennedy et al., 2001). Thus, socio-emotional selectivity is assumed to represent an adaptive ageing mechanism that primarily serves the function of emotion regulation, and it should become predominant in old age, because of its presumed functions in helping older people to cope with everyday life and the various kinds of threat to which they are exposed (Carstensen, 1995). Accordingly, it has been shown that most older people have a comparatively high proportion of emotionally very close people in their social network, and most studies have inferred the importance of these people from significant relationships to indicators of psychological well-being and social integration (Ferring and Filipp, 1999; Lang and Carstensen, 1994).

An inspection of the composition of social networks in old age shows that family members represent the majority of social relations (Ferring and Filipp, 1999; Lang and Carstensen, 1998; Wenger, 1997), and adult children not only stay in contact with their parents but also continue to share close emotional relationships with them (Lang and Carstensen, 1998). Between ageing parents and their adult children, at least weekly contact is the European norm (Burholt et al., 2003). This provides a number of occasions on which various kinds of parent–child interactions may unfold and these may contain positive emotional exchanges, the provision of financial help and gifts to the adult offspring as well as other forms of instrumental support on the one hand, and demands to assist the ageing parents as well as parental criticism or conflict on the other hand.

In the following sections two forms of kinship relations in old age will be highlighted: siblings, and grandparents with their grandchildren.

Sibling relations

Cicirelli (1985) has pointed out that sibling relationships occupy a unique position within the study of human relationships, and are of potentially longer duration than any other human relationship. They are, especially in comparison to parent–child relationships, egalitarian and the sibling role remains part of the individual's identity regardless of changes in life. These unique attributes contribute to the emotional and reciprocal influences that have been described among siblings at all stages in life. Geottings (1986) has elaborated a lifespan frame covering the developmental tasks of siblings and differentiates three underlying periods:

- Tasks during childhood and adolescence mainly comprise mutual emotional support, and the development and building of friendship and companionship. In general, older siblings help and support the younger ones, and demonstrate solidarity with one another against third parties (occasionally their parents).
- During early and middle adulthood, siblings may provide mutual emotional and financial support particularly in times of crises, as well as the joint care of the ageing parents.
- Tasks during late adulthood and old age comprise the integrative solution of their past common history. Instrumental as well as emotional support from siblings becomes even more important during this period since a partner may no longer be present.

Within this model, mutual support represents the constant link between siblings across the lifespan, and the assumed unidirectional sequence of support between siblings may seem idealistic in the light of findings indicating conflicts and rivalry in sibling relations (Bedford, 1995). Even conflicts initiated in childhood may have consequences for relationship quality towards parents and siblings in adulthood. Thus, it could be shown that retrospectively perceived differential parental treatment of siblings as well as presently perceived differential treatment of siblings by their ageing parents has consequences for currently experienced relationship with ones parents (Boll *et al.*, 2003). When it comes to rivalry of siblings in old age, it is assumed that these decrease across the lifespan if this is not hindered by underlying conditions and circumstances. Cicirelli (1985) reports that 85% of his elderly sample said that they got along very well with their siblings despite sibling conflict in childhood. He also found rivalries among elderly siblings to be quite low, with only 10% reporting arguments, 6% reporting bossy behaviour, 8% reporting feelings of competition and only a few reporting jealousy, hostility and snobbishness. This is in line with models assuming that sibling relations become increasingly symmetrical, as siblings grow older (Buhrmester and Furman, 1990).

In line with these findings, Gold (1989) has identified five types of sibling relationship in old age, which mainly reflect a positive relationship.

- Intimate siblings represent the first type. They have an especially close and extremely devoted relationship and give this high priority compared to other kin and non-kin relationships (14% fell into this category).
- Congenial siblings are close and caring but place a higher value on their marriage and parent–child relationships (34%).
- Loyal siblings base their relationship on the common family history. They have regular, periodic contact, participate in family gatherings, and support each other during times of crisis (30%).
- Apathetic siblings feel indifferent towards each other and are rarely in contact.
- Hostile siblings have relationships based on anger and resentment (only 11% came into the last two categories).

Findings about, and models of, sibling relationships underline the importance of these across the lifespan as a source of reciprocal instrumental and emotional support. Consequently, the experienced quality of siblings' relationships into old age seems to be positive even in the face of childhood conflicts and rivalry.

Grandparents and grandchildren

As has been pointed out above, the temporal frame for grandparents and their family, including sons and daughters and grandchildren, has extended during the last decade. Demographic and associated changes in family structure also give rise to a new definition of the roles assigned to grandparents during middle and late adulthood. The stereotypical image of the elderly grandparent is no longer true (if it ever was), since not all older people are grandparents, and not all grandparents are old, especially when their children experience teenage pregnancy, when they may well have to care for their children *and* grandchildren.

Nevertheless, grandparenthood is primarily defined by the option of generativity since the contact with grandchildren is inherent to grandparenthood, and this is clearly reflected in individual representations of this role. There have been a number of typologies of the social role of grandparenthood, many of them American. A recent European typology devised by Herlyn and Lehmann (1998) identified five styles in a sample of 573 German grandmothers:

- Duteous grandmothers represented 14% of the sample. They had a mean age of 59, the mean age of grandchildren being 7.6 years, and cared for their grandchildren on a regular basis. These grandmothers put a high value on 'immortality through clan'.
- Autonomous and highly engaged grandmothers (24%) had a mean age of 61 years with grandchildren having a mean age of 9.5 years. These grandmothers enjoyed common activities with the grandchildren but when able to choose give priority to their own extrafamilial activities.
- Integrated grandmothers (24%) with a mean age of 67 years and older grandchildren with a mean age of 14.8 years were well integrated in the family but showed less commitment, which may be attributed to the age of the grandchildren.
- Ambivalent grandmothers (21%) had a mean age of 67 years and grandchildren with a mean age of 17.7 years. They reported differing and conflicting needs of closeness and distance to the grandchildren, which possibly reflects the grandchild's individuation affecting not only the parents but also the generation of grandparents.
- Family-independent grandmothers (21%) had a mean age of 68 years and grandchildren of a mean age of 16.8 years, where the two did not have much in common and were described by a more or less detached relationship.

Although typologies can have heuristic value, they do suffer from over-simplification of what may be a dynamic and varied relationship with a number of different grandchildren. Nonetheless, grandparents are generally shown to have a positive relationship with their grandchildren, although the contact between them may decrease with growing age on both sides. Besides this, geographic proximity, gender and lineage, life stage, and timing of grandparenthood, marital status and employment status, race and ethnicity, and grandparents' relationships with their own grandparents have been identified as factors that exert a direct or indirect influence on the interaction between grandparents and grandchildren. Despite (a) diversity in the meaning of grandparenthood and styles of grandparenting, and (b) the social changes affecting it such as the increased tendency for grandparents to be in paid employment when their grandchildren are young, or conversely to become responsible for grandchild care, one may hold that grandparents provide a resource of emotional and financial support, and represent more indulgent social partners than do the parents. On the other side, grandparents also profit from the relationship through feelings of generativity and the sense of being valued.

Concluding remarks

In summary, findings about kinship relationships in old age show that most older people are well integrated in social networks strongly composed of family members. Findings on relationship quality indicate generally high satisfaction, and that interactions between ageing parents, their adult children, grandchildren and siblings focus mainly on the exchange of support and inter- and intra-generational solidarity. Nevertheless, this positive picture is confined to studies of older people still able to live an independent life. Other facets of family relationships in old age include phenomena such as ambivalence towards one's parents and children, and caregiver burden, elder abuse and violence, which have not been elaborated here. For an overview, see Pillemer and Lüscher (2004).

OLDER PEOPLE'S PERSONAL RELATIONSHIPS AND THE WIDER SOCIETY

Moving beyond family and kin relationships, we must address questions that, albeit relevant for all cohorts, assume particular relevance in older age.

- What are the links between the personal relationships of older people and the wider institutions in society, such as the economy, the state and healthcare and social care?
- How does each institution define, influence or constrain the behaviour of older people in their personal relationships?
- What are the societal values most likely to affect personal relationships and the commitment of older people within them?
- What are the differences between societies with more familistic values and those in which individualism is more dominant?

The social institutions of 'the wider society'

When we consider the influence exerted by the wider society on older people's personal relationships, we need to define what this means, and identify the main components in which it might be articulated. As with all human beings, older people develop in a variety of contexts and surrounding environments, with which they are in constant interaction, as for instance theoretically reconstructed by Bronfenbrenner (1979) in his 'socio-ecological model', which provides an inherent differentiation between the micro, meso and macro systems affecting individual behaviour.

Society can therefore be considered as made up of those *social institutions* that exert a significant impact on individuals' relationships. According to such definition (and excluding the family and kin relationships already dealt with in previous sections of this chapter), a relevant role is played in the first place by the *local community* – neighbours and other residents living in the same area – while *economic or market organisations*, relevant for the material security of individuals throughout life, exert a secondary influence even after retirement has reduced their direct involvement in the working world. Growing importance for personal relationships in older age must also be ascribed to care-related institutions, such as *health and social care organisations*, as age-related deterioration affects the individual's ability to remain independent in activities of daily living. While *cultural and educational institutions* tend to provide a framework for personal relationships especially for more autonomous older people, *religious affiliation* and *ethnic group membership* are two further factors that can exert a significant influence in shaping social networks. All the above categories can finally be usefully analysed within the background of the role played by the *state*, that is, any government or legal authority with responsibilities of administering public policy and affairs, usually under the impulse of political and non-governmental organisations (parties, trade unions, associations etc.). Their influence can be felt not only in the way governments encourage recognition of the role of family carers, but also in the way they put pressure on mothers of dependent children to seek paid employment, thus encouraging grandparents to become involved in childcare.

The local community

Neighbours play an important part in many older people's everyday lives in their community, contributing to their well-being and quality of life. Community participation, and the relationships it engenders, represent another relevant factor contributing to quality of life in older age, but probably also one less easily captured by empirical indicators (Wenger, 1989; Dykstra, 1990; Katz, 2000). When we try to measure it in terms of 'attendance at meetings' (community, neighbourhood, social groups, older people's clubs, lectures etc.), it seems to be higher among older Austrians and Dutch, and lower among Italians and Swedes (Burholt et al., 2003, pp. 50–52). If we measure it as 'volunteering activities and/or active membership in or use of civic organisations' (as churches, women's and older people's organisations, community centres, sports club etc.), involvement seems to be higher in the Netherlands, Italy and the UK (Droogleever Fortuijn et al., 2003). The first indicator, however, seems to be more sensitive than the second: while the latter varies only slightly between different groups of older individuals, the former is significantly associated to *age* (the older the more community oriented in Sweden, UK and Luxembourg, the less old in Austria and the Netherlands), *gender* (women showing higher community participation than men in the UK, Luxembourg and Sweden, the opposite being true in Austria), *type of location* (rural older inhabitants being more community oriented than those living in urban areas in the Netherlands and Luxembourg, but not in Austria), *household composition* (those living with a spouse only showing higher levels of community participation), *education* (the higher the educational level the higher the community participation) and *working status* (non-workers participating less in community meetings).

Relationships with neighbours and community participation in older age differ between rural and urban areas. Generally speaking, in most countries and with few exceptions, older people in rural areas seem to rely on broader or stronger networks of social support resources than is the case in urban areas (Burholt *et al.*, 2003, p. 35; Peeters *et al.*, 2004, p. 204).

The economy

One of the most relevant ways by which the economy exerts an influence on older people's personal relationships is through the impact of retirement (see Chapter 8). Older individuals strongly focused on working roles are more likely to face difficult adjustments after retirement, especially when their involvement in other social activities is low. This is more often the case for men than women, although even for the latter, when they show a strong occupational attachment, retirement is associated with loss of meaningful relationships, work being for many women an important source of social contacts (Price, 2002; Simmons, 2001). This impact is furthermore closely connected with social class (lower income groups making or maintaining rewarding relationships within the local community much more often than middle-class individuals) as well as with marital status (single men and women with a traditional gendered identity reporting poorer social relationships after retirement, compared to the most rewarding personal relationships experienced by older single people sharing more egalitarian gender roles). These results are confirmed by recent Italian data, where post-retirement experience is shown to be mainly one of 'having more time for home and social or family relationships', while the most common fear among pre-retirement female employees is 'to miss relationships with colleagues and contact with people', underlining once again the fact that 'work has represented, for many women of this generation, an achievement and a way to escape from the limitations of a housewife's life' (Polverini and Lamura, 2004, p. 772).

Economic forces also influence personal relationships in later life beyond retirement mechanisms, such as in the way poverty can strain social relations (Antonucci and Akiyama, 2002), or in the way socio-economic status affects supportive non-kin relationships in older age, with higher status being associated with a more positive impact (Broese van Groenou and van Tilburg, 2003). One striking example of this relatively universal phenomenon is provided by the impact of recent financial shortages in many eastern European countries following the breakdown of the Soviet Union (Tchernina and Tchernin, 2002, pp. 548–553). Increasing intergenerational tension between older cohorts – whose social attitudes are mainly based on the 'communal' value system of the soviet era – and more individualistic oriented younger people, is evident due to the economic pressure forcing many families to perform all domestic work by themselves, thus leaving little free time for meaningful communication with each other.

Cultural, educational and political institutions

'Third-age universities' and other life-long learning initiatives are currently providing in many European countries an undoubted contribution to promoting, among other things, social relationships in older age (Klercq, 2004), one of the main reasons for enrolling in them being for instance in Italy 'the research for new opportunities of socialisation' (Polverini and Lamura, 2004, p. 184). Although in many cases an age-restricted participation in adult education seems still to be the rule (Uhlenberg and de Jong Gierveld, 2004, p. 8), an increasing number of programmes open to all ages are currently being offered, in some cases involving very different fields of activities, but with the common aim of fostering intergenerational exchange (Davey, 2002).

Personal relationships in later age can benefit also from participation in other fields of activity. In the Netherlands, involvement in political parties, women's associations or music or theatre groups is higher in the 55- to 74-year age group than in the 35–54 group, thus revealing a high potential importance of such social activities for the development of personal relationships, especially of those related to the practice of hobbies (Peeters et al., 2004, p. 207). A recent trend observed in some countries is also the increasing engagement in older people's associations or retired people's trade unions, which in the Netherlands and Italy involve very large numbers of older people: a quarter of the Dutch (Peeters et al., 2004, p. 207) and 60% of Italians over 65 years (Polverini and Lamura, 2004). Although such engagement cannot be seen as an automatic impulse to foster deep personal relationships, it should be underlined that the several parallel activities and initiatives of a social and cultural nature developed thanks to these networks and associations often provide important opportunities for new meaningful contacts and longstanding relationships for many retired and older people. In Italy, for instance, where early retirement has been widespread until recently (with some people even retiring before reaching the age of 50; Polverini and Lamura, 2004, pp. 20–21), retirees' associations can be considered organisations of an almost intergenerational nature, with an increasing orientation to service provision and volunteering, which makes them also very powerful in the political arena.

The use of the Internet as a way of fostering social contacts remains much more underdeveloped in Mediterranean countries compared to most northern European ones, although 'silver surfers' using e-mails and Internet to get in touch with each other are not very widespread in the latter countries either (Selwyn *et al.*, 2003). This is confirmed, for instance, by the 'static' structure of many websites devoted to older people in Italy, which are aimed at providing information about studies concerning older age, rather than organised for an interactive use by a virtual community of older (and younger) people, who can find through the web a new 'social dimension' (Polverini and Lamura, 2004, p. 68).

Religious affiliation and ethnic group membership

Religious affiliation, through the involvement of individuals in activities organised by places of worship, represents another important channel for maintaining or starting new personal relationships in older age (Burholt *et al.*, 2003, p. 41; Polverini and Lamura, 2004, p. 183; Wenger, 1997, p. 7), even though in most cases of an age-homogeneous kind (Uhlenberg and de Jong Gierveld, 2004, p. 8). In the Mediterranean countries, characterised by a traditionally strong Roman Catholic tradition, the involvement of older people in confessional groups represents not only an important source of social contacts within the community life, but also helpful support to face loneliness in the event of reduced mobility or higher dependency (Polverini and Lamura, 2004, p. 186).

Ethnic group membership also affects personal relationships in later life. Today's presence of older ethnic minorities in European countries represents mainly a result, on the one hand, of the labour migration flows that occurred in the last half century – in many cases under deliberate support of national governments to sustain internal economic growth – and, on the other hand, to the 'amenity seeking' movement of 'northern Europeans who ... migrate to southern Europe for retirement' (Warnes *et al.*, 2004, pp. 309–312). While many older labour migrants are generally characterised by lower education and poorer linguistic skills, which are usually associated with higher risks of deprivation and social exclusion (Torres, 1999; Torres, 2001), current retirement migrants to southern Europe can more often count on more consistent socio-economic resources that allow them to make use of existing services and technologies, and to maintain close contacts with relatives and friends in the old homeland (Huber and O'Reilly, 2004). Empirical evidence seems to underpin the idea that older migrants' human capital, in terms of resources and preparedness for old age, is less influenced by personal social networks, and rather related to health and material security indicators such as income or assets (Warnes *et al.*, 2004, p. 313). This does not, however, contradict the fact that intergenerational and intra-ethnic support is traditionally quite strong in many ethnic minorities, especially in facilitating linguistically weak older members in contacts with local services and bureaucracy (Bolzman *et al.*, 2004, p. 420; Cylwik, 2002, p. 611; Weidekamp-Maicher and Reichert, 2004, p. 163), although the extent to which this occurs is very much affected by the timing, chronology and locations of the specific migration history of each ethnic group (Burholt, 2004, pp. 397–399).

With regard to the UK, community participation as a potential source of meaningful personal relationships – in terms of being politically active, a member of an organisation, or providing volunteer and informal care work – has been found to be weaker for older members of ethnic minorities than for national 'majorities', but this might be partly related also to the fact that community activities and contacts channelled through religion are often 'regarded by ethnic minority groups as integral to their faith ... rather than as voluntary participation in an organisation' (Bajekal et al., 2004).

FINAL COMMENTS

This chapter has covered a wide sweep of topics, from the discussion of self-disclosing intimacy with which it began to community participation with which it ended. This illustrates the necessary scope of a subject whose boundaries are widening and which up to now has been examined in a much more narrow way. Older people in Europe live within a complex array of personal relationships, changing not only as they grow older, but also as the world around them changes. As their behaviour changes so must the way in which we study it, including development of conceptual frameworks which can encompass many different types of relationship.

In this final section we reflect first on three themes of cross-cutting relevance. A first theme is the importance of the *subjective* experience – rather than 'objective' definitions – of personal relationships in older age. For example, at a societal level a telling example of the importance of subjective experience (though within the framework of societal values) is the fact that, despite the intensity and structural pervasiveness of family relationships, older people in Mediterranean countries seem to suffer from loneliness and lack of confidantes more often than is the case in central and northern European countries (Burholt et al., 2003, pp. 31–32; van Tilburg et al., 1998; Walker and Maltby, 1997, pp. 26–37). This might be explained by a weakening of the traditional 'amoral familism' of Mediterranean societies (Banfield, 1958) which, in times of renegotiation of inter-generational family relationships, makes it difficult for many older Italians, Greeks, Spaniards or Portuguese to change their 'familist' expectations, and rebalance 'disappointing' family ties through new meaningful non-kin relationships.

A second theme is the dynamic nature of personal relationships in later life. We have seen how the number and patterns of relationship in older people's social networks go on changing over time as does the nature of individual relationships, whether of friendship, kinship or partnership. In all these relationships as people age they are more likely to emphasise the caring and emotional closeness aspects, at the expense of other elements such as self-disclosure or shared activities.

A third theme is the *control* of older people over their relationships. Of course the factors over which they have no control (such as the death of partners or friends, the birth or non-birth of grandchildren, the divorce of children, their own physical ability to engage in social activities) have received a great deal of understandable attention, but beyond these older people are agents of their own relationships. They may become one of several different types of grandparent or sibling, they may be able to choose whether or not to live with their intimate partner (at least in northern Europe); they can pick new friends from among their local contacts and sever ties with others.

Finally we suggest several topics for future scrutiny or action. First is the continuing prevalence of age segregation in modern societies. Analysis of the age composition of personal social networks reveals widespread age segregation in later life, mainly related to the fact that few older people have regular contact with younger *non*-kin despite the evidence that newly contracted friendships in late old age appear to comprise more younger people (Jerrome and Wenger, 1999; Uhlenberg and de Jong Gierveld, 2004). This trend is a consequence of the age-segregating effects of both the education system and the labour market entry and exit mechanisms, structural expressions of the well-known phenomenon of the 'institutionalisation of the life-course' (Kohli, 1988). Older people who are still engaged in paid work or volunteering activities are more likely to have younger non-kin in their networks, thanks to the cross-age interaction stimulated by these activities, and a similar effect is reported for those who did not re-partner after divorce or widowhood, as well as for those living in a relatively young neighbourhood. With regard to this, the hindering effect of ageist attitudes and stereotypes in society for the formation of intergenerational non-kin relationships should not be underestimated (Giles *et al.*, 2003; Hummert *et al.*, 1994; Nelson 2002). Trends in this area need monitoring; it may be that as employment of older people becomes more flexible, as patterns of neighbouring, relationships with younger kin and community participation change, age segregation will lessen. But it is hard to say.

Second, we anticipate several areas where increased tensions are likely. We expect an increase of tensions in personal relationships around the key transitions in later life, such as retirement from paid employment. Retirement will become a more diverse and varied experience with less clear norms and patterns of behaviour and one which increasingly involves women equally with men. Even with traditional more rigid patterns of retirement this transition was a difficult one for people's personal relationships, especially friendship and marriage. This is likely to be exacerbated in the future. We expect that the blurring of boundaries between different kinds of relationship, such as those of friend or neighbour, friend or service provider, lover or partner, to cause tensions as the norms about these relationships remain unclear or are disputed, even though they also offer greater opportunities for integration of older people and the maintenance of a preferred sense of self.

A final aspect that should be considered is whether and how intervention programmes can be implemented to foster positive social relationships as a useful tool for helping people face the challenges arising in later life. Recent cross-national data from the European Study on Adult Well-being (ESAW) suggest that personal relationships are, besides material security and health, one of the main factors affecting well-being in older adults (Ferring *et al.*, 2003). As Hagestad (2002) puts it: 'Can we build social arenas, beyond the family, in which young and old build enough common understanding (and affection) that they can see beyond walkers, hearing aids, orange hair and piercing?' More generally, and not limiting the issue to inter-generational relationships, how is it possible to overcome communication difficulties, reaching shared relationships subjectively helpful in older age? The lack of meaningful personal relationships, also referred to as the 'risk of loneliness' or of social isolation, has been frequently associated, in older age, with conditions of (mainly female) widowhood, poor material security and (mainly male, but increasingly female too) post-retirement crisis. What is common to all these phenomena is their 'time'-related character, which suggests the need, at a micro, individual level, to have a flexible, dynamic approach to personal relationships but also, at a macro, institutional level, of adopting timely interventions able structurally to facilitate individuals in maintaining old relationships and building new ones. Recognition of the importance of the life-course and the subjective perspective may help towards developing a better, 'more civilised' conciliation between 'individualistic' and 'communitarian' styles of life, in terms of both opportunities for choice and for relationships between individuals within society.

CONCLUSIONS

It is often assumed that older people's habits and patterns of behaviour lag behind those of younger people and that they are slow to adapt to changing social circumstances. But as we look towards the uncertain future of personal relationships it is worth suggesting that older people may be in the vanguard here – with 'living apart together' or choosing lone living, and the increasing importance and flexibility of other kinds of friendly relationships – precisely because what deters change among younger people is the straitjacket of child-rearing and employment. Because they have lived longer, older people have longer experience of personal relationships than anyone else, and are thus more proficient at managing and even designing the living arrangements that suit them best.

FURTHER READING

Bornat, J., Dimmock B., Jones D & Peace, S. (1999) 'The Impact of Family Changes on Older People: The Case of Stepfamilies', *Ageing & Society*, Vol. 19, Part 2, March, pp. 239–410.

Davidson, K. (2001) Late life widowhood, selfishness and new partnership choices: a gendered perspective. *Ageing and Society* **21**, 297–317.

de Jong Gierveld, J. and Peeters, A.-M. (2003) The interweaving of re-partnered older adults' lives with their children and siblings. *Ageing and Society* **23**, 187–205.

Finch, J. and Mason, J. (1993) *Negotiating Family Responsibilities*. London: Routledge.

Jerrome, D. and Wenger, G. C. (1999) Stability and change in late-life friendships. *Ageing and Society* **19**, 661–676.

Phillipson, C., Bernard, M., Phillips, J. and Ogg, J. (2001) *The Family and Community Life of Older People*. London: Routledge.

10

Environment and ageing

Sheila Peace, Hans-Werner Wahl,
Heidrun Mollenkopf and Frank Oswald

INTRODUCTION

The types of environment in which older people live their lives form the context for continuing or maintaining activity, social interaction and developing personal identity. In relation to human ageing, the concept of 'environment' is therefore complex and may be seen as having physical/material, social/cultural and psychological dimensions.

- The *physical/material environment* includes the natural landscape, cultivated and open spaces, and the built environment, both domestic and non-domestic, developed over time.
- The *social environment* concerns the engagement of people to places – how spaces and places are used, organised and structured, from nations to neighbourhoods to homes displaying particular traditions and events within a particular culture.
- The *psychological environment* concerns the meaning of place, both current and across the life-course, and how it makes people feel about themselves.

Combinations of these environments make up ecological systems that can be seen as global, local or personal, or as macro, meso or micro (Bronfenbrenner, 1979; Lawton, 1980). In later life people will be affected at all these levels and their experiences and behaviours will reflect their own personal resources. A unique *social capital* based on cognitive and physical health, personality, individual relationships, social networks, education and financial resources will shape the person's well-being and morale. Understanding the relationship between environment and ageing can therefore range from global ageing to ageing in place.

Issues concerning the position of Europe within an ageing world were addressed in Chapter 1, so this chapter focuses on the relationship between person and environment (P–E) at the level of community, neighbourhood and accommodation (often equated with 'home'). This is a topic that utilises gerontological literature drawn from the fields of psychology, geography, anthropology, sociology, architectural design, engineering and health studies. It is also a topic guided by on-going theoretical development.

THEORETICAL PERSPECTIVES

Historical influences

From its inception, environmental gerontology has emphasised the theoretical understanding of person–environment relations as people age. For recent overviews see Oswald *et al.* (2006), Scheidt and Windley (1998, 2006), Wahl (2001) and Wahl and Weisman (2003). This is important because there is a tendency in scholarly work to 'de-contexualise' human ageing from the environment, the day-to-day surroundings in which a person's growing older really takes place. Environmental gerontology has focused particularly on the physical/material and spatial component of the context of ageing, while acknowledging that there are close links between physical, social, psychological and cultural environments. The 'Gestalt switch' from ageing persons to ageing person–environment systems has not occurred accidentally; it has taken a number of theoretical avenues and there is still a need to continue to develop and refine existing conceptualisations. That said, we begin by considering the historical roots of environmental gerontology, including a discussion and critique of currently well-accepted theoretical approaches, returning to suggestions for future theoretical development later in the chapter (Figure 10.1).

The 'birth' of environmental gerontology has been linked to the eminently readable contribution by Kleemeier (1959). However, this work was influenced by a range of earlier authors from sociological and ecological traditions, including the Chicago School of Urban Sociology in the 1920s and 1930s (Park *et al.*, 1925). Built environments such as run-down urban districts were regarded for the first time on an explicit level as having a negative impact on health and welfare. The theoretical writings of German psychologist Lewin in the 1930s and 1940s (see Lewin, 1951, for an overview) – which promoted the view that behaviour should be regarded as a function of the person *and* the environment – influenced contextual thinking in the behavioural and social sciences. At about the same time, Murray (1938), an American researcher of personality, introduced the term 'press' as an indication of how personal growth may be affected both objectively and subjectively by the context in which a person is situated. In

```
┌─────────────────────────────────────────────────────┐
│         Major historical influences on theories of   │
│          person–environment relations in old age     │
├─────────────────────────────────────────────────────┤
│                                                       │
│  • Chicago School of Urban Sociology/Human Ecology    │
│                                                       │
│  • Lewin's field theory                               │
│                                                       │
│  • Murray's environmental press model                 │
│                                                       │
│  • Learning theories                                  │
│                                                       │
│  • Evolution of social gerontology within gerontology │
│                                                       │
│  • Evolution of environmental psychology              │
│                                                       │
└─────────────────────────────────────────────────────┘
                           ↓
┌─────────────────────────────────────────────────────┐
│          Major person-environment theoretical        │
│      approaches in current environmental gerontology  │
├─────────────────────────────────────────────────────┤
│                                                       │
│  • Press–competence model/Environmental docility and  │
│    proactivity hypothesis                             │
│                                                       │
│  • Person–Environment fit model                       │
│                                                       │
│  • Social ecology concepts/Dependence–support script  │
│                                                       │
│  • Person–environment stress model not environment    │
│                                                       │
│  • Place attachment concepts/Place insideness         │
│                                                       │
│  • Place theory – dementia concepts                   │
│                                                       │
│  • Relocation concepts/Relocation trauma hypothesis   │
│                                                       │
└─────────────────────────────────────────────────────┘
                           ↓
┌─────────────────────────────────────────────────────┐
│              Critique and Future challenges           │
├─────────────────────────────────────────────────────┤
│                                                       │
│  • Better integration of environmental docility and   │
│    proactivity                                        │
│                                                       │
│  • Better integration of the micro and macro level of │
│    analysis                                           │
│                                                       │
│  • Better integration of temporality                  │
│                                                       │
│  • Better integration of physical and social environment │
│                                                       │
│  • Better integration of ongoing cohort dynamics      │
│                                                       │
└─────────────────────────────────────────────────────┘
```

Figure 10.1   Historical influences on theory development in environmental gerontology

addition, prominent learning theories in psychology and education during the 1950s and 1960s attributed much to the influence of environment in all stages of human development, and this proved an important stimulus for environmental perspectives in gerontology (see Baltes, 1996, for a review). In its most radical version, the message of learning theories applied to ageing is that it is not chrono-logical age per se but constraining environments that can be non-reinforcing or helplessness-provoking that lead to age-related loss in physical and mental functioning (Seligman, 1975).

The second half of the twentieth century saw these earlier developments over-shadowed by the impact of the social sciences within gerontology. Alongside the traditionally strong consideration of biology and medical conditions, social influences such as the role of economic circumstances, family and social sur-roundings, as well as housing and neighbourhood quality, became acknowledged as factors able to shape ageing. Finally, the emergence of environmental psy-chology in the 1960s and 1970s provided another set of roots for environmental gerontology. Old age became an attractive area for early work in this field (Pastalan and Carson, 1970) due to the assumed vulnerability of the ageing organism to environmental demands as well as the existence of specially designed environments for ageing people such as long-term care institutions. Such research influenced the development of ecological theories of ageing later in the twentieth century.

Ecological perspectives

The press–competence (PC) model
In Figure 10.1, the central box provides a synopsis of the major person–environment theoretical developments in environmental gerontology, a field that has been dom-inated by North American researchers. In the press–competence model suggested by Lawton and Nahemow (1973) with direct referral to Murray (1938) and Lewin (1951), there is a major assumption that the lowered competence of the older per-son in conjunction with strong 'environmental press' negatively impacts on behav-iour and well-being (Figure 10.2). In earlier conceptual and empirical work, the term 'environmental docility hypothesis' was coined to address this basic mecha-nism in person–environment relations (Lawton and Simon, 1968). Lawton and Simon revealed how the patterns of social interaction of older people in institu-tional settings depended on physical distances, with greater distances more strongly undermining social relations – thus pointing to the 'environmental docil-ity' of the older organism.

The press–competence model has been criticised for promoting a one-sided image of older people as 'pawns' of their environmental circumstances. In the 1980s, Lawton introduced the concepts of *proactivity* and *environmental rich-ness* (Lawton, 1985, 1998) in order to address this criticism.

The press–competence model takes quite a general approach in defining both 'competence' and 'environmental press'. For example, 'competence' could relate to sensory loss, loss in physical mobility, or cognitive decline; and 'environmen-tal press' could relate to low housing standard, bad neighbourhood conditions, or underdeveloped public transport. Also, 'behaviour' can mean basic activities of everyday living (such as dressing or washing) or leisure involvement; while

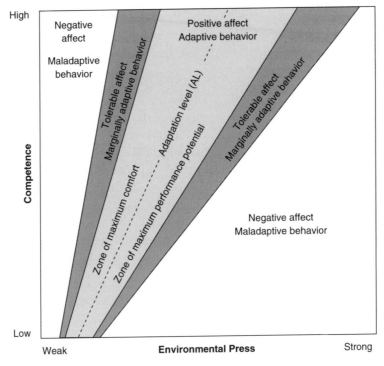

Figure 10.2 Ecological/Press–competence model

Source: Lawton and Nahemow (1973)

'well-being' covers positive and negative affect as well as cognitive evaluations such as satisfaction with life. The most central theoretical consequence of the PC model is that there exists for each ageing person an optimal combination of available competence and given environmental circumstances leading to the highest possible behavioural and emotional functioning for this person conceptualised by the adaptation level (Figure 10.2). Much empirical work in environmental gerontology, as well as practical work in terms of housing adaptation and designing institutions for the aged, directly or indirectly adheres to the PC model (Peace and Holland, 2001a; Scheidt and Windley, 2003; Wahl *et al.*, 2003).

However, while acknowledging the importance of environment, it should be noted that the model recognises the complexity of interaction beyond environmental determinism. There is also recognition that in different circumstances levels of environmental press can be seen as positive, as well as negative, being stimulating and promoting engagement (Weisman, 2003).

The person–environment fit (PEF) model

Complexity is also noted in the person–environment fit model, a parallel development that has strongly underlined the role of motivation and personal needs rather than competence within person–environment processes. The basic assumption is that there is a mismatch between personal needs and environmental options, leading to lowered behavioural functioning and well-being. Empirical support for this assumption has emerged from studies conducted in institutional settings (Kahana, 1982).

Carp and Carp (1984) suggested further differentiation for the PEF model in distinguishing between older people's basic and higher-order needs in relation to the potential and limits of a given environment. Here 'basic needs' are conceptualised in a similar way to 'competence' outlined above (for instance, facilitating sensory and walking ability), whereas 'higher-order needs' may relate to issues such as privacy and affiliation which facilitate greater self-actualisation – reflecting Maslow's (1964) model of human needs. According to the Carp and Carp extension of the PEF model, different outcomes of misfit in both of these domains are to be expected. While person–environment misfit in the basic needs domain will predominantly result in reduced behavioural autonomy, misfit in the higher-order realm will predominantly undermine emotional well-being and mental health.

Social ecology (SE) concepts and the person–environment stress (PS) model

The third theoretical perspective outlined here can be defined as *social ecology* (SE) concepts which assume close links between physical surroundings and the social behaviours of persons acting within these settings (Moos and Lemke, 1985). The study of institutional settings has also formed an ideal arena for applying the learning theory perspective to ageing within social ecology thinking, the assumption being that staff will have different reactions to residents' antecedent behaviours, leading to different outcomes.

The empirical application of this model has produced profound insights into the role of the social environment for dependent behaviour in old age by repeatedly identifying robust interaction patterns characterised as a 'dependence–support' script (Willcocks *et al.*, 1987; Baltes, 1996). According to this interaction script, staff tend to overly support dependent behaviours of residents, while independent behaviours are mostly overlooked. There are direct links here to Goffman's work on institutionalisation and the development of 'batch-living' (Goffman, 1961).

The interrelationship of all of these theoretical developments is apparent, nurtured by research that has been dominated by studies within age-segregated institutional settings. The person–environment stress (PS) model argues that environmental conditions, such as a lack of privacy or control due to the built or organisational environment specifically in institutions for the aged, should be regarded as stress-evoking (Schooler, 1982). How people cope with stress-inducing environments will vary. For instance, some ageing individuals may feel psychological threat, apathy or indifference when faced with similar 'environmental press', rather than the satisfaction of facing such a challenge. Where older people have experienced negative psychological reactions, supportive interventions such as the systematic enhancement of control in institutional settings may enable them to achieve an optimal level of behavioural and emotional functioning (Langer and Rodin, 1976; Rodin and Langer, 1977). However, as already mentioned, institutional control may devalue personal autonomy. Environmental gerontologists work with these issues both theoretically and practically. For example, in Britain, a national study of residential care homes in the early 1980s (Willcocks *et al.*, 1987) suggested the development of 'residential flatlets' that had potential for enhanced levels of privacy and autonomy for older people. This design and organisational innovation foreshadowed developments in both care homes and extra care housing (Netten, 2005; Parker *et al.*, 2004).

Place attachment

In contrast to the foregoing approaches that focus mainly on the role of the objective environment, research concerned with the concept of place attachment addresses the gamut of processes operating when ageing individuals form affective, cognitive and behavioural ties to their physical surroundings (Gurney and Means, 1993; Peace *et al.*, 2006; Oswald and Wahl, 2005; Rubinstein and Parmelee, 1992). Attachment to place may be reflected in the strength of such bonding, as well as in different meanings associated with places such as the home environment or specific landscapes.

One approach suggested by Rowles (1978, 1983) has focused on what he calls the many faces of *insideness of place* in old age. Whereas *social insideness* arises from everyday social exchange over long periods, *physical insideness* is characterised by familiarities and routines within given settings such as the home environment, such that the individual is able 'to wear the setting like a glove' (Rowles, 1983, p. 114). He labels the third element of place attachment as *autobiographical insideness* in that 'place becomes a landscape of memories, providing a sense of identity' (p. 114). Rubinstein (1989) focused on the more immediate environment of the home, developing a complimentary model of psycho-social processes linking person to place. According to his terminology, *social-centred processes* include social norms and relationships to other people, *person-centred processes* concern the expressions of one's life-course in features of the environment, and *body-centred processes* include the 'ongoing relationship of the body to the environmental features that surround it' (Rubinstein, 1989, p. 47).

Place theory and dementia concepts

The body of knowledge is always evolving and within environmental gerontology researchers are conscious of the changing characteristics and circumstances of older people within an ageing world. Gerontologists, particularly those living within developed nations, are concerned for those living with cognitive impairment, and the prevalence of dementing illnesses has increased from the late twentieth century. Consequently, 'place theory and dementia concepts' refers to the theoretical and practical challenge of providing good environments for older people with dementia, which optimise the person–environment interchange processes characteristic of this very specific human condition (Lawton, 2001). This work is driven not least by the hope that environmental design and re-design can make a difference for older people, even when major personal resources such as cognitive capacity are exhausted. Weisman's (1997, 2003) 'model of place' has received due recognition in this regard, and a cornerstone of this concept is its reference to environmental attributes important to secure the life quality of older people with dementia living in institutional settings. Numerous such environmental attributes have been suggested, covering the whole range from basic safety to stimulation, privacy and personal control (Marshall, 2001; Regnier and Pynoos, 1992; Weisman et al., 1996).

Relocation of older people

Finally, there has been a longstanding debate within environmental gerontology concerning residential decisions across the life-course. Early research in the 1960s and 1970s was mainly driven by the 'relocation trauma hypothesis' in which negative health effects of relocation from home to an institutionalised setting were stressed (Coffmann, 1981). The empirical evidence was controversial, however, and was plagued by methodological problems such as selectivity of study samples towards the more frail, and missing control groups. Focusing on later life, Litwak and Longino's (1987) distinction between first, second and third moves relied on the assumption of a substantial association between chronological age and the type of move and the motivation for it. Whereas first moves often take place early in the ageing process (close to retirement), and are usually prompted by the amenities associated with the desired place of residence, second moves (roughly appearing in the person's seventies or early eighties) are predominantly characterised by moving back to the place of origin, reflecting a higher need for support and proximity to kinship. Third moves often are to institutions in very old age (Oswald and Rowles, 2006).

Other ways of looking at relocation processes and their differential outcomes concern available coping resources (Golant, 1998) and the distinction between basic and higher-order needs (Carp and Carp, 1984) as motivations for moving (Oswald et al., 2002); while detailed housing histories (Holland, 2001; Peace et al., 2006) have also extended knowledge of the complexity of moving and 'staying put', showing stability and change across the life-course and identifying older people in the UK as migrants, movers and locals. To these debates there is a need to add more recent discussion of cross-national migration, both permanent and seasonal, and to reconsider 'relocation trauma' in the light of the position faced by the diversity of older migrants, whom as Warnes et al. (2004) have indicated (see Chapter 1) range from those who are deprived and socially excluded to those with wide personal resources but where all are currently disadvantaged through ageing as migrants.

Final remarks

In sum, pluralism seems to be essential to theorising within environmental gerontology (Wahl and Weisman, 2003). However, this should not be seen as a disadvantage or as an indication of weakness in the field. Instead, the complexity of person–environment relations in later life probably demands a diversity of perspectives and a level of methodological complexity which all contribute to a greater understanding of how environments impact on the course and outcomes of normal and frail ageing – contextualising ageing.

RESEARCHING PERSON–ENVIRONMENT INTERACTIONS

The relationship between context and individual behaviour offers a wide spectrum of situations for examination, and yet within the range of research that has underpinned this thinking certain settings and locations have been dominant whilst others are under-researched. Perhaps unsurprisingly much research has focused on interactions within specialised accommodation for frail older people.

During the second half of the twentieth century the development of age-segregated institutional and residential settings providing both housing and long-term care was of special interest to policymakers, providers and regulators in North America and Europe concerned with quality of care, capacity and finance. Consequently, for many years issues concerning these planned *micro environments* have overshadowed not only a wider interest in the general housing stock accommodating the majority of people in later life but also their engagement with and attachment to age-integrated communities – diverse *macro environments* in terms of urbanity, rurality and levels of amenity and deprivation.

Over the past decade, interest in the contextualisation of ageing has expanded and the need for methodological diversity and innovation (see Chapter 5) sits alongside the need for theoretical pluralism. Before moving on to consider what is known about the relationship between environment and ageing, comment is needed on the methods that underpin P–E interaction. Our first example comes from the study of planned environments for older people. As outlined above, Moos, Lemke and colleagues advanced their understanding of social ecology through research in residential facilities for older people. Their studies resulted in the development of a detailed assessment instrument – the Multiphasic Environmental Assessment Procedure (MEAP) – for evaluating the physical, social and organisational components of institutional environments. This has been tested and re-tested (Moos and Lemke, 1984, 1992, 1996). The MEAP is a well-used example of an instrument whose purpose is to unpack the dynamics of an organisation and measure the overall quality of a facility. They describe the MEAP as follows (Moos and Lemke, 1996, p. 1):

> [The MEAP] is a five-part procedure for evaluating the physical and social environments in residential settings for older adults. We designed the procedure to assess nursing homes, residential care facilities, and congregate apartments. The MEAP is designed to be used by qualified clinicians, consultants, program evaluators, and researchers to help them to describe and compare facilities, monitor program outcomes, and compare existing facilities with people's preferences.

The MEAP is based on a conceptual framework which combines objective data on environmental factors and personal factors relating to residents to consider how they may influence the social climate of the setting and how older people cope and adapt. The researchers use five instruments to measure different aspects of the model. For example, the Sheltered Care Environment Scale (SCES) considers *social climate*, which involves interviews with residents and staff, direct observation, and analysis of written documents leading primarily to statistical analysis.

In contrast, researchers interested in issues concerning *place attachment* or the relationship between environment and identity have developed in-depth qualitative methods focusing on the lives of particular individuals (e.g. Rowles, 1978; Rowles and Watkins, 2003; Rubinstein, 1989). Ethnographic methods (see Chapter 5) using observation and in-depth interviews have captured greater detail concerning social interaction, personal motivation and meaning within particular contexts, and this has evolved to include a greater level of participatory research by older people (Peace *et al.*, 2006). A greater understanding of the complexity of environmental context has also led researchers to become involved in multidisciplinary and cross-national studies where social gerontologists join with architects, engineers and IT specialists to bring the physical and social sciences together in order to develop instruments on both objective and perceived components of housing in later life, such as environmental barriers, housing accessibility and usability, and housing-related control beliefs (Hanson *et al.*, 2001; Iwarsson *et al.*, 2004; McCreadie and Tinker, 2005; Oswald *et al.*, 2003).

Within the following review the relationship between people and place is looked at, first in terms of living arrangements and accommodation, and second in terms of wider aspects of community living. The physical/material and social environments are discussed alongside each other and evidence is presented predominantly through survey research with some mixed-method studies using in-depth case material. Finally, examination of the psychological environment considers how the contextualisation of ageing is recognised within personal identity through attachment to and meaning of place.

ACCOMMODATING LATER LIFE

Living arrangements

Chapter 1 outlined the dynamics of the ageing population in Europe, reflecting on feminisation, diversity through migration, and the impact on urban and rural living, whilst Chapter 9 considered the changing nature of personal relations and the effects upon living arrangements. Such issues are of crucial importance to environmental gerontology. As noted, life expectancy for women and men varies across countries, but to date the consequences are similar: while a majority of older men are still married, older women are more often widowed and many more women than men form single-person households.

However, there is variation between countries in the proportion of older women and men living alone or with others. Using the classification of European countries outlined in Chapter 6, where distinction is made between Nordic, Continental and southern European countries, plus UK and Ireland, analysis of the European Community Household Panel survey 1994/95 shows that older men and women are more likely to live with a child (with or without their partner) in southern Europe than those living in Nordic or Continental countries where they tend to live with either their partner or alone – which is especially true of very old women (Iacovou, 2000). These arrangements are reflected in the patterns of informal care. Interestingly, those older people living with other adults, who may be relatives, but not partners or children, are most common in countries such as Ireland, and Iacovou comments that this reflects the number of people, especially men, who never married because they were waiting to inherit agricultural land on their father's death. These trends in living arrangements are confirmed by more recent EU statistics (European Commission, 2002, p. 127) as well as the EU-funded MOBILATE study in Finland, Germany, Hungary, Italy and the Netherlands (Mollenkopf *et al.*, 2005) where rural/urban differences were also identified with regard to multi-generational households and the proportion of older people living alone.

Housing history

Living arrangements reflect housing histories, and for older people the characteristics of the dwelling place and the area lived in are important prerequisites for autonomous living and well-being (Evans *et al.*, 2002). In later life a majority of older Europeans live in mainstream housing, with a proportion of those aged over 80 being most likely to move into age-related housing combining accommodation with a more supportive care environment. Design, accessibility and facilities within the home have all been identified as important factors determining quality of life – a part of the person–environment fit. However, in some European countries, housing tenure – whether owner-occupied (private housing) or rented (public/social housing) – has also been seen as an indicator of socio-economic status impacting on and reflected in the material environment, lifestyle and even mortality rates among older people (Huisman *et al.*, 2004).

Wider societal issues can impact upon individual decision-making regarding place of living and accommodation. In the UK, enormous changes in political ideology concerning housing tenure occurred in the last quarter of the twentieth century with particular consequences for the older generation, as the following comments from Peace and Holland (2001b, p. 9) show:

> [In] 1983, people aged over 60 and living alone were most likely to be in local authority housing. But, by 1997, following the general expansion of home ownership and the Right to Buy policies of the 1980s, they were most likely to be owner-occupiers (Forrest and Leather, 1998; Statsbase, 2000), with older couples more likely to own their own home than single people.

It is estimated that over three-quarters of British older people will be owner-occupiers by 2010 (DETR DoH, 2001). Home ownership can be seen as a capital asset, at least in those countries where rented apartments are not the general norm, but some people can become 'housing rich and income poor' (DETR, 2000) needing to find ways of releasing capital for maintenance and overhead costs in order to 'stay put'. Of course where property represents a form of capital it can also be used to fund a move to a different form of age-related housing or long-term care (Marcellini et al., 2005; Peace and Holland, 2001a).

However, some older people may deliberately make the decision to move from being an owner to being a tenant, which can affect housing-related responsibilities. This will also be the case in countries or regions, where ownership is culturally a less important factor. For instance, most people in Germany are not owners but live in privately rented accommodation (Scharf, 1998). Generally, rented houses or flats are more frequent in urban than in rural areas where there may be more house ownership, traditionally seen as a feature of agricultural society (Mollenkopf et al., 2004). Here we see how structural issues affecting decision-making during the life-course affect person–environment interaction.

Accommodation: domestic and special

The historical development of housing policy in every country impacts upon the subsequent housing infrastructure. Research shows that older Hungarians living in rural areas and older Italians, both urban and rural, are less well provided with basic housing amenities such as an inside toilet, bathroom or shower, and central heating, than their Finnish, Dutch and German contemporaries (Mollenkopf et al., 2004). However, in Germany, although significant improvements have undoubtedly taken place since reunification in 1990, some differences in housing quality have remained to the disadvantage of older people in the eastern rural regions; conversely, living arrangements in urban regions have achieved some level of parity (Mollenkopf and Kaspar, 2005).

Findings from the ENABLE-AGE Study demonstrate the great variation between countries in terms of their welfare systems and the integration of housing, healthcare and social care. In Sweden, the needs of older people and people with disabilities are recognised in universal policy, with building legislation prescribing housing that is accessible and usable. In Latvia, a welfare regime in transformation, a building programme is under way but the regime is slow to recognise the needs of older people beyond the improvement of social institutions. This research indicates the range of factors underpinning P–E interaction both cultural and societal, such as:

- the considerable east–west differences in housing investment
- the expertise in occupational therapy that exists in countries such as Sweden and to a lesser degree the UK, which can be used to manage housing adaptation
- the need to understand environmental barriers to accessibility both inside and outside the home in light of a person's functional limitations
- how housing is fundamental to the physical, social and psychological well-being of older people (Iwarsson et al., 2004).

Table 10.1   Overall space and allocation for daily living across a range of dwelling types, UK, 2001.

Housing type	Floor area (square metres)					
	Total	Habitable	Cooking	Bathing	Circulation	Storage
Terraced	82.20	51.38	9.50	4.89	12.52	3.91
Semi-detached	101.19	67.51	12.16	4.11	12.48	2.53
Bungalows (private)	74.22	44.82	10.83	4.24	6.13	6.40
Bungalows (sheltered)	38.86	23.02	7.59	3.30	3.86	1.10
Purpose-built low-rise flats	50.51	34.32	5.89	3.44	5.76	1.11
Sheltered flats	48.06	30.14	6.63	3.83	4.90	3.24
Converted flats	72.13	43.19	10.22	5.73	9.91	3.08
Nurs./resid. homes	16.61	15.18	-	1.42	0.00	0.00

Data are taken from the 60 household properties taking part in the EPSRC funded study 'From domesticity to care'.
Source: Adapted from Kellaher (2002, pp. 48–49).

The age of the housing stock can give a crude guide to the likelihood of physical deterioration and deficient amenities. In general, British housing stock is older than that of France and Germany; for example, data from 1998 show that 21% of the total housing stock in England at that time had been built before 1919 and a further 19% pre-dated 1944 (DETR, 1998a). However, the development of housing infrastructure is also reflected in the spatiality of housing/accommodation type having a direct impact on liveability, accessibility and visitability. By profiling the housing of older people in England through analysis of house plans, Hanson *et al.* (2001) have produced a measure of self-containment and a breakdown of space standards for the main activities of the home. The study shows that space declines within more recent designs, with the sharpest decrease being in purpose-built housing for older people within the social rented sector. In contrast, private sector space in bungalows and retirement flats is a third greater than in corresponding social accommodation (Kellaher, 2002). As Table.10.1 shows, space in mainstream housing is more highly differentiated than in age-related housing, which can affect behaviour and interaction; and on considering the needs of older people for housing, support and care, the researchers show how in practice not all homes are capable of facilitating variations in individual needs through adaptation.

Hanson *et al.* (2001) and the ENABLE-AGE study (Iwarsson *et al.*, 2005) show greater understanding of housing architecture and human experience through multidisciplinary research that provides important evidence of the way in which design can impact upon well-being – bringing a new dimension to both the press–competence model and the person–environment fit model. Findings from the ENABLE-AGE project on housing in very old age show that it is not the mere number of barriers but the individual housing accessibility that is related to outcomes of daily autonomy and well-being in different regions and settings. Such profiling also foregrounds the spatial reality of the material environment in which many older people will age in place, and is of value to those working to develop accessible housing and lifetime homes.

The development of assisted living environments that are age-related also varies between countries. (Assisted living environments involve accommodation plus care and include a diversity of settings such as: sheltered housing, very sheltered housing, extra care housing, residential care homes, care homes, nursing homes, and retirement communities.) In 1996, the OECD reported that the average figure for people aged over 65 living in residential care settings was less than 4.5% for Italy, Portugal, Spain and Greece; 4.5–5.4% for Austria, Belgium, France, Germany , Ireland and the UK; 5.5–6.4% for Denmark; and 9% for the Netherlands (OECD, 1996). While this variation will relate to cultural differences concerning the development of care between nuclear and extended families and the state, in all countries a percentage of very old and vulnerable people will move into housing with care and this is especially true for people with dementia and at the end of life.

These trends are seen in findings from the 1999 Eurobarometer Survey where people were posed the question:

> Some say that older people needing personal care should go into residential/nursing homes. [Others] say that the social services should help them to remain in their own homes for as long as possible. Which comes closest to your opinion?

Just under 90% of respondents felt that older people should be enabled to remain in their own homes, with the only countries where almost a quarter chose the residential care option being Denmark (23%) and Portugal (24%). Yet views concerning accommodation and care remained confused. For, whilst 'staying put' was seen as a primary goal for older people, the demand and need for assisted living was recognised by kin who may be able to offer only 'intimacy at a distance'. Consequently, in 11 out of 15 states involved in the survey at least a third of respondents saw co-residence as a response to the frailty of one of their parents (Walker, 1999a). Decisions over long-term care remain ambiguous.

Views on communal assisted living will develop during the twenty-first century as different forms of accommodation and care – retirement communities, co-housing, home-sharing – become available and acceptable in Europe. For example, at the turn of the century in the UK just 10% of people of pensionable age lived in accommodation such as sheltered housing, residential care homes and nursing homes; and this included approximately 25% of those aged over 85 years, predominantly women, living in residential care and nursing homes (Peace and Holland, 2001a). To add to this picture, the latest development in the UK is extra-care housing: one- or two-bedroomed apartments or houses with communal facilities such as restaurants and leisure services plus staff on site to provide up to 24-hour care as necessary. In some cases 'close care' may offer nursing home care on site. Only recently has evaluation begun to consider whether enhanced housing – with many units designed to lifetime home standards and access to additional services – may facilitate ageing in place for more vulnerable people (Netten, 2005).

These innovations in housing and care are indicative of the greater emphasis now being placed on developing person and relationship-centred care within what can be seen as institutional environments. Attention is now being paid to improving environmental quality in care institutions not only through the design of settings but also through the choice of activities and range of supportive services, leading to on-going debates concerning the funding of long-term care and the views of older people on the development of age-segregated retirement communities (Croucher, 2006; Wanless, 2006). Moreover, there are plans towards the development of a European standardisation of types of sheltered housing ('Betreutes Wohnen') based on the German, Swedish and other national norms, in order to provide better transparency and comparability for people who are interested in these types of service and housing across Europe.

For some older people, however, their changing levels of cognitive function may lead to enhanced environmental press which needs to be considered in the development of new forms of accommodation. A recent study in the UK (O'Malley and Croucher, 2005) shows that, given the predicted increase in morbidity through dementia within the next 50 years, attention needs to be paid to the very issues of where people should live, with whom and issues of press–competence within the environment. At present they estimate that between 20% and 45% of people with dementia are cared for in special or collective settings such as residential care or nursing homes, and that supported care in more segregated settings is more frequent. In these age-related settings, research is commonly concerned with issues of de-institutionalisation and developing best care practice.

Yet the experience of accommodation and care for people with dementia continues to be debated. As Cox (1998. p. 10) comments:

> People with dementia may sustain many of their strengths and abilities as well as their independence, if they have the right kind of physical environment, the right kind of social support and a daily pattern of living which supports their preferred lifestyle and a daily pattern of potential.

This environment could be their own home in the community, and research is focusing on enabling people to 'stay put' by adapting the environment and eliminating hazards through OT-based modification (Marshall, 2001). In contrast, the potential of sheltered housing may not have been fully explored (Cantley, 2001), and some commentators argue that very sheltered/extra-care housing may be most suitable for people with mild dementia or those who have developed this condition whilst ageing in place (Appleton and Porteous, 2003).

In both collective settings and 'ordinary' housing, innovation in design for people with dementia is under way (Clatworthy and Bjorneby, 1997). As Marshall (2001, p. 129) notes, such research has to understand a range of commonly experienced disabilities including: 'impaired memory; impaired learning; impaired reasoning; increasing dependence on the senses; and high levels of stress', all of which she feels can be compensated for through modifying the built environment.

This can be seen as a developing area within environmental gerontology where the press–competence model can be tested; and athough this is a specialist area the developing field of assistive technology has wider implications for exploring person–environment fit (Lawton, 2001).

TECHNOLOGICAL APPLICATIONS

The impact of technology is growing – household technology, communications technologies and rehabilitation aids can all affect the residential infrastructure. Whether older people's daily lives are facilitated or complicated by these technologies depends on the design, ease of handling, proliferation, and the acceptability and accessibility of these products and systems (Mollenkopf, 2003). *Gerontechnology*, a new scientific discipline established in the 1990s, addresses the broad scope of issues related to technology and ageing (Charness *et al.*, 2001; Fisk, 2001). Among the major features of this approach is its focus on the daily life domains of older people, rather than exclusively on illness and chronic conditions, as was the case with more traditional rehabilitation and assistive technology approaches (Buhler and Knops, 1999; Ramian, 1987).

Research in this field has long been focused on the problem-solving capacities of technology – on the design of technical products and interfaces, and on human–machine interactions (Charness and Bosman, 1990; Coleman, 1998; Smith *et al.*, 1999). In light of demographic change and the needs of the most vulnerable, the development and use of technical aids is being studied primarily with an eye to reducing costs by giving outpatient care rather than hospitalising the individual, and by facilitating the care of people with cognitive impairment. In the domestic environment, the application of technical products can make dealing with tiresome tasks easier and help older people run their homes independently, or alongside additional support (Czaja, 1997). The networking of previously isolated devices and systems into an 'intelligent house' or 'smart home' could also be of benefit in terms of ecology and economy, comfort and safety (Cooper and Ferreira, 1998; Fisk, 2001; van Berlo, 2002).

A recent consumer survey focusing on attitudes and preferences regarding smart technologies showed that people aged 53–83 years tend to expect more from this kind of technology than do younger people – a rather surprising finding. Older people imagine that the 'smart home' will simplify their lives, will improve and expand their access to information and communication resources, and make their home environment more fun. These expectations could be the result of a greater need for such assistance, but might also arise from relative inexperience with modern information technology – a situation that might change with future cohorts of older people (Meyer and Mollenkopf, 2003).

Until now, older people's access to domestic appliances and modern information and communication technologies (ICT) has depended strongly on aspects of *social structure* as well as on *individual attitudes* and *lifelong habits*. This has been confirmed in a German study which identified age, household composition, income and parenthood as important factors in relation to negative attitudes towards technology (Mollenkopf *et al.* 2000). In the domain of ICT, a high level of education and experience with technology turned out to be significant positive predictors. Gender was also a strong predictor with respect to household appliances, but had no impact on the equipment and use of information and communications technologies (Mollenkopf and Kaspar, 2002). Similar findings are reported by Selwyn *et al.* (2003) with respect to ICT access and use in the everyday lives of older adults in the West of England and South Wales. On the one hand, these findings suggest that the growing pace of technological developments may well create new social inequalities between the 'haves' and the 'have nots'. On the other hand, technological innovations are experienced by individual age generations at different stages of life and accepted in different ways (Docampo Rama *et al.*, 2001; Sackmann, 1996). To ensure that older people can use technology's positive opportunities for the preservation of independence, mobility and social participation, as well as for support in need of care, it will be crucial not only to improve design, but for developers, suppliers and promoters to consider older people's resources, competencies, interests and needs (Mollenkopf and Fozard, 2003). An understanding of factors affecting the complexity of P–E interaction (routines, space, technology) with implications for maintaining engagement and adapting lifestyles to support individual mastery is developing rapidly.

COMMUNITY LIVING

From the growing development of technology that may change aspects of future accommodation, we turn to the impact of the wider community in terms of environmental well-being. Peace *et al.* (2006) have recognised that research concerning ageing in place has to address a 'layered environment'. While biological aspects of human ageing may lead to spatial restriction and a lifestyle centred on the home, personal autonomy in a broad sense is connected to the structures, facilities and opportunities allowing the individual to engage beyond the self. For this reason, engagement with the residential area around the dwelling, the natural environment (park, garden or yard), the availability of transport, the presence of services, characteristics of the resident population, and aspects of security and safety within an area are all factors that may affect an individual's well-being. Before moving on to consider environmental meaning, consideration is given to research that identifies wider issues relating to the urban/rural nature of place, the impact of deprivation on engagement and well-being, and the importance of transport and mobility within studies of environment and ageing.

In the British ethnography *Environment and Identity in Later Life*, the researchers worked with 54 older people in three locations seen as metropolitan, urban and semi-rural (Peace *et al.*, 2006). They identified particular aspects of location as central to person–environment fit at the level of the community or neighbourhood, including the convenience and activities of the town, the loss of public transport and amenities in rural areas, the litter and 'dirt' associated with the physical environment in the city, and the high density of housing versus the intimacy of 'village life' – all based on comments through which people developed their own environmental biography (see also Rowles and Watkins, 2003).

These views have resonance with survey findings from the MOBILATE project, outlined earlier, based on urban and rural areas in Germany, Italy, the Netherlands, Hungary and Finland. While most older people interviewed had access to fundamental services such as a food store, doctor, pharmacy, bank, post office, bus or tram stop etc., the western German city had the greatest number of services (9 out of 11) that could be reached within 15 minutes by more than 80% of the interviewees (aged between 55 and 79 years). In contrast, the availability of services in rural areas decreased sharply, with essential services such as food stores, pharmacies and doctors proving most difficult to access particularly in rural areas of Hungary, eastern Germany and Finland (Mollenkopf et al., 2005). The study shows that for older people looking after their basic needs – food, health and savings – is essential. Interestingly, the presence of a bus or tram stop, whilst a service common in all areas, was seen as less important, perhaps indicating both the importance of using independent, private transport and the immediate proximity of services. Indeed, distance to services was a major deterrent across the study and locations within the Netherlands proved most accessible.

Mobility, transport and traffic

Despite the importance of accessible locations, research has revealed the importance of transport in facilitating community participation. Public or private means of transportation can compensate for physical decline and to a certain degree help to bridge distances. Several studies have shown that outdoor mobility decreases with advancing age, but that those who are able to use a car clearly perform more trips than persons who cannot (Hakamies-Blomquistm and Wahlstrom, 1998; Marottoli et al., 1993). Indeed, people owning and driving a car themselves show a significantly higher satisfaction with their possibilities to get around even if they are physically impaired (Mollenkopf et al., 2002). Consequently, whilst transport studies have their own history, within studies of environment and ageing, transport and personal mobility need to be incorporated in discussions of environmental press.

Whether public transport is used depends greatly on location and the quality of service. Unfortunately, the preconditions for mobility do not hold fully for all older European citizens. In rural areas, there are generally less public transport modes available than in urban areas. In the UK, for instance, Tinker (2002) reports that 75% of rural areas have no daily bus service. It is true that older people participating in the comparative European MOBILATE study generally expressed high satisfaction with mobility-related aspects such as leisure activities, accessibility of services and facilities, public transport, travelling, or overall mobility. However, there were clear differences between subgroups and between urban and rural areas. In Italy and western Germany, public transport in the country was evaluated particularly negatively, and in eastern Germany, both urban and rural elders bemoaned the lack of services and facilities. These evaluations clearly indicate a discrepancy between what people want or need and what is available to them (Mollenkopf et al., 2005).

While the possession of a driver's licence and a private motor vehicle by older European citizens is still strongly age- and gender-dependent, driving will become a natural element of everyday life experience for the coming generations. However, the rise in individual transportation will have differing effects: on one hand, easier access to private cars contributes to an increase in the mobility of the older individuals who often avoid driving under poor or complex conditions (Tacken and van Lamoen, 2005); whilst on the other hand, the increasing volume, density and speed of traffic, especially in cities, can lead to older people feeling uncertain and unsure of maintaining their driving capacity (Schlag, 2003). In addition, the shift to individual transportation also increases the risk of further reduction in public transport services. In parallel with this, if important societal areas such as services, shopping, cultural and sport facilities continue to be oriented towards the car user, then the danger exists that inequality will increasingly lead to greater social exclusion (Mollenkopf et al., 2002).

Neighbourhood security

The usability of the residential area is influenced not only by accessibility but also by how people feel about their neighbourhood. The respondents of the MOBILATE study commented on having a quiet living area and a clean environment as well as the need for a sense of security. These comments relate to those raised by Peace et al. (2006), outlined above. Fear can become a psychological barrier which influences mobility-related decisions and inhibits outdoor behaviour. Yet, for most of the older respondents in either of these studies security did not seem to be a disincentive. In the MOBILATE study, older people in Finland felt most secure whilst the highest percentages of insecurity were found in the Hungarian rural area, both by day and night. The level of insecurity increased at night in the urban areas in all countries, with the highest percentages in eastern Germany (39%), Italy (37%) and western Germany (32%), and comments such as these from all locations indicate the relationship between time and security (Marcellini et al., 2005): 'I'm afraid to leave the house/apartment when it is dark'; 'I'm afraid of being mugged when it is dark'; 'I'm afraid of burglars during my absence.'

Issues of crime and fear were commonly raised across the British study, but as the researchers comment this could become an issue where people's behaviour demonstrates the mastery of environmental press. Peace et al. (2006, pp. 68–9) comment:

> [The] older people we spoke to recognized where they had control in relation to risk and safety both inside and outside their homes. They felt unable to have much influence on the behaviour of other people and some of them felt their control of their own bodies was compromised by disabilities or illnesses. The consequences for them of, for example, a fall caused by a street crime ... were potentially very high. ... In this light the defensive

behaviour of many of our respondents within the world outside their homes appears much more rational than the image of the unreasonably fearful older person. It also helps to explain in part why they can, on the one hand, express a fear of going out into their neighbourhoods at night and, on the other hand, express attachment to their same neighbourhoods.

Of course, both people and places change over time and, in 2000, Mollenkopf *et al.* (2003) were able to carry out a follow-up study in three European cities (Germany, Italy, Finland) that had taken part in the original MOBILATE research. They found that the most frequent changes in the environment between 1995 and 2000 were negative ones and respondents commented on access to shops, services and transport connections. More shops and services had closed than opened, and in every city there had been a reduction in the use of modes of transport and the range of different outdoor activities undertaken. The picture was especially negative for those whose health had declined.

Impact of deprivation

While reflecting on aspects of environmental press within the wider community, it should be noted that neither of the foregoing studies deliberately set out to consider the lives of older people experiencing levels of social exclusion. However, this was not the case for Scharf *et al.* (2004) whose study of older people living in deprived urban neighbourhoods has contributed to British policy development concerning quality of life and multiple exclusion in old age (Smith *et al.*, 2004; Scharf *et al.*, 2005). This research included a survey of 600 people aged 60 and over in the UK living in Liverpool, Manchester and a London Borough as well as in-depth interviews with a smaller sub-sample. The areas chosen ranked among England's top 50 most deprived in 1998 as classified by the Index of Deprivation (DETR, 1998b) which included characteristics such as high unemployment, drug problems, poor public transport, poor housing, low income and poverty, high crime rate and feeling unsafe. The study indicates how a significant minority of older people are excluded from basic services, material resources, civic activities, social relations and other aspects of the wider neighbourhood. They are people who in later life suffer from restricted income, poor health and a lack of social ties which may be compounded by a life history of relative disadvantage which undermines personal mastery. However, increasing environmental press associated with population change, economic decline and rising levels of crime and instability can enhance vulnerability amongst people who may still remain strongly attached to ageing in place, a feature also noted in rural areas (Scharf & Bartlam, 2006).

ENVIRONMENTAL MEANING

When questioned about the meaning of home, older people in the MOBILATE and ENABLE-AGE research projects were quite satisfied with the area in which they were living (Mollenkopf *et al.*, 2005). Although it is true that there is often a connection between objective contextual factors and subjective understandings, the relationship is far from simple and there is still conceptual and empirical diversity between different aspects such as residential satisfaction, meaning of home domains, perceived usability or even housing-related control beliefs. While discussion so far has centred on more objective aspects of environment, the complex interface between material, social and psychological aspects is seldom far away and here we turn to focus on meaning.

Place attachment has been conceptualised as a process of transforming space into place (Altman and Low, 1992) as individuals or groups form affective, cognitive and behavioural bonds to a particular socio-physical setting or location (Brown and Perkins, 1992). Across the life-course, people interact with their social and physical environments, leading to a meaningful representation of the self (see earlier discussion of work by Rowles). Within the context of life-long development, it is assumed that the transaction between person and environment becomes increasingly complex from childhood to adult life (Baltes, 1987; Bronfenbrenner, 1999). Among the driving forces for this increasingly complexity is the challenge for each developing individual to find a balance between basic needs for a secure, safe and stable base, on the one hand, and higher-order needs toward exploration, stimulation and environmental mastery on the other hand as their action range increases. Later in the human life-course, as the action range may decrease again, place attachment remains quite complex and comprises much more than mere reminiscence and nostalgia. Moreover, there is evidence that – beside processes of housing-related environmental agency – place attachment and processes of belonging to home are linked to outcome of autonomy and well-being (Oswald *et al.*, 2006).

Place attachment and meaning in old age

The meaning of place and place attachment have become increasingly relevant in old age (Rowles and Chaudhury, 2005; Rubinstein and Parmelee, 1992). As people grow older, not only do the number of experienced and cognitively represented places increase, but the immediate home environment and the close neighbourhood become more important, both in terms of the time people spend at home, and in terms of the place where most of the daily activities occur. It is a well-replicated finding that ageing coincides with a reduction in action range, which is especially true for very old age (Baltes *et al.*, 1999a). The home can acquire new meaning, because it may serve to compensate for the reduced functional capacity of the ageing individuals (Rowles *et al.*, 2004). Indeed, either environmental changes or behavioural adaptations may be needed in order to maintain autonomy and to avoid institutionalisation (Peace *et al.*, 2006; Oswald and Rowles, 2006).

Research based on the 'environmental docility' hypothesis (Lawton and Nahemow, 1973; Lawton, 1987) has shown a strong correlation between reduced environmental competence, such as vision loss or mobility impairment, and objective living arrangements (Wahl *et al.*, 1999). As a result, research and application often reduce questions regarding the meaning of home to whether or not the home environment is accessible and forget about other more psychological effects such as those relating to attachment, well-being and autonomy. Observational data have shown that a tendency for environmental centralisation exists among older people, especially around the most favoured places in the home. The adaptive potential of this lies in maintaining and enhancing control over the immediate environment and thus establishing areas that may be called *control centres or living centres* (Hanson *et al.*, 2001; Kellaher, 2002; Lawton, 1985; Rubinstein and Parmelee, 1992). Typically, these are the most comfortable places at home that also afford a good view outside as well as the placement of many necessary and preferred things close at hand (Peace *et al.*, 2006; Oswald *et al.*, 2006).

However, an increasing number of older people are far from being home or house-bound and the home itself is a place of continued engagement. Indeed, Lawton recognised that the stimulation provided by the home environment should also be considered (Lawton, 1989a), producing 'environmental proactivity' (Lawton, 1989b). Thus, how the individual interprets the meaning of home may vary, reflecting behavioural adaptations and modifications of the home environment to stay independent as well as cognitive representation of a lifestyle, developed over years (Thomae, 1988). As Peace *et al.* (2006, p. 95) note, the domestic home may permit older people 'to be the selves they wish to be', and by presenting a secure base for daily activities through routines that enable identity construction and maintenance, as people age they remain active decision-makers. Again, European data with very old elders revealed that perceived usability and meaning of home is related to healthy ageing. Participants who perceive their home as useful and meaningful and who perceive themselves to be in charge at home (i.e. low external control beliefs), are more independent in daily life, have a better well-being and suffer less from depressive symptoms in different European regions (Oswald *et al.*, 2006).

An increasing portion of older adults decide to relocate voluntarily, many of them not for basic needs to stay independent, but to fulfil preferences and wishes and thus to actively seek new options for place attachment in the years of life remaining (Oswald *et al.*, 2002; Oswald and Rowles, 2006). But this is not always the case, and in studying people across a range of age-integrated and age-related housing in England, Peace *et al.* (2006) are able to consider how people use their knowledge of age-related housing to frame their decisions about engagement and disengagement through 'option recognition' towards the end of life. They comment (p. 130):

> Environmental press will push people towards option recognition and many older people will be able to take action, but for those who are not able, the press of the environment will ultimately require compensatory action, perhaps by carers. But most people want to optimize their mastery over environment and constantly, if subtly, evaluate their circumstances and, when it appears right to do so, consider the next best step.

Physical aspects

'physical home' (Sixsmith, 1986)

'community' (Feldman, 1990)

'physical insideness' (Rowles, 1983)

'body-centered process' (Rubinstein, 1989)

(...)

Personal aspects

Personal (Sixsmith, 1986)

'Person-centered process' (Rubinstein, 1989)
(...)

Behavioral aspects
'centeredness' (Feldman, 1990)
'activity' (Harris *et al.,* 1996)
'body-centered process' (Rubinstein, 1989)
'Control' (Zingmark *et al.*, 1995)

Cognitive aspects
'identity' (Harris *et al.*, 1996)
'autobiographical insideness' (Rowles, 1983)
'safety' (Zingmark *et al.*, 1995)
'recognition' (Zingmark *et al.*, 1995)

Emotional aspects
'embededness' (Feldman, 1990)
'positive evaluations' (Harris *et al.*, 1996)
'rootedness' (Zingmark *et al.*, 1995)
'joy' (Zingmark *et al.*, 1995)

Social aspects

'social home' (Sixsmith, 1986)

'connection' (Harris *et al.,* 1986)

'social insideness' (Rowles, 1983)

'social-centered process' (Rubinstein, 1989)

'togetherness' (Zingmark *et al.,* (1995)

(...)

Figure 10.3   Heuristic framework for domains of meaning of home in old age.

Source: Oswald and Wahl (2005)

On-going developments

As noted earlier, the work of gerontologists such as Rowles and Rubinstein has provided an essential base for developing work on place attachment and environmental meaning in later life. Subsequent research, from various disciplines, has contributed to this debate extending coverage to different types of location and setting with a range of respondents. In particular, research by Zingmark *et al.* (1995), in a study with 150 participants aged from 2 to 102, offers a lifespan trajectory identifying several common aspects of place attachment to home, such as *safety, rootedness, joy, privacy, togetherness, recognition* and *control*. In contrast, Oswald and Wahl (Oswald, 2003; Oswald and Wahl, 2005) have considered whether aspects of meaning of home differ for older people with different levels of physical competence. Here 126 older people (from 61 to 92 years of age) were interviewed – one-third in good health, one-third suffering from severe mobility impairment, and one-third who were blind; and analysis reveals a range of meaning: physical, behavioural, cognitive, emotional and social (Figure 10.3).

In all of these studies the question can be raised: 'Do the psychological processes of place attachment and meanings of place or home fulfil a particular purpose'? Based on data for children as well as people in their middle and late adulthood, Marcus (1992) was able to extract three main functions of place attachment:

- gaining cognitive and behavioural *control* over space
- manipulating, moulding or decorating space in order to *create* a setting of physical comfort and well-being
- perceiving *continuity* with significant places and people of the past.

In addition, a relationship was found between place attachment and the ability to maintain *privacy.*

However, the cultural specificity of research should be noted here given the dominance of North American and western European literature. In future the impact of globalisation will need to be addressed in research on place attachment and meaning of home in later life. Older people who have migrated between countries at various stages of their lives will offer different views of place attachment, as a respondent from the Peace *et al.* (2006, p. 147) study suggests:

> In many ways mentally and in my thinking processes I am more like British but culturally I am Indian, so I am in a sort of limbo, in between. So I could say that I belong to both of them or none of them, completely. So it's just one of those states you've got to make the best of the situation and adapt yourself. (Harjit, aged 66 at interview living in sheltered housing, Haringey, London)

CONCLUSIONS

Critical reflections on theories and concepts in environmental gerontology stimulate developmental thinking. If you return to Figure 10.1, you will see that the final box outlines five ways in which existing theoretical approaches can and are being extended. First, there is a need to examine the tension for people as they age which exists between environments that encourage *docility and proactivity.* The dynamic between docility and proactivity which probably reflects a daily challenge for the fast-growing portion of very old people is still not treated well in any environmental gerontology concept and needs further development (Oswald *et al.*, 2006).

A second point of critique relates to the *better integration of the micro- and macro-levels in person–environment analysis.* Theoretical accounts as described above primarily operate on the micro level in old age (a typical example is the press–competence model) and do not theoretically consider the interfaces between in homes, technology, neighbourhoods, communities, states or even globalisation (Wahl & Mollenkopf, 2003). For example, future housing options are shaped by community resources and different housing options as well as – for a growing portion of older people – by the ease of moving from one's home country to another country permanently or for intermittent periods. Unfortunately, Bronfenbrenner's (1979, 1999) strong theoretical suggestion to consider different levels of analysis in any social-ecological work (including spheres of influence not physically inhabited by the subject in question, such as culture, society and the law) has not found much resonance in environmental gerontology so far. However there are some important recent developments, and research by Peace *et al.* (2006) is not only one of the first British studies to involve older people living in different locations – urban and rural – as well as both 'ordinary' age-integrated housing and 'special' age-related housing, but also focuses on the impact of environment on identity which incorporates the temporal dimension of life history past and future alongside the present. Consequently attachment to place adopts greater fluidity and cultural dynamism, addressing the third point of *better integration of temporality.*

Our understanding of the relationship between *the physical and the social environments* is the fourth area in need of development. Although there is a clear consensus that both physical and social environments are closely interwoven, ageing research has tended to separate both of these 'worlds'. To date, pragmatics has played a major role here. It has been convenient to separate the professional world into those working on the social environment (such as network research, social support research, family studies etc.) and those working on physical environments (e.g. concerned with building design, community development, transport engineering). Future theoretical work should aim to simultaneously analyse both person–environment system changes in the physical/spatial and social domains and the interactions of these changes as people age (Wahl and Lang, 2003). This demands interdisciplinary research and the development of greater communication between researchers alongside the greater input of the user perspective from those already sophisticated in integrating these environments within their everyday lives.

Finally, there is a need for *better integration of ongoing cohort dynamics* into existing theoretical accounts of person–environment relations in ageing. For example, tomorrow older people will probably be more flexible in their housing options, more mobile in terms of car-driving and long-distance travelling, more alert to environmental change, and more eager to use 'new' technology such as the Internet and high-tech solutions to improve their housing quality and care needs. These changes challenge present theories in environmental gerontology in acknowledging and incorporating new potential for autonomy, health and well-being provided by these new possibilities for the enhancement of person–environment fit. In the ideal case, theoretical development should possess a built-in dynamic mechanism able to adjust major components (such as competence, environmental press, person–environment fit) to on-going cohort changes.

FURTHER READING

Mollenkopf, H., Marcellini, F., Ruoppila, I., Szeman, Z. and Tacken, M. (eds.) (2005) *Enhancing Mobility in Later Life: Personal Coping, Environmental Resources, and Technical Support*. Amsterdam: IOS Press.

Peace, S. and Holland, C. (2001) Housing in an ageing society. In: Peace, S. M. and Holland, C. (eds) *Inclusive Housing in an Ageing Society*, 1–26. Bristol: Policy Press.

Peace, S., Holland, C. and Kellaher, L. (2006) *Environment and Identity in Later Life*. Maidenhead: Open University Press.

Oswald, F. and Wahl, H-W. (2005) Dimensions of the meaning of home in later life. In G.D.Rowles and Chaudhury, H. (eds) *Home and Identity in Later Life: International Perspectives*, 21–46. New York: Springer.

Scharf, T. and Bartlam, B. (2006) Rural Disadvantage: Quality of life and disadvantage among older people – a pilot study, CR 19, London: Commission for Rural Communities.

Wahl, H-W., Scheidt, R. and Windley, P. G. (eds) (2003) *Annual Review of Gerontology and Geriatrics. Aging in Context: Socio-physical Environments*, vol. 23. New York: Springer.

11

Meanings of ageing and old age: Discursive contexts, social attitudes and personal identities

Gerben J. Westerhof and
Emmanuelle Tulle

INTRODUCTION

Among the most important questions that have to be addressed in social gerontology are 'what are ageing and old age?' and 'who counts as old and why?' At first sight, the answers seem to be rather straightforward. In western culture, ageing is most often seen as a biological process of decline of bodily functions (Gullette, 2003). Greying hair, changing skin texture, failing eyesight, waning muscular strength, or reduced vitality – all these biological signs are commonly thought of as the defining features of old age. Consequently, older people are viewed as having frail health, as being unproductive and in need of support (see Chapter 6). This perspective on ageing appears to be all the more convincing as it is related to biological and presumably natural processes of ageing (see Chapter 2).

However, the almost inevitable association of ageing with biological decline does not do justice to the large diversity in the experience of old age. At present, lifespan theories see ageing as an individualised, unique process involving changes in many aspects of life, not just failing health (see Chapter 3). Hence, any generalising statement about ageing, old age and older people does not recognise the complexities of everyday life. Whereas the view of ageing as biological decline is highly dominant in western cultures, other constructions of ageing and old age come to the fore when studying other cultures (Keith *et al.*, 1994; Shweder, 1998; Westerhof *et al.*, 2001b). However natural the link between ageing and a failing body may seem at first sight, it is in fact a culturally specific interpretation of the intricacies of the ageing process (Gergen and Gergen, 2000).

In this chapter we describe how the confounding of ageing with bodily decline is part and parcel of our culture, which takes place and is reinforced in many settings, from larger institutional settings through everyday social interactions, to individual experiences of ageing people. We explore the particular meanings of this perspective in different fields (medicine, policies, media, care settings, work settings) as well as the recent changes in this perspective on ageing. We propose to draw upon both sociological and psychological perspectives, on the one hand, to bring to the fore the broader context in which the meanings of ageing and old age have emerged and, on the other, to explore the patterns of behaviour through which these meanings are appropriated, perhaps transgressed and even transformed by older people themselves.

Crucially, this particular approach allows us to explore how the interaction between cultural processes and actual social practices shape opportunities for self and identity construction. Cultural meanings have real consequences for individual lives and identities (Hepworth, 2000). Individuals are fully involved in the perpetuation of cultural meanings, through various processes of self-regulation (Tulle and Mooney, 2002). This implies that ageing people may find ways in which alternative meanings about old age are negotiated. In the last part of this chapter we will deal with our underlying concern, which is to highlight the ways in which the dominant perspective on ageing and old age can be resisted, giving rise to more positive approaches to the experience of growing older and the formation of identity.

DISCURSIVE CONTEXT

This first section discusses the ways in which the complexities of ageing and old age are reduced in the creation of meaningful symbols, ideals and practices concerning old age. We will mainly use the work of Michel Foucault (1970, 1974) and the concept of 'discourse' (Smart, 1985). Discourse refers to sets of institutional and cultural systems that provide meaning, map out the space in which social practices are made possible and constitute 'official' knowledge or truth.

According to Foucault we can only know the world and engage in social action through specific discourses. The Foucauldian concept of discourse allows us first to identify the social fields and institutions in which ageing and old age are constructed. These encompass biomedicine, social policy-making, the mass media, fiction, less prominently the arts, as well as social gerontological knowledge! Later we will show that a close reading of Foucault's work also allows us to propose that individual social actors are fully implicated in the negotiation of meanings and therefore in the consolidation of normative ideas about old age and ageing. But we will first explore the most important frameworks that have provided the underpinning for contemporary meanings of ageing and old age: medicine, social policy and the mass media.

Medicalisation

From the mid-eighteenth century and throughout the nineteenth century, clinicians like Charcot started to take an interest in ageing processes, charting their clinical features (Haber, 2001). In effect they helped establish a new discursive space in which new kinds of questions could be asked about ageing and old age. Terms like 'senescence' were coined to denote the changes in function that take place in the human organism in the later years. This helped consolidate the scientific legitimacy of the new medicine of ageing whilst also naturalising the close link drawn between ageing and inevitable decline (Tulle-Winton, 2000).

   Clinicians were also engaged in a debate about the status of disease in old age, a debate which continues to animate what is now referred to as 'bio-gerontology'. The nature of change in the ageing organism was ambiguous; although pathology was a normal feature of ageing, the latter could not be easily conceived of as pathological, that is as deviation from the norm (Katz, 1996). As Charcot and Loomis (1881, quoted in Katz, 1996, p. 81) put it:

> [The] textual changes which old age induces in the organism sometimes attain such a point that the physiological and the pathological states seem to mingle in an imperceptible transition and to be no longer sharply distinguishable.

This led Katz (1996, p. 81) to conclude:

> Thus the aged medicalised body was neither diseased nor healthy, but both normal and pathological since both conditions in old age were expressions of the same physiological laws.

This paradox persists in contemporary bio-gerontology today. It is not unusual to find ageing equated with deterioration or debilitation in gerontological and geriatric texts (Palmore, 2000). Vincent (2003b) conducted a textual analysis of an academic paper describing the biochemistry of ageing. He found descriptions of 'older' molecules which reinforced the construction of ageing as disorder, failure, abnormality, alteration, run down, incorrect, damaged, defective, unstable, diminished, even dangerous and deleterious. In contrast, adult cells were young, integrated, developing, normal, in a state of homeostasis, accurate, fitter and prone to healing and repair. The author of the paper concluded that 'natural ageing and disease in old age are not different'.

Stretching this argument even further, a strand of biomedicine, known as 'anti-ageing medicine', has set itself the task of combating the biological signs of ageing by treating it as a disease. In contrast, Hayflick (2001) and a number of increasingly influential bio-gerontologists proclaim that ageing is not a disease, and they have become vocal in their criticism of 'anti-ageing' approaches (see Chapter 2).

As we can see, the nature of the relationship between ageing and disease is up for grabs. Nevertheless what is well established is the naturalisation of deficiency, which the medicalisation of ageing has legitimated. Thus we have a paradox here: disease is an inherent part of ageing but ageing may or may not itself be a disease. This conundrum is crucial because in theory diseases can be addressed and perhaps even cured; on the other hand, if ageing is constructed as inevitable descent into disease state, then there is as yet little that can be done. This has implications not only for medical care, but also for the role of ageing people themselves in the prevention of illness and disability. Regardless of which side of the debate one stands on, older people are now under pressure to minimise the risk of illness and disability and to take on the financial responsibility of managing physical dependency. The privatisation and individualisation of responsibility for health maintenance has echoes in the social policy arena, an issue to which we now turn.

Social policies

Social policies have certainly drawn from the biomedical decline perspective. It is not the nature of ageing and disease that is disputed in this field, but the social consequences of ageing as a natural process of decline. Here consequences, such as increasing dependency and decreasing productivity, are constructed as inherent aspects of old age posing social problems that have to be solved (see Chapter 6). Yet, the particular ways of dealing with these social problems have changed, partly in response to earlier social policy 'solutions'. In what follows we explore the decline perspective in relation to the content and context of European social policies.

Although each European country has its own history of social policies towards ageing and old age, a number of common trends can be discerned, in particular in north-western Europe. Whereas some provision for older people already existed on a smaller scale, national old age policies mainly started to develop with the rising welfare states after the Second World War (Phillipson, 2003b). Policies were mainly directed towards retirement and pensions, as well as the provision of housing and health and social services. These policies proceeded from a conception of older people as less productive and in need of financial, medical and social support. Older people were recognised as social citizens, albeit largely passive ones. In essence this political discourse assumed that ageing was a natural process of disengagement from work (see Chapter 4) and social life which was in turn related to decline in health status. Although variable in the generosity of support structures, the legitimacy of taking care of the old, as a collective responsibility, appeared to be firmly established across Europe.

In response to the economic recession of the 1980s, brought on by globalising forces, and the related mass redundancies, early retirement programmes were introduced throughout the European Union (except in Sweden; see Chapter 8). At the same time the principle of funding provision for age-related welfare products from collective resources was questioned (Naafs, 1993). As Katz (1992) describes, an alarmist discourse constructed the greying of society as a process in which increasing numbers of older people would put a financial strain on existing retirement and health provisions. In this alarmist discourse we find once again old age as a period of health problems, which are related to a loss of productivity and independence. Yet, the problem is no longer how to support older people adequately, but how to deal with the strains on the very same welfare products that were seen as the solution to the needs of older people in the previous period. The reactions to this recent way of dealing with age-related problems give rise to new meanings as well.

A first solution is to introduce greater individual responsibility. Changing the generous schemes for early retirement goes hand in hand with introducing more flexible retirement arrangements. Access to welfare services becomes 'marketised' (Powell and Biggs, 2000). Services are no longer guaranteed by the state nor will there be an automatic right to support. The relationship between service providers and service users is being reconstructed in market terms. Service users become customers: they are expected not only to make a contribution to their care but also to make financial decisions based on the anticipation of physical disability (Tulle and Mooney, 2002), such as taking up private pensions to fund everyday living expenses and care products or moving to age-appropriate housing. (For a detailed account of these trends, see Chapters 6 and 7.)

Another solution was to stress the resources of older people. As an example, the Charter of Fundamental Rights of the European Union states in Article 25: 'The Union recognises and respects the rights of older people to lead a life of dignity and independence and to participate in social and cultural life.' Policies were therefore moving from traditional concerns with discrete problems in the fields of work, healthcare and housing to more integrated policies on ageing that touch on the lifestyles of older people more generally (Walker and Naegele, 1999). In doing so, the basic discourse of disengagement and decline which was related to state support was increasingly supplemented by a discourse of autonomy and participation, related to the value of individual responsibility. Both discourses continue to co-exist. For example, in the Netherlands, an integrated policy for older people is being developed that will be characterised by support for frail people on the one hand and active ageing on the other (Roelfsema, 2003).

The social policy discourse has clear consequences for older people as it contributes to shaping the opportunities for and constraints on individual lives. The social policies of the welfare state have often been hailed for alleviating poverty and hardship among older people. Critical gerontologists have pointed out that there were also other effects (see Chapter 4). Policies used chronological age boundaries and treated older people as a rather homogenous social category. In this way they contributed to the standardisation of the life-course, in particular for men, and to the construction of older people as a separate category (Kohli, 1985; Walker, 2000). By drawing boundaries, they also contributed to excluding older people from society (Bijsterveld, 1996). This is most clearly seen in the spatial separation realised in institutional living arrangements, and also in the exclusion of older people from the workforce. By identifying old age primarily as a time of reliance on the welfare state, older people were put in a situation of 'structured dependency' (Townsend, 1981). What was believed to be a natural process of disengagement was in fact also a result of social policies creating disengagement.

The dismantling of post-war welfare contracts described above is accompanied by a shift in the discourse of old age from social citizenship based on collective responsibility to individual responsibility. The age boundaries are being redrawn and are becoming more permeable. Laslett (1989) has argued that a third phase of life came into being, characterised by relatively healthy, active and autonomous lifestyles. This has opened the door for the construction of later life as a more uncertain time, perhaps promising greater freedom, affluence and choice. However, the risk of poverty amongst those whose socio-economic position does not permit financial independence in old age might become greater (Krause, 2000). Social gerontologists have also pointed out that this might serve to further marginalise those who do not conform to images of active, healthy and independent agers (Blaikie, 1999). Whereas the shift from the association of ageing with bodily decline to one that emphasises choice has often been welcomed, one should be careful in evaluating the meanings of ageing implicit in this new political discourse.

Besides helping to shape individual lives, this new discourse has infused public debates, thus influencing lay perceptions about older people. The mass media provide an important stage for public opinion to be formed and rehearsed, so it is worthwhile to study in some detail how older people are represented there.

Mass media

Arguably the media provide a cosmos that reflects general attitudes towards old age in our cultures (Roy and Harwood, 1997). The programmes, stories and images that are broadcast are evaluated in terms of their appeal to the general public, driven by the imperative to increase viewing figures or readership in the visual and written media. Media images about older people are also related to selling products to older people through advertisements. In this sense, the messages found in the mass media are a hyperbole of cultural concepts of ageing and old age. One might therefore expect that the discourse about ageing as biological decline will be highly visible in this field.

Almost all studies on older people in the media have found that they are not well covered, whether in popular films, TV series, advertisements, fiction or comics (Filipp and Mayer, 1999; Tews, 1991; Robinson and Skill, 1995; Vasil and Wass, 1993). Programmes are more often *about* older people than for older people and they seldom give older people their own voice (Filipp and Mayer, 1999). It has also been found that older people play main characters less often than people of other ages (Robinson and Skill, 1995). Although there are minor variations according to the type of media and programmes, the percentage of older people in the mass media is well below their actual proportion in the general population. This applies even more strongly to women than men and to people in their fourth as compared to those in the third age. This clear underrepresentation of older people in the media has been attributed to the youth orientation that prevails there. Older people and their bodies do not meet the criteria of beauty and vitality that are valued in the 'cult of youth'.

Even when they are present, some studies have found that older characters are negatively portrayed, for example as asexual, incompetent or having health problems. There have been marked differences in the portrayal of older men and women. Markson and Taylor (2000), in a study of Hollywood movies, showed that the range of roles was wider for ageing male actors than for their female counterparts. These roles tended to conform to mainstream images of masculinity: sexual potency, physical strength and power. In contrast, roles for actresses were more restricted. Older actresses were rarely cast in leading, let alone romantic, roles, and the power they might have held was more covert. However, neither actors nor actresses were protected from their characters being at risk of downfall, caused by either physical, cognitive deterioration or simply from ridicule and obsolescence. Bytheway and Johnson (1998) showed that, in the main, very old women were invisible or represented in very restricted, stereotypical ways, such as in care situations, receiving assistance. Hearn (1995) argued that there was a corresponding built-in ambivalence in the portrayal of older men in the media, either as powerful or whose hold on power was increasingly placed at risk. In other words the portrayal of ageing and old age is gendered and at the same time reinforces the tenuous position of older people. It is also worth remembering that 'fourth-agers' (Gilleard and Higgs, 2000) – that is, very old, disabled or financially insecure people – are rarely depicted in the mass media, and when they are indeed featured, usually it is as the object of pity or as the victim of scandalous practices.

Yet, there is also clear evidence of more varied images of older people which may even be positive, such as in the portrayal of older people as grandparents or of older men as authority figures (Miller *et al.*, 2003; Van Selm *et al.*, 1996; Vasil and Wass, 1993). In general, it may be unwarranted to conclude that older people, in particular older men, are always negatively portrayed in the mass media (Roy and Harwood, 1997).

The evidence regarding the number of older people appearing in the mass media over time is somewhat inconsistent. Ursic *et al.* (1986) found an increase in older individuals in magazine advertisements between 1950 and 1980, but Robinson and Skill (1995) found no evidence of increased coverage of older people in prime-time fictional TV programmes between 1970 and 1990. Van Selm and Westerhof (2004) also found no clear increase in the percentage of older people in Dutch TV commercials between 1993 and 2003. Yet, the portrayal of older people appears to be changing. Featherstone and Hepworth (1995) analysed the *Retirement Choice* magazine and found that, over a period of a few years, pictures had changed from the disengaged retiree to the active pensioner. The name of the magazine changed, in a way portraying this transition. In the first editions of the early 1970s, *Retirement* was given prominence over *Choice*. In later editions, *Choice* became the more prominent aspect of the title and nowadays it is called *Choice: Britain's Magazine for Successful Retirement*. Although combating negative images of old age was important from the start, the magazine has focused more and more on consumerist and active lifestyles.

Again, we have to be careful in evaluating the change in discourse. The American TV comedy series Golden Girls, for example, intended to introduce positive role models of older women. However, Harwood and Giles (1992) argue that the use of humour in this series contributes to negative stereotypes of older people. Although the characters in Golden Girls behaved in counter-stereotypical ways, the fact that they were the object of laughter undermined the aims of the series to provide positive role models of old age. The humorous portrayal of older people has been documented in a number of other studies (Gerbner *et al.*, 1980; Roy and Harwood, 1997; Van Selm *et al.*, 1996).

To summarise, older people are relatively absent in the mass media and we find a lot of negative imagery as soon as the ageing body comes into play. This applies in particular to older women and to fourth-agers. Yet, not all images are negative and there is some evidence of more varied older identities being represented in the mass media over the past few years.

This representation of older identities is related to broader cultural changes that are held to be among the defining features of late or post-modernity, such as the turn to consumption (Shilling, 2003) and the blurring of traditional life-course boundaries (Featherstone and Hepworth, 1995). Gilleard and Higgs (2000) proposed that consumption would postpone cultural and social marginalisation in later life, till the fourth age. Post-modernity would foster new ways of imagining later life, no longer based on a period of disengagement but on an extended midlife, during which new roles and obligations could be negotiated (Featherstone and Hepworth, 1995). In contrast, the contemporary obsession with the 'body beautiful' (Turner, 1996) – that is, the cult of youthful and beautiful bodies – is particularly problematic for the status of people who are ageing and their bodies.

These considerations are all the more salient given that, as Hearn (1995) has argued, representations of later life and ageing are coterminous with *imaging* later life and ageing, thus influencing the ways in which we apprehend later life. There is clearly a lack of positive role models for older people to identify with. Negative portrayals may result in negative self-concepts and identities, in particular because older people are among the most frequent users of the media (Robinson and Skill, 1995). An additional effect is the inculcation of negative attitudes about old age among younger groups (Roy and Harwood, 1997). These images are not benign and we propose that they influence social interactions with older people, an issue to which we turn next.

We have seen that the association of ageing with biological decline plays an important role in the discursive contexts discussed in this section. The medical discourse mainly served to legitimise and naturalise this meaning of ageing, by making it worthy of scientific study. The social policy discourse used the concept of ageing as biological decline to shape the opportunity structures in which social actors can envisage their old age. The mass media was found to promote largely stereotypical portrayals of older characters, thus contributing to their exclusion. We have also seen that the understanding of ageing as decline does not have a fixed and single meaning in bio-medical science, social policies nor the mass media. In recent years, understandings of old age as physical frailty, poor health, dependency and loss of productivity are complemented by concepts of societal participation, autonomy and consumption in the third age. Choice plays a more prominent role and older adults are increasingly made responsible for their own health and life.

SOCIAL ATTITUDES

The previous section focused on the wider institutional contexts in which ageing and later life have been given meaning. Taking a symbolic interactionist perspective, we could argue that the meanings of ageing and the context in which these are produced contribute to the production of a range of symbolic resources and shared meanings which social actors themselves draw upon to rehearse their own understandings of ageing and old age (Hepworth, 2000). Before turning to the different ways in which older individuals themselves make use of these meanings for interpreting their own ageing process, we will focus in this section on understandings of old age and their influence on interactions of younger with older adults.

Research suggests that, from infancy, children are sensitive to age differences and are socialised into the dominant meanings of ageing and old age (Montepare and Zebrowitz, 2002). Thus, arguably, broader cultural contexts influence the attitudes and behaviours that individuals have towards older people. This influence is even stronger due to the age-segregated nature of our society (Riley and

Riley, 1994). About two in three older people mentioned that they had little or no contact with people younger than 25 in a Eurobarometer study (Walker and Maltby, 1997). This lack of intergenerational contact results in a lack of individualised experience with older people, thus leaving young people more likely to be influenced by the institutional discourses discussed before.

The wider cultural context would not have an influence on the attitudes and behaviours of people towards ageing and older people unless they fell on some fertile psychological ground. Taking a social cognitive perspective, one can understand why the complex social reality of ageing is reduced and schematised from an individual perspective. General psychological motives for comprehension and social distinction as well as a fear of death have been proposed as explanations.

First, social psychology has shown how individuals try to prevent cognitive overload and to maintain order and comprehensibility by processing information in a biased and simplified way. Once particular attitudes have become established, individuals reinforce them again and again. Even when they are confronted with experiences that do not fit their cognitive models, they assimilate them into the existing models where they are treated as exceptions to the general rules (Cuddy and Fiske, 2002). Second, it has been found that a large part of our understandings of the world is derived from our membership of different social groups, among them age groups (Harwood et al., 1995). Individuals accentuate differences between in-groups and out-groups, they downplay differences within out-groups and they favour their in-group over out-groups. This process of social distinction mainly serves to enhance self-esteem. Third, individuals are said to have a fear of death for which they build up all kinds of ego defences (Greenberg et al., 2002). As old age reminds us of our own mortality, the induced fear is projected in negative stereotypes and behaviours towards older people, in order not to blame the ageing process as such but older people.

Given the need for order, social distinction and the fear of death, one might expect that an emphasis on ageing as bodily decline as found in the broader discursive context would indeed inform individual attitudes and behaviours. In the following review of research evidence, it should be kept in mind that most of it comes from the USA and does not differentiate between third and fourth ages. Furthermore, we could not find any studies addressing changes in attitudes across the last decades. It is therefore not possible to draw conclusions about the question whether the changes in discursive contexts described above are mirrored in changes in social attitudes.

Kite and Johnson (1988) conducted a meta-analysis of studies on attitudes towards older and younger adults. They found that attitudes towards old age and older people in general are more negative than attitudes towards younger people. However, it also matters on which dimension older adults are judged. Older adults were judged negatively mainly on dimensions of physical attractiveness and competence. No differences from younger adults were found on the dimensions of desirability of contact and personality. Similarly, Cuddy and Fiske (2002) found that older people as a stereotyped group scored low on a dimension of competence, but high on a dimension of social warmth. The work of Heckhausen and colleagues (1989) on perceptions of lifespan development also shows that young and old individuals still find positive aspects in the later phases of life, although the balance between positive and negative traits across the life-course becomes more skewed towards negative perceptions.

Other studies have found evidence of multiple stereotypes of older people. Brewer *et al.* (1981) were the first to argue that the category 'elderly' represents a number of subordinate categories: grandmother, senior citizen and elder statesman. Schmidt and Boland (1986), and later Hummert *et al.* (1994), expanded on this work. Hummert (1999) identified seven types of 'elders': 'Perfect Grandparent', 'John Wayne Conservative', 'Golden Ager', which are positively laden, whereas in contrast 'Severely Impaired', 'Shrew/Curmudgeon', 'Despondent' and 'Recluse' are negatively laden types. Besides aspects of physical decline, it can be seen that social characteristics are important in these subtypes. This is reflected in the 'Golden Ager' who reminds us of the discursive interpretations of old age in terms of choice, autonomy and participation.

Studies have shown that attitudes towards older people are situation-specific. Simplistic attitudes towards older people are more relevant in situations where no other information about a person is present. As soon as individuating information becomes available, people tend to rely less on their attitudes (Kite and Wagner, 2002). Furthermore, attitudes towards old age are more negative in studies where individuals of different ages were compared (Kite and Johnson, 1988). Stimuli that may serve as markers of old age in social interactions include cues of posture and gait, facial physiognomy and voice (Montepare and Zebrowitz, 1998). Positive stereotypes are more easily activated when photographs of faces of younger older people are shown, whereas negative stereotypes are more easily activated when photos of very old people are shown (Hummert, 1999).

Taken together, these studies show that bodily ageing is an important aspect of the largely negative attitudes towards old age and ageing. Bodily attractiveness and competence are major dimensions of negative judgements about old age as well as defining components of negative prototypes of older people. These attitudes are mainly triggered in situations involving some aspect of bodily appearance or functioning. However, bodily ageing is not the only component that influences attitudes about old age and ageing. Social and psychological aspects, such as warmth and personality, and roles such as grandparenthood, are important as well. Crucially, these latter aspects are often judged in more positive ways.

Consequences of negative attitudes

It is one thing to hold negative attitudes towards ageing and old age, yet another whether such attitudes have any substantial effects in everyday life. Social psychological studies addressing this question have focused on the influence of attitudes on information processing about older people as well as on behaviour towards them.

Studies have documented differences in information seeking and attribution vis-à-vis younger and older adults. Carver and de la Garza (1984) asked students to read the same brief description of a car accident. When the driver was characterised as old (84 years), they were seeking information about the physical, mental and sensory inadequacies of the driver. When the driver was young (22 years), they were looking for information about speeding and alcohol consumption. In the studies summarised by Erber and Prager (1999), memory failure was attributed to different causes in younger and older subjects. The failures of younger subjects were mainly attributed to lack of effort, whereas those of older subjects were attributed to lack of ability. These studies document the impact that stereotypes about the competencies of older people have on the cognitive processing of information.

Attitudes may also direct our behaviour towards older adults. Most studies in this domain have been carried out on social interactions in the fields of care, medicine and work. Much work in the field of care has addressed what Williams and Nussbaum (2001) describe as over-accommodative communication: the over-playing of particular communication styles relative to the needs of the interlocutor. Patronising speech (Ryan et al., 1995), also identified as displaced baby talk (Caporael and Culbertson, 1986) or 'elderspeak' (Kemper and Harden, 1999), is prototypical of over-accommodation. This kind of communicative style is characterised by a high pitch, overly prone intonation, loud voice, the use of concrete and familiar words, an easy grammar, and a directive and childish way of speaking, such as the use of 'we' when referring to an individual. Non-verbally, it is signalled by frowning, little eye contact, raised eyebrows, hands on the hips and abrupt gestures. Sachweh (1998), studying German nursing homes, found high pitch and exaggerated intonation in almost half of the conversations and the use of 'we' in almost every two out of three conversations between nurses and residents.

Patronising interaction is mediated by negative stereotypes of older people being incompetent or having sensory decrements (Ryan et al., 1986). It is mostly motivated by a wish to make an impression of nurturance and support, but it may also be related to motives of staying in control. Although it is not always perceived as negative, in particular not by frail older adults, over-accommodation may have strong effects on the lives of older adults. Margaret Baltes (1995) found that among institutionalised people it was the need for assistance with personal care that was rewarded with high levels of interaction, whereas displays of independence in personal care and social behaviours were largely ignored. This eventually resulted in a vicious circle of dependency.

In line with the problems in medical science to disentangle ageing and disease, it has been observed in medical practice that physicians ascribe the symptoms experienced by older patients to advanced age, rather than to disease.

Summarising the findings of several studies in the field of medicine, Pasupathi and Löckenhoff (2002, p. 210) conclude:

> Taken together, there is substantial evidence that physicians treat older patients differently from younger patients. Specifically, this differential treatment involves the potential for mis-interpretation of symptoms and inappropriate treatment, is reflected in less open and recep-tive communication practices, and results in poor concordance between patient and physician about what has been accomplished in the interview.

In the domain of work there is evidence of negative effects of attitudes about older workers. McCann and Giles (2002) have argued that stereotypes about the physical and mental decline of older workers go hand in hand with ideas about their lowered productivity, inability to cope with change and pining for retire-ment. This may result in denigrating remarks being made towards older people, fewer possibilities for continuing education, age-discriminatory hiring practices and forced early retirement.

In general, information processing with regard to older people as well as behaviours towards older adults have been associated with negative stereotypes about older adults. Research has focused on stereotypes regarding physical and mental competences and autonomy of older people, identifying the social set-tings in which these competences are highly relevant (care, medicine, work). One should be aware that negative stereotypes are not the only reason for nega-tive behaviours towards older people. In some cases age differentiation may be justified as in speaking louder to an older individual who does indeed hear less well. Aspects of over-accommodation may also be found in communication with younger people who are ill or dependent. It has been pointed out that other motives may be important as well, such as time pressures in care situations. However, a counter-argument would be that time pressures are present in care settings in the first place because of understaffing justified by the relatively low priority accorded to the care of older people.

The existing research shows how the competencies and the bodies of ageing individuals are shaped by the interpretations and behaviours that result from schematised ways of constructing the social reality of ageing and old age. As we also found in the consequences of political discourse about disengagement, there is a self-fulfilling component in attitudes about ageing and old age. As depend-ency and incompetence are treated as characteristics of old age, exactly these aspects of ageing are reinforced.

One might question how this would affect the beliefs of older individuals themselves. Most studies have found that younger and older adults are remark-ably similar in their attitudes towards ageing and older people. The only sys-tematic difference is that older adults hold more complex attitudes towards ageing (Heckhausen et al., 1989) and older people (Hummert et al., 1994). Does this also mean that the identities of older people, and of those in the fourth age in particular, are negatively influenced by the meanings that emanate from the broader discursive context and social interactions? Are individuals in their third and fourth ages mere victims of the cultural context and social attitudes or is there also a possibility for resistance? We address these questions in the next sections.

PERSONAL IDENTITIES

Until now we have described research on the discursive context and social attitudes about ageing. We have seen that the understanding of ageing as physical decline is an important aspect of the institutional arrangements, social attitudes and interactions with older people. We have also seen that the consequences of this view of ageing are manifold for ageing individuals. How, then, do they construe the meanings of their own ageing process? We are now entering the domain of research into self and identity.

From a Foucauldian perspective, discourses provide us with the frameworks in which we order the world and from which we derive our subjectivity. Tulle and Mooney (2002) have argued that, in the field of ageing, discourse provides us with a set of age-appropriate, that is normative, expectations and identities. From a symbolic interactionist perspective, older individuals learn about their own identities through everyday interactions with others. Here, age identities are mainly conceived of as threatened or even spoiled (Goffman, 1968) as people grow older. From a cognitive psychological perspective, individuals interpret their experiences of growing older through the templates and schemes about self and ageing acquired earlier in life (Levy, 2003).

Research has shown that the experience of growing older is a multifaceted process (Von Faber, 2002; Keller *et al.*, 1989; Steverink *et al.*, 2001; Westerhof, 2003). Older people distinguish between positive and negative aspects of their own ageing and they hold different age identities in different domains of functioning, such as physical, social and psychological functioning (Montepare and Zebrowitz, 1998). Keller *et al.* (1989) conducted in-depth interviews on the ageing experience with 32 American community-dwelling adults aged 50 to 80 years and identified five major categories of positive and negative experiences:

- ageing as a natural and gradual process without remarkable features
- ageing as a period of life evaluation, philosophical reflection, or increased wisdom and maturity
- ageing as a period of increased freedom, new interests and fewer demands
- ageing as a period associated with physical health difficulties or concerns about health
- ageing as a period of losses, both interpersonal and job-related.

In the Dutch Ageing Survey, respondents were asked about positive and negative aspects of their own ageing (Westerhof, 2003). Similar results to Keller *et al.* (1989) were found: positive aspects were mainly found in the social domain (e.g. freedom, fewer responsibilities, respect, relationships with grandchildren) and the psychological domain (e.g. life experience, wisdom, inner calmness), whereas negative aspects of one's own ageing process were found in the physical domain (e.g. losses of psychophysical functioning, vitality, mobility, strength, as well as changes in appearance) and in the social domain (e.g. attrition in one's social position, losses in personal relationships and loss of independence).

Studies have found that self-views are consonant with the cultural patterning of the life-course (Cross and Markus, 1991; Dittmann-Kohli, 1995a; Dittmann-Kohli *et al.*, 2001; Freund and Smith, 1999; Westerhof *et al.*, 2003a). These studies and others (Hooker, 1999; Westerhof *et al.*, 1998) have found that health and psychophysical functioning become more important aspects of self-concepts as people age. Not only do older people complain more about problems in psychophysical functioning, such as reduced vitality and mobility, but they also construe their future more in terms of remaining healthy and maintaining fitness. Interestingly, in these qualitative studies older people also brought up more often the fact that they were still in good condition and health, showing that this aspect of life becomes more salient in how individuals perceive themselves (see Chapter 13).

Extending this perspective, it has been argued that as individuals age, the stereotypes they previously held about older people are turned towards themselves; that is, they become self-stereotypes. In a series of laboratory studies and longitudinal surveys, Levy (2003) investigated the effects of such self-stereotypes. She primed older people with positive or negative stereotypical words about old age (e.g. wisdom or decrepitude) at speeds below conscious awareness. She found that the older subjects who were primed with the negative stereotypes performed worse on different cognitive memory tasks and motor tasks (handwriting and walking). They also tended to reject life-prolonging interventions that were accepted by subjects who were primed with positive age-stereotypes. The first group also showed higher cardiovascular stress directly after the priming task, as well as after anxiety-producing challenges. In her longitudinal studies she found that individuals who have more positive self-perceptions of ageing had better functional health and were more likely to survive during the 20-year period of the longitudinal study, even when controlling for other factors related to health and survival (age, functional and subjective health, gender, loneliness, race, socio-economic status).

Cross-sectional studies have shown that self-perceptions of ageing are related to subjective well-being. People who feel younger than their actual age report higher levels of life satisfaction, self-esteem, morale, locus of control and positive affect (Barak and Stern, 1986). People who experience their own ageing process more in terms of physical or social decline report lower levels of subjective well-being, whereas those who see their own ageing more in terms of continuous growth report higher levels of subjective well-being, controlling for a number of resources that are related to well-being (Steverink *et al.*, 2001; Westerhof, 2003).

We can conclude from these studies that bodily decline is an important aspect of the self-concepts and identities of older individuals, reflecting its salience in the wider discursive context and behaviours that older adults experience in their everyday social interactions. The role played by the decline model in how individuals give meaning to themselves as they grow older has clear-cut effects on well-being, health and longevity: a view of ageing as physical decline may function as a self-fulfilling prophecy, indeed giving rise to more decline. At the same time, they show that there are individual differences in dealing with the ageing experience. Apparently some people, in particular in their third age, are able to resist the dominant view, showing that older people are not mere victims of negative discourses, attitudes and behaviours.

Resistance

Our Foucauldian perspective and the cognitive and symbolic interactionist approaches drawn from social psychology lead us to explore the possibilities for resistance. The notion of 'techniques of the self', borrowed from Foucault and in some cases associated with compliance and social regulation (see Tulle and Mooney, 2002), draws our attention to the agency of ageing individuals themselves (Markula, 2003). Possibilities for resistance are also found in the relative autonomy which symbolic interactionism accords to individuals managing their identities in social situations. Last, the self-regulatory competences which cognitive psychology grants individuals also play a role in producing their own development and life-course trajectories (see Chapter 13). We will provide an overview of the different strategies of self-management which might count as resistance.

A first strategy would be the denial of one's age. Everyone knows of an older resident in a nursing home exclaiming, 'what am I doing here amongst all these oldies?' Systematic research has shown that individuals tend to feel younger than their actual age, and this discrepancy is larger in older groups (Barak and Stern, 1986). Kaufman and Elder (2002), Öberg and Tornstam (2001), Uotinen (1998) and Westerhof et al. (2003b) more recently reported similar findings from studies carried out in the USA, Sweden, Finland and Germany, respectively. In all studies, it was found that respondents feel subjectively younger than their chronological age, although the discrepancy was larger in the United States than in Europe. As in the studies reviewed by Barak and Stern (1986) the discrepancy increased in line with chronological age. Some studies found that there was a gender effect at play: men wanted to be on average 26 years younger than they were, compared to 19 years for women (Kaufman and Elder, 2002). Researchers have interpreted the strategy of identifying with younger ages in a culture that devalues old age as a way to maximise self-esteem and well-being (Filipp and Ferring, 1989; Montepare and Lachman, 1989; Staats, 1996). The relationship between feeling younger and subjective well-being is more pronounced in the United States than in Germany, however (Westerhof and Barrett, 2005).

This strategy may become more difficult as individuals experience declines in bodily functioning and appearance. Health status is indeed found to be one of the strongest predictors of subjective age (Barrett, 2003), proving that as soon as individuals are experiencing worse health, it becomes more difficult for them to dissociate themselves from old age. For example, a person who experiences an illness, particularly a chronic one that tends to be associated with older age, might use a cultural meaning such as 'old age doesn't come alone' and conclude that he or she is really becoming old now (Coupland and Coupland, 1994).

Bodily changes may be a source of ontological insecurity in later life (Wainwright and Turner, 2003). That is, they threaten identity because they unsettle the mind–body unity, where physical integrity reflects and coincides with self-recognition (Leder, 1984). Although Leder's analysis is based on the experience of illness, it could also be applied to the changes in appearance and functioning brought on by biological ageing. In a bid to restore the integrity of the body–mind relationship, older people either tinker with bodily appearance or deny bodily ageing.

As regards the first alternative, we could interpret interventions such as exercise and workouts, hormone replacement therapies, dyeing one's hair, wearing make-up, skin peels, tummy tucks, forehead lifts, hair transplants, botox injections and facial fat grafting as ways not only of improving bodily appearance, of restoring mind–body integrity, but also of fulfilling the demands of post-modern society to look after the self through the care of the body (Gilleard and Higgs, 2000). Öberg and Tornstam (2001) reported that only 8% of men and 16% of women would resort to cosmetic surgery to maintain a youthful appearance. Nevertheless, both men and women, regardless of age, associated slenderness and bodily appearance with youthfulness. They all reported wanting to be fitter and healthy in order to maintain mind–body integrity. This emphasis on bodily aesthetics and the attendant rejection of the old body was a noteworthy finding, showing that here resistance means beating bodily ageing.

The other road would be to distance oneself from bodily ageing. Featherstone and Hepworth (1991) argued that older people made sense of age-related physical changes as a mask that concealed the ageless self. The ageing body in effect was reported as distorting people's true self and the only way to reclaim ontological security was by claiming that the true self was ageless. In other words, the claim to agelessness appeared to fulfil the need to draw attention away from an unwanted outer shell.

Different strategies of presenting the self have been described that divert attention away from ageing bodies. Hazan (1986; 1994) vividly reported on his ethnographic study of a Jewish daycare centre in the East End of London. He found that centre users collectively managed bodily deterioration by 'toning down', or drawing attention away from, differences in physical and cognitive abilities. They also shunned contact with other 'disabled' groups, to avoid any association of centre members with them. On one occasion they enthusiastically allowed themselves to be photographed but only chose photographs that did not render their frailty visible. The centre itself was also run in such a way so as not to assign labels of dependency to centre users. The centre allowed users to maintain their sense of belonging, regardless of physical ability. In contrast, Gubrium and Holstein (1999) found that mentally alert and physically fit residents in a long-stay institution referred to demented residents as vegetables. In both loci, older people distanced themselves from frailty because of its association with the loss of competence. However, they did this in contrasting ways, because of the different ethos and organisational structure of each setting: by finding ways not to draw attention to increasing frailty among centre members, in the former, and by using negatively laden language towards those who had become frail, in the latter. Twigg (2003) has interpreted cantankerous or unhelpful behaviour among very dependent residents in care institutions in a similar way. She has argued that it may in fact be seen as a set of strategies to resist the disempowerment that their physical limitations, on the one hand, and their subjection to the rules and regulations of the institutions, on the other, may be fostering.

We can re-interpret these attempts to efface bodily ageing and of managing the visible signs of age as techniques of the self (Tulle, 2003). Although these strategies serve to restore one's sense of self-worth and well-being, they all make use of the negative discourse of ageing and old age as physical decline. They appear to reproduce and give legitimacy to dominant sets of meanings of ageing and they force older people into compliant behaviours that in the end may only serve to reinforce their marginalisation. The meanings of old age are pushed ever further into 'deep old age', or the fourth age, so that they may even become more, rather than less, negative and skewed.

Thus what is needed is the elaboration of techniques of the self that challenge the dominant view of ageing and being old by offering alternative constructions not based on the achievement of near-youth. Resistance might not simply be about beating regulatory pressures at their own game but about changing the game. In other words, are there other ways for older people to change the game?

Post-modern identities

Hepworth (2004), in a bid to revise the mask of ageing approach, now argues that older people do not necessarily experience themselves as ageless all the time but in response to particular situations. Tulle (2003) found that veteran ageing runners did indeed claim that they felt younger than their unfit contemporaries because of their exceptional physical abilities. On the other hand they were also acutely aware of physical ageing, for instance when they compared their running times over time or when they attempted to anticipate their future as elite athletes. Thus the mask of ageing and the claim to agelessness that appears to go with it is only one response to ageing and one that depends on the situation.

We have seen that although the perspective on ageing as physical decline is dominant, ageing has other meanings as well at all three levels described in this chapter. Autonomy, participation, activity and consumption were found to play a role in recent political and media discourses on ageing; attitudes towards older individuals were not found to be negative on social and personality dimensions; and older people experienced gains in social and psychological domains of functioning. One way of resisting ageing as physical decline consists of bringing these other meanings of ageing more to the fore. When such reconstructions of ageing are not derived from our youth-oriented culture, but value these aspects of life that are inherent to ageing in our present-day culture, such as life experience, grandparenthood, individual freedom and responsibility, then there is an opportunity to foster 'agefulness' instead of agelessness (Andrews, 1999).

A strategy of resistance that is significant here is the reframing of the concepts of ageing and older people in a more positive way. A representative survey showed that older individuals residing in the EU preferred the terms 'senior citizens' (31%), 'older people' (27%), or 'retired people' (15%). These terms appear to have positive connotations of integration and activity. They stress citizenship, personhood and the restoration of social capital and they see age only as an attribute, rather than as a defining characteristic. In contrast, the term most commonly used by policy-makers, the media and social gerontologists – that is, 'the elderly' – is firmly rejected (Walker and Maltby, 1997). Such a strategy is similar to the change from Negroes to Blacks to African Americans in the United States. Indeed, terms like 'grey power' and the 'Gray Panthers' have already been used by politically active organisations of older people.

Post-modern, consumerist culture has been both praised and criticised for its complexity. Some scholars see this complexity as liberating, opening up new opportunities and flexibility (Gergen and Gergen, 2000). Others describe it in terms of fragmentation, leading to an empty, superficial self without any real commitments (Cushman, 1990). Inspired by Carl Gustav Jung, Biggs (1999, 2003) has argued that masquerade plays an important role in reconciling social exigencies with a more deeply rooted sense of self that is hidden in public life. Masks are mainly developed in early adulthood, but during midlife individuals experience more and more discomfort with these masks as they increasingly cease to represent the deeper rooted sense of identity. After midlife, individuals develop a more playful type of masquerade that, far from rejecting the ageing of identity, in fact embraces the process, thus opening the way for more authentic ageing (Biggs, 2004).

CONCLUSIONS

Accentuating the positive meanings of ageing and old age, reframing these concepts and making visible the flexible adjustments of identities of people growing older, may pave the way for a less homogenous treatment of ageing and old age. They make clear that ageing and being old are just one aspect of one's life. They also point out that it is important to realise diversity among older people as well as flexibility of identities across different situations. In this sense, the complexities of the ageing process are not reduced to a single perspective of ageing as physical decline, however natural and insuperable the latter may seem to us.

However, the self cannot be reconstructed purely in individual terms, without taking account of the context in which ageing is experienced and ageing identities made possible. The changes in the discursive contexts that we have seen mainly in social policies and the media in the post-modern era may give rise to the development of more diverse ways of looking at ageing and old age. As we have seen before, a new phase of life, the third age, has developed over the past decades (Laslett, 1989). This new phase is linked to recent social policies and media images and it is experienced by a group of rather well-educated, financially secure and healthy baby-boomers whose experiences contrast with those of earlier cohorts but more importantly with many of their age contemporaries. For third-agers, the retirement phase is no longer construed as a period of disengagement from society, but as a period of active re-engagement and consumption. Together with a change from the standard biography to a choice biography in post-modern culture, the importance of freedom and individual choice in the third phase of life is an important aspect of the cultural change that has affected old age.

Nevertheless, there continue to be more structurally based obstacles to experiencing meaningful ageing and constructing ageing identities: gender and class inequalities continue to marginalise older people. The very old, or fourth-agers, are at particular continuing risk of exclusion. Thus the call to positive well-being is meaningless without tackling these inequalities of opportunities. Only if older people themselves have power and control in bringing these positive meanings to the fore and, in the process, improve their own social and cultural capital (Tulle, 2004), can individual and social acts be understood as resistance. In other words, changing meanings is not thinkable without corresponding improvements in the structural location of older people.

FURTHER READING

Featherstone, M. and Wernick, A. (eds) (1995) *Images of Ageing: Cultural Respresentation of Later Life.* London: Routledge.

Nelson, T. D. (ed.) (2002) *Ageism: Stereotyping and Prejudice Against Older Persons.* Cambridge, MA: MIT Press.

Steverink, N., Westerhof, G. J., Bode, C. and Dittmann-Kohli, F. (2001) The personal experience of growing old: resources and subjective well-being. *Journal of Gerontology* **56B**, P364–373.

Tulle, E. (ed.) (2004) *Old Age and Agency.* Hauppauge, NY: Novascience.

Westerhof, G. J., Dittmann-Kohli, F. and Bode, C. (2003) The aging paradox: towards personal meaning in gerontological theory. In: Biggs, S., Lowenstein, A. and Hendricks, J. (eds) *The Need for Theory: Social Gerontology for the 21st Century,* 127–143. Amityville, NY: Baywood Publishing.

12

Competence and cognition

Ralf Th. Krampe and Lynn McInnes

INTRODUCTION

As we have seen in a number of earlier chapters, the concepts of 'age', 'old' and 'ageing' enjoy a diversity of meanings and connotations from the perspectives of different scientists engaged in gerontology, different cultures and social groups experiencing ageing in their day-to-day lives and within the development and implementation of public policy. In particular, scientific attempts to categorise life-periods and people's experience and self-perception seem to be at odds with employment strategies and social policies. One well-documented form of institutionalised ageism (see Chapter 6) is that older employees are considered less flexible and less competent than younger adults when it comes to mastering new professional challenges and developing new skills. The chances of older workers being rehired after unemployment are much lower than for younger workers. To accommodate these trends, some European states have passed protective laws for older employees but, in some countries, early retirement continues to be promoted although the trend is declining (see Chapter 8). This is in contrast to apprehension about the increasing gerontic dependency ratios in most European countries and concerns about the immense waste of skill and productivity accompanying early withdrawal from the labour market. A key factor here is the continuing stereotypes about older people and older workers in particular about competencies and the ability of older people to learn new skills.

This chapter reviews the extant models and empirical findings related to competencies and learning in adulthood. It discusses potentials and limitations of younger and older adults and highlights some of the ecological constraints on older adults' performances. Its starting point is the paradox of how to reconcile general age-related declines in basic cognitive functions with expert performances in later life in the context of societal stereotypes of older people and the different perspectives on ageing provided by older people themselves, public policy in relation to employment and some of the challenges of different 'scientific' theories. The chapter continues with different theoretical accounts and data from age-comparative studies on expertise and high-level skills. Evidence from studies investigating learnability for new skills (cognitive plasticity) in younger and older adults is presented. The role of physical and bodily constraints on cognitive performance in later life is investigated. Finally the chapter examines the role of older people in the workforce given what is known about competencies in later life, and considers some of the challenges for employers and older adults themselves. The chapter concludes with a summary of key findings and offers some implications for future challenges faced by ageing societies.

AGEISM, GENERAL SLOWING AND OLDER EXPERTS

Studies from occupational psychology appear to defy negative stereotypes about older employees. Two meta-analyses (McEvoy and Cascio, 1989; Waldman and Avolio, 1986) of cross-sectional comparisons found the relationship between age and productivity in work settings to be near zero or even slightly positive. Experimental ageing research and psychometric intelligence testing portray a less optimistic picture. The ubiquitous outcome in age-comparative studies with normal adults is that the *cognitive mechanics* (reaction time, speed of memory search, reasoning speed, motor speed and precision) undergo systematic age-related declines from young to late adulthood (Baltes *et al.*, 1999b; Li *et al.*, 2004; Rabbitt, 1993a; Rabbitt *et al.*, 2004). Older adults in their seventh decade of life typically need about 1.6 to 2 times as long to process the same tasks as adults in their twenties do, a phenomenon referred to as *general age-related slowing* or the processing-speed mediation of adult age differences in cognition (Salthouse, 1996). Likewise, large-scale cross-sectional studies revealed sizeable age-graded declines in performances on subscales of IQ-tests, which measure speed and accuracy of performance, starting as early as age 30 (Kaufman, 2001). Language abilities (word knowledge) and competencies based on declarative knowledge show more gentle (if any) deteriorations with advanced age (Kaufman, 2001; Li *et al.*, 2004; Rabbitt, 1993a; Rabbitt *et al.*, 2004).

The bottom line is that 'normal' ageing tends to reduce the speed and efficiency of cognitive, perceptual and psychomotor functions. From the assumption that these processes form the building blocks or integrate components of expert performance, one would expect such age-related reductions to affect professional competence. Thus, from the perspectives of experimental ageing research the impressive accomplishments of elderly experts (like virtuouso musical performances of older musicians) or successful entrepreneurs and business people present a puzzle. One potential explanation (and a valid criticism of most studies in occupational psychology or expertise research) is that competent older individuals in cross-sectional comparisons are the rare survivors of long-term selection processes and thus are hardly representative for their age groups (e.g. Salthouse and Maurer, 1996). For example, professionals whose performance declines with advancing age might be forced to retire or move to less challenging occupations. In societies that appreciate experience and social networks over actual accomplishment, the same effects are typically achieved by promotion to better paid though less challenging positions. An approach to shed light on these issues is to combine experimental investigations of skilled performance with assessments of general processing speed or psychometric marker tests of basic abilities in samples of younger and older experts. These empirical studies and related theoretical accounts are addressed in the next section.

AGEING AND EXPERTISE

Throughout history, common sense or folk psychology has valued outstanding accomplishments by older individuals like the wisdom of elderly politicians and statesmen and stateswomen or the swan-song oeuvres of famous composers. In the public's opinion, advanced age is typically identified with maturity or heightened levels of experience, which complement the exceptional talents or gifts that had presumably enabled outstanding individuals to surpass ordinary people in the first place. The key questions in scientific research have been whether older experts or highly competent older individuals are exempt from general age-graded declines in cognitive functioning or have they maintained their competencies in spite of age-related declines demonstrated for general abilities in the 'normal' population. Three different accounts related to these questions have been proposed (compare Krampe and Baltes, 2003; Krampe and Charness, 2006; Salthouse, 1991b).

The first account maintains that the highly competent or experts among older people have always been superior in skill-relevant abilities such that their advantages at any age could be attributed to inter-individual differences with long-term stability that existed prior to expertise acquisition. This account shares similarities with talent accounts of exceptional levels of performance equally applicable at younger ages. For example, specific talents or dispositions for visuo-spatial processing might motivate a gifted individual to pursue a career as an architect or graphic designer and benefit her professional success. Assuming that the critical abilities undergo the same age-related decline as general functions, this individual will still excel in her age group as older adult. This account is also referred to as 'preserved differentiation' in the literature (Salthouse et al., 1990).

Critical dispositions need not necessarily be innate, however, they are assumed to precede skill acquisition.

The second position assumes that the process of competence development involves gradual improvements in those abilities that constrain normal performance (like working memory span) such that specific skills or even expertise should transfer to some (but not all) broader cognitive functions. As in the first theoretical position, the implication of this account is that older experts should differ from non-expert individuals not only in measures relevant to their domain of expertise, but also in other measures, like speeded processing of any type of materials.

Finally, the third account posits that high levels of competence or expertise at any age rest on specific mechanisms that must be acquired and maintained through individual efforts directed at long-term adaptation to internal constraints (e.g. age-related changes in cognitive functions) and external constraints (e.g. task-domain, professional environment) (Ericsson et al., 1993; Ericsson and Charness, 1994; Ericsson and Lehmann, 1996; Krampe and Ericsson, 1996). This account maintains that expertise and high levels of professional competence are domain-specific, that is older experts differ from controls only in tasks closely related to their area of skill, but they show the typical age-related decline in basic cognitive motor functions with speed aspects (i.e. they experience age-related slowing).

Age-comparative studies with individuals differing in their levels of expertise have been conducted in such diverse domains as typewriting (Bosman, 1993; Salthouse, 1984), chess (Charness, 1981a; Charness, 1981b; Charness et al., 1996), bridge (Charness, 1989), GO (a Japanese board game similar to chess; Masunaga and Horn, 2001), piloting (Morrow et al., 1994; Morrow et al., 2001), Mastermind (Maylor, 1994), crossword-puzzle solving (Hambrick et al., 1999; Rabbitt, 1993b), management skills (Colonia-Willner, 1998; Walsh and Hershey, 1993), and music (Krampe and Ericsson, 1996; Meinz, 2000). The general picture emerging from these studies was that older experts show 'normal' (i.e., similar to non-expert controls) age-graded declines in general measures of processing speed, cognitive abilities as measured through psychometric tests, and performance on unfamiliar materials. At the same time, older experts show reduced, if any, age-related declines in the efficiencies or the speed at which they perform skill-related tasks. One exception is the poorer air traffic control message recall performance of older pilots compared to younger pilots. However, when the task was changed to a realistic one that allowed note-taking, Morrow et al. (2003) showed that age differences disappeared.

Related studies are subject to the same criticism of selection effects that we described earlier. However, they successfully demonstrated older experts' high levels of functionality in *specific* processes (even if assessed under laboratory conditions) despite obvious 'normal' age-related declines in speeded types of general information processing. Thus, general information processing speed and performance IQ must not be considered good correlates of professional skill in later adulthood. A distinctive prediction of the third account is that levels of performance at each stage of development or age should be a direct function of deliberate practice (Ericsson *et al.,* 1993). Deliberate practice refers to an individual's investment of time and effort to improve or maintain skills. This notion is distinct from 'experience' in a given domain, like extended routine performance of the same activities or leisurely exercise without trying to optimise one's performance (Krampe and Ericsson, 1996).

Two studies have explicitly addressed the role of deliberate maintenance practice in older experts. Krampe and Ericsson (1996) studied young (aged 20–29 years) and older (aged 55–65 years) expert and amateur pianists. They used a combination of experimental and psychometric methods of ability assessment along with self-report and diary data measuring the time investment into deliberate practice and other activities. The expertise-related abilities tested comprised not only virtuoso skills like maximum repetitive tapping and speeded multi-finger sequencing tasks, but also non-speeded tasks like memorisation of sequences and (rated) expressive musical interpretation. In line with the results summarised earlier, the authors found that older professional pianists showed normal age-related declines in measures of general processing speed like choice reaction time or performance IQ. Age effects in expertise-related measures of multi-finger coordination speed were similar to the above pattern in the amateur group, but were reduced or fully absent in the expert sample. Taken together these findings led to an age-by-expertise dissociation of mechanisms supporting general processing and expertise-specific processing, respectively.

Krampe and Ericsson (1996) argued that this dissociation reflects older experts' selective maintenance of acquired, expertise-specific mechanisms like the advance preparation of movements. Consistent with this interpretation, the degree to which levels of performance in speeded expertise tasks was maintained depended on the amounts of deliberate practice invested at the later stages of expertise development, namely in the fifth and sixth decades of life. Note that measures of general processing speed did not relate to the inter-individual differences in skilled performance in the expert group. In contrast, however, such measures correlated with performance in the amateur group, suggesting that expertise decouples itself from the negative age-related decline in general abilities (Krampe and Baltes, 2003).

In a similar vein, Charness *et al.* (1996) found that chess ratings (based on chess tournament performance) in a large sample of rated players covering ages from 20 to 80 years depended on amounts of deliberate practice far more than on chronological age (standardised coefficients in a regression equation were −0.38 for age and 0.62 for deliberate practice). In addition, regression analyses revealed that older players needed more current deliberate practice than younger players to reach equivalent skill levels, again pointing to the continued need to invest deliberate efforts into the maintenance of skills at advanced ages. A second interaction suggested a law of diminishing returns for deliberate practice later in life: additional amounts of cumulative deliberate practice did not reap the same gains in skill level for older players. Continued effects of maintenance practice were also demonstrated in the domain of sports (Ericsson, 1990).

These studies, though correlational in their approaches, demonstrate the importance of active maintenance of competencies through individual efforts in terms of investments of mental and physical efforts; that is, deliberate practice. They also show that mere experience (staying on the job) is not sufficient to this end and that leisurely engagement (as with the older amateurs) with low levels of goal-directed practice distributed over decades does not suffice towards this end.

For some time, researchers have expressed concerns about the *decontextualisation* of tests designed in the IQ-based tradition and standard laboratory tasks as valid indicators of competencies and cognition in older adults (Dixon and Baltes, 1986; Horn and Masunaga, 2000; Sternberg and Wagner, 1986). As a result, more ecologically based approaches focusing on everyday competencies and real-life expertise have emerged. Research agendas have changed from finding correlates or causes of age-related decline to identifying mechanisms that support successful ageing in those individuals that maintain competencies at high levels, or to design interventions suitable for developing older adults' potentials. The next section summarises the evidence from one type of intervention, namely cognitive training specifically designed for older adults, and then examines the ecological constraints on developing cognitive competencies in older adults.

COGNITIVE PLASTICITY AND TRAINING OLDER ADULTS

Cognitive plasticity is the central concept motivating extensive skill acquisition and training studies with older adults. At the neural level, the concept of plasticity refers to the capacity of the brain to change cortical representations as a function of experience. At the behavioural level, plasticity denotes the (reserve) capacity to extend the behavioural repertoire by acquiring new skills or behaviours through experience or practice (Baltes and Singer, 2001; Buonomano and Merzenich, 1998; Singer, 1995). Over the last decades, cognitive-ageing research has generated much optimism by showing that older adults in their sixties and seventies continue to profit from learning and can clearly improve their performances even in psychometric tests of fluid intelligence (Baltes *et al.*, 1996; Baltes and Willis, 1982; Hofland *et al.*, 1981; Schaie and Willis, 1986; Willis, 1990). Likewise, neuropsychological studies (e.g. Kaas, 1991; Karni *et al.*, 1995; Wang *et al.*, 1995) support the view that brain plasticity extends into later adulthood and may be considered a life-long phenomenon. This is in contrast to the stereotypical view that ageing is a period of cognitive decline where new skills cannot be learnt. Plasticity in late adulthood is not limited to the acquisition of knowledge-based skills. Playing a musical instrument increases the cortical representation of the hand and single fingers and the size of the effect correlates to the years of training (Elbert *et al.,* 1995). Plasticity of related brain areas has also been demonstrated for older adults who take up playing the violin or intensify their practice regime later in life (Elbert *et al.,* 1996).

Although older people can learn new skills and behaviours, there are caveats to their performance. Cavallini *et al.* (2003) showed that while older adults can be trained to use memory strategies, and that training using the method of loci and strategic training both led to an improvement in memory performance, younger adults still outperformed older adults following training. Training was most beneficial when used with ecological tasks, which was supported by Auffray and Juhel's (2001) research showing that older people benefit most when cognitive programmes use less abstract exercises.

The amount of reserve capacity or the degree of plasticity appears to be subject to age-related changes. Compared with younger adults, older adults tend to benefit less from performance-enhancing training programmes, need more cognitive support during training, comply less with instructions, apply the methods correctly less often, and their ultimate levels of performance attained after training is below that of younger adults (Baltes and Baltes, 1997; Camp, 1998; Verhaeghen and Marcoen, 1996; Verhaeghen *et al.,* 1992). The latter point is most evident from studies applying the testing-the-limits paradigm (Kliegl and Baltes, 1987) in which healthy younger and older adults were extensively trained with a mnemonic technique (the method of loci). Older adults' memory performance after training clearly surpassed that of untrained younger adults. A comparison of groups after training showed, however, that age effects were magnified: after 38 sessions of training there was almost no overlap of the distributions of young and older participants (Baltes and Kliegl, 1992; Kliegl *et al.,* 1989; Kliegl *et al.,* 1990).

One implication of these findings is that older adults in their third age (aged 60–79 years) can quite successfully master new skills – 'old dogs can learn new tricks' – but their ultimate potential for high levels of functioning is reduced relative to younger adults. Such reductions in cognitive plasticity and learning potential are even more pronounced during the fourth age (aged 80 years or more). Singer *et al.* (2003) conducted memory training with a large sample of adults ranging in their ages between 75 and 105. Not all participants in this group were able to profit from the instruction with the mnemonic technique. Moreover, following the basic initiation to the method, even most among those who had benefited from instruction failed to further improve their performance. In contrast, younger adults continuously improved their performance through continued training. Auffray and Juhel (2001) suggested that cognitive plasticity may not be possible for those in their fourth age especially with low cognitive levels and limited educational background. More recently, Yang *et al.* (2006) showed that older adults in their fourth age could improve existing abilities, like performances on reasoning tests or markers of fluid intelligence, but their learning potential was significantly smaller than in younger adults and older adults in their sixties and seventies.

Two other age-related limitations in older adults' learning potential became evident from recent training and intervention studies, namely:

- older adults' failure to optimise learning benefits to the level of flawless performances in certain tasks
- older adults' increasing need for specific tutoring, feedback and training methods.

The latter characteristic, typical of older adults' limitations in acquiring new skills, emerged from a series of intervention studies focusing on face–name memory (Kliegl *et al.*, 2001). Everyday problems with associating faces with names or locations are among the top complaints in healthy older adults, and several experiments failed to demonstrate substantial training benefits in laboratory tasks even with older adults who were from the top-percentiles of their age-graded distributions in fluid intelligence (Kliegl *et al.*, 2001). In their intervention study of face–place memory, Kliegl *et al.* (2001) used a cognitive-engineering approach based on the concept of deliberate practice proposed by Ericsson *et al.* (1993). Older participants were not only trained in a mnemonic skill, but were also given extensive tutoring in elaborating memory cues specific to the trained materials (i.e. details in the pictures of faces presented and associative cues for the landmarks). A noticeable difference from earlier laboratory studies was that participants could repeatedly work on the same lists thereby optimising their encoding strategies using computers for practice at their homes. The authors observed a clear positive intervention effect after such extensive coaching. However, the levels of performance achieved were still considerably below that typical of younger adults after much less practice and limited tutoring conditions.

These findings indicate that continued everyday experiences with a task and even repeated exercise under laboratory training conditions are not sufficient to mobilise older adults' reserve capacities. Compensating for age-related declines in specific processes like episodic encoding of visuo-spatial materials requires extensive deliberate efforts on the part of older individuals. At the same time, the outcome falls short of what young adults can achieve with far less effort. Kliegl *et al.* (2001) proposed that perfecting certain everyday skills in older adults might involve as much effort and training as required from a young individual who starts to learn playing a musical instrument. As a general rule, the potential to acquire new skills appears to be far more constrained in older adults than the potential to maintain existing competencies.

In conclusion, reviews of the memory training literature (e.g. Whitbourne, 2001) showed that while older people can be successfully trained to use mnemonics, to organise material to aid memory and to use environmental supports, once training has ended they often fail to use them in the 'real world'. For memory training strategies to be more effective and actually used they should assist older people in devising their own strategies and take into account their learning styles (Whitbourne, 2001). Boosting self-efficacy and beliefs about their memory is often just as important for improving memory as actual strategies. Indeed, Hayslip's (1989) work showed that reducing anxiety when people take intelligence tests can be just as effective in leading to gains in intelligence as training.

The next section highlights factors influencing intellectual functioning in later adulthood to degrees that match cognitive constraints – but which received far less attention until recently.

BODILY CONSTRAINTS ON COGNITIVE FUNCTIONING IN OLDER ADULTS

Coordinating multiple activities in time or adapting to concurrent task demands is a frequent characteristic in everyday life and, even more so, in professional settings. Consider, as examples, navigating through an unfamiliar environment while conducting an on-going conversation, or arising at important decisions while listening (or at least pretending to listen) to endless statements at committee meetings. The metaphor employed by psychological theories addressing related problems is that of an individual commanding a limited pool of cognitive resources, which must be efficiently allocated to concurrent processing demands. To investigate resource demands and resource allocation processes, experimentors use the dual-task paradigm, in which concurrent-task performances are contrasted with single-task performances for the same individual. Performance decrements in dual- as compared to single-tasks are referred to as dual-task costs (DTCs). The general finding in the literature is that DTCs are larger in older than in younger adults (Hartley and Little, 1999; see Li *et al.*, 2005, for an overview). From these results we may conclude that older adults have specific problems in coordinating concurrent activities, both in terms of the challenge such situations provide and also in terms of the speed and accuracy of performances. Multi-tasking is considered a special instance of executive control (Baddeley, 1996) and recent neuro-psychological evidence has linked negative age effects in such functions to changes in certain brain areas, like the dorsolateral prefrontal cortex (Baddeley *et al.*, 1997).

Most dual-task studies used combinations of two cognitive tasks (e.g. reaction time and memorisation). More recently, researchers have systematically investigated the interplay of cognitive processes and bodily functions that were considered largely automatic. Particularly, in the domain of cognitive ageing sensorimotor functions with high ecological validity for certain age groups have received growing attention. Maintaining postural stability is a task of high ecological validity for older adults, because the risk of falling is alarmingly high in the older population (Fuller, 2000) and falls can have dramatic consequences at advanced ages. Epidemiological studies in different countries revealed that more than a third of the individuals above the age of 65 years experience at least one involuntary fall per year. Different from traditional approaches focusing exclusively on vestibular functions, postural control has recently been linked to higher-level (cortical) control processes, particularly in older adults. In a typical dual-task study involving postural control, participants perform cognitive tasks (memorisation, problem-solving, visual search) under standard laboratory conditions (single-task condition: sitting in front of a computer screen) as well as concurrently with a postural control task (dual-task situation: standing on a force platform that measures postural sway). Comparisons of performances under single- and dual-task conditions reveal the costs (dual-task costs) that concurrent cognitive demands impose on postural stability and vice versa.

Related studies for the most part replicated the finding of increased DTCs in older adults and suggested that postural control is in fact cognitively demanding in older participants (Woollacott and Shumway-Cook, 2002). For example, Rapp et al. (2006) found that healthy adults in their sixties and seventies could produce only 90% of the memory performances they had produced sitting when they were standing. Importantly, concurrent performance of a challenging memory task also reduced older participants' postural stability to 80% of their baseline performances (simple standing and doing a cognitively undemanding task). Memory performance in older participants was further reduced, when the supporting platform was regularly tilting at small angles and relatively modest velocities. In contrast, younger participants showed no reductions in memory performances under dual-task conditions and only small increases in postural sway. Even the sensory and motor aspects of a task such as walking need attentional resources as age advances, which reduces cognitive resources for memorising (Lindenberger et al., 2000).

Increasing difficulty to simultaneously accommodate everyday sensorimotor demands and mental activities are now considered a prime candidate explanation for the alarmingly high prevalence of incidental falls among older people. Sensorimotor functions that appear automatic in younger adults become increasingly demanding in terms of cognitive resources when we grow older. Aggravating factors impairing postural control are obesity and diabetes type 2 (which are, naturally, related). From the perspective of appreciating and optimising adults' cognitive performances in professional and everyday contexts, such ecological constraints warrant more attention at levels preceding physical handicaps or diagnosed diseases. The impact of physical conditions on cognitive performance and the potential of physical training as a means of improving cognitive functioning in older adults are also evident from recent work by Kramer and colleagues (Kramer et al., 1999). Training studies demonstrated that older adults can indeed improve and reduce multi-task coordination costs (Kramer et al., 1995). At the level of daily activities, the constraints of bodily functions were illustrated by one finding in the aforementioned study on expert pianists (Krampe and Ericsson, 1996): according to their diary data, older experts spent reliably more time on health and body care than did their young counterparts (Krampe, 1994). From the perspective of adaptive resource allocation, such increased time demands for health maintenance must limit the available time for maintaining expert levels of performance.

THE OLDER WORKER

With the ageing population there is likely to be a significant increase in the number of older people in the future workforce (Brooke, 2003; Williamson and Crumpton, 1997) and older people will be expected to work past what is generally now accepted to be retirement age. This has implications for organisations; how will they manage older employees in an ever changing workplace where advances in technology mean that job roles can change rapidly and retraining is needed. Organisations need to know if their older employees can meet the demands placed upon them: can they adapt, can they be retrained, how should training be structured and at what cost (Brooke, 2003)? The stereotypical view held by both employees and employers is that, due to cognitive and physical changes as people age, many older people will not be able to make effective contributions and keep up to date in the workforce. Yeatts *et al.* (2000) noted that many older workers indeed prefer to retire rather than adapt to new working roles, but this leaves the employer with a lack of employees with the knowledge and skills gained through experience. Employers are now therefore realising the value of older, experienced workers as reflected in a change to more positive perceptions about an ageing workforce by managers (Lyon and Pollard, 1997).

The training of older workers is going to become an area of rapid development and, given that age discrimination laws have been introduced, the view – noted by Goldstein (1993) – that older workers cannot perform as well on the job and cannot acquire new skills will no longer be admissible by organisations for failing to provide adequate training for the older workforce. The evidence discussed in this chapter indeed suggests that such views are unfounded. Goldstein (1993) reports a meta-analysis by McEvoy and Cascio and a review by Rhodes which both led to the conclusion that age and performance are, for the most part, unrelated, especially when experience is taken into account. Age and performance relationships are to be found only when the job requires speed or accuracy of movement. These reviews therefore suggest that training is viable for older workers but it needs to take into account the changes that laboratory studies have identified that take place with ageing in the areas of memory, intellect and speed of processing.

Goldstein (1993) reports a review of training literature by Sterns and Doverspike who concluded that, for older people to achieve most success from training programmes, the training needs to be job relevant, to build on tasks that the person is familiar with, to ensure mastery at a lower level before preceding to the next level, to be organized to reduce load on memory, and to reduce demands for speed and time pressure. Older people may also need more time and assistance to meet the required standards. The effects of this differential training for younger and older workers needs further research to determine how well such strategies work, how well it is accepted and how beneficial it is to all parties (Thayer, 1997). The fear of age discrimination with regard to training and development offered to its workers is real (Maurer and Rafuse, 2001) and will prompt research to determine the most appropriate way for training to take place given what is known about the capabilities and limits of the ageing brain.

Whatever studies take place with older participants, be they of intervention, plasticity or occupational training, it must be remembered that as sample age increases cognitive variability among the sample also increases. Rabbitt's longitudinal studies into cognitive ageing (Rabbitt, 1993a; Rabbitt et al., 2001a, 2004) have demonstrated a most important point about cognitive changes with age, in that individuals differ markedly in the rates and so amounts of change on cognitive tests as they grow older. Individuals age 'cognitively' at different rates in such a way that knowing someone's chronological age tells us little about their cognitive skills. Similarly, Singer et al. (2003) found there are large individual differences in cognitive plasticity in old age. Rabbitt et al. (2004) suggested two reasons for this increase in variability. First, a person's genetic inheritance, health and life history mean that people of the same age will show variability; and second, as people age their performance varies more from day to day (Rabbitt, 1999b; Rabbitt et al., 2001b). It is of great practical importance for employers and older people themselves to be aware of this variability for it emphasises that people must be treated as individuals; and that, while one person may show cognitive decline, another of the same age may not. Organisations should therefore try to develop individual training plans for their older workers to suit the skills and abilities of each of its members.

CONCLUSIONS

This chapter started out from the paradox of feeling old and being treated as 'old' and the seeming contradiction between age-related declines in basic cognitive motor functions and high-level competencies in older experts. The conceptual approach was informed by a lifespan developmental perspective and models of real-life expertise development. Both frameworks emphasise the additive value of individual resource allocation; that is, the investment of time and effort into the development of skills. The review of empirical evidence converged on the decoupling of specific skills from more general abilities during adult development. Individual resource investments in terms of time and effort spent on the acquisition or maintenance of specific skills shape the trajectories of changes in professional and everyday competencies. The bottom line is that individuals in their third age have considerable control over the development of their skills, and cognitive plasticity enables them to learn new, even complex, skills and to largely maintain existing competencies. None of this comes freely; mere 'experience' does not give protection from age-related decline.

Resource investments are constrained by age-graded changes, both in terms of the overall resources available and in terms of reduced cognitive plasticity. Among the key factors constraining cognitive resources is bodily functioning, which limits the effort that older individuals can invest into the maintenance of their skills and into acquiring new skills. In addition, in older adults their bodily functions, like maintaining a stable posture, place a burden on cognitive resources, which are no longer available for concurrent mental tasks. As to plasticity, older adults require more time, and more intense, qualitatively different coaching support to acquire new skills. The outcome of extended training in older adults is typically below the level of performance attained by younger adults. This is problematic in professions like piloting, but can be acceptable in most professional domains.

This largely positive perspective applies to what is called the third age, which is roughly the period between ages 60 and 80. The prospects for the so-called fourth age are far less optimistic. Individuals differ substantially with respect to the onset of this latter phase of more rapid decline and increased impairment. Ageing societies must face the challenge of accommodating the potentials and the constraints of the third age, while providing flexible transitions to the fourth age that take account of individual differences. Chronological age tells us little about a person's ability, so generalisations should not be made about how a 'typical' 60-year-old, 70-year-old or 80-year-old will perform. In each age group some individuals will have changed very little and will learn effectively while others will have shown marked decline. It is of great practical importance for employers and those working with older members of the population to treat people as individuals and not be influenced by negative age stereotypes.

There is nothing wrong with universities offering senior degrees for retirees, but this is not what lifelong learning should be about. Much teaching of basic skills in schools, universities and industry could be done by those 'older' professionals (aged 55–70 years) if they are given a reduction in workload and a shift in criteria for evaluating their contributions. Naturally, this societal commitment to individual differences has to go along with a flexibility in salaries – potential reductions included.

FURTHER READING

Cavallini, E., Pagnin, A. and Vecchi, T. (2003) Aging and everyday memory: the beneficial effect of memory training. *Archives of Gerontology and Geriatrics* **37**, 241–257.

Rabbitt, P. M. A., McInnes, L., Diggle, P., Holland, F., Bent, N., Abson, V., Pendleton, N. and Horan, M. (2004) The University of Manchester longitudinal study of cognition in normal healthy old age, 1983 through 2003. *Aging, Neuropsychology and Cognition* **11**, 245–279.

13

Self and life management: Wholesome knowledge for the third age

Freya Dittmann-Kohli and Daniela Jopp

INTRODUCTION

The term 'wholesome knowledge' (Assmann, 1994) designates types of knowledge and cognitive activity that are intended to improve or preserve human beings. Our focus here is on knowledge that may be beneficial for older individuals and may help to develop new thought content. To be beneficial, knowledge should help to enhance broad goals like the development and management of the inner self and one's (outer) life. Such development is planned and intentional (Brandtstädter, 1999a), as well as intuitively growth-oriented. In this process, inner and outer resources are used, suitable goals are generated, barriers and difficulties are overcome.

Self-determined action to promote personal growth and life management is a relatively new phenomenon in European history (Taylor, 1989). For many centuries, the church dominated and decided what was wholesome and valuable in individuals' lives. Ordinary life was not considered important or under individuals' control. Nowadays, ordinary life is considered as being 'the real thing', in which individuals develop their own life goals and make their own life choices. Life quality is taken to be a relevant primary goal with individuals seeking greater life fulfilment. Wholesome knowledge for personal development serves individual needs and helps develop desired characteristics. Individuals are assumed to profit from wholesome knowledge since it inspires them and helps them to grow, unfold, and learn to lead a personally meaningful life. Self and life management are here understood as processes that utilise knowledge and cognitive skills to improve or reconstruct identity and life (style).

Since the Enlightenment, scientific enquiry has contributed to the systematic development of 'wholesome knowledge'. In psychological research a starting point has been the observation of factors that are linked to psychological well-being in the broadest sense. From a psychological perspective, the purpose of wholesome knowledge is to facilitate and promote healthy development, to prevent disturbances and to restore normal and optimal functioning. Such 'positive psychology' is a relatively new movement that explicitly aims to reach such goals (e.g. Aspinwall and Staudinger, 2003; Seligman, 1991). In addition to such knowledge for individual ends, wholesome knowledge for collective ends, for groups, institutions, countries and world communities is produced systematically.

Our modern scientific efforts to identify and generate wholesome knowledge for individual and social ends can be traced back to times in ancient civilization, when questions of individual goals, choices and conduct were in need of answers; the answers found have been summarised often under the term 'wisdom'. According to research of an historical anthropologist, wisdom is a domain of very ancient knowledge (Assmann, 1994). Though under different societal, cultural and economic conditions, certain trans-historical aspects of individual life tasks and problems of self and life management surfaced thousands of years ago. Ancient texts contain advice on how to lead a good and respected life, and how to keep the right orientations. In ancient Egypt, groups of teaching-for-life texts were transferred to educational books and used widely (Baumgartner, 1933). Wisdom or the so-called *Lebenslehren* (teaching for life) have been centred on core aspects as well as on more superficial sides of human conduct, beliefs and value orientations. They were presented as coming from father to son, or from wise teachers or elders to the young. In the Old Testament, we also find wisdom books. Greek and Roman efforts in respect to defining and reconstructing the meaning of wisdom are described by various authors. In early medieval times, scholars also were interested in understanding and developing further the idea of age-related wisdom as wholesome knowledge (Assmann, 1994; cf. Brandt, 2002). Before psychology developed as a science, wise insights were generated in philosophy and theology; religious advice especially often provided wholesome knowledge on existential situations.

Nowadays, such domains of knowledge have been subsumed and investigated under the term 'pragmatic wisdom' by Baltes and colleagues (see Chapter 3). Advice for self and life management emerges to a large extent from many differentiated spheres of psychological research and knowledge production (e.g. Brower and Nurius, 1993; Steverink *et al.*, 2005) and is transmitted through books and other media. Psychotherapies consist of wholesome knowledge used to solve personal problems and to restore mental health. Print and other mass media are used to diffuse and implement wholesome knowledge for the larger public, and many institutions and practices exist that support and direct wholesome individual education and development.

WHOLESOME KNOWLEDGE AND THE THIRD AGE

The idea that later stages of the lifespan are most suitable to develop wisdom was set forth clearly in early medieval Christian writings (Burrow, 1986) and was common also to Eastern teachings, religions and philosophies. However, attitudes like personal responsibility for and knowledge of self-development emerged in ancient Rome and Greece but were not typical for medieval times. In recent psychological theory and research, both the topic of wisdom and its application to development and guidance (management) of the individual self and life have reappeared and became popular. Though the bulk of such wholesome knowledge is derived from and applied to people in the first half of life, we shall focus here on wholesome knowledge for self-development in the second half of life, in particular for people in their third age (see Chapter 11).

In our view, the third age is *the* time for learning and applying wholesome knowledge for self and life management. It is the stage of life when men and women become free to pursue a more contemplative lifestyle after having been released from many societal duties and may have disengaged from work- and family-related personal ambitions. From that perspective, one can assume that they may be open and ready to develop wisdom-related mental orientations and competencies. Since changes in social roles and orientations become necessary with their exit from the workforce or as a consequence of children leaving the home, individuals may take the chance to focus on redesigning self and life. It is also a time when body and mind are changing through age-related processes, but, in order to maintain a positive identity and meaning of life, alternative life goals that can be pursued in the third and the fourth ages must be established. Our knowledge society provides ample possibilities and resources that can help to develop new identities, life goals and competencies that could not be pursued in earlier phases of the lifespan.

Older people's strengths such as integrative thinking, ill-defined problem-solving and synthesised intelligence (Dittmann-Kohli, 1984) can be brought to bear in work and family life. In family life, there may be demands on stress resistance and vitality, when empathy, accumulated expertise and experience are called for. Interpersonal wisdom (i.e. understanding others) can benefit children, partnership, friends and others. In addition, intrapersonal competence and psychological autonomy tend to increase with maturity. This includes understanding of one's inner and outer world. Autonomy implies that compliance with a large range of social norms is reflected on critically and may give way to individual freedom. Self-confidence concerning personal choices of values, standards, opinions and likes may grow, and feelings of dependency on others' opinions and judgements may wane. In other words, self-realisation may become easier than it was during earlier life when success depended on compliance with societal institutions and when biological needs propelled many actions (cf. Ridley, 1982). Emotional intelligence is needed to gain insight into needs, feelings and valuations of self and others that come with maturity and change considerably with age (Grewal and Salovey, 2005).

Aldwin and Levenson (2001) proposed that wisdom may alter one's style of life management. Even if coping ability per se does not improve, accumulated experience is likely to translate into better life management. The authors presented findings that testify to a more careful and efficient type of coping in late midlife, characterised by avoiding problems or by letting them be solved by time – which requires less effort. The third age may also be a sensitive period for acquisition of wholesome knowledge about emotional functioning and emotional coping; this is important not only in dealing with cycles of loss, depression and frustration, and finding new meanings in life (Klinger, 1977), but also to life planning (Smith *et al.*, 1989).

Generally speaking, wisdom is a form of higher knowledge with certain features related to personal growth and coping with life. Wisdom is helpful in solving existential problems and developmental tasks in the third and fourth ages. For instance, it is considered wise to give up unattainable ambitions and to detach oneself from pleasures that can no longer be obtained in the social world because of biological changes. Wisdom (and wholesome knowledge) is required to construct new perspectives for gains and benefits, and to understand present potentials and social resources. Practical wisdom is sometimes needed to seek help and support in order to deal with difficult times. Wisdom will lead creative people to gather needed information and understanding from other people, books, philosophies, religious beliefs and others' life experiences. Creativity depends in part at least on one's attitude – to an open mind, to learning and to experimenting.

Modern Western societies provide easy access to means for self-development, for further learning and training (Dittmann-Kohli, 1981). Governmental and educational institutions in western Europe offer a range of programmes. Exchange-of-knowledge projects have been organised for experienced older people, and universities offer courses and seminars specifically designed for this age group. Self-development projects and training programmes are produced in research on the lifespan and on old age.

In this chapter, we hope to contribute to the acquisition of wise and wholesome knowledge in the third age. This we shall attempt through examining theories and research about lifespan development and self and life management. We shall describe models of lifespan development and life management strategies that can be translated into 'wholesome knowledge' that can lead to a desired lifestyle. We will illustrate how people in the second half of life perceive themselves, and how the opportunities and challenges are reflected in self-reports. We offer proposals on how such findings may be used to enhance the development and the application of wholesome knowledge, and how some training programmes were designed and tested with middle-aged and older adults.

LIFESPAN ADAPTATION AND STRATEGIES: POSSIBLE CONCEPTS FOR SELF-DEVELOPMENT

General principles governing (adult) individual development and the human life-course have been established for many decades. In the last two or three decades, theoretical models of adaptation over the lifespan have been developed and empirically tested. Three models developed in Germany were conceptualised as universal processes of adaptation valid across life situations and possibly cultures, based on the assumption that individuals regulated their developmental activity (Lerner and Bush-Rassnagel, 1981).

- A model of assimilation and accommodation has been proposed by Brandtstädter. This encompasses general tendencies of personality or self-development, complemented by so-called immunisation strategies that protect the self from threat (Brandtstädter, 1999a).
- The lifespan developmental theory by P. and M. Baltes focuses on the selection, optimisation and compensation (SOC) model. It includes intuitive strategies to select goals, to enhance one's functioning, and to compensate for losses and deficits (Baltes and Baltes, 1990) and an adaptation to the shifting balance of growth and decline over the lifespan (Freund and Baltes, 1998; Freund and Baltes, 2002).
- A third model of lifespan adaptation (Heckhausen and Schulz, 1993, 1995; Schultz and Heckhausen, 1996) stresses the discrimination between primary and secondary control (Rothbaum et al., 1982). The concept of primary control can be used to identify events and situations to be changed directly, while secondary control consists of adapting one's aspirations, goals and feelings to new situations.

We shall not describe the third model here in detail, but suggest that it can be converted into a guideline for self-development in the third age in a similar way as the other two.

COPING: ASSIMILATION, ACCOMMODATION AND IMMUNISATION

The model of assimilative and accommodative coping developed by Brandtstädter and colleagues focuses explicitly on the mechanism that guides lifelong development of the self (Brandtstädter and Renner, 1990; Brandtstädter and Greve, 1994; Brandtstädter, 1999a). According to this model, the central goal of human development is the attainment and maintenance of a positive self-identity. Critical events or age-related constraints compromise the self, because they produce a discrepancy between actual and desired pathways of development.

In order to maintain stability of the self despite such developmental losses, the individual has at least three ways to re-establish congruence:

- the developmental context (e.g. situational conditions) can be modified actively
- internal aspects of the situation (e.g. the goal) can be changed
- information about the critical event or constraint could be processed (e.g. evaluated) in a way such that no discrepancy occurs.

In Brandtstädter's theory, the individual's endeavours to react to situations critical for the positive self are determined primarily by the first two processes, assimilation and accommodation.

Assimilation represents an active modification of the developmental context and life situation of the individual that is based on individual values, goals and expectations (e.g. use reading glasses or follow the news on TV in place of a newspaper). Assimilative coping is dependent on the availability and efficiency of means. If such active changes of the context are not possible, the process of accommodation is employed.

Accommodative coping refers to internal processes that regulate thoughts, feelings and actions. It involves adaptation of expectations, values and goals to external conditions and requirements, such as environmental resources and developmental opportunities (e.g. develop a taste for radio if eye problems cannot be compensated). The amount of adaptation by accommodation is limited by the extent to which self and life concepts are flexible. If a self-concept is complex, having many domains or roles, accommodative coping can be more widely and more successfully applied, because a multifaceted self gives more possibilities for restructuring goal hierarchies.

Stability of the self can also be fostered by a third mechanism, *immunisation*. This refers to changes of interpretation of self-relevant information, or feedback that endangers the self-concept. Self-protecting cognitive information processing represents a typical immunisation process (e.g. Brandtstädter, 1999b). One way of protecting the ageing self against negative age stereotypes is, for example, to integrate more positive aspects into the category 'old'. This type of immunisation has been demonstrated in a priming experiment by Wentura *et al.* (1995), showing that older adults link more positive connotations to the word 'old' than do younger adults. Choosing developmental contexts carefully represents a mechanism of immunisation. For example, doing sports in a group of young adults is predestined to make an older adult clearly aware of age-related constraints and limits, whereas training in a group of people of the same age might facilitate self-enhancing comparison processes (Brandtstädter and Greve, 1994).

Assimilative, accommodative and immunising processes are assumed to work in a complementary fashion. As long as individuals have the opportunity to shape their development actively by changing environmental conditions, assimilative coping will be the central process. If such active changes become impossible, either because resources are constrained (e.g. because of illness) or because the situation is not alterable (e.g. on the death of a loved one), accommodative coping will take the lead together with immunising processes. Nevertheless, all mechanisms can occur at the same time on different self-regulatory levels.

It is also assumed that inter-individual differences on a dispositional level exist. Although less controllable conditions are expected to be dealt with by accommodation, and assimilation is expected to have a leading role in actively changeable circumstances, people are thought to have either an assimilative or accommodative *style* in regulating discrepancies between the reality and desired development. However, there is clear evidence that, with advancing age, adults are prone to shift their preference from assimilative to accommodative coping (Brandtstädter and Renner, 1990; Brandtstädter, 1999b). It is assumed that this shift enables adjustment to the reality of old age, and allows the perception of continuity of the self over the years (Brandtstädter and Rothermund, 2002).

LIFE MANAGEMENT: SELECTION, OPTIMISATION AND COMPENSATION

Life management strategies such as selection, optimisation and compensation (SOC) represent a content-free way of selecting goals and investing resources in order to achieve them. As such, they focus not only on how personal goals are set, but also how such goals are pursued and realised by the individual.

Selection is defined as the process of choosing personal goals from a set of possible projects and committing oneself to a hierarchy of goals. Selection is either based on individual preferences (i.e. elective selection), or triggered by resource constraints impeding goal realisation, so that the blocked goal is abandoned (i.e. loss-based selection). Choosing and committing to one specific goal, such as deciding on a specific professional career, represents a typical instance for elective selection. Examples of loss-based selection are giving up a goal due to resource restriction (e.g. stop marathon running because training is too exhausting) and replacing it by a new goal (e.g. swimming regularly), or restructuring the goal hierarchy after resource loss (e.g. running is downgraded in the goal hierarchy, whereas spending time with the family increases in importance).

Life management strategies involve *optimisation* and *compensation*. Both strategies focus on the use and the application of resources in order to reach a selected goal. Optimisation represents the acquisition, the refinement and the investment of personal resources that are, in essence, action means used to achieve selected goals. Acquiring a new language, learning a technique to improve one's capacity (e.g. how to type with a 10-finger system), or training and practice of physical or mental skills (e.g. weight lifting to increase muscle strength or yoga to augment concentration), represent typical optimisation strategies. Compensation involves strategies by which lost action means are creatively replaced by other resources so that the original action goal can be pursued further. Typical compensations are the activation of alternative action means to ensure goal realisation (e.g. use of social support) or the application of external technical aids (e.g. wearing glasses when reading becomes difficult due to changes in vision).

The SOC life management strategies are understood as a system of strategies that are closely interwoven. In order to create and stabilise the self, goal selection and goal achievement are necessary. The SOC theory assumes, therefore, that the strategies might be applied at once or in timed sequences, but always in a coordinated manner – called 'orchestration'. Given that changes in multiple domains of living do occur when growing older, successful adaptation over the lifespan – the maximisation of positive outcomes and gains while minimising negative outcomes and losses (Freund and Baltes, 1998) – requires strategies that both enhance positive development (elective selection, optimisation) as well as regulating losses (loss-based selection, compensation). In contrast to models of stress and coping, SOC life management strategies focus on developmental regulation as a whole. Their application is not only restricted to situations of loss regulation but they are equally important for growth and improvement of the self.

Empirical studies show that application of the SOC life management strategies develops differentially over the lifespan. During adolescence and young adulthood, selection is increasingly applied, probably because the individual has to decide on major developmental paths (e.g. family planning). Optimisation and compensation are thus applied and knowledge about the use of these strategies is consolidated. In midlife, SOC life management strategies are applied most often (Freund and Baltes, 2002).

In the second half of the lifespan, there is some evidence that SOC life management strategies are used less often than in midlife. Based on a lifespan sample, Freund and Baltes (1999) found that only elective selection was increasingly used whereas loss-based selection, optimisation and compensation were applied less often. Whether this trend is still continuing in the last phase of life is still an open question. In the Berlin Ageing Study, negative correlation with age indicated a further decline in SOC use, except for elective selection, which was unrelated to age (Freund and Baltes, 1997). In contrast, no age differences in SOC use were found between young-old and old-old adults in another representative sample (Jopp, 2003). Only elective selection was correlated with age, indicating that the older a person was the more goals were chosen based on individual preferences, which would mirror the often mentioned new liberty in old age. Furthermore, there is evidence that the availability of resources (as action means) might be more decisive for using SOC strategies than age per se: resource-poor older adults used significantly fewer SOC strategies than those who were resource-rich (Jopp and Smith, 2006).

SOC life management strategies can be understood as mechanisms to stabilise the self and personal identity in the sense that they allow the individual to rearrange his or her goal hierarchy according to the action means available; they enable the individual to gain by working on personal potentials; and they make it possible to pursue goals through other means when the previously used means are lost. Thus, not surprisingly, the use of SOC strategies was found to be positively related to indicators of positive development and successful ageing such as subjective well-being (Freund and Baltes, 1997, 2002) over the lifespan. For example, life management strategies displayed positive correlations to positive affect and psychological well-being as assessed by Ryff's (1989) scales, 'positive relations' and 'purpose in life'.

LIFE PLANNING

Planning techniques have been adapted specifically not only for collaborative activities in, for instance, business, government and education, but also for individuals in the sense of life planning (Smith, 1999). Planning can be used not only with short-term goals but also for long-term strivings such as reaching desired developmental goals. Planning refers to the strategic processes involved in specifying what has to be done and when action has to be taken in order to attain a selected goal. A main feature of the planning process is that it is deliberate and goal-directed, and that it is an attempt to 'solve a problem', reach a goal or achieve a task along preconceived steps. When having an intention to achieve a long-term goal in ordinary life, such as 'better self and life management', one has to deal with complexity and uncertainty. In that case, a so-called 'ill-defined problem situation' has to be thoroughly analysed and understood before a realistic goal can be selected and a multiple-step plan made (Dittmann-Kohli, 1986). Resources must be recognised, probabilities estimated, pathways found, and barriers identified.

Motivational theories suggest that anticipatory planning serves several purposes. For instance, it reduces uncertainty, helps to get over initial problems in starting work on a goal, establishes a mindset conducive to achieving the goal, and helps to minimise stress. Planning also provides a means to test alternative actions in imagination, without actually using up physical resources and incurring social and personal costs. An important advantage results when a plan is created and stored for multiple access in long-term memory. In that case, cognitive capacity can be focused on directing and monitoring behaviour. People generally feel satisfied when they have developed a plan towards an important future life goal; the expectation of reaching the goal becomes more prominent, and positive affect may emerge in anticipation of the outcome and in feeling good about being in control. Also, the effort taken to mentally explore the future goal event may help to render it much more realistic, making advantages and disadvantages clearer, and even pointing out alternative routes to the same goals (Smith, 1999).

A high degree of planning is a characteristic of societies with complex economies and political systems. In modern societies, the institutionalisation of the life-course, and of adult work and family life, is such that the individual is also forced to do some planning, in order to prepare for important transitions, and to ensure that not too many chances for fulfilment are overlooked. Clearly, this involves getting to know the typical characteristics of different periods of life.

Having reviewed strategies and knowledge about planning processes on a general level, we next provide a description of what people have reported about their everyday lives. Empirical findings of self-representations of young, middle-aged and older adults will be presented, because by reading descriptions of other individuals' self and life perceptions a 'cognitive map' of these life stages can be constructed. That is, the task of identifying which aspects and areas of one's life and self should be changed and improved can be guided by learning about other people's experiences of ageing. A large number of specific empirical findings will be integrated into a 'story' of how individuals understand and interpret themselves. Thereafter, we will suggest a procedure for identifying the life tasks of different age groups where assimilation and accommodation processes may take place and where available resources, strategies and planning techniques must be explored.

SELF-UNDERSTANDING OVER THE LIFESPAN: EMPIRICAL FINDINGS

Research procedures linking concepts and data

Particular levels of data gathering, instruments and procedures are needed to tap characteristic thoughts and feelings in people's everyday mental activity and interpersonal communication. Identity and the personal meaning of self and life have been conceptualised as being mentally represented in a form that can be activated by verbal reports, as for example in the form of self-narratives (McAdams, 1996). Thus, spontaneous verbal statements about self and life constructions can be elicited and collected in written form.

Some psychological instruments provide spontaneous probes of self-knowledge that allow us to combine qualitative and quantitative analysis. The SELE (SElf and LifE) instrument (Dittmann-Kohli, 1990) does just this. It is a structured sentence completion instrument that requires the subjects to provide information about themselves that they consider as important and characteristic. Sentence stems are used to trigger spontaneous self-reports about desires, hopes, goals and needs, about concerns like fears and worries, and about beliefs on self and life. Both person–environment relations and person–self relations are assembled in this way, with references to future, past and present.

With a very complex, systematic content analysis, the type and number of semantic meanings are counted to portray the ideas of older men and women about themselves and their lives. Using general principles of classification (a systematic hierarchical content analysis) the sentences are grouped according to similarity and logical consistency. In general, domains of relevance for self-development and life management are work, family, leisure, physical self, psychological self and life satisfaction. Cross-age changes in the self can be captured by comparing the frequencies (centrality) of semantic meanings in spontaneous self-reports collected with the SELE instrument. For instance, the number of specific aspects or topics about health and illness mentioned in a person's responses is an indicator of how important (i.e. central) these are in a person and age group.

Over the last two decades a considerable number of studies have used the SELE instrument and provided evidence for its usefulness in natural and cross-cultural research. The majority of findings summarised below pertain to the German Ageing Survey that studies personal meaning of self and life in a representative German sample of about 3000 people (Dittmann-Kohli *et al.*, 2001) and an earlier, more exploratory age-comparative study on young and older adults (600 subjects) (Dittmann-Kohli, 1995a). The Ageing Survey was carried out in western and eastern Germany. A parallel study in the Netherlands (the Dutch Ageing Survey) comprised a representative sample of about 1000 people; its results are occasionally also called upon (Bode, 2003).

The survey data represent a cross-sectional pattern of three age groups (40–54, 55–69 and 70–85 years) covering the second half of life. For some analyses, participants were divided into six age groups. Interviewers collected spontaneous self-reports with the 28 low-structured sentence stems of the SELE instrument. In addition, standard psychological instruments and sociological interviews and questionnaires were used. The spontaneous self-reports were analysed with an adapted systematic content analysis originally developed in the age comparative study of 300 young adults (18- to 25-year-old vocational and university students) and 300 older people (60–90, average age 74).

Overall, the survey sample demonstrated that age is the factor that accounts for most of the differences observed in the self descriptions, compared to all other demographic markers such as gender, region of living, family and work status. Ageing has thus the strongest developmental influence on self and life constructions (identity) on the 'middle level of personality' situated between traits and life story; these are uncovered by the SELE instrument. Apart from age, subjective health proved to be the strongest influence on self and life constructions among the psychological variables. Findings are presented in clusters corresponding to the most salient domains of personal meaning of self and life. These are:

- the existential self (i.e. the physical and temporal self)
- the social self
- the activity domain (combining work and leisure)
- the psychological self.

The existential self

Physical integrity (the physical self) and the temporal self have been integrated here to form the 'existential self' because of their strong link to biological ageing. Both domains consist of several sub-domains, and these in turn comprise several categories.

Physical integrity: body, health and functioning

The findings on the physical self suggest that the biological aspects of human existence and ageing are reflected in personal identity in an analogous way to the psychological self, where personality traits and processes are represented. The age-comparative study (Dittmann-Kohli, 1995a) showed that, in young adulthood, male and female students describe their physical features and their body in terms of concerns associated with sexual and interpersonal attractiveness in a positive and in a critical sense (e.g. romance, beauty, weight). Physical integrity, however, is very rarely mentioned as being of concern. Older adults in the third and fourth ages, on the other hand, speak so often about this aspect of themselves that it amounts to the main feature of their identity. Older adults mentioned general psychophysical functioning (e.g. competence, fitness), health, illness and frailty very frequently. The typical complaints and hopes of later life occupy a large space in the network of thoughts and feelings on self and life. In other words, physical integrity is central in the older person's self-concept and personal identity. Spontaneous self-reports about death and dying were also referred to more often by older than by younger adults, but their absolute frequency was much lower than those about the physical self. The qualitative aspects of statements regarding death are more impressive than differences in frequencies. For example, only older adults referred to death in a positive sense (e.g. wanting it or waiting for it), and only older adults were concerned about the quality of the process of dying (Dittmann-Kohli, 1995a). Motoric activity is another example. The absolute number of statements about sports and other physical activities, physical anxieties and being tired does not show very large age differences, but the content of statements is again typical for early and late adulthood, reflecting age-related concerns. For the young, such concerns were about tough sports, being exhausted from learning, and the fear of mice and snakes. Older adults thought of gardening or taking daily walks, being tired too quickly and too often, and the fear of physical decline.

The German Ageing Survey (Kuin et al., 2001; Westerhof et al., 1998) provided the possibility to test whether the physical self increased in centrality over the second half of life. As expected from other cross-sectional studies over the lifespan, this was the case. Again, physical integrity was the largest domain of meaning of self and life, and frequencies increased regularly with age. Physical integrity as part of the self-concept was associated with beliefs about subjective health and psychological well-being measured by scales. In contrast, gender was not related to the number of spontaneous statements about physical integrity. Thus, thoughts and feelings about health, illness and psychophysical functioning occupy a more and more central part of the self-concept. The association of the frequency and the content of the spontaneous physical self-concept with objective age and with the reported experience of ageing (Steverink et al., 2001) suggests that the typical western concept of biological ageing is adopted in the second half of life to construct one's own identity and to interpret one's own experience of ageing (see Chapter 11).

Of interest for intentional self-development and for self and life management in the area of health is the observation that men and women speak less often of anticipated illness as a negative event and more often about maintaining or hoping for long-term preservation of good health, fitness, mobility and energy. In other words, this is one example of a tendency for positive thinking when there is an alternative.

The temporal self

A temporal frame of reference, for instance the concept of the lifespan, is applied to understand the changes in the self from life to death, and to integrate the perceived past and present life with that of the expected future (Dittmann-Kohli, 2006; Whitbourne, 1985). The self-localisation and positioning of an individual on a chronologically structured lifeline is reflected in self-narratives, such as autobiographical stories (Brockmeier, 2001), but the non-sequential temporal order of the SELE responses also reflects the dimension of subjective time. Life stage and temporal frame of reference are evident in a wide array of semantic elements in the SELE statements (Dittmann-Kohli, 1995b; Dittmann-Kohli, 2006). Our language contains semantic and grammatical terms to speak about time by assigning a temporal specification to an event or thing (Klein, 1984). Thus, self-reports allude to the temporal extension of the self into the past and future by referring to memories and by using verbal expressions for things lying ahead. Statements also contain terms for the stage of life one is in, so that the individual's position on the lifeline is indicated. Various temporal expressions (like 'still' or 'furthermore') exist that indicate certain types of changes or stability.

Spontaneous references to past self and life were found to be rare in young adults, but were brought up, often repeatedly, by nearly all older adults (Dittmann-Kohli, 1995a). References to the future, on the other hand, were uttered 20 times more often by the younger adults, compared to the older age group. Complementing the results of statements reflecting the past and future autobiographical perspective, additional types of temporal references appeared with great frequency. These included statements on 'subjective age', such as wanting to be younger, being already old, being too old, being a retired person, of living at the dusk of life. Young adults (students) were much less time-conscious in their self statements, showing a type of lifespan construct with a tightly populated personal future containing education, job entry and partnership or family establishment, combined with a subjectively short and insignificant past. In contrast, older adults put forth self-descriptions that indicate their identity is built on a long past with many good and bad life events, and contains the memories of their changing experiences, personality and outlook. Their present is the most important part of life because they must experience fulfilment and meaningfulness *now*, and not wait for the future. An additional class of categories refers to change, transition and development. Whereas thoughts about personal growth were more typical for young adulthood, references to maintenance, to reduction/decline, to limited continuation and to the finiteness of life were ten times as often given in the older adults' spontaneous self-reports.

Complementing the above studies, an investigation of the temporal expressions used in all of the sentence completions (falling into different content categories) in the German Ageing Survey showed that there was a steady increase of such terms over the second half of life. These expressions refer to cognitive representations of (hoped for) preservation, limited continuation and decline/loss (Dittmann-Kohli, 2006). Analysis that focused on the content and number of anticipated gains, maintenance and losses mentioned in six sentence stems implying a future time perspective found that most frequently mentioned gains (future-related themes of possible enrichment) were lifestyle and leisure activities (Timmer *et al.*, 2002, 2003). Future-oriented themes on generativity, caring for others, societal commitment and vocational ambitions showed substantial decreases around 50 years of age. The analysis of personal projects and anticipations expressing the desire for maintenance (continuation, stability), in contrast, expressed very different desires than the spontaneous self-reports coded as gains. Desires for maintenance are expressed in respect to physical and behavioural resources and to life circumstances where age-related decline is expected. Statements about expected loss refer to age-related decline, especially concerns about the possible decrease in quality of external living conditions and psychophysical functioning.

The conclusion from these findings is that identity changes over the lifespan are strongly linked to temporal self-location in various domains of self and life. It is evident that the awareness of having a temporary, transitional existence, and therefore a transitory 'I' and 'me', is much more intense as well as prominent in self-narratives of the older adults, compared to the younger ones.

Summary
It can be concluded that the experience and understanding of one's ageing process are reflected markedly in personal identity. In middle and later life, biological ageing and the temporal condition of existence play a greater role in spontaneous thought and mental self-representations than do psychological features of the self. The ageing survey has affirmed that the existential self-concept increases strongly and changes its content continuously over the second half of life, and probably over the whole lifespan, to grow into the strongest component of the self. Together with scientific and lay knowledge about biological ageing, this must be reflected in wholesome knowledge for self-development and self and life management. The findings also imply that the third age is experienced as a period of shifting self-definitions when the question of one's true age is concerned. Finding out about age-identity and one's potential for desired self-enhancement should be taken into account as issues when planning for intentional self-development and the ensuing self and life management.

The social self: people and interpersonal relations

In this section, the interpersonal or social themes in the third age are our focus of interest; responses referring to the collective self (regarding people in general, society or humanity) are included in the domain of social self. Overall, spontaneous self-reports provide evidence of the significance of other people and interpersonal relations in younger adults and over the second half of life (Bode, 2001, 2003; Dittmann-Kohli, 1995a; cf. Nuttin, 1984). Social contacts appear to be meaningful and central throughout life, to men and women, and across social classes and cultures, but are stronger in women than in men. Over the second half of life, however, there is some decrease in the salience of the social self, especially if the number of themes subsumed under the social self is constrained.

In self-reports to incomplete sentences, the spontaneous naming of other people can be easily coded. In two studies (Bode, 2001; Dittmann-Kohli, 1995a) when people were mentioned, the great majority of references made concerned the family in general or specific family members, in contrast to friends and acquaintances. Even older people living in urban centres did not mention friends very often, while the family occupied the central space of the social self. Older people without children, however, mentioned friends somewhat more often than those having children. Gender differences were found to be in the usual direction. As expected and in line with findings on interdependence and gender, women mentioned their partner and children more often in their self-accounts than did the men; this applies to young adults as well as to middle-aged and older adults. In the German Ageing Survey, women's reports also included more frequently all other categories of the social self, which refer to interpersonal relations and to social personality characteristics. Unexpectedly, however, the larger extension of the female social self is accounted for by a certain type of interpersonal topic. More negative and ambivalent ideas and feelings were expressed with respect to social contact, social competence and interactions. This was observed for the whole female group of participants aged between 40 and 85 years.

In stating that the social self is of similar importance to younger adults as for older adults, qualifications must be made. First, how frequent the social categories are – and thus how extended the social self is within an individual's personal identity – depends on the type of categories included. In the German Ageing Survey, social categories included responses about loss of autonomy and fears of becoming dependent. This type of social meaning did not appear in younger adults' answers, and less often in early middle age (40–54) than in young-old (55–64 years) and old age (65–85). In old age, fears and other concerns about becoming dependent on other people were related to life conditions following biological decline. In younger adults (18–25 years), exactly the opposite concern was salient within their social self, namely becoming independent financially, or from parents. Their statements on independence were also semantically related with the desire for personal growth and success in education and work. It is thus a matter of how the boundaries of the social self were delineated (i.e. how the set of categories is defined) whether spontaneous self-reports on social themes become less central (less frequent) from early to middle and late adulthood. If fears and concerns about becoming dependent on other people are not considered as belonging to the social self (but rather as a personal trait and thus as a category of the psychological self), the changes over the lifespan appear to follow a different pattern. In that case, the conclusions from our cross-sectional findings with the SELE instrument are that the social self is less central in later life.

Apart from the question about the (possible or real) lifespan decline in the size of the social self, the social self in the second half of life is qualitatively different from that of younger adults. First, the differential content is a reflection of the different social ecology at early and later adult life stages. Individuals in different age groups are necessarily oriented towards and interacting with persons of their own age; therefore, their interaction partners also have the characteristics of people at the various life stages, and together they share age-segregated settings in their environments. Even if interaction partners and reference groups include different generations, each age group will have their age-specific bio-cultural needs, interests, competences and habits, reflecting biological and social life-cycles of friends and family. For instance, while vocational school students (apprentices) dream of being with a partner in a romantic situation on an island, middle-aged and older parents may be worried about their children's development or marriage partners. Younger adults are fearful of being left by their girlfriend or boyfriend, older people express concerns about being left alone, about the illness of their partner, or about becoming dependent on their children. The content of the social self varies thus with the stage of life. Although significant differences were found in centrality of social selves of individuals with different family status (widowed, separated, married, never married), the age differences found are much more remarkable.

Bode (2003) studied age differences in the centrality and content of dependent and interdependent selves based on Markus' conceptions about cultures that produce individuality oriented versus social-collective selves (Markus and Kitayama, 1991; Markus *et al.*, 1997). Using a broad range of subcategories within these basic motivational orientations, changes over the second half of life were observed that were in agreement with other findings of studies analysing the SELE-data from the German Ageing Survey. The major concerns (themes) within the interdependent social self showed significant age-related decreases in centrality. Statements in the interdependent, socially oriented categories included concerns about societal and national issues, interpersonal and social traits, concerns about the life and well-being of other family members, social behaviour of the other toward the respondent, common experiences of projects and events, and quality of interpersonal relationships. The one exception to the decreases in the frequencies of the subcategories was the component 'social contact and relations', which maintained the same number of statements from middle to later life.

Thus, while social contact and relations stay central to the social self and personal identity over the lifespan, other social meaning content decreases in significance. Various subcategories become less frequent with higher age, while others, relating to dependence and loneliness, increase in number. Regarding intentional self-development for the third age, social contact and interpersonal relations must be considered an important source of positive meaning. Strategies and resources which may be useful for preventing or reducing the fear of loneliness, of increasing loss of autonomy and dependence on others, are important in optimising self and life management. Family and friends are often resources for emotional and material support, but most older people also have a need for supporting and helping others. Planning and the choice of developmental strategies should take this into account. One choice may be to participate in a training for widows and women who feel isolated or desire more satisfying social contact (see later).

Work and leisure: activities in self-reports

The second half of life is the period when more and more working people change their status from (self-)employment to retirement. Also, home-making women experience a change in their everyday life setting because of the 'empty nest' or the partner staying at home. This is reflected in the representation of the activity domain in the second half of life. Institutional structures, type of work status, stage of life and biological status are clearly visible in the type and number of spontaneous statements made in the identity domains of work and leisure (Dittmann-Kohli, 1995b; Westerhof, 2001a, 2001b; Westerhof and Dittmann-Kohli, 2000). The main category of this meaning domain has again numerous sub-domains. Statements on work include possible improvements in self and work environment, deficits in competencies, work motivation, and work-related feelings.

Westerhof (2001a) found in the analyses of the survey data that the spontaneous self-statements differ according to work status (employee, unemployed, retiree and housewife). They reflect that being employed is considered as desirable, and unemployment is not. Housework was acceptable to non-working women, but they still hope to get paid work sometime in the future. In the youngest age group of the sample, from 40 to 54 years, housewives and workless people indicated that they would like to have at least a part-time paid job. In the next age-group (55–64), identity components reflecting the transition to retirement and being a retiree were much more frequent for employed early and late middle-aged adults and for 'transitional' men and women (those working fewer hours or retiring soon), while a status change in female home-makers is not reflected in their narrative self-reports.

With regard to retirement, both positive and negative perspectives emerged. Regret is expressed about leaving work, but in general individuals are looking forward to retirement and to enjoying freedom and rest. During working age, those who have paid work perceive their status as positive, having work is considered as valuable; only during retirement the status of not working can be wholeheartedly appreciated, while identification with one's former occupation may persist.

As in the case of work status, significant socio-cultural (regional) differences between eastern and western Germany were found that reflect age group differences related to institutional factors. East and West Germans work identity reflects the ideological differences that gradually developed because of contrasting political systems. Within the group of the unemployed and those in transition to retirement, East Germans see unemployment in an even more negative way than West Germans; the former hope to take up paid work significantly more often. This regional effect, however, is not evident in retired people, who seem to accept the socially defined non-work status as retiree as much as those in West Germany.

Underlining the regional ideological features of East Germans' work identity is the following finding. None of the East German women define themselves as being pure housewives, but those in West Germany do. In both East and West Germany, there are practically no men who consider themselves as being 'house husbands'. Women without paid work (the groups of the unemployed, the retirees and in transition to retirement) mention the topic of housework much more often than men. The differential traditional role definition for men and women is evident again.

Overall, references to the domain of leisure increase in frequency compared to those to work. Noteworthy, the evidence points to a continuity of the leisure time self in terms of type of activities. Thus, radically new designs for life after work are not common. A significant reduction of statements about travel, the most popular leisure time project, was found in the age-comparative study between the third age and the fourth age. In the age-comparative study (Dittmann-Kohli, 1995a), those aged 75–90 years were found to mention self-related thoughts in the category 'travel' significantly less often than those aged 60–74. In all age groups of the Ageing Survey, travel was the most frequent preference in hobbies and future leisure plans (Timmer *et al.*, 2003; Westerhof, 2001a). A decline in frequency is presumably a reflection of worsening health status and lower physical fitness expectations in the fourth age.

A further affirmation on the decreasing significance of the work- and achievement-related self-concept with age was obtained. In the study cited in the context of the social self, Bode (2003) found a significant drop in the frequencies of all ten subcategories of the individuality centred orientation called 'independent' self. Over six consecutive age groups from 40 to 85 years, a significant gradual decrease in the number of work-related statements occurred, including personal characteristics, work environment, retrospective thoughts, and leisure activities or projects. The drop in the interdependent self also reflects the decline in psychophysical functioning.

The subjective life situation (subjective life space) during the third age is, according to the self-narratives of the Ageing Survey, marked by the transition to retirement and the gradual accommodation of goals and activities to the new setting and roles. In contrast to the now dominant pattern of continuing leisure activities, intentional self-development can be planned in regard to finding a new identity, complete with goals and strategies. Projects can be planned for developing new skills and learning activities. Activities for participation in neighbourhood or communal voluntary work can be planned, and/or new hobbies can be developed or neglected projects identified. The subjective life situation in the third age is thus prompted by retirement regulations, but biological ageing affecting physical strength and skills will also direct preferences and choices. Intellectual interest, education and values will affect choices of voluntary work and leisure activities, while many older people will just extend former leisure activities.

The psychological self

The psychological self comprises various aspects of personality characteristics, psychological states and processes, and attitudes and feelings toward oneself (positive and negative valuation of oneself). One important finding is that feeling satisfied, happy, relaxed and balanced or integrated is of concern to the large majority of men and women in their second half of life, reporting they either feel that way or that they lack it, implying they should have it. A further important finding is that the overall level of self-evaluation and life satisfaction does not decline with higher age. Also, the general positive and negative quality of all psychological traits, states and processes ascribed to one's own person remains stable over the second half of life; that is, it does not decline. It is rather the oldest group that spontaneously expresses more often to be satisfied, and the youngest group states to be dissatisfied (with some aspect of the self). In spite of this finding, the comparison of the number of answers classified under the psychological self declines with age; the overall number of psychological traits and (feeling) states mentioned becomes smaller. Older people have more interest in being satisfied and content and show less concern for character or competence. The members of the age group from 40 to 55 years describe themselves more often in terms of (intra- and inter-personal) competence.

Gender differences exist, in that men have a more positive self-evaluation. Women, in contrast, show a more ambivalent and more negative self-image because more of them perceive themselves as unhappy and lonely. But women also see themselves more often as socially and psychologically competent. With regard to the experience of subjective well-being and life satisfaction, however, there are no gender differences. For both men and women, satisfaction is the most central aspect of their psychological self. This underlines that older people are more concerned with their own well-being than are younger adults (cf. Dittmann-Kohli and Westerhof, 2000).

Lifespan development and social change: effects on identity

The findings on self and life highlight the age-related increase and qualitative change in the existential self. An overall picture emerges of how western or middle European identity is transformed over the adult lifespan.

While thoughts about the existential self comprising physical integrity and temporal identity gain more salience with increasing age, their number decreases in the activity domain. The social self (the interdependent orientation of self-reports) and especially the independent self (categories on activity and autonomy) decrease in centrality. The independent self comprises ten major themes or concerns of which just one does not decline significantly: statements about control, individual achievements and goals, autonomy, self-reflection, personal projects and activities decrease over the second half of life. The exception lies in the category psychological well-being and restful life. This category, of course, comprises exactly those individual concerns that are to remain important with higher age. The category frequencies within the social (interdependent) self also decreased, but less so, indicating the preservation of concerns related to social contact and isolation. Plans to improve self and life management will have to build on such changes in identity and life situation.

Are these trajectories of lifespan development permanent or will they be different in the future? The SELE instrument has the advantage that it is sensitive to and captures self-relevant reactions to social change that influence life conditions. If the future economic situation of older people becomes much worse than it is now, it would affect answers in the respective subdomains of meaning. In a similar vein, social changes such as the rising number of single and divorced persons and childlessness would be reflected in the personal meaning. It can also be assumed that the higher educational level of younger generations will influence the self-concept and the readiness to look for new goals and identities. This follows from our findings about the context specificity of self-narratives. They reflect not only demographic facts such as age and gender, but also, to a certain extent, regional characteristics such as nationality and politico-economic systems (Bode, 2003; Dittmann-Kohli, 2001).

SELF-DEVELOPMENT AND LIFE MANAGEMENT IN THE THIRD AGE

As described above, theory and data are available about how individuals, on average, develop in the second half of life and how specific strategies can be beneficial. The development of wholesome knowledge and its application in practice require taking into account a series of additional considerations. We shall discuss a series of issues related to conditions, limitations and possibilities of developing and applying wholesome knowledge.

Clarifying what the third age could mean

The development of wholesome knowledge useful for translation into training and development can start with exploring the situation during the third age. As we suggested earlier, the third age has potential for further development of identity and redirection of life. Since individuals experience a considerable deal of change and discontinuity, the third age seems predestined for developing new life directions, orientations and goals. Although not all individuals may feel the need to change their lives in the third age, change of internal and external conditions such as mandatory retirement may open up opportunities to more easily adopt a new lifestyle that provides more meaning and is more fulfilling – for instance, through learning how to enjoy nature, art and literature in more depth. Not only the search for something new, but also the focus on forgotten plans and dreams, may provide inspiration. Unfulfilled projects can be rediscovered, open and closed paths can be explored. In order to successfully shape this transition, the concepts of assimilation and accommodation may be used in combination with developmental tasks and SOC life management.

With regard to intentional self-development, one may explore how to achieve further personal growth, develop new skills, more psychological autonomy and emotional intelligence. New sources of meaning can be found in regard to leisure, adult children and grandchildren, and a more positive way of living can perhaps be achieved in social relations, productive work, creative activity, leisure and sport. Planning for intentional self-development may also include getting rid of bad habits (e.g. stress, smoking), or adopting new habits to decrease health risks. Finally, self-development may serve the purpose of getting relief from despair and depression – these are cost-intensive for society and individuals not only in younger people but also older people because of the latter's possible contribution and (non-monetary) benefits for society.

The third age not only provides enormous potential but is also a burden in that it represents the time to face the developments that will accompany the fourth age. For instance, when it comes to negative changes in health, cognitive functioning, or the loss of social partners, preparations and precautions should be taken. This may include getting on a waiting list for assisted living, making a will, thinking about possible care situations, and whether one wants others (e.g. family) to get involved.

Translating wholesome knowledge into goals

The development or choice of new or altered goals plays a central role in planning and using strategies for self and life management. Goals cannot just be picked up like a book; psychological laws must be recognised. To increase the likelihood of being realised, goals should be selected on the basis of affective preferences, needs, interests and existing motivations, and of these underlying motives one must become aware in a process of self-understanding. Another psychological mechanism to take into account is automatisation of motivation and behaviour (Bargh, 1997). In other words, new goals must be 'exercised', integrated and fitted into existing motive systems. This may be a major requirement in a period of life where the personal meaning system is being reorganised in its overall structure (Dittmann-Kohli, 1995a).

Goal-setting is one of the central procedures in training schemes and in choosing strategies. Before a suitable and realistic goal and corresponding strategies can be found, a rich and insightful knowledge about person and life situation is important, because goals should be reachable. Realistic goals must be in agreement with situational and personal resources and costs. Checking goals for reachability is important to prevent frustrations. Old goals should be addressed again if they are necessary to give the individual the impression that they must be fulfilled in order to find freedom. Goals could also stay dreams that are worth keeping. For instance, a woman had the dream to go to Tuscany. Now she is too frail for the trip, but she enjoys sitting in front of her wall portraying a Tuscany landscape. Thus, dream-goals can still promote well-being, and sometimes fantasy and feeling may be more rewarding than 'reality'. To find and adopt goals, observation of other people and their lives can help in addition to systematic self-observation and self-understanding. Elderly friends, relatives and strangers can be observed, films and literary resources can be used.

Some new goals should be picked in accordance with anticipated changes and developmental tasks in the fourth age (e.g. better travel to Asia now, since the physical constitution may prevent this later). With advancing age, goals may have to be selected more carefully and modestly because of shrinking competences and sensory abilities (to enjoy). Worsening life conditions as a consequence of social changes will have serious impact on an individual in the fourth age. Health, financial and social status, economic recession or growth are crucial when it comes to choosing goals for the fourth age.

Finding goals in domains of meaning

For a practical way to define life tasks and find appropriate goals for the third age, concepts from research on problem-solving can be used (Dittmann-Kohli, 1986). Domains of self and life can be seen as a set of situations with ill-defined problems whose diagnosis is difficult regarding the identification of positive components, the conditional factors and the barriers. The 'problem definition' will specify which goals and solutions are applicable in order to change the situation into one that is desirable for the individual. Procedures to explore systematically the domains of self and life for the purpose of determining priority goals and tasks for self-development may thus be helpful.

In this process, concepts for discrimination between basic types of activities (intrapersonal, interpersonal and extrapersonal behaviour and competences) and age-related domains/settings can be profitably applied (Dittmann-Kohli, 1986). Creating a taxonomy, life tasks of a given individual (or group) can be sorted into distinct cells. In each of the domains, the number of settings and life tasks are identified. In the next step, these are classified regarding the three basic types of behaviour and competences. The resulting life tasks represent ill-defined problem situations that need thorough analysis in respect of barriers and resources before goals are chosen. Many settings and life situations (e.g. those containing certain activity patterns and social relations) will be shared by individuals according to gender, former work, and educational level, so the diagnosis can proceed in common. Personality and personal domains, such as the psychological and physical self, should be screened separately for possible gains as well as preventive and maintenance goals, and the compensation of losses. In the selection of training programmes for self-development, individual goals can further be identified through checking systematically present and future, in addition to present, life tasks. A final step for goal identification and programme development is to check and integrate overlapping and related goals and plans.

Another programme element may be an identification of life management strategies that individuals already use. The empirically observed SOC strategies and planning techniques can be translated into one's own case. A group or an individual can develop a procedure in order to learn how to find and use them. Strategies and techniques identified as being in use should be labelled and scrutinised in how they promote well-being and successful ageing. This can create a new awareness and may activate motivation to translate the familiar strategies into new ones, or transfer them into other domains of living and functioning.

Guidelines for learning

Useful knowledge for a specific type of personal project has been brought together in an educational research setting in Toronto, Canada, for adults who want to plan a so-called learning project (Tough, 1971). Essential to learning projects is that the objective is to learn something – for instance, a specific skill, or a broad area of knowledge – or improve existing abilities. Although learning projects can be part of many other life plans and strategies, when setting up the project the learning process, the means for learning, and the learner characteristics are important to consider. Tough (1971) has conceived a programme that helps to structure, plan and implement deliberate learning episodes for adult men and women. In his guidelines and programme instructions, Tough has assembled knowledge necessary to understand the psychological process of learning. The programme was originally not designed for older adults but adult learners and their motivations in general. The usefulness of this type of intervention lies in its comprehensive consideration of how to organise learning, taking into account the personal characteristics of the learner, the possible structure and content of learning projects, types of learning materials, and types of settings (e.g. self-planned versus group learning). The author also provides information about possible motives and reasons for learning, on preparatory steps, institutions, instructors, and cost and time needed.

Forms and techniques for learning and development

Some of the important principles of self-directed learning in organised group training need to be mentioned. Group sessions will show how other people deal with certain issues and induce openness to other solutions and new paths in handling day-to-day problems. Moreover, being a member of such a group can serve its own purpose in that new people can be met and new social contacts made. A training programme might include an intense phase in the beginning with a focus on education and self-exploration. The next steps involve development of goals, feedback by group and trainers, and implementation in real life. Weekly meetings can accompany progress and make corrections if necessary. In a later phase, monthly meetings may suffice to motivate participants to stick to their plans. The group is thus used as a support team in charge of supervision. Individuals could be encouraged to organise weekly meetings without the trainer between monthly meetings.

Learner characteristics

Training programmes need to be tailored to individual needs and life situations. Learning and development projects must depart from personal dispositions and goals. Professionals who are interested in becoming a facilitator for self-development and self and life management of older adults must attend to the learner characteristics of the target group or individual. Important features are, in addition to age, educational and occupational level, attitudes to self-development, type of former work, and gender. A cluster of personality characteristics are important in the context of self-development, such as intrapersonal competence and emotional intelligence, openness and curiosity, and creativity. Strong traditional beliefs and a clinging to conventional rules can hinder intentional self-development efforts and personal growth.

Initial steps for self-directed learning

If individuals want to plan their own identity development, an easy way to start is non-scientific literature and easy-to-read psychological literature about what people in the third age feel, think and do. New role identities can be 'tried on' in the sense of imagining oneself in certain roles. Novels and autobiographies are particularly helpful in this respect. Autobiographical accounts on the experience of ageing exist that can be used in this way. Also, descriptions of behaviour and life conditions can be easy and interesting to read. Films and books are available that are suitable in this respect. Améry (1971), Berman (1994) and Sturm (1992) provide the reader with personal experiences. Such accounts demonstrate how older individuals have dealt with tasks of accommodation while keeping up morale, identity and self-esteem (cf. Rothermund and Brandtstädter, 2003).

Useful knowledge for the domain of work and activity

Intra- and inter-personal development have been the preferred fields for psychologists interested in wholesome knowledge and the construction of self-development and training programmes. The domain of work and psychophysical functioning will become central for professionals and scientists who are concerned with later life in the coming decades, as a consequence of mounting demands for a longer working life (see Chapters 7 and 8). Creativity and productive potential are valuable dispositions for many adults who want to stay active in extra-personal commitments after retirement. Research has shown that both of these 'traits' can be actively maintained and promoted. A type of literature of special interest for older adults who want to educate themselves are books that propose an active third age. For instance, there are texts that provide information about possible activities, roles, engagements, hobbies, voluntary work etc. for retirees in their third age (e.g. Cusack and Thomson, 1999; Kerscher and Hansan, 1996). Psychological findings on lifespan development of creativity and productivity may be attractive to those who want to be creative and want to plan for intellectual self-development. The role of creativity and productivity in later life is not simply decreasing with age but has been found to be dependent on personal efforts (e.g. Adams-Price, 1998; Kelly, 1993).

Examples of training schemes

There have been innumerable attempts to design and carry out more or less elaborate and standardised training schemes for psychological growth and coping with life. A quarter of a century ago in Europe, and much earlier in the USA, a wave of books and programmes for psychological change and development surged forth, providing experts and lay persons with the means for initiating beneficial circles of development. Devices specifically constructed for the older population have become popular more recently. Because of increasing numbers of very old people in need of help, research on development and evaluation of training has been promoted through scientific grants to psychologists during the last ten years or so. New trainings schedules are being developed that use specific or more general theories on ageing or on general strategies. Three of them are selected here to illustrate their approach to self-development and the chosen area of life management.

A training programme for the social self

The first example concerns social skills and interpersonal identity in the third age. Stevens (2001) has developed and evaluated training programmes to combat loneliness, a problem often mentioned by older people. The training programme's main goal is to facilitate making new friends through developing suitable goals, skills and orientations. It helps women (often widowed) to clarify their needs for friendship, to analyse their current social network, to set goals for winning new friends, and to develop strategies to achieve various types of interpersonal goal. The conceptual framework of the programme is based on the concept of successful ageing and the increase of well-being. Old friends often help to sustain self and identity in a changing world. According to Stevens (2001, p. 184): 'they do this by sharing experiences and contributing to interpretations of both past and present life events'. Other functions and conditions of friendship were examined to combat loneliness.

A training programme to enhance coping

The identification of goals, problems and strategies is necessary in training programmes for the maintenance of well-being and optimisation of coping. 'Proactive coping' is the leading concept of a training scheme developed in the Department of Health Psychology, University of Utrecht (Bode and de Ridder, 2003). In the training course, future threats and problems have to be anticipated by participants, and positive goals need to be developed. The proactive coping approach emerged in clinical psychology; and was tested initially with chronically ill older people. The new training is designed for persons aged from 50 to 75 years; its purpose is to learn a proactive coping style addressing life in general. The training is focused on tasks like preparing for the third and the fourth ages, development of goals and plans for those life periods, anticipation of possible negative situations, barriers and conflicts, and careful evaluation of goals along several criteria of usefulness and risk. Furthermore, action plans are prepared and behavioural alternatives are explored through mental simulations. In the finalising steps, action plans are elaborated after feedback by trainer and group has been examined and evaluated with regard to the progress the individual has made in implementing the (project) plans.

Preparation for the fourth age

The last example from the work of Dutch researchers is based on an integrated psycho-sociological lifespan model of successful ageing (Steverink et al., 1998). The training programme was designed to increase the self-management ability of slightly to moderately frail older adults. Guidance and instructions on how to understand and improve successful self-management of ageing (Steverink et al., 2005) have also been prepared. An evaluation study of this learning device has been carried out by Frieswijk (2004). Whereas prior self-management training programmes focused on targeting just one age-related problem (like depression, falling, insomnia, or chronic illness) separately, the new programme was designed for people with a mixture of problems in multiple life domains. The training programme is constructed with modules intended to help people develop a positive frame of mind, to be self-efficacious, to take initiative, to invest in a variety of resources and to maintain them for long-term benefits. As in the proactive coping and in the social empowerment models of training, goal-setting, planning and overcoming barriers were important features. The importance of initiative and self-efficacy is stressed in the areas of physical comfort and mental stimulation. Plans to increase physical comfort and mental stimulation have to be imagined and executed individually. In addition to physical comfort and mental stimulations, interpersonal concerns and need satisfaction are part of the training schedule. Participants were asked to think about comfortable and stimulating substitutes for their favourite activities and alternative persons for social contact. If substitutions were not available, individuals were encouraged to develop new activities and to meet new people in order to be less dependent on their already existing resources.

CONCLUSIONS

We have presented examples of training programmes for the third and fourth ages that are designed to compensate for or shield against losses in later life. Also, procedures and considerations were presented that can direct the construction of learning and training schemes for the third age. In concluding this chapter, we state the hope to have contributed to an integration of wholesome knowledge on interventions, and on lifespan theory and research. Results from lifespan research are useful and necessary to conceptualise existing and alternative ways of development, and models of development over the lifespan can serve as a guide for the design of organised group learning as well as individual self-directed learning and development.

Research on identity development and the third age suggests that this period of life is suited for using creativity and wisdom in discovering new potentials and ways of life. The third age is a time for a new type of self-integration and growth in ways not feasible in the more active phases of adult life. At the same time, self-understanding is required to absorb and redefine the changes in the existential and psychological self. New constraints in functioning and feeling have to be integrated into self-definition, and most people seem to be successful in so far as they can accept negative aspects of ageing while being satisfied with themselves and their lives. Conceding limitations does not imply self-doubts and feeling threatened, but increases the focus on development of hidden or neglected skills, especially on the level of awareness and delight in life.

Wholesome knowledge for self-development can be deduced from examining the experience of ageing in relation to the physical and the psychological self, and from understanding how the self relates to work, leisure and other people. Any kind of intentional self-development and organised training must consider the individual's idiosyncratic goal structure and basic personal resources. These can be identified against the background of self-accounts that are useful as a basis for learning about 'what is generally the case' in mid and later life. Understanding the experience of ageing should be fused with structural and action concepts, such as dealing with developmental tasks in special socio-cultural (sub-)systems and settings and their influence on the type of adaptation possible. It is important to take into account the socio-cultural conditions in which individuals live and in which their identities were originally 'programmed' in helping them to identify strategies and resources for self- and life management. It is hoped that gerontologists will be able to extend their understanding of development in the second half of life in the future, and retain sufficient financial means to continue research and the study of self-development schemes and interventions.

FURTHER READING

Dittmann-Kohli, F. (1990) The construction of meaning in old age: possibilities and constraints. *Ageing and Society* **10**, 279–294.

Freund, A. M. and Baltes, P. B. (2002) Life management strategies of selection, optimization and compensation: measurement by self-report and construct validity. *Journal of Personality and Social Psychology* **82**, 642–662.

Steverink, N., Westerhof, G. J., Bode, C. and Dittmann-Kohli, F. (2001) The personal experience of growing old: resources and subjective well-being. *Journals of Gerontology* **56B**, P364–373.

14

Ageing into the future

John Bond, Freya Dittmann-Kohli, Gerben
J Westerhof and Sheila Peace

INTRODUCTION

In Chapter 1, we documented the ageing of European populations and high-lighted that this was a global phenomenon. Although the nature of human age-ing and the experience of later life has seen considerable change during the twentieth century, individuals, organisations and states appear ill-equipped or unwilling to prepare for the changes likely in the present century. Within the European Union the proportion of the population will increase considerably. By 2050 the dependency ratio will increase from one person aged 65 years or over to four people of working age (15–64 years) to one person aged 65 years or over to two people of working age. In absolute terms over the same period there will be a tripling of people aged 80 years or over (from 18 million in 2004 to about 50 million in 2051) as the baby-boomer generation reach their eighth decade (Lanzieri, 2006). This 'greying' of society will have profound implications for individuals in all walks of life and how we organise our societies in the future. Of course, human ageing is only one aspect of human experience that may change markedly in this century. If we take the last 100 years as a guide we should expect in the next 100 years continuing changes to the natural environ-ment reflecting both the serendipity of nature and the impact of human activity; rapid development of technological and scientific innovation that will change the way we organise our lives; and with increasing globalisation changes in our cultural, political and social insitutions. It is within these contexts that individuals and societies will experience human ageing.

The unpredictability of natural events such as earthquakes, volcanic disruption, tsunamis, hurricanes, typhoons and droughts make some areas of the globe more inhospitable to human existence than others. Such events habitually bring misery to the local populations that are affected and it is the most vulnerable – children, disabled people, older people and the poor – who are most at risk from the devastating impacts of such 'natural' disasters. In many parts of the world natural disasters are an inevitable aspect of some communities' psyche and culture. They are a way of life. Human societies have always gambled with nature, for example living on flood plains and around the foothills of volcanoes, which have provided rich fertile land for farming; or developing industry and commerce in earthquake zones because of the proximity of resources and markets. Richer societies like the USA and Japan have used their wealth to invest in built environments that withstand much of the onslaught of nature, for example reinforced buildings in earthquake zones and flood defences and early warning systems. But in these societies it is the vulnerable who suffer most from the vicissitudes of nature – as the experience of New Orleans in the wake of hurricane Katrina in 2005 illustrates so clearly. Forecasting or predicting natural disasters in the twenty-first century may, with technology, become more widely available, but human ingenuity is not equipped to overcome the awesome power of nature. So the vulnerable, including older people, will continue to suffer.

Much of Europe, especially northern Europe, is relatively unaffected by natural disasters. But global warming has introduced elements of natural disasters through extremes in climate patterns, such as the hot summer of 2003 that claimed the lives of many older people in France and other parts of central Europe and the increasing number of floods following exceptionally high rainfall in Britain and across the north European plain. The long-term impact of global warming still remains unknown although there exists some consensus about rising sea levels with the inevitable consequences for low-lying areas and vulnerable members of the population living in them. As with other natural disasters, investment in infrastructure can mediate the effects of such events, but as with sea-cliff erosion there will come a time when nature will impose her will over human ingenuity and indifference.

The industrial revolution and the subsequent development of science and technology has benefited most citizens of Europe. As we saw in Chapter 2, expectation of life increased markedly in the last century and this was a direct consequence of increasing human understanding of the natural world. Westendorp and Kirkwood predict that life expectancy will continue to increase for the foreseeable future (see Chapter 2). But the impact of science and technology on our European lives has been wider than simply extending the length of the average life. It has affected us all in so many ways: in the nature of our built environments; in our approach to war; in the organisation of work, leisure and family life; in the way we think about ourselves and in the way we communicate with others. Looking back through history we can see the increasing pace of scientific and technological change with key discoveries changing the course of history: the development of the wheel; steam, electric and nuclear power, and of course most recently the Internet. With each major discovery a quantum leap in technological development has increased the pace of change. But it is not only these landmarks in scientific developments that have changed the European landscape. Technological innovation in devices aimed at the consumer market has opened up the lives of some older people who have embraced technology and, for the cognitively intact, increased their independence. For example, fast freeze food and the microwave oven has revolutionised the organisation of meals services for individuals who are housebound, and alarm systems and mobile phones have made communication easier, although often technologies developed for the mass market have not been designed with the partially sighted or physically frail in mind. Throughout history, scientific and technological development has impacted on the cultural, political and social life of European citizens; the industrial revolution and the mass migration of people from small towns and villages into the large cities and migration overseas would be just one example.

The second half of the twentieth century saw an accelerated increase in the rate of cultural, economic, political and social changes. In the political sphere, two key processes stand out: the fall of communism in Europe and the emergence of Islam as a political force. Both processes have had enormous impact on the lives of many European citizens. The fall of communism and the democratic revolution in Europe has reinforced the hegemony of capitalism in the organisation of economic life, strengthening the role of the expanded European Union and World Trade Organization in supporting 'free' trade and the development of a globalised world economy. Globalisation has resulted in changes in the world of work across Europe with a shift away from a manufacturing-based economy toward a service economy in which tourism and international finance play a major role. As we saw in Chapter 8, these changes had serious consequences for the older worker who was encouraged to retire earlier but without the resources always to enjoy life outside work. Across Europe the new economic world has seen the emergence of a new set of 'class' relations based on income and wealth which has been described by the speech-writers for George W. Bush as the division between the 'have nots', the 'haves' and the 'have mores'. The emergence of Islam is likely to be more central to the political landscape of the world in the future than it has been in the recent past, but Islam has played an important role in diversifying European culture. Economic migration over the second half of the twentieth century has left a legacy of diverse cultures, many of them Islamic, within a number of European countries. This has influenced popular culture, dietary habits as well as religious expression. This diversity is reflected in the variety of eating outlets to be found in most towns and cities across Europe. It is perhaps a paradox that while the processes of globalisation are producing standardisation and harmonisation in much of our lives, the development of diverse ethnic communities is producing a richer cultural and social environment. But for older people such change in their communities is difficult to accept such that in many inner city areas they are isolated from their families and friends. Of course, in the future the characteristics of older people will become diversified further along ethnic lines, reflecting both greater secularisation and increased multi-culturalism.

LOOKING INTO THE FUTURE

This book has highlighted some of the key ideas and understandings of contemporary gerontological knowledge. In this chapter we want to look into the future and suggest some ways in which ageing and the experience of later life might develop as the rate of change increases through out the globalised world. It is not our intention to attempt an overview of the future of old age. Another text has been produced in parallel with this volume for that purpose (Vincent *et al.*, 2006). Rather we will focus on a number of selected issues, relating to many of the topics addressed in different chapters of this book.

In thinking about the future it is relevant to draw a distinction between short-term projections, medium-term forecasts and longer-term speculation. As individuals most of us think in the short term, reflecting the cyclical pattern of the seasons and key milestones along the life-course. We will plan our next holiday, prepare for that landmark birthday or as we approach retirement what we are going to do afterwards. And as societies we also think in the short term. Although there is some discussion about the future of our planet it is usually in terms of thinking about life for our grandchildren's generation. In policy terms most governments focus on short-term projections, which are usually based on assumptions rooted firmly in the present day. Medium-term forecasting is rarely a public activity with think-tanks and Delphi activities (Linstone and Turoff, 1975) being done in private by private organisations or small groups of individuals. Forecasting will be based less on the current state of knowledge and will involve a degree of professional guesswork. Long-term speculation is left to the science-fiction writers, philosophers and some scientists.

Our approach to this chapter is to present our thoughts for the medium and long term, and although we are starting from a contemporary knowledge base our thoughts are based on informed speculation and wise guesswork. We will try to extrapolate from changes that are already underway, such as globalisation, but recognise that the nature of ageing and later life will depend on the way future generations respond to the changing environment and personal development.

LONGEVITY AND HUMAN AGEING

A key issue for gerontology is how the science of human ageing will develop and implications of future gerontological knowledge for individuals and societies. In forecasting the effects of the science of human ageing at least three scenarios can be suggested.

The first that follows on from the predictions of Westendorp and Kirkwood (see Chapter 2) is that gradual but persistent increases in life expectancy will continue through improved healthcare, and scientific and technological intervention in fixing failures of individual bodies and individual lifestyle management. It is unclear whether the advantages experienced by women in the last century will be maintained throughout the present century. In recent years men have extended their average life expectancies faster than women and the gender ratio is becoming less unbalanced in later life. Much will depend on the effects of future lifestyles of men and women and the impact of choosing the gender of children in the future. At present, compared with differences between men and women, greater inequalities in life expectancy also exist between the 'haves' and the 'have nots' and in this scenario there is no expected convergence.

The second scenario suggests that, at least for some social groups, increasing life expectancy is halted because of detrimental lifestyle behaviours, serious economic or political disruption such as war or revolution, and natural disasters such as pandemics. In this scenario a divergence in the experience of life expectancy would be expected.

The final scenario suggests dramatic increases in life expectancy because of genetic and biomedical engineering of the human body from designer babies and biological engineering throughout the life-course (de Grey, 2003). As with the other scenarios, inequality in life expectancy will persist because of inequalities in access to the appropriate resources from which to gain the benefits. At the societal level, increasing life expectancy within Europe, even at the modest rate proposed by Westendorp and Kirkwood, will increase pressure on the dependency ratios (see Chapter 6) and potentially the way European states organise social protection systems in the future; particularly in terms of pension policy, healthcare and long-term care (see later). For individuals, as at present, increasing length of life will be associated with increasing quality of life – adding life to years not just adding years to life.

AGEING AND THE GLOBAL POLITICAL ECONOMY

Globalised capitalism has been strengthened in recent years by the fall of communism in the Soviet Union and eastern Europe and China's embracement of some of its key elements. Globalised capitalism therefore looks set to stay as the dominant economic system for the foreseeable future. Whether it remains dominated by the imperialist trends in the United States or emerges in different clothes within the tiger economies of China and south-east Asia is unclear, as is the role of Islam in the development of African and Asian economies.

More certain is the inevitable march of globalisation – the interconnectedness of global economic, political and social orders characterised by global hierarchies of power and inequality that challenge the power of the nation state and individual citizenship. Phillipson (2006b) has highlighted a number of aspects of globalisation that will impact on older people. Central here is the idea that the ageing of the population is no longer a burden on national or European economies but a global 'problem'.

Worldwide dependency ratios are greater than ever, reflecting not only increasing life expectancy for older people but also the devastating impact of AIDS on the younger populations in many areas of the world. As Phillipson argues, this ideological perspective influences the way that social policies in response to ageing have privatised the risks of ageing. The decline of collectivism and the sharing of risks have placed the responsibility of financial security and healthcare and long-term care firmly on the individual. In the future, increasing social exclusion and inequality between the 'haves', 'have nots' and 'have mores' is inevitable as there will be an accumulative disadvantage over the life-course for those who are poor or less educated. The development may also give rise to ever more powerful multinational companies in providing health insurance and pensions.

PRODUCTION AND CONSUMPTION

In *Future Shock*, Toffler (1970) forecast the leisure society. Since then there has been a reduction in average working hours and increasing holiday entitlement for people in work across Europe. But changing working practices in recent years has not seen the predicted improvement in work/life balance and shorter working hours in all European countries. Toffler's predictions, however, are reflected in the current cohorts of early-retiring third-agers (see Chapter 8), a significant minority are relatively wealthy (see Chapter 7) and can afford the consumption lifestyles described by Gilleard and Higgs (2000). But will future generational cohorts be able to afford similar lifestyles? Patterns of work are changing and those currently economically active will change jobs (as opposed to employers) many times in their lifetime and will require continuous retraining and life-long learning to keep up with changing production technologies and products. Greater flexibility in employment regulations associated with increasing portfolio working will increase the risks of unemployment and poverty in old age, limiting the opportunities for consumption. Unless men and women can maintain relatively stable work patterns in full-time employment and above-average wages, then their ability to achieve financial independence and maintain an acceptable lifestyle in later life will be seriously limited.

How might ageing individuals respond to these new risks of ageing? One potential approach supported by global institutions and states is to stop early retirement and increase formal retirement ages, thus extending working life for future generations of older people. Ageism remains a barrier to this process, particularly as employers are reluctant to employ older workers because of stereotypes about individual productivity and the perceived increased costs of employing older people (see Chapter 8). But future cohorts of older workers will have worked in a labour market in which they will have been expected to change jobs or occupations, retire and re-enter the labour market and be reskilled at regular intervals. The habit of having to reskill new employees may facilitate a change in stereotypes about older workers' potential. Given the scarcity of labour in many European economies, increasing experience of using older workers may also overcome traditional stereotypes. Both employers and employees will be forced by labour market and personal circumstances to increase the age of retirement for future cohorts. Of course the difficulty with these forecasts is a lack of knowledge about the kind of economies that will exist into the future and other factors such as the economic migration of younger workers into Europe to fill gaps in the labour market produced by the ageing of the population.

SOCIAL PROTECTION

An enduring feature of the last 25 years of the twentieth century was the decline of European welfare states. A key challenge for social protection in Europe has not simply been an increase in the numbers of older people demanding support but also the nature of that support. For example, the healthcare landscape changed dramatically during this period. New treatments and services have escalated in recent years and inevitably rationing has been necessary in order to contain costs. Approaches to rationing have included the provision of only those treatments that are seen as cost-effective; delaying or denying treatments according to some priority order and the encouragement of individuals to opt out of the welfare state and privately purchased treatment. Of course the development of the private market to respond to such demands increases the likelihood that other treatments will be contracted out to provider organisations, so the decline of state provision for healthcare becomes a self-fulfilling prophesy. As we saw in Chapters 6 and 7, this process has resulted in different levels and systems of social protection across Europe for health and pensions. Some diversity is likely to persist, but the decline in collectivist solutions and the increasing acceptance of individualistic market-based solutions to managing individual healthcare and long-term care, and income provision in later life, is likely to lead to the destruction of the 'welfare state' in most countries of Europe – with increasing demand placed on informal care and family and kinship networks. The impact of this would be increased inequalities in income, healthcare and social care and the provision of informal care (Evandrou and Falkingham, 2006; Price and Ginn, 2006). Although this forecast challenges current political rhetoric to maintain some vestiges of the welfare state, there are few indicators that recent trends can be reversed with social protection being a right of all European citizens. Of course such forecasts are self-fulfilling, but the destruction of the welfare state is only likely to be resisted by concerted action by European citizens.

BUILDING ENVIRONMENTS FOR ALL

The built environment is the context in which we all age. It is also a major barrier to ageing in place. In the same way that people are not disabled – it is the environments that disable them (Oliver, 1996) – so with older people it is not age that is the barrier to life fulfilment but the environment in which they live. For many years gerontologists have been arguing that the environment should be built for all ages (and disabilities) to facilitate ageing in place. This implies designing and building life-long housing, transport systems and public spaces that are accessible to all ages. Better design standards that make accessible to older people different environments inevitably require formal regulation. But old and relatively simple technologies were often not incorporated into new 'builds' because of short-term cost containment. Urban suburbs are inadequate for the needs of older people and are an increasing aspect of their social isolation. One solution preferred by some older people has been the development of retirement communities. But from the perspective of others such segregation may lead to the ghettoisation of the older population and the reinvention of a different type of 'asylum' (Goffman, 1961).

New technologies provide opportunities to achieve ageing in place, to enhance the quality of older people's environments and to increase life fulfilment and quality of life. Yet relatively more older people are slow adopters of new technologies, in part due to cost but also attitudes. Older people are traditionally seen to be conservative or norm-oriented, this is likely to change as the baby-boomers generation takes over 'old age' and therefore in the future may not be characterised as slow adopters. Manufacturers accept these stereotypes and are also slow to realise market opportunities for technologies that would enhance older people's lives. For example, much of the recent communications technology has been aimed at younger age groups in advertising campaigns and little attempt has been made to recognise special needs, such as the visual impairment experienced by all older people. In recent years the EU and individual states have recognised the potential for harnessing new technologies in improving the lives of older people and have provided incentives for manufacturers to consider this market. 'Smart' houses have been developed and evaluated (Fisk, 2001) but not widely built. This suggests that developing the built environment, and technologies that are convenient and suitable to older people, needs a collective drive something that is at odds with the individualistic ideologies of late modernity. The development and introduction of new environments or technologies requires understanding barriers to their 'market' exploitation and implementation. The quality of the built environment, transportation systems and access to public spaces will continue to be key factors differentiating the 'haves' and 'have nots' in later life.

SOCIAL RELATIONS AND SOCIAL NETWORKS

We saw in Chapter 9 how social relations and social networks in later life are diversifying. A key question is whether the post-modern view of the fluidity of social relations will prevail within European societies. Traditional family and kinship structures, religious and political institutions and the influence of the local 'community' still remain strong in some parts of most countries, particularly in rural areas, and in some cultures. These may continue to underpin social networks and relationships in the future. But what impact will social and geographical mobility have on these structures? We have seen how social relationships which are predominantly built around the world of work during middle age are transformed on retirement. No longer is there a single set of relationships. Rather relationships are increasingly compartmentalised to specific contexts and settings in which they occur. We would anticipate that this would be the pattern for the future.

A key set of social relationships in later life are those built around friendship (Jerrome and Wenger, 1999). In the future, with the continuing feminisation of later life, the decline in the size of family and kinship networks, the creation of 'patchwork families' due to increasing divorce and separation rates, and the emergence of a sizeable proportion of older people living independently alone (or 'flying solo' – Davidson, 2006), friendship relationships will become increasingly important. Fluidity in friendships are more likely with serial relationships developing in line with different later life-course experiences around the interests and needs of older people. Of course, with the changing face of communication, particularly Internet technology, more widespread social networks and individual relationships will be established and developed.

THE MEANING OF OLD AGE

In Chapter 11, Westerhof and Tulle examined the diversity of meanings of ageing and old age in European cultures. A common feature of constructions of ageing and old age is the inevitable decline in physical appearance and fitness, and cognitive performance. The emphasis on decline rather than change underpins the almost universal negative stereotypes and attitudes of ageing and older people that appear to be held by most people of all ages and cultures. The enduring nature of ageism, like sexism, racism and disabilism, seems set to continue into the future. With the increasing diversity and unpredictability of individual life-courses, understanding of ageing and what constitutes old age may conceivably change. As populations become healthier and fitter, the hallmarks of ageing bodies may become less visible – particularly with wider use of anti-ageing products and technologies such as hair colouring or body sculpting (lipo suction) by the 'botox generation'.

So although ageism will continue to reflect the way societies think about ageing, there could be a redefinition of old age away from chronological age to one reflecting frailty of individuals and the increasing youth-oriented behaviour of middle-aged adults. Increasingly activity among older people, particularly 'third-agers', will be facilitated by the increasing use of replacement body parts from hips and knees to kidneys and hearts. At an individual level, ageing will continue to be associated with the experience of age-associated decline of the human body and age-associated disease, but mediated by changes to healthier lifestyles and the use of technology and biomedical engineering. Negative stereotypes may be postponed until later years, into the fourth age or deep old age.

Stereotypes of ageing may also be redefined by changing the official retirement age. On top of physical appearance, employment status is a key characteristic considered by others when stereotyping older people. The label 'pensioner' was one of the more positive terms for older people in the twentieth century but it still holds negative connotations not least because of the negative rhetoric of dependency ratios and the pensions burden. By increasing the official retirement age, society decreases the proportion of older people by the stroke of a pen!

For the foreseeable future, cognitive decline and dementia are likely to remain the experience of a substantial minority of very old people (currently those aged 80 years or over, but like physical disease the age of onset may get later.) Of course, being demented remains one of the most negative stereotypes of old age and one that is increasingly in the public eye because of increasing prevalence in the community and the role of advocate organisations to raise awareness.

FUTURE ROLES FOR OLDER PEOPLE

A positive trend in recent years, which may change the way individuals and societies see ageing and old age, has been the emergence of a self and the development of individual identities. In late modernity, individuals no longer have a life-course mapped out from birth. Of course, social structure will continue to play a central role in the moulding of individual life-courses; but within this context, nowadays and into the future, people will have the potential for more control over the development of their own identities and life-course experiences. Consequently they will have more control over the course of their later life. Laslett (1987; 1996) first highlighted the opportunities for older people in managing their later life in his identification of the *third age*. Although it has been argued that self-identities for some in their third age are constructed by patterns of consumption (Gilleard and Higgs, 2000), the potential for making other contributions to society remains considerable (see Chapter 13).

Across the life-course, developmental patterns are becoming more complex. The trend towards continuing education into the twenties, and the desire of young adults (especially young women) to develop independent careers, means that the family formation stage of the life career is delayed – and as a result serial relationships often elongated. These patterns are also increasingly complex because of the different experiences of the 'haves' and 'have nots' in educational experience and subsequent employment. But the extension of the family-building and career-establishing phase of life, the increasing demands of the labour market due to world competition, along with the selfishness of the consumption culture, means that second-agers have little time to devote to activities outside work, family and leisure.

We forecast that older people, particularly those in their third age, in the future will make substantial contributions to wealth creation in European economies. Ageism in employment will *have* to be overcome, with demand for skilled labour facilitating this to some extent. The positive roles and functions of older workers will *have* to be recognised. Employers will *have* to be as flexible with their older employees as they have had to become for women and part-time workers in order that older employees can recharge their physical and psychological energies, as well as fulfil their own caring and family responsibilities. Increasing the retirement age will increase the potential for age-related mental and physical health problems if the limitations of older workers' energies are not recognised. But careful consideration by employees and employers of the potential contribution and strengths of individual older workers to the organisation will prevent work-related morbidity among older workers.

Although retirement will be delayed in the future, third-agers who have retired from formal paid employment will continue to have more time to spend on other activities. Aside from leisure and consumption, this may often be in carer or grandparenting roles, active roles in political or religious organisations and other forms of civic and community participation. But future third-agers will also need to play a greater role in the transmission of European culture and in bridging the gap between the 'haves' and 'have nots' through increased civic and community roles such as educational assistants in schools as well as the more traditional caring roles into people's homes and caring institutions. Increasing the role of older people in society will happen only when traditional organisations such as the churches and political parties recognise their potential for contributing to the wider society.

PERSONAL FULFILMENT AND THE FUTURE OF AGEING

The 'third age' will continue to be important for the development of personal integrity and growth. Social support roles in the widest sense will continue to be ways of maintaining self-fulfilment and personal well-being. For those with intellectual, artistic and scientific backgrounds, particularly those with a flexible and creative outlook on life, the task of ensuring fulfilment, personal well-being and a positive meaning for later life will be relatively straightforward. Those who have artisan, manual and technical skills will also be well positioned to develop productive and creative activities that will enhance their general well-being in later life. Those who lack such skills or experience will continue to find old age as a period of life lacking fulfilment and positive well-being. A general shift to more positive attitudes toward one's own age and other people's ageing, however, may provide more people with a sense of possibility and may enhance creative reinventions of the self in intrapersonal and interpersonal processes. Here again, the further increase of predominance of women aged 80 years or over calls attention to the dangers of their 'social obsolescence'. There is a continuing necessity to establish their voice in society and address the need to support active contributions to the shaping of their lives (Cruickshank, 2003).

To ensure that later life is fulfilling, more direct information programmes for older people experiencing ageing are needed to promote self-education of the threats and opportunities in later life. These might take the form of elementary courses in the basic facts and trends of ageing reflecting the needs of people of different educational backgrounds. As familiarity with the Internet increases, wider use of its potential as an educational vehicle will be exploited, but there will be a need to ensure that users have the skills to make use of such a resource. For even in self-awareness and self-education programmes there is a risk of widening the gap between the 'haves' and the 'have nots'. However, as we saw in Chapter 13, self management of the ageing process is in the reach of everyone as long as he or she has and can develop the resources to do it. The habit of life-long learning among future generations will facilitate optimal self management of ageing processes.

THE FUTURE OF GERONTOLOGY

The opportunities for gerontology as an interdisciplinary activity should be enhanced by current understandings of the ageing population. Yet investment in research on ageing is not the highest of priorities (House of Lords Science and Technology Committee, 2005). Basic research on ageing and old age, whether from bio-gerontology, psycho-gerontolology or social gerontology, is not prioritised if it focuses on 'normal' ageing. Biomedical research is driven by cures and treatments of age-associated disease; psycho-gerontology reflects psychology's focus on neuroscience and the brave new world of being able to develop mechanisms for controlling the human brain; while within social gerontology evaluative and government policy-oriented research dominate. To date the survival of social gerontology has been its roots within the 'ageing as a social problem' paradigm with many social and behavioural scientists offering an applied view of their discipline in order to develop the discipline in the direction that they feel is more appropriate. Basic research that seeks to understand the future of human ageing is poorly funded unless there is a clear commercial opportunity.

Promoting the agenda for ageing research remains a major challenge for gerontology. Of course, the position of gerontology is handicapped by the problematising of ageing and the need to respond to funding opportunities. In order to promote our discipline and justify our existence within a market-driven economy, there is a risk that gerontology – like many other sciences – overstates the short-term implications of basic research. But the basic bio-psycho-social understandings of ageing remain an important scientific area to support. In the future, social and human aspects of psychology, including psycho-gerontology, could re-emerge if a more spiritual perspective on life were to re-emerge within European societies. Sociology will continue to challenge the hegemony of capitalism and should continue to play a central role in the development of central gerontology. The continuing development of critical gerontology (political economy, feminism and post-modernism), a perspective that highlights human agency as well as social structure and one that in recent years has taken an increasing interest in ideas of self and identity, will remain central to the gerontological project. However, as with psycho-gerontology, funding for this enterprise is seen as a luxury for a capitalist consumer culture and is limited. The future is not rosy but there is a future for gerontology. In its development we expect to see increasing interdisciplinary working and a parallel eclectic approach to method with greater use of mixed-method designs. At a theoretical level is a vision of continuing and imaginative development in psychological and social theories of ageing.

FURTHER READING

Vincent, J. A., Phillipson, C. and Downs, M. (2006) *The Futures of Old Age.* London: Sage.

References

Achenbaum, W. A. (1995) *Crossing Frontiers: Gerontology Emerges as a Science*. New York: Cambridge University Press.

Adams-Price, C. E. (ed.) (1998) *Creativity and Successful Aging: Theoretical and Empirical Approaches*. New York: Springer.

Ainsworth, M. D. (1989) Attachments beyond infancy. *American Psychologist* **44**, 709–116.

Ainsworth, M. D. S., Blehar, M. C., Waters, E. and Wall, S. (1978) *Patterns of Attachment: A Psychological Study of the Strange Situation*. Hillsdale, NJ: Erlbaum.

Aldwin, C. M. and Levenson, M. R. (2001) Stress, coping, and health at midlife: a developmental perspective. In: Lachman, M. E. (ed.) *Handbook of Midlife Development*, 188–214. New York: Wiley.

Aldwin, C. M., Sutton, K. J., Chiara, G. and Spiro, A. (1996) Age differences in stress, coping and appraisal: findings from the Normative Aging Study. *Journal of Gerontology* **51B**, P179–188

Alliance for Health and the Future (2006) Health and the Future website: www.healthandfuture.org. Date accessed 22/5/2006.

Altman, B. M. (2001) Disability definitions, models, classification schemes, and applications. In: Albrecht, G. L., Seelman, K. D. and Bury, M. (eds) *Handbook of Disability Studies*, Chapter 3, 97–122. Thousand Oaks, CA: Sage.

Altman, I. and Low, S. M. (eds) (1992) *Human Behaviour and Environment. Vol. 12 – Place Attachment*. New York: Plenum.

Amann, A. (1984) *Social Gerontological Research in European Countries: History and Current Trends*. West Berlin and Vienna: German Centre of Gerontology and Ludwig–Boltzmann Institute of Social Gerontology and Life Span Research.

Andersson, L. (ed.) (2003) *Cultural Gerontology*. Westport, CT: Auburn House.

Andrews, M. (1999) The seductiveness of agelessness. *Ageing and Society* **19**, 301–318.

Antonucci, T. C. and Akiyama, H. (2002) The effect of social relations with children on the education–health link in men and women aged 40 and over. *International Society for the Study of Behavioural Development, Newsletter* 1 (41), 2–6.

Appleton, N. and Porteous, J. (2003) *Extra Care Housing for Older People: An Introduction for Commissioners*. London: Department of Health.

Arber, S., Davidson, K. and Ginn, J. (eds) (2003) *Genders and Ageing: Changing Roles and Relationships*. Buckingham: Open University Press.

Arber, S. and Ginn, J. (1991) *Gender and Later Life. A Sociological Analysis of Resources and Constraints*. London: Sage.

Arber, S. and Ginn, J. (2004) Ageing and gender: diversity and change. In: Summerfield, C. and Baab, P. (eds) *Social Trends*, issue 34, 1–15. London: Office for National Statistics. Stationery Office.

Ardelt, M. (2003) Empirical assessment of a three-dimensional wisdom scale. *Research on Aging* **25**, 275–324.

Arnds, P. and Bonin, H. (2003) Institutionelle Faktoren des Rentenzugangs: Ein Überblick aus ökonomischer Perspektive. In: Herfurth, M., Kohli, M. and Zimmerman, K. F. (eds) *Arbeit in einer alternden Gesellschaft*, 65–91. Opladen: Leske & Budrich.

Arts, W. A. and Gelissen, J. (2002) Three worlds of welfare capitalism or more? A state-of-the-art report. *Journal of European Social Policy* **12**(2), 137–158.

Aspinwall, L. G. and Staudinger, U. M. (2003) A psychology of human strength: some central issues of an emerging field. In: Aspinwall, L. G. and Staudinger, U. M. (eds) *A Psychology of Human Strengths: Fundamental Questions and Future Directions for a Positive Psychology*, 9–22. Washington, DC: APA Books.

Assmann, A. (1994) Wholesome knowledge: concepts of wisdom in a historical and cross-cultural perspective. In: Featherman, D. L., Lerner, R. M. and Perlmutter, M. (eds) *Life-span Development and Behavior*, vol 12, 187–224. Hillsdale, NJ: Lawrence Erlbaum.

Atchley, R. (1976) *The Sociology of Retirement*. Cambridge, MA: Schenkman.

Atchley, R. C. (1971) Retirement and leisure participation: continuity or crisis. *Gerontologist* **11**, 13–17.

Atchley, R. C. (1989) A continuity theory of normal aging. *Gerontologist* **29**(2), 183–190.

Atchley, R. C. (1991) The influence of aging or frailty on perceptions and expressions of the self: theoretical and methodological issues. In: Birren, J. E., Lubben, J. E., Rowe, J. C. and Deutchman, D. E. (eds) *The Concept and Measurement of Quality of Life in the Frail Elderly*, 207–225. New York: Academic Press.

Atkinson, R. (2002) The life story interview. In: Gubrium, J. and Holstein, J. A. (eds) *Handbook of Interview Research: Context and Method*, Chapter. 6, 121–140. London: Sage.

Auffray, C. and Juhel, J. (2001) General and differential effects of a multimodal cognitive training program for the elderly. *Année Psychologique* **101**, 65–89.

Augusztinovics, M. (2002) Issues in pension system design. *International Social Security Review* 55(1), 21–35.

Austad, S. N. (1997) Comparative aging and life histories in mammals. *Experimental Gerontology* **32**, 23–38.

Baars, J., Dannefer, D., Phillipson, C. and Walker, A. (eds) (2006) *Globalization and Inequality*. Amityville, NY: Baywood Publishing.

Bäcker, G. (2004) Der Ausstieg aus der Sozialversicherung: Das Beispiel Rentenversicherung [Exit from the social security system: the example of the statutory pension system]. *WSI-Mitteilungen* **57**(9), 483–488.

Bäcker, G., Bispinck, R., Hofemann, K. and Naegele, G. (2006) *Sozialpolitik und soziale Lage* [Social policy and social reality], 4th edn. Wiesbaden: Westdeutscher Verlag.

Baddeley, A. (1996) Exploring the central executive. *Quarterly Journal of Experimental Psychology* **49A**, 5–28.

Baddeley, A. D., Della Sala, S., Papgno, C. and Spinnler, H. (1997) Dual-task performance in dysexecutive and nondysexecutive persons with frontal lesions. *Neuropsychology* **11**, 187–194.

Baddeley, A. D. and Hitch, G. J. (1974) Working memory. In: Bower, G. H. (ed.) *The Psychology of Learning and Motivation*, vol 8, 47–90. New York: Academic Press.

Bajekal, M., Blane, D., Grewal, I., Karlsen, S. and Nazroo, J. (2004) Ethnic differences in influences on quality of life at older ages: a quantitative analysis. *Ageing and Society* **24**(5), 709–728.

Bakan, D. (1966) *The Duality of Human Existence: Isolation and Communion in Western Man*. Boston MA: Baecon Press.

Ballinger, C. and Payne, S. (2002) The construction of the risk of falling among and by older people. *Ageing and Society* **22**(3), 305–324.

Baltes, M. M. (1995) Dependency in old age: gains and losses. *Current Directions in Psychological Science* **4**, 14–19.

Baltes, M. M. (1996) *The Many Faces of Dependency in Old Age*. Cambridge: Cambridge University Press.

Baltes, M. M. and Baltes, P. B. (1986) *The Psychology of Control and Aging*. Hillsdale, NJ: Erlbaum.

Baltes, M. M. and Baltes, P. B. (1997) Normal versus pathological cognitive functioning in old age: plasticity and testing-the-limits of cognitive/brain reserve capacity. In: Forette, F., Christen, Y. and Boller, F. (eds) *Démences et longévité*, 77–101. Paris: Fondation Nationale de Gérontologie.

Baltes, M. M., Neumann, E.-V. and Zank, S. (1994) Maintenance and rehabilitation of independence in old age: an intervention program for staff. *Psychology and Aging* 9, 179–188.

Baltes, M. M., Maas, I., Wilms, H.-U. and Borchelt, M. (1999a) Everyday competence in old age: theoretical considerations and empirical findings. In: Baltes, P. B. and Mayers, K. U. (eds) *The Berlin Aging Study*, 384–402. Cambridge: Cambridge University Press.

Baltes, P. B. (1979) Life-span developmental psychology: some converging observations on history and theory. In: Baltes, P. B. and Brim, O. G. (eds) *Life-span Development and Behavior*, vol. **2**, 255–279. New York: Academic Press.

Baltes, P. B. (1987) Theoretical propositions of life-span developmental psychology: on the dynamics between growth and decline. *Developmental Psychology* **23**(5), 611–626.

Baltes, P. B. (1993) The aging mind: potential and limits. *Gerontologist* **33**, 580–594.

Baltes, P. B. (1997) On the incomplete architecture of human ontogeny: selection, optimization and compensation as foundation of developmental theory. *American Psychologist* **52**, 366–380.

Baltes, P. B. and Baltes, M. M. (1990a) Psychological perspectives on successful aging: the model of selective optimization with compensation. In: Baltes, P. B. and Baltes, M. M. (eds) *Successful Aging: Perspectives from the Behavioral Sciences*, Chapter 1, 1–34. New York: Cambridge University Press.

Baltes, P. B. and Baltes, M. M. (eds) (1990b) *Successful Aging: Perspectives from the Behavioural Sciences*. New York: Cambridge University Press.

Baltes, P. B. and Carstensen, L. (1996) The process of successful ageing. *Ageing and Society* **16**, 397–422.

Baltes, P. B. and Kliegl, R. (1992) Further testing of limits of cognitive plasticity: negative age differences in a mnemonic skill are robust. *Developmental Psychology* **28**, 121–125.

Baltes, P. B. and Lindenberger, U. (1997) Emergence of a powerful connection between sensory and cognitive functions across the adult life span: a new window to the study of cognitive aging? *Psychology and Aging* **12**, 12–21.

Baltes, P. B. and Mayer, K. U. (eds) (1999) *The Berlin Aging Study: Aging from 70 to 100*. New York: Cambridge University Press.

Baltes, P. B. and Singer, T. (2001) Plasticity and the ageing mind: an exemplar of the bio-cultural orchestration of brain and behaviour. *European Review* **9**, 59–76.

Baltes, P. B. and Staudinger, U. M. (2000) Wisdom: a meta-heuristic (pragmatic) to orchestrate mind and virtue towards excellence. *American Psychologist* **55**, 122–136.

Baltes, P. B. and Willis, S. L. (1982) Plasticity and enhancement of intellectual functioning in old age: Penn state's adult development and enrichment program (adept). In: Craik, F. I. M. and Trehub, S. E. (eds) *Aging and Cognitive Processes*, 353–389. New York: Plenum Press.

Baltes, P. B., Smith, J. and Staudinger, U. M. (1992) Wisdom and successful aging. *Nebraska Symposium on Motivation* **39**, 123–167.

Baltes, P. B., Staudinger, U. M., Maercker, A. and Smith, J. (1995) People nominated as wise: a comparative study of wisdom-related knowledge. *Psychology and Aging* **10**, 155–166.

Baltes, P. B., Dittmann-Kohli, F. and Kliegl, R. (1996) Reserve capacity of the elderly in aging-sensitive tests of fluid intelligence: replication and extension. *Psychology and Aging* **1**(172), 177.

Baltes, P. B., Lindenberger, U. and Staudinger, U. M. (1998) Life-span theory in developmental psychology. In: Damon, W. and Lerner, R. M. (eds) *Handbook of Child Psychology. Vol. 1 – Theoretical Models of Human Development*, 1029–1143. New York: Wiley.

Baltes, P. B., Staudinger, U. M. and Lindenberger, U. (1999b) Lifespan psychology: theory and application to intellectual functioning. *Annual Review of Psychology* **50**, 471–507.

Banfield, E. C. (1958) *The Moral Basis of a Backward Society*. Glencoe, IL: Free Press.

Barak, B. and Stern, B. (1986) Subjective age correlates: a research note. *Gerontologist* **26**, 571–578.

Barford, A., Dorling, D., Davey Smith, G. and Shaw, M. (2006) Life expectancy: women now on top everywhere. *BMJ* **332**, 808.

Bargh, J. A. (1997) The automaticity of everyday life. In: Wyer, R. S. (ed.) *The Automaticity of Everyday Life. Advances in Social Cognition*, vol. x, 1–62. Mahwah: Erlbaum.

Barker, D. J. (2002) Fetal programming of coronary heart disease. *Trends in Endocrinology and Metabolism* **13**, 364–368.

Barker, D. J. P. (2004) The developmental origins of well-being. *Philosophical Transactions of the Royal Society of London Series B – Biological Sciences* **359**, 1359–1366.

Barr, N. (2000) *Reforming Pensions: Myths, Truths and Policy Choices.* Washington, DC: International Monetary Fund.

Barrett, A. E. (2003) Socioeconomic status and age identity: the role of dimensions of health in the subjective construction of age. *Journals of Gerontology* **58B**, S92–100.

Bauman, Z. (1998) *Globalization: The Human Consequences.* Cambridge: Polity Press.

Baumgartner, W. (1933) *Israelitische und alterorientalische Weisheit.* Tübingen: Verlag J.C.B. Mohr (Paul Siebeck).

Bayley, J. (1998) *Iris: A Memoir of Iris Murdoch.* London: Duckworth.

Beck, U. (1992) *Risk Society.* London: Sage.

Becker, H. (1963) *The Outsiders.* New York: Free Press.

Bedford, V. H. (1995) Sibling relationships in middle and old age. In: Blieszner, R. and Bedford, V. H. (eds) *Handbook of Aging and the Family*, 201–222. Westport, CO: Greenwood Press.

Bengtson, V., Biblarz, T. and Roberts, R. (2002) *How Families Still Matter: A Longitudinal Study of Youth in Two Generations.* Cambridge: Cambridge University Press.

Bengtson, V., Rosenthal, C. and Burton, L. (1990) Families and aging: diversity and heterogeneity. In: Binstock, R. and George, L. (eds) *Handbook of Aging and the Social Sciences*, 3rd edn. New York: Academic Press.

Bengtson, V. L. and Schaie, K. W. (eds) (1999) *Handbook of the Theories of Aging.* New York: Springer.

Berger, P. and Luckmann, T. (1966) *The Social Construction of Reality.* New York: Doubleday.

Berman, H. J. (1994) *Interpreting the Aging Self. Personal Journals in Later Life.* New York: Springer.

Berman, W. H. and Sperling, M. B. (1994) The structure and function of adult attachment. In: Sperling, M. B. and Berman, W. H. (eds) *Attachment in Adults: Clinical and Developmental Perspectives*, 3–28. New York: Guilford Press.

Bernard, M., Phillips, J., Machin, L. and Harding Davies, V. (eds) (2000) *Women Ageing: Changing Identities, Challenging Myths.* London: Routledge.

Beveridge, W. (1942) *Social Insurance and Allied Services* (Beveridge Report). London: HMSO.

Bidwell, J., Keen, L., Gallagher, G., Kimberly, R., Huizinga, T. *et al.* (1999) Cytokine gene polymorphism in human disease: on-line databases. *Genes and Immunity* **1**, 3–19.

Biggs, S. (1999) *The Mature Imagination: Dynamics of Identity in Midlife and Beyond.* Buckingham: Open University Press.

Biggs, S. (2003) Negotiating aging identity: surface, depth, and masquerade. In: Biggs, S., Lowenstein, A. and Hendricks, J. (eds) *The Need for Theory: Social Gerontology for the 21st Century*, 145–159. Amityville, NY: Baywood.

Biggs, S. (2004) In pursuit of successful identities and authentic aging. In: Tulle, E. (ed.) *Old Age and Agency*, 137–155. Hauppauge, NY: Nova Science.

Biggs, S. (2006) New ageism: age imperialism, personal experience and ageing policy. In: Biggs, S. and Daatland, S. (eds) *Ageing and Diversity: Multiple Pathways and Cultural Migrations*, 95–106. Bristol: Policy Press.

Biggs, S., Lowenstein, A. and Hendricks, J. (2003) *The Need for Theory: Critical Approaches to Social Gerontology.* Amityville, NY: Baywood.

Bijsterveld, K. (1996) *Geen kwestie van leeftijd: Verzorgingsstaat, wetenschap en discussies rond ouderen in Nederland, 1945–1982.* Amsterdam: Van Gennep.

Birren, J. E. and Fisher, L. M. (1990) The elements of wisdom: overview and integration. In: Sternberg, R. J. (ed.) *Wisdom: Its Nature, Origins and Development.* Cambridge: Cambridge University Press.

Birren, J. E. and Schroots, J. J. F. (1984) Steps to an ontogenetic psychology. *Academic Psychology Bulletin* 6, 177–190.

Blaikie, A. (1999) *Ageing and Popular Culture.* Cambridge: Cambridge University Press.

Blaikie, A. (2002) Using documentary material: research the past. In: Jamieson, A. and Victor, C. (eds) *Researching Ageing and Later Life: The Practice of Social Gerontology*, Chapter 3, 35–50. Buckingham: Open University Press.

Blaikie, A. and Hepworth, M. (1997) Representations of old age in painting and photography. In: Jamieson, A., Harper, S. and Victor, C. (eds) *Critical Approaches to Ageing and Later Life*, Chapter 9, 102–117. Buckingham: Open University Press.

Blakemore, K. and Boneham, M. (1994) *Age, Race and Ethnicity. A Comparative Approach.* Buckingham: Open University Press.

Blaxter, M. (1983) The causes of disease: women talking. *Social Science and Medicine* **17**, 59–69.

Blaxter, M. (1990) *Health and Lifestyles.* London: Routledge.

Blazer, D. G., Burchett, B., Service, C. and George, L. K. (1991) The association of age and depression among the elderly: an epidemiological exploration. *Journal of Gerontology* **46**, M210–215

Bode, C. (2001) Wenn ich bestimmte Dinge nicht mehr kann: der antizipierte Umgang mit Einbussen im Kompetenz- und Fähigkeitsbereich. In: Dittmann-Kohli, F., Bode, C. and Westerhof, G. (eds) *Die zweite Lebenshälfte – Psychologische Perspektiven: Ergebnisse des Alters-Survey*, 169–191. Stuttgart: Kohlhammer.

Bode, C. (2003) *Individuality and Relatedness in Middle and Late Adulthood: A Study of Women and Men in the Netherlands, East and West Germany.* Enschede, Netherlands: Print Partners Ipskamp.

Bode, C. and de Ridder, D. T. D. (2003) *'Op weg naar de gouden jaren': Handleiding, Design en Instrumenten* ['Towards the golden years': manual, design and instruments]. Internal Report, Department of Health Psychology: Utrecht University.

Bograd, R. and Splika, B. (1996) Self-disclosure and marital satisfaction in mid-life and late-life remarriages. *International Journal of Aging and Human Development* **42**, 161–172.

Boll, T., Ferring, D. and Filipp, S.-H. (2003) Perceived parental differenital treatment in middle adulthood: curvilinear relations with relationship quality to sibling and parents. *Journal of Family Psychology* **17**, 472–487.

Bolzman, C., Poncioni-Derigo, R., Vial, M. and Fibbi, R. (2004) Older labour migrants' well-being in Europe: the case of Switzerland. *Ageing and Society* **24**, 411–429.

Bond, J. (1992) The politics of caregiving: the professionalisation of informal support. *Ageing and Society* **12**, 5–21.

Bond, J. (1997) Health care reform in the UK: unrealistic or broken promises to older citizens. *Journal of Aging Studies* **11**(3), 195–210.

Bond, J. and Carstairs, V. (1982) *Services for the Elderly: A Survey of the Characteristics and Needs of a Population of 5000 Old People* (Scottish Health Service Studies no. 42). Edinburgh: Scottish Home and Health Department.

Bond, J. and Corner, L. (2004) *Quality of Life and Older People.* Buckingham: Open University Press.

Bond, J., Bond, S., Donaldson, C., Gregson, B. and Atkinson, A. (1989) Evaluation of an innovation in the continuing care of very frail elderly people. *Ageing and Society* **9**, 347–381.

Bond, J., Corner, L. and Graham, R. (2004) Social science theory on dementia research: normal ageing, cultural representation and social exclusion. In: Innes, A., Archibald, C. and Murphy, C. (eds) *Dementia and Social Inclusion. Marginalised Groups and Marginalised Areas of Dementia Research, Care and Practice*, Chapter 14, 220–236. London: Jessica Kingsley Publishers.

Bonnesen, J. L. and Burgess, E. O. (2004) Senior moments: the acceptability of an ageist phrase. *Journal of Aging Studies* **18**(2), 123–142.

Boote, J., Telford, R. and Cooper, C. (2002) Consumer involvement in health research: a review and research agenda. *Health Policy* **61**, 213–236.

Bornat, J. (2002) Doing life history research. In: Jamieson, A. and Victor, C. R. (eds) *Researching Ageing and Later Life: The Practice of Social Gerontology*, Chapter 8, 117–134. Buckingham: Open University Press.

Börsch-Supan, A., Brugiviani, A., Jurges, H., Mackenbach, J., Siegrist, J. *et al.* (eds) (2005) *Health, Ageing and Retirement in Europe: First Results from the Survey of Health, Ageing and Retirement in Europe.* Mannheim: Mannheim Research Institute for the Economics of Aging.

Bosman, E. A. (1993) Age-related differences in the motoric aspects of transcription typing skill. *Psychology and Aging* **8**, 87–102.

Bourdieu, P. (1992) *An Invitation to Reflexive Sociology.* Cambridge: Polity Press.

Bowlby, J. (1973) *Attachment and Loss. Vol. 2 – Separation: Anxiety and Anger.* New York: Basic Books.

Bowlby, J. (1980) *Attachment and Loss. Vol. 3 – Loss: Sadness and Depression.* New York: Basic Books.

Bowlby, J. (1982) *Attachment and Loss. Vol. 1 – Attachment,* 2nd edn [first published 1969]. New York: Basic Books.

Bowling, A. (1995) The most important things in life – comparisons between older and younger population age groups by gender: results from a national survey of the public's judgements. *International Journal of Health Sciences* **6**(4), 169–175.

Bowling, A. (1999) Ageism in cardiology. *British Medical Journal* **319**, 1353–1355.

Bowling, A. and Grundy, E. (1997) Activities of daily living: changes in functional ability in three samples of elderly and very elderly people. *Age and Ageing* **26**, 107–114.

Bowling, A., Formby, J., Grant, K. and Ebrahim, S. (1991) A randomised controlled trial of nursing home and long-stay geriatric ward care for elderly people. *Age and Ageing* **20**, 316–324.

Bradbury, B. and Jäntti, M. (1999) *Child Poverty Across Industrialized Nations.* Florence: UNICEF Innocenti Research Centre.

Bradley, J. M. and Cafferty, T. P. (2001) Attachment among older adults: current issues and directions for future research. *Attachment and Human Development* **3**, 200–221.

Brakefield, P. M., Gems, D., Cowen, T., Christensen, K., Grubeck-Loebenstein, B. *et al.* (2005) What are the effects of maternal and pre-adult environments on ageing in humans, and are there lessons from animal models? *Mechanisms of Ageing and Development* **126**(3), 431–438.

Brandt, H. (2002) *Wird auch silbern mein Haar: Eine Geschichte des Alters in der Antike.* München: Verlag CH Beck.

Brandtstädter, J. (1999a) The self in action and development: cultural, biosocial, and ontogenetic bases of intentional self-development. In: Brandtstädter, J. and Lerner, R. M. (eds) *Action and Development: Theory and Research Through the Life Span,* 37–65. London: Sage.

Brandtstädter, J. (1999b) Sources of resilience in the aging self. In: Hess, T. M. and Blanchard-Fields, F. (eds) *Social Cognition and Aging,* 123–141. San Diego, CA: Academic Press.

Brandtstädter, J. and Greve, W. (1994) The aging self: stabilizing and protective processes. *Developmental Review* **14**, 52–80.

Brandtstädter, J. and Renner, G. (1990) Tenacious goal pursuit and flexible goal adjustment: explication and age-related analysis of assimilative and accommodative strategies of coping. *Psychology and Aging* 5, 58–67.

Brandtstädter, J. and Rothermund, K. (1994) Self-precepts of control in middle and later adulthood: buffering losses by rescaling goals. *Psychology and Aging* **9**, 265–273.

Brandtstädter, J. and Rothermund, K. (2002) The life-course dynamics of goal pursuit and goal adjustment: a two-process framework. *Developmental Review* **22**(117), 150.

Braungart, R. G. and Braungart, M. M. (1986) Life-course and generational politics. *Annual Review of Sociology* **12**, 205–231.

Brewer, M. B., Dull, V. and Lui, L. (1981) Perceptions of the elderly: stereotypes as prototypes. *Journal of Personality and Social Psychology* **41**, 656–670.

Brierley, E. J., Johnson, M. A., Lightowlers, R. N., James, O. F. W. and Turnbull, D. M. (1998) Role of mitochondrial DNA mutations in human aging: implications for the central nervous system and muscle. *Annals of Neurology* **43**, 217–223.

Brockmeier, J. (2001) Identity. In: *Encyclopedia of Life Writing: Autobiographical and Biographical Forms,* vol. 1, 455–456. London: Fitzroy Dearborn.

Brod, S. A. (2000) Unregulated inflammation shortens human functional longevity. *Inflammation Research* **49**, 561–570.

Brody, E. M. (1999) *Women in the Middle: Their Parent-care Years.* New York: Springer.

Broese van Groenou, M. I. and van Tilburg, T. (2003) Network size and support in old age: differentials by socio-economic status in childhood and adulthood. *Ageing and Society* **23**, 625–645.

Bromley, D. B. (1986) *The Case-study Method in Psychology and Related Disciplines.* Chichester: Wiley.

Bronfenbrenner, U. (1979) *The Ecology of Human Development: Experiments by Nature and Design.* Cambridge, MA: Harvard University Press.

Bronfenbrenner, U. (1999) Environments in developmental perspective: theoretical and operational models. In: Friedman, S. L. and Wachs, T. D. (eds) *Measuring Environment Across the Life Span*, 3–28. Washington, DC: American Psychological Association.

Bronfenbrenner, U. and Crouter, A. C. (1983) The evolution of environmental models in developmental research. In: Mussen, P. H. (ed.) *Handbook of Child Psychology. Vol. 1 – History, Theory, and Methods*, 357–414. New York: Wiley.

Bronfenbrenner, U. and Morris, P. A. (1998) The ecology of developmental processes. In: Damon, W. and Lerner, R. M. (eds) *Handbook of Child Psychology. Vol. 1 –Theoretical Models of Human Development*, 993–1028. New York: Wiley.

Brooke, L. (2003) Human resource costs and benefits of maintaining a mature-age workforce. *International Journal of Manpower* **24**, 260–283.

Brooker, D., Foster, N., Banner, A., Payne, M. and Jackson, L. (1998) The efficacy of Dementia Care Mapping as an audit tool: report of a 3-year British NHS evaluation. *Aging and Mental Health* **2**, 60–70.

Brower, A. M. and Nurius, P. S. (1993) *Social Cognition and Individual Change: Current Theory and Counseling Guidelines*. London: Sage.

Brown, B. and Perkins, D. (1992) Disruptions in place attachment. In: Altman, I. and Low, S. M. (eds) *Human Behaviour and Environment. Vol. 12 – Place Attachment*, 279–304. New York: Plenum Press.

Brown, J. D. (1998) *The Self*. New York: McGraw-Hill.

Brugman, G. and Heymans, P. (1994) *Psychogerontology: Een Levensloopbenadering* [Psychogerontology: a lifespan approach]. Bussum: Coutinho.

Bruunsgaard, H., Pedersen, M. and Pedersen, B. K. (2001) Aging and proinflammatory cytokines. *Current Opinion in Hematology* **8**, 131–136.

Buhler, C. and Knops, H. (eds) (1999) *Assistive Technology on the Threshold of the New Millenium*. Amsterdam: IOS Press.

Buhrmester, D. and Furman, W. (1990) Perceptions of sibling relationships during middle childhood and adolescence. *Child Development* **61**, 1387–1398.

Bundesministerium für Familie, Senioren, Frauen und Jugend (ed.) (2006) *Potenziale des Alters in Wirtschaft und Gesellschaft: Der Beitrag älterer Menschen zum Zusammenhalt der Generationen. Fünfter Bericht zur Lage der älteren Generation in der Bundesrepublik Deutschland. Bericht der Sachverständigenkommission* [Fifth report of the situation of the elderly in Germany – the potential of an ageing population for economy and society]. Berlin.

Buonomano, D. V. and Merzenich, M. M. (1998) Cortical plasticity: from synapses to maps. *Annual Review of Neuroscience* **21**, 149–186.

Burgess, E. W. (1960) Aging in western culture. In: Burgess, E. W. (ed.) *Aging in Western Societies*, 3–28. Chicago: Chicago University Press.

Burholt, V. (2004) The settlement pattern and residential histories of older Gujaratis, Punjabis and Sylhetis in Birmingham, England. *Ageing and Society* **24**(3), 383–409.

Burholt, V., Wenger, G., Lamura, G., Paulsson, C., van der Meer, M. *et al.* (2003) *European Study of Adult Well-Being: Comparative Report on Social Support Resources*. Report to European Commission, Brussels, Centre for Social Policy Research and Development, Institute for Medical and Social Care Research, University of Wales, Bangor.

Burkle, A., Beneke, S., Brabeck, C., Leake, A., Meyer, R. *et al.* (2002) Poly(ADP-ribose) polymerase-1, DNA repair and mammalian longevity. *Experimental Gerontology* **37**, 1203–1205.

Burrow, J. A. (1986) *The Ages of Man: A Study in Medieval Writing and Thought*. Oxford: Clarendon Press.

Butler, R. N. (1987) Ageism. In: *The Encyclopedia of Aging*, 22–23. New York: Springer.

Bytheway, B. (1995) *Rethinking Ageing*. Buckingham: Open University Press.

Bytheway, B. and Johnson, J. (1998) The sight of age. In: Nettleton, S. and Watson, J. (eds) *The Body in Everyday Life*, 243–257. London: Routledge.

Callahan, D. (1987) *Setting Limits: Medical Goals on an Aging Society*. New York: Simon & Schuster.

Calnan, M. (1987) *Health and Illness: The Lay Perspective.* London: Tavistock.

Camp, C. J. (1998) Memory intervention for normal and pathological older adults. *Annual Review of Gerontology and Geriatrics* **18**, 155–189.

Campbell, A. J. and Buchner, D. M. (1997) Unstable disability and the fluctuations of frailty. *Age and Ageing* **26**, 315–318.

Campisi, J. (1997) Aging and cancer: the double-edged sword of replicative senescence. *Journal of the American Geriatrics Society* **45**, 482–488.

Cantley, C. (2001) Understanding the policy context. In: Cantley, C. (ed.) *A Handbook of Dementia Care,* 201–219. Buckingham: Open University Press.

Caporael, L. R. and Culbertson, G. H. (1986) Verbal response modes of baby talk and other speech at institutions for the aged. *Language and Communication* **6**, 99–112.

Carp, F. M. and Carp, A. (1984) A complementary/congruence model of well-being or mental health for the community elderly. In: Altman, I. and Lawton, M. P. (eds) *Human Behavior and Environment. Vol. 7 – Elderly People and the Enviornment,* 279–336. New York: Plenum Press.

Carr, D. (2004) Gender, pre-loss marital dependence and older adults' adjustment to widowhood. *Journal of Marriage and the Family* **66**, 220–235.

Carstensen, L. L. (1991) Selectivity theory: social activity in life-span context. In: Schaie, K. W. and Powell Lawton, M. (eds) *Annual Review of Gerontology and Geriatrics: Behavioral Science and Aging,* vol. 11, 195–217. New York: Springer.

Carstensen, L. L. (1993) Motivation for social contact across the life span: a theory of socioemotional selectivity. In: Jacobs, J. E. (ed.) *Developmental Perspectives on Motivation* [Nebraska Symposium on Motivation, 1992], 209–254. Lincoln, NE: University of Nebraska Press.

Carstensen, L. L. (1995) Evidence for a life-span theory of socioemotional selectivity. *Current Directions in Psychological Science* **4**, 151–156.

Carstensen, L. L., Fung, H. and Charles, S. T. (2003) Socioemotional selectivity theory and the regulation of emotions in the second half of life. *Motivation and Emotion* **27**, 103–123.

Carstensen, L. L., Isaacowitz, D. M. and Charles, S. T. (1999) Taking time seriously: a theory of socioemotional selectivity. *American Psychologist* **54**, 165–181.

Carter, B. and McGoldrick, M. (eds) (1999) *The Expanded Family Life Cycle,* 5th edn. Boston: Allyn & Bacon.

Carver, C. S. and de la Garza, N. H. (1984) Schema-guided information search in stereotyping of the elderly. *Journal of Applied Social Psychology* **14**, 69–81.

Cavallini, E., Pagnin, A. and Vecchi, T. (2003) Aging and everyday memory: the beneficial effect of memory training. *Archives of Gerontology and Geriatrics* **37**, 241–257.

Cavan, R. S. (1963) Self and role in adjustment during old age. In: Vedder, C. B. (ed.) *Gerontology: A Book of Readings,* Springfield, Ill.: Thomas.

Cavan, R. S., Burgess, E. W., Havighurst, R. J. and Goldhamer, H. (1949) *Personal Adjustment in Old Age.* Chicago: Social Science Research Associates.

Cawthon, R. M., Smith, K. R., O'Brien, E., Sivatchenko, A. and Kerber, R. A. (2003) Association between telomere length in blood and mortality in people aged 60 years or older. *Lancet* **361**, 393–395.

CEHR (2006) Commission for Equality and Human Rights website: www.cehr.org.uk/content/purpose.rhtm. Date accessed 22/6/2006.

Cerny, P. G. and Evans, M. (2004) Globalization and public policy under new labour. *Policy Studies* **25**(1), 51–65.

Charles, S. T., Reynolds, C. and Gatz, M. (2001) Age-related differences and change in positive and negative affect over twenty-five years. *Journal of Personality and Social Psychology* **80**, 136–151.

Charmaz, K. (1983) Loss of self: a fundamental form of suffering in the chronically ill. *Sociology of Health and Illness* **5**(2), 168–195.

Charmaz, K. (2000) Experiencing chronic illness. In: Albrecht, G. L., Fitzpatrick, R. and Scrimshaw, S. C. (eds) *Handbook of Social Studies in Health and Medicine,* Chapter 2.6, 277–292. London: Sage.

Charness, N. (1981a) Aging and skilled problem solving. *Journal of Experimental Psychology: General* **110**, 21–38.

Charness, N. (1981b) Search in chess: age and skill differences. *Journal of Experimental Psychology: Human Perception and Performance* **7**, 467–476.

Charness, N. (1989) Expertise in chess and bridge. In: Klahr, D. and Kotovsky, K. (eds) *Complex Information Processing: The Impact of Herbert A. Simon*, 183–208. Hillsdale, NJ: Erlbaum.

Charness, N. and Bosman, E. A. (1990) Human factors and design for older adults. In: Birren, J. E. and Schaie, K. W. (eds) *Handbook of Psychology of Aging*, 446–464. New York: Academic Press.

Charness, N., Czaja, S., Fisk, A. D. and Rogers, W. (2001) Why gerontechnology? *Gerontechnology* **1**(2), 85–87.

Charness, N., Krampe, R. T. and Mayr, U. (1996) The role of practice and coaching in entrepreneural skill domains: an international comparison of life-span chess skill acquisition. In: Ericsson, K. A. (ed.) *The Road to Excellence: The Acquisition of Expert Performance in the Arts, Sciences, Sports, and games*, 51–80. Mahwah, NJ: Erlbaum.

Chevan, A. (1996) As cheaply as one: cohabitation in the older population. *Journal of Marriage and the Family* **58**, 656–667.

Cicirelli, V. G. (1985) Sibling relationships throughout the life cycle. In: Abate, L. L. (ed.) *The Handbook of Family Psychology and Therapy*, 177–214. Homewood, IL: Dorsey Press.

Cicirelli, V. G. (1987) Locus of control and patient role adjustment of the elderly in acute-care hospitals. *Psychology and Aging* **2**, 138–143.

Clark, R. and Spengler, J. (1980) Dependency ratios: their use in economic analysis. In: Simon, J. and Devanzo, J. (eds) *Research in Population Economics*, vol 2, chap. 6. Greenwich, CT: JAI Press.

Clatworthy, S. and Bjorneby, S. (1997) Smart house installations in Tonsberg. In: Bjorneby, S. and van Berlo, A. (eds) *Ethical Issues in Use of Technology for Dementia Care*, 67–72. Knegsel: Akontes Publishing.

Clausen, J. (1972) The life course of individuals. In: Riley, M. W., Johnson, M. and Foner, A. (eds) *Aging and Society. Vol. 3 – A. Sociology of Age Stratification*, 457–514. New York: Russell Sage Foundation.

Clemens, W. (2003) Wissenschaftsentwicklung und Forschungsstand. In: Herfurth, M., Kohli, M. and Zimmermann, K. F. (eds) *Arbeit in einer alternden Gesellschaft: Problemereiche und Entwicklungstendenzen der Erwerbsbeteiligung Älterer*, 179–193. Opladen: Leske & Budrich.

Coffmann, T. L. (1981) Relocation and survival of institutionalized aged: a re-examination of the evidence. *Gerontologist* **21**, 483–500.

Cohen, J. (1960) A coefficient of agreement for nominal scales. *Educational and Psychological Measurement* **XX**, 37–46.

Cole, T., Van Tassel, D. and Kastenbaum, R. (eds) (1992) *Handbook of the Humanities and Aging*. New York: Springer.

Cole, T. R., Achenbaum, W. A., Jakobi, P. L. and Kastenbaum, R. (eds) (1993) *Voices and Visions of Aging: Toward a Critical Gerontology*. New York: Springer.

Coleman, K. A. (1995) The value of productive activities of older Americans. In: Bass, S. A. (ed.) *Older and Active: How Americans Over 55 are Contributing to Society*, 169–203. New Haven: Yale University Press.

Coleman, P. G. (1999) Creating a life story: the task of reconciliation. *Gerontologist* **39**, 135–154.

Coleman, P. G. (2002) Doing case study research in psychology. In: Jamieson, A. and Victor, C. R. (eds) *Researching Ageing in Later Life*, 135–154. Buckingham: Open University Press.

Coleman, P. G. and O'Hanlon, A. (2004) *Ageing and Development: Theories and Research*. London: Arnold.

Coleman, R. (1998) Improving the quality of life for older people by design. In: Graafmans, J., Taipale, V. and Charness, N. (eds) *Gerontechnology: A Sustainable Investment in the Future*, 74–83. Amsterdam: IOS Press.

Colonia-Willner, R. (1998) Practical intelligence at work: relationship between aging and cognitive efficiency among managers in a bank environment. *Psychology and Aging* **13**, 45–57.

Commission of the European Communities (2003) *Commission Staff Working Paper 'Draft Joint Inclusion Report', Statistical Annex*. COM (2003) 773 final, Brussels: Commission of the European Communities.

Commons, M. L., Armon, C., Kohlberg, L., Richards, F. A., Grotzer, T. A. *et al.* (eds) (1990) *Adult Development. Vol 2 – Models and Methods in the Study of Adult and Adolescent Thought.* New York: Praeger.

Commons, M. L., Richards, F. A. and Armon, C. (eds) (1984) *Beyond Formal Operations.* New York: Praeger.

Cooney, T. and Dunne, K. (2001) Intimate relationships in later life. *Journal of Family Issues* **22**, 838–858.

Cooney, T. M. and Smith, L. A. (1996) Young adults relation with grandparents following recent parental divorce. *Journals of Gerontology* **51**, S91–95.

Cooper, M. and Ferreira, J. (1998) Home networks for independent living, support and care services, issues impinging on the successful introduction of products and services. In: Placencia Porrero, I. and Ballabio, E. (eds) *Improving the Quality of Life for the European Citizen*, 359–363. Amsterdam: IOA Press.

Corner, L. (1999) Developing approaches to person-centred outcome measures for older people in rehabilitation settings. Unpublished PhD thesis, University of Newcastle upon Tyne, UK.

Cornwell, J. (1984) *Hard-earned Lives: Accounts of Health and Illness from East London.* London: Tavistock.

Costa, P. T. and McCrae, R. R. (1997) Longitudinal stability of adult personality. In: Hogan, R., Johnson, J. A. and Briggs, S. R. (eds) *Handbook of Personality Psychology*, 269–290. New York: Academic Press.

Cottrell, D. A., Blakely, E. L., Johnson, M. A., Ince, P. G., Borthwick, G. M. *et al.* (2000) Cytochrome c oxidase deficient cells accumulate in the hippocampus and choroid plexus with age. *Neurobiology of Aging* **22**, 265–272.

Coupland, J. and Coupland, N. (1994) 'Old age doesn't come alone': discursive representations of health-in-aging in geriatric medicine. *International Journal of Aging and Human Development* **39**, 81–95.

Cournil, A. and Kirkwood, T. B. L. (2001) If you would live long, choose your parents well. *Trends in Genetics* **17**, 233–235.

Cowgill, D. O. and Holmes, L. D. (eds) (1972) *Aging and Modernization.* New York: Appleton Century–Crofts.

Cox, S. (1998) *Home Solutions: Housing and Support for People with Dementia.* London: Housing Associations Charitable Trust.

Craib, I. (1984) *Modern Social Theory.* Brighton: Wheatsheaf.

Crawford, R. (1984) A cultural account of 'health': control, release, and the social body. In: McKinlay, J. B. (ed.) *Issues in the Political Economy of Health Care*, Chapter. 2, 60–103. New York: Tavistock.

Cresswell, J. W. (2003) *Research Design: Qualitative, Quantitative and Mixed Methods Approaches*, 2nd edn. Thousand Oaks, CA: Sage.

Crimmins, E. M. (1996) Mixed trends in population health among older adults. *Journal of Gerontology* **51B**, S223–225

Crimmins, E. M., Hayward, M. D. and Saito, Y. (1996) Differentials in active life expectancy in the older population of the United States. *Journal of Gerontology* **51B**, S111–120.

Crittenden, P. M. (1995) Attachment and the risk for psychopathology: the early years. *Journal of Developmental and Behavioral Paediatrics* **16** (suppl. 3), S12–16.

Crittenden, P. M. (1997) The effect of early relationship experiences on relationships in adulthood. In: Duck, S. (ed.) *Handbook of Personal Relationships*, 2nd edn, 99–119. Chichester: Wiley.

Crittenden, P. M. (2002) *Adult Attachment Interview Coding Manual.* Unpublished manual available from the author.

Cross, S. and Markus, H. (1991) Possible selves across the life-span. *Human Development* **34**, 230–255.

Croucher, K. (2006) *Making the Case for Retirement Communities.* York: Joseph Rowntree Foundation. Website: www.jrf.org.uk/knowledge/findings/socialcare/0166.asp.

Croucher, K., Hicks, L. and Jackson, K. (2006) *Housing with Care for Later Life: A Literature Review.* York: Joseph Rowntree Foundation.

Crow, G., Allan, G. and Summers, M. (2002) Neither busybodies nor nobodies: managing proximity and distance in neighbourly relations. *Sociology* **36**(1), 127–145.

Cruickshank, M. (2003) *Learning To Be Old: Gender, Culture and Aging.* Lanham: Rowman & Littlefield.

Crystal, S. (2006) Dynamics of later life inequality: modelling the interplay of health disparities, economic resources. In: Baars, J., Dannefer, D., Phillipson, C. and Walker, A. (eds) *Globalization and Inequality*, 205–213. Amityville, NY: Baywood Publishing.

Crystal,S. and O'Shea,D. (2002) Economic outcomes in later life: public policy, health and cumulative advantages. *Annual Review of Gerontology and Geriatrics*, vol. 22. New York: Springer.

Cuddy, A. J. C. and Fiske, S. T. (2002) Doddering but dear: process, content, and function in stereotyping of older persons. In: Nelson, T. D. (ed.) *Ageism: Stereotyping and Prejudice Against Older Persons*, 3–26. Cambridge, MA: MIT Press.

Cumming, E. and Henry, W. E. (1961) *Growing Old: The Process of Disengagement.* New York: Basic Books.

Cusack, S. A. and Thomson, W. J. A. (1999) *Leadership for Older Adults. Aging with Purpose and Passion.* Philadelphia, PA: G. H. Buchanan.

Cushman, P. (1990) Why the self is empty: toward a historically situated psychology. *American Psychologist* **45**, 599–611.

Cylwik, H. (2002) Expectations of inter-generational reciprocity among older Greek Cypriot migrants in London. *Ageing and Society* **22**(5), 599–613.

Czaja, S. J. (1997) Using technologies to aid the performance of home tasks. In: Fisk, A. D. and Rogers, W. A. (eds) *Handbook of Human Factors and the Older Adult*, 311–334. San Diego, CA: Academic Press.

Daatland, S. O. (2002) Time to pay back? Is there something for psychology and sociology in gerontology. In: Andersson, L. (ed.) *Cultural Gerontology*, 1–12. Westport, CT: Auburn House.

Daatland, S. O. and Biggs, S. (eds) (2006) *Ageing and Diversity: Multiple Pathways and Cultural Migrations.* University of Bristol: Policy Press.

Dannefer, D. (1999) Neoteny, naturalization and other constituents of human development. In: Ryff, C. D. and Marshall, V. W. (eds) *The Self and Society in Aging Processes*, 67–93. New York: Springer.

Dannefer, D. (2003a) Cumulative advantage/disadvantage and the life course: cross-fertilizing age and social science theory. *Journal of Gerontology* **58B**(6), S327–337.

Dannefer, D. (2003b) Toward a global geography of the life course: challenges of late modernity for life course theory. In: Mortimer, J. T. and Shanahan, M. J. (eds) *Handbook of the Life Course*, 647–659. New York: Kluwer Academic/Plenum Publishers.

Dannefer, D. (2006) Reciprocal co-optation: the relationship of critical theory and social gerontology. In: Baars, J., Dannefer, D., Phillipson, C. and Walker, P. (eds) *Aging, Globalization and Inequality*, 103–120. Amityville, NY: Baywood Publishing.

Davey, J. A. (2002) Active ageing and education in mid and later life. *Ageing and Society* **22**, 95–113.

Davidson, K. (2001) Late life widowhood, selfishness and new partnership choices: a gendered perspective. *Ageing and Society* **21**, 297–317.

Davidson, K. (2006) Flying solo in old age: widowed and divorced men and women in later life. In: Vincent, J. A., Phillipson, C. and Downs, M. (eds) *The Futures of Old Age*, 182–189. London: Sage.

Dawe, A. (1970) The two sociologies. *British Journal of Sociology* **21**, 207–218.

de Grey, A. (2003) The forseeability of real anti-aging medicine: focusing the debate. *Experimental Gerontology* **38**(9), 927–934.

de Jong Gierveld, J. and Peeters, A.-M. (2003) The interweaving of re-partnered older adults' lives with their children and siblings. *Ageing and Society* **23**, 187–205.

de Vaus, D. (2001) *Research Design in Social Research.* London: Sage.

Deci, E. L. and Ryan, R. M. (2000) The 'what' and 'why' of goal pursuits: human needs and self-determination of behaviour. *Psychological Inquiry* **11**, 227–268.

Department for Work and Pensions (2006) *Security in Retirement: Towards a New Pensions System.* London: Stationery Office. Website: www.dwp.gov.uk/pensionsreform/whitepaper.asp.

Department of Health (2001) *National Service Framework for Older People.* London: NHS Executive.

DETR (1998a) *English Housing Condition Survey 1996.* London: DETR (Department of the Environment, Transport and the Regions).

DETR (1998b) *Updating and Revising the Index of Deprivation.* London: Stationery Office.

DETR (2000) *Quality and Choice: A Decent Home For All* [Housing Green Paper]. London: Stationery Office.

DETR and DoH (2001) *Quality and Choice for Older People's Housing.* London: Stationery Office.

Dex, S. (2003) *Families and Work in the Twenty-first Century.* York: Joseph Rowntree Foundation/York Publishing Services.

Dittmann-Kohli, F. (1981) Learning how to learn: a psychological approach to self-directed learning. *Education* **24**, 23–33.

Dittmann-Kohli, F. (1984) Weisheit als mögliches Ergebnis der Intelligenzentwicklung im Erwachsenenalter. *Sprache und Kognition* **3**, 112–132.

Dittmann-Kohli, F. (1986) Problem identification and definition as important aspects of adolescent's coping with normative life tasks. In: Silbereisen, R. K., Eyfert, K. and Rudinger, G. (eds) *Development as Action in Context*, 19–37. New York: Springer.

Dittmann-Kohli, F. (1990) The construction of meaning in old age: possibilities and constraints. *Ageing and Society* **10**, 279–294.

Dittmann-Kohli, F. (1995a) *Das persönliche Sinnsystem: Ein Vergleich zwischen frühem und spätem Erwachsenenalter.* Göttingen: Hogrefe.

Dittmann-Kohli, F. (1995b) Das SELE-Verfahren: Eine neue Methode zur Erhebung und Analyse von Selbstbeschreibungen. In: König, E. and Zedler, P. (eds) *Bilanz qualitativer Forschung. Vol II – Methoden*, 101–132. Weinheim: Deutscher Studienverlag.

Dittmann-Kohli, F. (2001) Selbst- und Lebensvorstellungen in der zweiten Lebenshälfte: Ergebnisse aus dem Alterssurvey. In: Dittmann-Kohli, F., Westerhof, G. J. and Bode, C. (eds) *Die zweite Lebenshälfte: Psychologische Perspectiven*, 549–584. Stuttgart: Kohlhammer.

Dittmann-Kohli, F. (2007) Temporal references in the construction of self-identity: a life span approach. In: Baars, J. and Visser, H. (eds) *Aging and Time: Multidisciplinary Perspectives*[n1]. Amityville, NY: Baywood Publishing (in press).

Dittmann-Kohli, F., Bode, C. and Westerhof, G. J. (eds) (2001) *Die zweite Lebenshälfte – Psychologische Perspektiven – Ergebnisse des Alters-Survey [The second half of life – psychological perspectives: results of the German Aging Survey].* Stuttgart: Kohlhammer.

Dittmann-Kohli, F. and van der Heijden, B. (1996) *Leistungsfähigkeit älterer Arbeitnehmer: interne und externe Einflußfaktoren [Performance capacity of elderly workers: internal and external influencing factors].* Zeitschrift für Gerontologie und Geriatrie **29**(5), 323–327.

Dittmann-Kohli, F. and Westerhof, G. J. (2000) The personal meaning system in a life span perspective. In: Reker, G. T. and Chamberlain, K. (eds) *Exploring Existential Meaning: Optimizing Human Development across the Life Span*, 107–123. Thousand Oaks, CA: Sage.

Dixon, R. A. (2000) Concepts and mechanisms of gains in cognitive aging. In: Park, D. C. and Schwarz, N. (eds) *Cognitive Aging: A Primer*, 23–41. Philadelphia: Psychology Press.

Dixon, R. A. and Bäckman, L. (eds) (1995) *Compensating for Psychological Deficits and Declines: Managing Losses and Promoting Gains.* Hillsdale, NJ: Erlbaum.

Dixon, R. A. and Baltes, P. B. (1986) Toward life-span research on the functions and pragmatics of intelligence. In: Sternberg, R. J. and Wagner, R. K. (eds) *Practical Intelligence: Nature and Origins of Competence in the Everyday World*, 203–235. New York: Cambridge University Press.

Docampo Rama, M., de Ridder, H. and Bouma, H. (2001) Technology generation and age in using layered interfaces. *Gerontechnology* **1**, 25–40.

Dowd, J. J. (1975) Aging as exchange: a preface to theory. *Journal of Gerontology* **30**, 584–594.

Dowd, J. J. (1987) The rectification of age: age stratification theory and the passing of autonomous subject. *Journal of Aging Studies* **1**, 317–335.

Dressel, P. L. (1988) Gender, race, class and aging: advances and opportunities. In: Minkler, M. and Estes, C. L. (eds) *Critical Gerontology*, 584–594.

Droogleever Fortuijn, J., van der Meer, M., Sassenrath, S., Quattrini, S., Ferring, D. *et al.* (2003) *Comparative Report on Ageing Well and Life Activities* [Report to European Commission]. University of Wales, Bangor: Centre for Social Policy Research and Development, Institute for Medical and Social Care Research.

Dudley, M. J. and Burns, E. (1992) The influence of age on policies for admission and thrombolysis in coronary care units in the United Kingdom. *Age and Ageing* **21**, 95–98.

Dumazedier, J. (1984) Social time and leisure in retirement. In: International Center of Social Gerontology (ed.) *Ageing Well Through Living Better*, 39–49. Paris: International Centre of Social Gerontology.

Durkheim, E. (1964) *The Division of Labour in Society*. New York: Free Press.

Dykstra, P. (1990) *Next of (Non)Kin: The Importance of Primary Relationships for Older Adults' Well-being*. Amsterdam: Swets & Zeitlinger.

Dykstra, P. (1995) Loneliness among the never and formerly married: the importance of supportive friendships and a desire for independence. *Journals of Gerontology* **50B**, S321–329.

Ehmer, J. (1990) *Sozialgeschichte des Alters*. Frankfurt: Suhrkamp.

Ekerdt, D. J. (1998) Workplace norms for the timing of retirement. In: Warner Schaie, K. and Schooler, C. (eds) *Impact of Work on Older Adults*, 101–123. New York: Springer.

Ekerdt, D. J. (2004) Born to retire: the foreshortened life course. *Gerontologist* **44**, 3–9.

Ekstrom, R. B., French, J. W., Harman, H. and Derman, D. (1976) *Kit of Factor-referenced Cognitive Tests*, rev. edn. Princeton, NJ: Educational Testing Service.

Elbert, T., Pantev, C., Wienbruch, C., Rockstroh, B. and Taub, E. (1995) Increased cortical representation of the fingers of the left hand in string players. *Science* **270**, 305–307.

Elbert, T., Sterr, A. and Rockstroh, B. (1996) Untersuchungen zu corticaler plastizitat beim erwachsenen menschen: was lernt das gehirn beim geige spielen? [Studies of cortical plasticity in adults: what does the brain learn from playing the violin?]. *Musikphysiologie und Musikmedizin* **3**, 57–65.

Elder, G. H. (1974) *Children of the Great Depression*. Chicago: University of Chicago Press.

Elder, G. H., Jr (1982) Historical experiences in the later years. In: Hareven, T. K. and Adams, K. J. (eds) *Ageing and Life Course Transitions: An Interdisciplinary Perspective*, 75–109. New York: Guilford Press.

Elder, G. H. (1991) Lives and social change. In: Heinz, W. R. (ed.) *Theoretical Advances in Llife Course Research*, 58–85. Weinheim: Deutscher Studien Verlag.

Elliot, R., Fischer, C. T. and Rennie, D. L. (1999) Evolving guidelines for publication of qualitative research studies in psychology and related fields. *British Journal of Clinical Psychology* **38**, 215–229.

Epel, E. S., Blackburn, E. H., Lin, J., Dhabhou, F. S., Adler, N. E. *et al.* (2004) Accelerated telomere shortening in response to life stress. *Proceedings of the National Academy of Science of the United States of America* **101**, 17312–17315.

Erber, J. T. and Prager, I. G. (1999) Age and memory: perceptions of forgetful young and older adults. In: Hess, T. M. and Blanchard-Fields, F. (eds) *Social Cognition and Aging*, 197–217. San Diego, CA: Academic Press.

Ericsson, K. A. (1990) Peak performance and age: an examination of peak performance in sports. In: Baltes, P. B. and Baltes, M. M. (eds) *Successful Aging: Perspectives from the Behavioral Sciences*, 164–196. New York: Cambridge University Press.

Ericsson, K. A. and Charness, N. (1994) Expert performance: its structure and acquisition. *American Psychologist* **49**, 725–747.

Ericsson, K. A. and Lehmann, A. C. (1996) Expert and exceptional performance: evidence on maximal adaptations on task constraints. *Annual Review of Psychology* **47**, 273–305.

Ericsson, K. A., Krampe, R. T. and Tesch-Römer, C. (1993) The role of deliberate practice in the acquisition of expert performance. *Psychological Review* **100**, 363–406.

Erikson, E. H. (1950) *Childhood and Society*. New York: Norton & Co.

Erikson, E. H. (1963) *Childhood and Society*, 2nd edn. New York: W. W. Norton.

Erikson, E. H. (1982) *The Life Cycle Completed: A Review*. New York: Norton.

Erikson, E. H., Erikson, J. M. and Kivnick, H. Q. (1986) *Vital Involvement in Old Age: The Experience of Old Age in Our Time*. New York: Norton.

Esiri, M. M., Matthews, F., Brayne, C., Ince, P. G., Matthews, F. E. *et al.* (2001) Pathological correlates of late-onset dementia in a multicentre, community-based population in England and Wales. *Lancet* **357**, 169–175.

Esping-Andersen, G. (1990) *The Three Worlds of Welfare Capitalism.* Cambridge: Polity Press.

Estes, C. (2006) Critical feminist perspectives, aging and social policy. In: Baars, J., Dannefer, D., Phillipson, C. and Walker, A. (eds) *Globalization and inequality*, 81–102. Amityville, NY: Baywood Publishing.

Estes, C. and Phillipson, C. (2002) The globalization of capital, the Welfare State and old age policy. *International Journal of Health Services* **32**(2), 279–297.

Estes, C., Swan, J. and Gerard, L. (1982) Dominant and competing paradigms in gerontology: towards a political economy of ageing. *Ageing and Society* **12**, 151–164.

Estes, C., Biggs, S. and Phillipson, C. (2003) *Social Theory, Social Policy and Ageing.* Buckingham: Open University Press.

Estes, C. L. (1979) *The Aging Enterprise.* San Francisco: Jossey Bass.

Estes, C. L. (1981) The social construction of reality: a framework for inquiry. In: Lee, P. R., Ramsay, N. B. and Red, I. (eds) *The Nation's Health*, 395–402. San Francisco: Boyd & Fraser.

Estes, C. L. (1999) Critical gerontology and the new political economy of aging. In: Minkler, M. and Estes, C. L. (eds) *Critical Gerontology: Perspectives from Political and Moral Economy*, 17–35. New York: Baywood Publishing.

Estes, C. L., Alford, R. R., Binney, E. A., Bradsher, J. E., Close, L. *et al.* (2001) *Social Policy and Aging: A Critical Perspective.* Thousand Oaks, CA: Sage.

Estes, C. L. and Binney, E. A. (1989) The biomedicalization of aging: dangers and dilemmas. *Gerontologist* **29**(5), 587–596.

Europa (2006) The history of the European Union. Website: http://europa.eu/abc/history/index_en.htm. Date accessed 22/5/2006

European Commission (1983) *Schlussbericht der Kommission an den Rat über das erste Programm vonn Modellvorhaben und Modellstudien zur Bekämpfung der Armut* [Final Report on the First Programme: Fighting Poverty in the European Member States]. Brussels.

European Commission (2002) *The life of women and men in Europe: a statistical portrait – Data 1980-2000.* Luxembourg: Office for Publications of the European Communities.

European Commission (2003a) *Health in Europe. Results from 1997–2000 surveys.* Luxembourg: Office for Official Publications of the European Communities.

European Commission (2003b) *Die soziale Lage in der Europäische Union* [Social reality in the European Union Member States]. Brussels.

European Commission (2005) *Pensions in Europe 2002.* Brussels: EC.

European Commission and the Council (2003) *Supporting National Strategies for the Future of Health Care and Care for the Elderly.* Brussels: European Commission.

EUROSTAT (1999) European Community Household Panel (ECHP) wave 6. Website: http://forum.europa. eu.int/irc/dsis/echpanel/info/data/information.html. Date accessed 30/5/2006

EUROSTAT (2003a) Self perceived health by sex, age, education and activity status. *European Community Household Panel UDB, Eurostat, 06/2003.* Website: http://epp.eurostat.cec.eu.int/ portal/page?_pageid=1073,46870091&_dad=portal&_schema=PORTAL&p_product_code=SPH1. Date accessed 30/5/2006

EUROSTAT (2003b) *Time Use at Different Stages of Life: Results from 13 European Countries.* Luxembourg: Office for Official Publications of the European Communities.

EUROSTAT (2004a) At risk of poverty rates by age and gender. Website: http://epp.eurostat.cec.eu.int/ portal/page?_pageid=1073,46870091&_dad=portal&_schema=PORTAL&p_product_code=ILC_LI 02. Date accessed 30/5/2006.

EUROSTAT (2004b) At-risk-of-poverty rate by gender and selected age groups. Website: http://epp. eurostat.cec.eu.int/portal/page?_pageid=1073,46870091&_dad=portal&_schema=PORTAL&p_ product_code=ILC_PN02. Date accessed 29/5/2006.

EUROSTAT (2004c) *Eurostat Yearbook 2004: The Statistical Guide to Europe.* Luxembourg: Eurostat.

EUROSTAT (2004d) Statistics EU: old age dependency ratios. Website: http://europa.eu.int/comm/employment_social/eoss/eurostat7_en.html. Date accessed 30/5/2006.

EUROSTAT (2006) A statistical view of the life of women and men in the EU25. *STAT/06/29*, 6 March 2006. Website: http://europa.eu.int/rapid/pressReleasesAction.do?reference=STAT/06/29&format=HTML&aged=0&language=EN&guiLanguage=en. Date accessed 22/5/2006.

Eurostat News Release (2004) *Demographic, Economic and Social Data on 258 Cities across Europe.* 82/2004, 25 June 2004, Eurostat. Website: http://epp.eurostat.cec.eu.int/.

Eurostat News Release (2005) *EU25 Population Rises Until 2025, Then Falls.* 48/2005, 8 April 2005, Eurostat. Website: http://epp.eurostat.cec.eu.int/.

Evandrou, M. and Falkingham, J. (2006) Will the baby-boomers be better off than their parents in retirement? In: Vincent, J. A., Phillipson, C. and Downs, M. (eds) *The Futures of Old Age,* 90–102. London: Sage.

Evans, G. W., Kantrowitz, E. and Eshelman, P. (2002) Housing quality and psychological well-being among the elderly population. *Journal of Gerontology* **57B**(4), 381–383.

Evans, J. G. (1991) Aging and rationing. *British Medical Journal* **303**, 869–870.

Farquhar, M. (1994) Quality of life in older people. In: Fitzpatrick, R. (ed.) *Advances in Medical Sociology,* Chapter 7, 139–158. Greenwich, CT: JAI Press.

Farquhar, M. (1995) Elderly people's definitions of quality of life. *Social Science and Medicine* **41**(10), 1439–1446.

Featherstone, M. and Hepworth, M. (1991) The mask of ageing and the postmodern lifecourse. In: *The Body: Social Process and Cultural Theory,* 371–389. London: Sage.

Featherstone, M. and Hepworth, M. (1995) Images of positive ageing: a case study of *Retirement Choice* magazine. In: Featherstone, M. and Wernick, A. (eds) *Images of Ageing: Cultural Respresentation of Later Life,* 29–48. London: Routledge.

Featherstone, M. and Wernick, A. (eds) (1995) *Images of Ageing: Cultural Representations of Later Life.* London: Routledge.

Felton, B. and Kahana, E. (1974) Adjustment and situationally bound locus of control among institutionalized aged. *Journal of Gerontology* **29**, 295–301.

Fennell, G., Phillipson, C. and Evers, H. (1988) *The Sociology of Old Age.* Milton Keynes: Open University Press.

Ferge, Z. (1997) A central European perspective on the social quality of Europe. In: Beck, W., van der Maesen, L. and Walker, A. (eds) *The Social Quality of Europe,* 187–206. The Hague: Kluwer International.

Ferge, Z. (2001) European integration and the reform of social security in the accession countries. *European Journal of Social Quality* 3(1/2), 9–25.

Ferrera, M. (1996) The southern model of welfare in social Europe. *Journal of European Social Policy* **6**(1), 17–37.

Ferring, D., Boll, T. and Filipp, S.-H. (2003) Elterliche Ungleichbehandlung in Kindheit und Jugend aus der Perspektive des mittleren Erwachsenenalters. [Parental differential treatment in childhood and adolescence from the perspective of middle-aged adults]. *Zeitschrift für Entwicklungspsychologie und Pädagogische Psychologie* **35**, 83–97.

Ferring, D. and Filipp, S.-H. (1999) Soziale Netze im Alter: Selektivität in der Netzwerkgestaltung und Prävalenz positiver und negativer Sozialbeziehungen [Social networks in old age: socioemotional selectivity, perceived quality of social interactions, and affect]. *Zeitschrift für Entwicklungspsychologie und Pädagogische Psychologie* **31**, 127–137.

Field, D. and Millsap, R. E. (1991) Personality in advanced old age: continuity or change? *Journal of Gerontology* **46**, 299–308.

Fielding, N. G. and Fielding, J. L. (1986) *Linking Data: The Articulation of Qualitative and Quantitative Methods in Social Research.* Beverley Hills, CA: Sage.

Filipp, S.-H. and Ferring, D. (1989) Zur Alters – und Bereichsspezifität subjektiven Alterserlebens. *Zeitschrift für Entwicklungspsychologie und Pädagogische Psychologie* **21**, 279–293.

Filipp, S.-H. and Mayer, A. K. (1999) *Bilder des Alters: Altersstereotypes und die Beziehungen zwischen den Generationen*. Stuttgart: Kohlhammer.

Finch, C. E. and Tanzi, R. (1997) The genetics of aging. *Science* **278**, 407–411.

Finch, J. and Mason, J. (1993) *Negotiating Family Responsibilities*. London: Routledge.

Fishman, D. B. (1999) *The Case of Pragmatic Psychology*. New York: NY University Press.

Fisk, M. J. (2001) The implications of SMART home technologies. In: Peace, S. M. and Holland, C. (eds) *Inclusive Housing in an Ageing Society*, 101–124. Bristol: Policy Press.

Folkman, S., Lazarus, R. S., Pimley, S. and Novacek, J. (1987) Age differences in stress and coping processes. *Psychology and Aging* **2**, 171–184.

Fonseca, M. L., Caldeira, M. J. and Esteves, A. (2002) New forms of migration into the European south: challenges for citizenship and governance: the Portuguese case. *International Journal of Population Geography* **8**(2), 135–152.

Forrest, R. and Leather, P. (1998) The ageing of the property owning democracy. *Ageing and Society* **18**(1), 35–63.

Foucault, M. (1970) *L'Orde du discourse*. Paris: Gallimard.

Foucault, M. (1973) *The Birth of the Clinic*. London: Tavistock.

Foucault, M. (1974) *The Order of Things: An Archaeology of the Human Sciences*. London: Tavistock.

Franz, C. E. and White, K. M. (1985) Individuation and attachment in personality development: extending Erikson's theory. *Journal of Personality* 53, 224–256.

Freidson, E. (1975) *Profession of Medicine. A Study of the Sociology of Applied Knowledge*. New York: Dodd, Mead & Co.

Freund, A. M. and Baltes, P. B. (1998) Selection, optimization and compensation as strategies of life-management: correlations with subjective indicators of successful aging. *Psychology and Aging* 13, 531–543.

Freund, A. M. and Baltes, P. B. (2002) Life management strategies of selection, optimization and compensation: measurement by self-report and construct validity. *Journal of Personality and Social Psychology* 82, 642–662.

Freund, A. M. and Smith, J. (1999) Content and function of the self-definition in old and very old age. *Journal of Gerontology* **54B**, P55–67.

Fries, J. F. (1980) Aging, natural death, and compression of morbidity. *New England Journal of Medicine* **303**, 130–135.

Frieswijk, N. (2004) Frail but happy: the importance of self-management ability and social comparison for the subjective well-being of elderly persons [doctoral dissertation]. University of Groningen.

Fuller, G. F. (2000) Falls in the elderly. *American Family Physician* **61**, 2159–2168.

Gabriel, S. E., Brigman, K. N., Koller, B. H., Bonches, R. C. and Stutts, M. (1994) Cystic fibrosis heterozygote resistance to cholera toxin in the cystic fibrosis mouse model. *Science* **266**, 107–109.

Gabriel, Z. and Bowling, A. (2004) Quality of life from the perspectives of older people. *Ageing and Society* **24**(5), 675–691.

Gems, D. and Partridge, L. (2001) Insulin/IGF signalling and ageing: seeing the bigger picture. *Current Opinion in Genetics and Development* 11, 287–292.

George, C., Kaplan, N. and Main, M. (1985) An adult attachment interview: interview protocol. Unpublished manuscript, Department of Psychology, University of California, Berkeley.

George, L. K. (1990) Social structure, social processes, and social psychological states. In: Binstock, R. H. and George, L. K. (eds) *Handbook of Aging and the Social Sciences*, 186–200. San Diego, CA: Academic Press.

George, L. K. (1993) Sociological perspectives on life course transitions. *Annual Review of Sociology* **19**, 353–373.

Geottings, A. (1986) The development tasks of siblings over the life cycle. *Journal of Marriage and the Family* **48**, 703–714.

Gerbner, G., Gross, L., Signorielli, N. and Morgan, M. (1980) Aging with television: images on television drama and conceptions of social reality. *Journal of Communication* **30**, 37–47.

Gergen, K. J. and Gergen, M. M. (2000) The new aging: self construction and social values. In: Schaie, K. W. and Hendricks, J. (eds) *The Evolution of the Aging Self: The Societal Impact on the Aging Process*, 281–306. New York: Springer.

Gerth, H. H. and Mills, C. W. (1948) *From Max Weber: Essays in Sociology*. London: Routledge & Kegan Paul.

Giddens, A. (1984) *The Constitution of Society*. Cambridge: Polity Press.

Giddens, A. (1991) *Modernity and Self Identity*. Cambridge: Polity Press.

Giddens, A. (1992) *The Transformation of Intimacy: Sexuality, Love and Eroticism in Modern Societies*. Cambridge: Polity Press.

Giles, H., Noels, K. A., Williams, A., Ota, H., Lim, T. *et al.* (2003) Intergenerational communication across cultures: young people's perceptions of conversations with family elders, non-family elders and same-age peers. *Journal of Cross Cultural Gerontology* **18**, 1–32.

Gilleard, C. and Higgs, P. (2000) *Cultures of Ageing: Self, Citizen and the Body*. Harlow: Prentice-Hall.

Glaser, B. G. and Strauss, A. L. (1967) *The Discovery of Grounded Theory: Strategies for Qualitative Research*. New York: Aldine.

Glendinning, C. and Millar, J. (eds) (2002) *Women and Poverty in Britain in the 1990s*. Brighton: Harvester Wheatsheaf.

Goffman, E. (1961) *Asylums: Essays on the Social Situation of Mental Patients and Other Inmates*. New York: Anchor Books.

Goffman, E. (1968) *Stigma: Notes on the Management of Spoiled Identity*. Harmondsworth: Penguin.

Golant, S. M. (1998) Changing an older person's shelter and care setting: a model to explain personal and environmental outcomes. In: Scheidt, R. J. and Windley, P. G. (eds) *Environment and Aging Theory: A Focus on Housing*, 33–60. Westport, CT: Greenwood Press.

Gold, D. T. (1989) Sibling relationships in old age: a typology. *International Journal of Aging and Human Development* **28**, 37–51.

Goldstein, I. L. (1993) *Training in Oorganisations*, 3rd edn. California: Brooks/Cole.

Gouldner, A. (1970) *The Coming Crisis of Western Sociology*. London: Heinemann.

Graebner, W. (1980) *A History of Retirement*. New Haven: Yale University Press.

Greenberg, J., Schimel, J. and Mertens, A. (2002) Ageism: denying the face of the future. In: Nelson, T. D. (ed.) *Ageism: Stereotyping and Prejudice Against Older Persons*, 27–48. Cambridge, MA: MIT Press.

Grewal, D. and Salovey, P. (2005) Feeling smart: the science of emotional intelligence. *American Scientist* **93**, 330–339.

Grewal, I., Lewis, J., Flynn, T., Brown, J. and Bond, J. (2005) Developing attributes for a generic quality of life measure for older people: preferences or capabilities? *Social Science and Medicine* **62**, 1891–1901.

Groombridge, B. (1982) Learning, education and later life. *Adult Education* **54**, 314–325.

Grube, K. and Bürkle, A. (1992) Poly(ADP-ribose) polymerase activity in mononuclear leukocytes of 13 mammalian species correlates with species-specific life span. *Proceedings of the National Academy of Sciences of the USA* **89**, 11759–11763.

Gruber, J. and Wise, D. A. (2002) Social security programs and retirement around the world: micro estimation [NBER working paper w9407]. Cambridge MA.: National Bureau of Economic Research.

Gubrium, J. F. (1986) *Oldtimers and Alzheimer's: The Descriptive Organization of Senility*. Greenwith, CT: JAI Press.

Gubrium, J. F. (1993) Voice and context in a new gerontology. In: Cole, T., Achenbaum, W. A., Jakobi, P. and Kastenbaum, R. (eds) *Voices and Visions of Aging: Toward a Critical Gerontology*. New York: Springer.

Gubrium, J. F. and Holstein, J. A. (1999) The nursing home as a discursive anchor for the ageing body. *Ageing and Society* **19**, 519–538.

Gullette, M. M. (2003) From lifestory telling to age autobiography. *Journal of Aging Studies* **17**, 101–111.

Gurney, C. and Means, R. (1993) The meaning of home in later life. In: Arber, S. and Evandrou, M. (eds) *Ageing, Independence and the Life Course*. London: Jessica Kingsley Publishers.

Gutmann, D. (1987) *Reclaimed Powers: Towards a New Psychology of Men and Women in Later Life*, 2nd edn. New York: Basic Books.

Haan, N., Millsap, R. and Hartka, E. (1986) As time goes by: change and stability in personality over fifty years. *Psychology and Aging* **1**, 220–232.

Haber, C. (2001) Anti-aging: why now? A historical framework for understanding the comtemporary enthusiasm. *Generations* **25**, 9–14.

Hagestad, G. (1991) Trends and dilemmas in life course research: an international perspective. In: Heinz, W. R. (ed.) *Theoretical Advances in Life Course Research*, 23–57. Weinheim: Deutscher Studien Verlag.

Hagestad, G. (2002) Commentary: relationships in time and space. *International Society for the Study of Behavioural Development, Newsletter* **1**(41), 17–18.

Hagestad, G. and Dannefer, D. (2001) Concepts and theories of aging: beyond microfication in social science approaches. In: Binstock, R. and George, L. (eds) *Handbook of Aging and the Social Sciences*, 5th edn, 3–21. San Diego, CA: Academic Press.

Hakamies-Blomquistm, L. and Wahlstrom, B. (1998) Why do older drivers give up driving? *Accidents Analysis and Prevention* **30**(3), 305–312.

Halpert, B. P. and Zimmerman, M. K. (1986) The health status of the 'old-old': a reconsideration. *Social Science and Medicine* **22**, 893–899.

Hambrick, D. Z., Salthouse, T. A. and Meinz, E. J. (1999) Predictors of crossword puzzle proficiency and moderators of age-cognition relations. *Journal of Experimental Psychology: General* **128**, 131–164.

Hamerman, D. (1999) Toward an understanding of frailty. *Annals of Internal Medicine* **130**, 945–950.

Hammersley, M. and Atkinson, P. (1983) *Ethnography: Principles in Practice*. London: Tavistock.

Hanson, J., Kellaher, L. and Rowlands, M. (2001) *Profiling the Housing Stock for Older People: The Transition from Domesticity to Care* [Final report of EPSRC EQUAL research]. University College London.

Hart, E. and Bond, M. (1995) *Action Research for Health and Social Care: A Guide to Practice*. Buckingham: Open University Press.

Hartley, A. A. and Little, D. M. (1999) Age-related differences and similarities in dual-task interference. *Journal of Experimental Psychology: General* **128**, 416–449.

Harwood, J. and Giles, H. (1992) 'Don't make me laugh': representations of age in a humourous context. *Discourse and Society* **3**, 403–426.

Harwood, J., Giles, H. and Ryan, E. B. (1995) Aging, communication, and intergroup theory: social identity and intergenerational communication. In: Nussbaum, J. and Coupland, J. (eds) *Handbook of Communication and Aging Research*, 133–159. Mahwah: Lawrence Erlbaum.

Hasher, L. and Zacks, R. T. (1988) Working memory, comprehension, and aging: a review and a new view. In: Bower, G. H. (ed.) *The Psychology of Learning and Motivation: Advances in Research and Theory*, Chapter 22, 193–225. New York: Academic Press.

Hatch, L. and Bulcroft, K. (1992) Contact with friends in later life: disentangling the effects of gender and marital status. *Journal of Marriage and the Family* **54**, 222–232.

Hautamäki, A. and Coleman, P. G. (2001) Explanation for low prevalence of PTSD among older Finnish war veterans: social solidarity and continued significance given to wartime sufferings. *Aging and Mental Health* **5**, 165–174.

Havighurst, R. J. (1961) The nature and values of meaningful free-time activity. In: Kleemeier, R. W. (ed.) *Aging and Leisure*, 309–344. New York: Oxford University Press.

Havighurst, R. J. (1968) Personality and patterns of aging. *Gerontologist* **8**, 20–23.

Havighurst, R. J. and Albrecht, R. (1953) *Older People*. London: Longman.

Hayes, V., Morris, J., Wolfe, C. and Morgan, M. (1995) The SF-36 Health Survey Questionnaire: is it suitable for use with older adults? *Age and Ageing* **24**, 120–125.

Hayflick, L. (2001) Anti-aging medicine: hype, hope, and reality. *Generations* **25**, 20–26.

Haynie, D. A., Berg, S., Johannsson, B., Gatz, M. and Zarit, S. H. (2001) Symptoms of depression in the oldest old: a longitudinal study. *Journal of Gerontology* **56B**, P111–118

Hayslip, B. J. (1989) Alternative mechanisms for improvements in fluid ability performance among older adults. *Psychology and Aging* **4**, 122–124.

Hazan, C. and Shaver, P. R. (1987) Romantic love conceptualized as an attachment process. *Journal of Personality and Social Psychology* **52**, 511–524.

Hazan, H. (1980) *The Limbo People: A Study of the Constitution of the Time Universe Among the Aged*. London: Routledge & Kegan Paul.

Hazan, H. (1986) Body image and temporality among the aged: a case study of an ambivalent symbol. *Studies in Symbolic Interaction* **7**, 305–329.

Hazan, H. (1994) *Old Age: Constructions and Deconstructions*. Cambridge: Cambridge University Press.

Hearn, J. (1995) Imaging the aging of men. In: Featherstone, M. and Wernick, A. (eds) *Images of Aging: Cultural Representations of Later Life*, 61–75. London: Routledge.

Heaton, T. B., Jacobson, C. K. and Holland, K. (1999) Persistence and change in decisions to remain child-less. *Journal of Marriage and the Family* **61**, 531–539.

Heckhausen, J. (1999) *Developmental Regulation in Adulthood: Age-normative and Sociostructural Constraints as Adaptive Challenges?* New York: Cambridge University Press.

Heckhausen, J., Dixon, R. A. and Baltes, P. B. (1989) Gains and losses in development throughout adult-hood as perceived by different adult age groups. *Developmental Psychology* **25**, 109–121.

Heckhausen, J. and Schulz, R. (1993) Optimisation by selection and compensation: balancing primary and secondary control in life-span development. *International Journal of Behavioral Development* **16**, 87–303.

Heckhausen, J. and Schulz, R. (1995) A life-span theory of control. *Psychological Review* **102**, 284–304.

Heckhausen, J., Wrosch, C. and Fleeson, W. (2001) Developmental regulation before and after a devel-opmental deadline: the sample case of 'biological clock' for child-bearing. *Psychology and Aging* **16**, 400–413.

Held, D. and McGrew, A. (2002) *Governing Globalization: Power, Authority and Global Governance*. Cambridge: Polity Press.

Held, D., McGrew, A., Goldblatt, D. and Perraton, J. (1999) *Global Transformations*. Oxford: Polity Press.

Helson, R. and Kwan, V. S. Y. (2000) Personality change in adulthood: the broad picture and processes in one longitudinal sample. In: Hampson, S. E. (ed.) *Advances in Personality and Psychology*, vol. 1, 77–166. Philadelphia: Psychology Press/Taylor & Francis.

Hendricks, J. and Hendricks, C. D. (1986) Theories of social gerontology. In: Hendricks, J. and Hendricks, C. D. (eds) *Aging in Mass Society: Myth and Reality*, 3rd edn, 80–122. Boston: Little, Brown.

Henretta, J. C. (1994) Social structure and age-based careers. In: Riley, M. W., Kahn, R. L. and Foner, A. (eds) *Age and Structural Lag*, 57–79. New York: Wiley.

Henretta, J. C. and Campbell, R. T. (1976) Status attainment and status maintenance: a study of strati-fication in old age. *American Sociological Review* **41**, 981–992.

Henry, J. P. (1988) The archetypes of power and intimacy. In: Birren, J. E. and Bengtson, V. L. (eds) *Emergent Theories of Ageing*, 269–298. New York: Springer.

Henwood, K. L. and Pidgeon, N. F. (1992) Qualitative research and psychological theorizing. *British Journal of Psychology* **83**, 97–111.

Henwood, M. (1990) No sense of urgency: age discrimination in health care. In: McEwen, E. (ed.) *The Unrecognised Discrimination*. London: Age Concern.

Hepworth, M. (2000) *Stories of Ageing*. Buckingham: Open University Press.

Hepworth, M. (2004) Embodied agency, decline and the masks of aging. In: Tulle, E. (ed.) *Old Age and Agency*, 125–135. Hauppauge, NY: Nova Science.

Herlyn, I. and Lehmann, B. (1998) Grossmutterschaft im Mehrgenerationenzusammenhang: Eine empirische Untersuchung aus der Perspektive von Grossmüttern. *Zeitschrift für Familienforschung* **10**, 27–45.

Hertogh, C. M. P. M., The, B. A. M., Miesen, B. M. L. and Eefsting, J. A. (2004) Truth telling and truthful-ness in the care for patients with advanced dementia: an ethnographic study in Dutch nursing homes. *Social Science and Medicine* **59**, 1685–1693.

Hertzman, C. and Hayes, M. (1985) Will the elderly really bankrupt us with increased health care costs? *Canadian Journal of Public Health* **76**(6), 373–377.

Herzlich, C. (1973) *Health and Illness*. London: Academic Press.

Herzlich, C. and Pierret, J. (1985) The social construction of the patient: patients and illnesses in other ages. *Social Science and Medicine* **20**(2), 145–151.

Herzlich, C. and Pierret, J. (1987) *Illness and Self in Society*. Baltimore: Johns Hopkins University Press.

Herzog, R. A., Franks, M. M., Markus, H. R. and Holmberg, D. (1996) Productive activities and agency in older age. In: Baltes, M. M. and Montada, L. (eds) *Produktives Leben im Alter*, 323–343. Frankfurt: Campus.

Herzog, R. A. and Morgan, J. N. (1992) Age and gender differences in the value of productive activities: four different approaches. *Research on Aging* **14**, 169–198.

Herzog, R. A., Kahn, R. L., Morgan, J. N., Jackson, J. S. and Antonucci, T. C. (1989) Age differences in productive activities. *Journal of Gerontology* **44**, S129–138

Hicks, P. (2001) Neue Tendenzen der Rentenreformen in Europa. In: Stiftung, F. E. (ed.) *Rentenpolitik in Europa: Welches Modell wird zur Leitidee von Reformen?* [Pension policy in Europe: what is the leading model for reforms?]. Bonn: FES-library.

Hinrichs, K. (2000) Rentenreformpolitik in OECD-Ländern: Die Bundesrepublik Deutschland im internationalen Vergleich [Pension policy in the OECD countries: Germany international comparison]. In: *Deutsche Rentenversicherung*, 3/4.

Hirst, M. (2001) Trends in informal care in Great Britain during the 1990s. *Health and Social Care in the Community* **9**(6), 348–357.

Hochschild, A. R. (1975) Disengagement theory: a critique and proposal. *American Sociological Review* **40**, 533–569.

Hockey, J. and James, A. (1993) *Growing Up and Growing Old: Ageing and Dependency in the Life Course*. London: Sage.

Hoerder, D. (2001) Reconstructing life courses: a historical perspective on migrant experiences. In: Marshall, V., Heinz, W., Kruger, H. and Verma, A. (eds) *Reconstructing Work and the Life Course*. Toronto: University of Toronto Press.

Hofland, B. F., Willis, S. L. and Baltes, P. B. (1981) Fluid intelligence performance in the elderly: intraindividual variability and conditions of assessment. *Journal of Educational Psychology* **73**, 573–586.

Holland, C. A. (2001) *Housing Histories: The Experience of Older Women Across the Life Course* [PhD thesis]. Milton Keynes: Open University.

Holland, C. A., Clark, A., Katz, J. and Peace, S. (2006) *Social Interactions in Urban Public Places* [research report]. York: Joseph Rowntree Foundation.

Holliday, S. G. and Chandler, M. J. (1986) *Wisdom: Explorations in Adult Competence*. Basel: Karger.

Holstein, J. A. and Gubrium, J. F. (1995) *The Active Interview*. Thousand Oaks, CA: Sage.

Holstein, J. A. and Gubrium, J. F. (2000) *The Self We Live By: Narrative Identity in a Post-modern World*. Oxford: Oxford University Press.

Hooker, K. (1999) Possible selves in adulthood: incorporating teleonomic relevance into studies of the self. In: Hess, T. M. and Blanchard-Fields, F. (eds) *Social Cognition and Aging*, 97–122. San Diego, CA: Academic Press.

Horn, J. L. (1982) The theory of fluid and crystallized intelligence in relation to concepts of cognitive psychology and aging in adulthood. In: Craik, F. I. M. and Trehub, S. (eds) *Aging and Cognitive Processes*, 237–278. New York: Plenum.

Horn, J. L. and Cattell, R. B. (1976) Age differences in fluid and crystallized intelligence. *Acta Psychologica* **26**, 107–129.

Horn, J. L. and Masunaga, H. (2000) New directions for reserach into aging and intelligence: the development of expertise. In: Perfect, T. J. and Maylor, E. A. (eds) *Models of Cognitive Aging*, 125–159. New York: Oxford University Press.

House of Lords Science and Technology Committee (2005) *Ageing: Scientific Aspects*. London: Stationery Office.

Huber, A. and O'Reilly, K. (2004) The construction of Heimat under conditions of individualised modernity: Swiss and British elderly migrants in Spain. *Ageing and Society* **24**, 327–351.

Hui, H. C. and Yee, C. (1994) The Shortened Individualism–Collectivism Scale: its relationship to demographic and work-related variables. *Journal of Research in Personality* **28**, 409–424.

Huisman, M., Kunst, A. E., Andersen, O., Bopp, M., Borgan, J.-K. *et al.* (2004) Socioeconomic inequalities in mortality among elderly people in 11 European populations. *Journal of Epidemiology and Community Health* **58**, 468–475.

Hulko, W. (2002) Making the links: social theories, experiences of people with dementia, and intersectionality. In: Leibing, A. and Scheinkman, L. (eds) *The Diversity of Alzheimer's Disease: Different Approaches and Contexts*, 231–264. Rio de Janeiro: CUCA–IPUB.

Hummert, M. L. (1999) A social cognitive perspective on age stereotypes. In: Hess, T. M. and Blanchard-Fields, F. (eds) *Social Cognition and Aging*, 175–196. San Diego, CA: Academic Press.

Hummert, M. L., Garstka, T. A., Shaner, J. L. and Strahm, S. (1994) Stereotypes of the elderly held by young, middle-aged, and elderly adults. *Journal of Gerontology* **49**(5), P240–249

Humphrey, R. (1993) Life stories and social careers: ageing and social life in an ex-mining town. *Sociology* **27**(1), 166–178.

Hutton, W. and Giddens, A. (2000) *On the Edge: Living with Global Capitalism*. London: Jonathan Cape.

Iacovou, M. (2000) *The Living Arrangements of Elderly Europeans*. University of Essex: Institute for Social and Economic Research. Website: www.iser.essex.ac.uk/pubs/workpaps/pdf/2000-09.pdf.

Idler, E. L. and Benyamini, Y. (1997) Self-rated health and mortality: a review of twenty-seven community studies. *Journal of Health and Social Behavior* **38**, 21–37.

Ingebretsen, R. and Solem, P. E. (1998) Spouses of persons with dementia: attachment, loss and coping. *Norwegian Journal of Epidemiology* **8**, 149–156.

International Association of Gerontology (1954) *Old Age in the Modern World: Report of the Third Congress*. London: E&S Livingstone.

Isaacs, B. and Neville, Y. (1976) The needs of old people: 'interval' as a method of measurement. *British Journal of Preventive and Social Medicine* **30**, 79–85.

Iwarsson, S., Sixsmith, J., Oswald, F., Wahl, H.-W., Nygren, C. *et al.* (2005) The ENABLE-AGE Project: multi-dimensional methodology for European housing research. In: Vestbro, D. J., Hurol, Y. and Wilkinson, N. (eds) *Methodologies in Housing Research*, 70–90. Gateshead: Urban International Press.

Iwarsson, S., Wahl, H.-W. and Nygren, C. (2004) Challenges of cross-national housing research with older people: lessons learned from the ENABLE-AGE Project. *European Journal of Ageing* **1**(79), 88.

Izaks, G. J. and Westendorp, R. G. (2003) Ill or just old? Towards a conceptual framework of the relation between ageing and disease. *BMC Geriatrics* **3**, 1–6.

Jacobs, K., Kohli, M. and Rein, M. (1991) The evolution of early exit: a comparative analysis of labor force participation patterns. In: Kohli, M., Rein, M., Guillemard, A.-M. and van Gunsteren, H. (eds) *Time for Retirement: Comparative Studies of Early Exit from the Labor Force*, 36–66. Cambridge: Cambridge University Press.

Jamieson, A. and Victor, C. R. (2002) *Researching Ageing and Later Life: The Practice of Social Gerontology*. Buckingham: Open University Press.

Jamieson, L. (1998) *Intimacy: Personal Relationships in Modern Societies*. Cambridge: Polity Press.

Jennett, B. (1995) High technology therapies and older people. *Ageing and Society* **15**, 185–198.

Jerrome, D. (1992) *Good Company: An Anthropological Study of Old People in Groups*. Edinburgh: Edinburgh University Press.

Jerrome, D. and Wenger, G. C. (1999) Stability and change in late-life friendships. *Ageing and Society* **19**, 661–676.

John, O. P. (1990) The 'big five' factor taxonomy: dimensions of personality in the natural language and in questionnaires. In: Pervin, L. A. (ed.) *Handbook of Personality: Theory and Research*, 66–100. New York: Guilford Press.

John, R. (1984) Prerequisites of an adequate theory of aging: a critique and a reconceptualisation. *Mid-American Review of Sociology* **9**(2), 79–108.

Johnson, C. L. and Barer, B. M. (1997) *Life Beyond 85 Years: The Aura of Survivorship*. New York: Springer.

Joint Taskforce on Older People (2000) *Healthcare and Ageing Population Panels*. London: Department of Trade and Industry.

Jopp, D. (2003) Erfolgreiches Altern: zum Funktionalen Zusammenspiel von personalen Ressourcen und adaptiven Stategien des Lebensmanagements [Successful aging: on the functional interplay between personal resources and adaptive life-management strategies]. Freie Universität Berlin, Germany. Electronic version: www.diss.fu-berlin.de/2003/50/indexe/html.

Jopp, D. and Smith, J. (2006) Resources and life-management strategies as determinants of successful aging: on the protective effect of selection, optimization, and compensation (SOC). Psychological Aging, 21, 253–265.

Judt, T. (2005) *Post War: A History of Europe Since 1945*. London: Heinemann.

Jung, C. G. (1972) The transcendent function. In: Read, H., Fordham, M., Adler, G. and McGuire, W. (eds) *The Collected Works of C.G. Jung. Vol. 8 – The Structure and Dynamics of the Psyche*, London: Routledge & Kegan Paul.

Kaas, J. H. (1991) Plasticity of sensory and motor maps in adult mammals. *Reviews of Neuroscience* **14**, 137–167.

Kahana, E. (1982) A congruence model of person–environment interaction. In: Lawton, M. P., Windley, P. G. and Byerts, T. O. (eds) *Aging and the Environment: Theoretical Approaches*, 97–121. New York: Springer.

Kahn, R. L. and Antonucci, T. C. (1980) Convoys over the life course: attachment, roles, and social support. In: Baltes, P. B. and Brim, O. (eds) *Life-span Development and Behavior*, vol. 3, 253–286. New York: Academic Press.

Karni, A., Meyer, G., Jezzard, P., Adams, M. M., Turner, R. *et al.* (1995) Functional MRI evidence for adult motor cortex plasticity during motor skill learning. *Nature* **377**, 155–158.

Kart, C. S. (1987) The end of conventional gerontology. *Sociology of Health and Illness* **9**, 76–87.

Katz, S. (1992) Alarmist demography: power, knowledge and the elderly population. *Journal of Aging Studies* 6(3), 203–225.

Katz, S. (1996) *Disciplining Old Age: The Formation of Gerontological Knowledge*. Charlottesville, VA.: University Press of Virginia.

Katz, S. (2000) Busy bodies: activity, aging, and the management of everyday life. *Journal of Aging Studies* **14**, 135–152.

Katz, S. (2003) Critical gerontological theory: intellectual fieldwork and the nomadic life of ideas. In: Biggs, S., Lowenstein, A. and Hendricks, J. (eds) *The Need for Theory: Critical Approaches to Social Gerontology*, 15–31. Amityville, NY: Baywood Publishing.

Kaufman, A. S. (2001) WAIS-III IQs, Horn's theory, and generational changes from young adulthood to old age. *Intelligence* **29**, 131–167.

Kaufman, G. and Elder, G. H., Jr (2002) Revisiting age identity: a research note. *Journal of Aging Studies* **16**, 169–176.

Kaufman, S. R. (1987) *The Ageless Self: Sources of Meaning in Late Life*. Madison: University of Wisconsin.

Keith, J., Fry, C. L., Glascock, A. P., Ikels, C., Dickerson-Putman, J. *et al.* (1994) *The Aging Experience: Diversity and Commonality Across Cultures*. Thousand Oaks, CA: Sage.

Kellaher, L., Peace, S. and Willcocks, D. (1990) Triangulating data. In: Peace, S. (ed.) *Researching Social Gerontology: Concepts, Methods and Issues*, 115–128. London: Sage.

Kellaher, L. A. (2002) Is genuine choice a reality? The range and adequacy of living arrangements available to older people. In: Sumner, K. (ed.) *Our Homes, Our Lives*. London: Centre for Policy on Ageing and the Housing Corporation.

Keller, L. and Genoud, M. (1997) Extraordinary lifespans in ants: a test of evolutionary theories of ageing. *Nature* **389**, 958.

Keller, M. L., Leventhal, E. A. and Larson, B. (1989) Aging: the lived experience. *International Journal of Aging and Human Development* **29**, 67–82.

Kelly, J. R. (1993) *Activity and Aging: Staying Involved in Later Life*. Newbury Park, CA: Sage.

Kelly, J. R. and Freysinger, V. J. (2000) *21st Century Leisure*. Boston: Allyn & Bacon.

Kemper, S. and Harden, T. (1999) Experimentally disentangling what's beneficial about elderspeak from what's not. *Psychology and Aging* **14**, 656–670.

Kennedy, Q., Fung, H. H. and Carstensen, L. L. (2001) Aging, time estimation, and emotion. In: McFadden, S. H. and Atchley, R. C. (eds) *Aging and the Meaning of Time: A Multidisciplinary Exploration*, 51–73. New York: Springer.

Kenyon, C., Chang, J., Gensch, E., Rudner, A. and Tabtiang, R. (1993) A *C. elegans* mutant that lives twice as long as wild-type. *Nature* **366**, 461–464.

Kerscher, H. K. and Hansan, J. E. (eds) (1996) *365 Ways ... Retiree's Resource Guide for Productive Lifestyles*. London: Greenwood Press.

Kim, S., Kaminker, P. and Campisi, J. (2002) Telomeres, aging and cancer: in search of a happy ending. *Oncogene* **21**, 503–511.

Kimura, K. D., Tissenbaum, H. A., Liu, Y. X. and Ruvkun, G. (1997) *daf-2*, an insulin receptor-like gene that regulates longevity and diapause in *Caenorhabditis elegans*. *Science* **277**, 942–946.

King, R. (2002) Towards a new map of European migration. *International Journal of Population Geography* **8**(2), 89–106.

Kirkwood, T. B. L. (1977) Evolution of ageing. *Nature* 270, 301–304.

Kirkwood, T. B. L. (1997) The origins of human ageing. *Philosophical Transactions of the Royal Society of London Series B – Biological Sciences* **352**, 1765–1772.

Kirkwood, T. B. L. (2005) Understanding the odd science of ageing. *Cell* **120**, 437–447.

Kirkwood, T. B. L. and Austad, S. N. (2000) Why do we age? *Nature* **408**, 233–238.

Kite, M. E. and Johnson, B. T. (1988) Attitudes towards older and younger adults: a meta-analysis. *Psychology and Aging* **3**, 233–244.

Kite, M. E. and Wagner, L. S. (2002) Attitudes towards older adults. In: Nelson, T. D. (ed.) *Ageism: Stereotyping and Prejudice Against Older Persons*, 129–162. Cambridge, MA: MIT Press.

Kitwood, T. (1993) Towards a theory of dementia care: the interpersonal process. *Ageing and Society* **13**, 51–67.

Kitwood, T. (1997) *Dementia Reconsidered: The Person Comes First*. Buckingham: Open University Press.

Kitwood, T. and Bredin, K. (1992) Towards a theory of dementia care: personhood and well-being. *Ageing and Society* **12**, 269–287.

Kitzinger, J. (1994) The methodology of focus groups: the importance of interaction between research participants. *Sociology of Health and Illness* **16**(1), 103–121.

Kleemeier, R. W. (1959) Behavior and the organization of the bodily and external environment. In: Birren, J. E. (ed.) *Handbook of Aging and the Individual*, 400–451. Chicago: University of Chicago Press.

Klein, W. (1984) *Time in Language*. London: Routledge.

Klercq, J. (2004) *Learning in Later Life in an Ageing Society: Observations and Recommendations for Policy Makers from the PEFETE Network*. Brussels: European Commission.

Kliegl, R. and Baltes, P. B. (1987) Theory-guided analysis of mechanisms of development and aging through testing-the-limits and research on expertise. In: Schooler, C. and Schaie, K. W. (eds) *Cognitive Functioning and Social Structure Over the Life Course*, 95–119. Norwood, NJ: Ablex.

Kliegl, R., Smith, J. and Baltes, P. B. (1989) Testing-the-limits and the study of adult age differences in cognitive plasticity of a mnemonic skill. *Developmental Psychology* **25**, 247–256.

Kliegl, R., Smith, J. and Baltes, P. B. (1990) On the locus and process of magnification of adult age differences during mnemonic training. *Developmental Psychology* **26**(894), 904.

Kliegl, R., Phillipp, D., Luckner, M. and Krampe, R. T. (2001) Face memory skill acquisition. In: Charness, N., Park, D. C. and Sabel, B. A. (eds) *Communication, Technology and Aging: Opportunities and Challenges for the Future*, 169–186. New York: Springer.

Klinger, E. (1977) *Meaning and Void: Inner Experience and the Incentives in People's Lives*. Minneapolis, MI: University of Minnesota Press.

Knäuper, B. (1998) Age differences in question and response order effects. In: Schwarz, N., Park, D. C., Knäuper, B. and Sudman, S. (eds) *Cognition, Aging, and Self-reports*, vol. 17, 341–363. Philadelphia: Psychology Press.

Knipscheer, C. P. M., de Jong Gierveld, J., van Tilburg, T. G. and Dykstra, P. A. (eds) (1995) *Living Arrangements and Social Networks of Older Adults*. Amsterdam: Free University Press.

Kohli, M. (1985) Die Institutionalisierung des Lebenslaufs. *Kölner Zeitschrift für Soziologie und Sozialpsycholgie* **37**, 1–29.

Kohli, M. (1986) The world we forgot: a historical review of the life course. In: Marshall, V. (ed.) *Later Life: The Social Psychology of Aging*, 271–303. Beverly Hills: Sage.

Kohli, M. (1988) Social organisation and subjective construction of the life course. In: Sorensen, A. B., Weiner, F. E. and Sherrod, L. R. (eds) *Human Development and the Life Cycle*, 271–292. Hillsdale, NJ: Erlbaum.

Kohli, M. and Kunemund, H. (2000) *Die zweite Lebenshalfte: Gesellschaftliche Lage und Partizipation im Spiegel des Alters-Survey* [The second half of life: societal position and participation from the ageing survey perspective]. Opladen: Leske & Budrich.

Kohli, M., Rein, M., Guillemard, A.-M. and van Gunsteren, H. (eds) (1991) *Time for Retirement: Comparative Studies of Early Exit from the Labor Force*. Cambridge: Cambridge University Press.

Kohli, M., Künemund, H., Motel, A. and Szydlik, M. (2000) Families apart? Intergenerational transfers in East and West Germany. In: Arber, S. and Attias-Donfut, C. (eds) *The Myth of Generational Conflict: Family and State in Ageing Societies*, 88–99. London: Routledge.

Kolland, F. (1984) Bildungsbenachteiligung älterer Menschen. *Berichte aus Forschung und Praxis* **1**, 1–35.

Kolland, F. (2004) *The New Leisure World of Modern Old Age: New Aging on the Bright Side of the Street*. Vienna: University of Vienna (mimeo).

Kramer, A. F., Larish, J. F. and Strayer, D. L. (1995) Training for attentional control in dual task settings: a comparison of young and old adults. *Journal of Experimental Psychology: Applied* **1**, 50–76.

Kramer, A. F., Hahn, S., Cohen, N. J., Banich, M. T., McAuley, E. *et al.* (1999) Ageing, fitness and neurocognitive function. *Nature* **400**, 418–419.

Kramer, D. A. (1990) Conceptualizing wisdom: the primacy of affect-cognition relations. In: Sternberg, R. J. (ed.) *Wisdom: Its Nature, Origins and Development*, 279–313. Cambridge: Cambridge University Press.

Kramer, D. A. (2000) Wisdom as a classical source of human strength: conceptualization and empirical inquiry. *Journal of Social and Clinical Psychology* **19**, 83–101.

Krampe, R. T. (1994) *Maintaining Excellence: Cognitive–Motor Performance in Pianists Differing in Age and Skill Level*. Berlin: Edition Sigma.

Krampe, R. T. and Baltes, P. B. (2003) Intelligence as adaptive resource development and resource allocation: a new look through the lenses of SOC and expertise. In: Sternberg, R. J. and Grigorenko, E. L. (eds) *The Psychology of Abilities, Competencies and Expertise*, 31–69. New York: Cambridge University Press.

Krampe, R. T. and Charness, N. (2006) Aging and expertise. In: Ericsson, K. A., Charness, N., Feltovich, P. and Hoffman, R. (eds) *Cambridge Handbook on Expertise and Expert Performance*. New York: Cambridge University Press.

Krampe, R. T. and Ericsson, K. A. (1996) Maintaining excellence: cognitive–motor performance in pianists differing in age and skill level. *Journal of Experimental Psychology: General* **125**, 331–359.

Krause, N. (1995) Assessing stress-buffering effects: a cautionary note. *Psychology and Aging* **10**, 518–526.

Krause, N. (2000) Commentary: are we really entering a new era of aging? In: Schaie, K. W. and Hendricks, J. (eds) *The Evolution of the Aging Self: The Societal Impact on the Aging Process*, 307–318. New York: Springer.

Kuin, Y., Westerhof, G. J., Dittmann-Kohli, F. and Gerritsen, D. (2001) Psychophysische Integrität und Gesundheitserleben [Psychophysical integrity and health experience]. In: *Die zweite Lebenshälfte – Psychologische Perspektiven: Ergebnisse des Alters-Survey* [The second half of life – psychological perspectives: results of the German Aging Survey], 343–399. Stuttgart: Kohlhammer.

Kulik, L. (2002) Marital equality and the quality of long-term marriage in later life. *Ageing and Society* **22**, 459–481.

Künemund, H. (1999) Entpflichtung und Produktivität des Alters [Productivity, pensions and an ageing population]. *WSI-Mitteilungen* **52**(1), 26–31.

Künemund, H. (2000) Produktive Tätigkeiten. In: Kohli, M. and Künemund, H. (eds) *Die zweite Lebenshälfte. Gesellschaftliche Lage und Partizipation im Spiegel des Alters-Survey*, 277–317. Opladen: Leske & Budrich.

Künemund, H. (2001) *Gesellschaftliche Partizipation und Engagement in der zweiten Lebenshälfte. Empirische Befunde zu Tätigkeitsformen im Alter und Prognosen ihrer zukünftigen Entwicklung.* Berlin: Weißensee-Verlag.

Labouvie-Vief, G. (2003) Without gender, without self. In: Staudinger, U. M. and Lindenberger, U. (eds) *Understanding Human Development: Dialogues with Lifespan Psychology*, 401–412. Dordrecht, Netherlands: Kluwer.

Labouvie-Vief, G. (2005) The psychology of emotions and ageing. In: Johnson, M., Bengtson, V. L., Coleman, P. G. and Kirkwood, T. (eds) *The Cambridge Handbook of Age and Ageing*. Cambridge: Cambridge University Press.

Labouvie-Vief, G. and Marquez Gonzales, M. (2004) Dynamic integration: affect optimization and differentiation in development. In: Dai, D. Y. and Sternberg, R. J. (eds) *Motivation, Emotion, and Cognition: Integrative Perspectives on Intellectual Functioning and Development*. Mahwah, NJ: Erlbaum.

Labouvie-Vief, G. and Medler, M. (2002) Affect optimization and affect complexity: modes and styles of regulation in adulthood. *Psychology and Aging* **17**, 571–588.

Lamprecht, M. and Stamm, H. (1994) *Die soziale Ordnung der Freizeit*. Zurich: Seismo.

Lang, F. (2001) Regulation of social relationships in later adulthood. *Journal of Gerontology* **63**(6), 321–326.

Lang, F. R. and Carstensen, L. L. (1994) Close emotional relationships in late life: further support for proactive aging in the social domain. *Psychology and Aging* **9**, 315–324.

Lang, F. R. and Carstensen, L. L. (1998) Social relationships and adaptation in late life. In: Bellack, A. S. and Hersen, M. (eds) *Comprehensive Clinical Psychology*, vol. 7, 55–72. Oxford: Pergamon.

Langer, E. J. (1983) *The Psychology of Control*. Beverly Hills: Sage.

Langer, E. J. (1989) Minding matters: the consequences of mindlessness–mindfulness. *Advances in Experimental Social Psychology* **22**, 137–173.

Langer, E. J. and Rodin, J. (1976) The effects of choice and enhanced personal responsibility for the aged: a field experiment in an institutional setting. *Journal of Personality and Social Psychology* **34**(2), 191–198.

Lanzieri, G. (2006) *Long-term Population Projections at National Level*. Luxembourg: OPOCE.

Larsen, P. L., Albert, P. and Riddle, D. L. (1995) Genes that regulate both development and longevity in *Caenorhabditis elegans*. *Genetics* **139**, 1567–1583.

Lash, S. and Urry, J. (1986) Dissolution of the social? In: Wardell, M. L. and Turner, S. P. (eds) *Sociological Theory in Transition*. London: Sage.

Lash, S. and Urry, J. (1994) *Economics of Signs and Space*. London: Sage.

Laslett, P. (1965) *The World We Have Lost*. London: Methuen.

Laslett, P. (1977) The history of ageing and the aged. In: *Family Life and Illicit Love in Earlier Generations*, 174–213. Cambridge University Press.

Laslett, P. (1987) The emergence of the third age. *Ageing and Society* **7**, 133–160.

Laslett, P. (1989) *A Fresh Map of Life: The Emergence of the Third Age*. London: Weidenfeld & Nicolson.

Laslett, P. (1996) *A Fresh Map of Life: The Emergence of the Third Age*, 2nd edn. London: Weidenfeld & Nicolson.

Lawton, M. P. (1980) *Environment and Aging*. Belmont, CA: Brooks-Cole.

Lawton, M. P. (1985) The elderly in context: perspectives from environmental psychology and gerontology. *Environment and Behavior* **17**(4), 501–519.

Lawton, M. P. (1987) Environment and the need satisfaction of the aging. In: Carstensen, L. L. and Edelstein, B. A. (eds) *Handbook of Clinical Gerontology*, 33–40. New York: Pergamon Press.

Lawton, M. P. (1989a) Three functions of the residential environment. *Journal of Housing for the Elderly* **5**, 35–50.

Lawton, M. P. (1989b) Environmental proactivity in older people. In: Bengston, V. L. and Schaie, K. W. (eds) *The Course of Later Life*, 15–23. New York: Springer.

Lawton, M. P. (1998) Environment and aging: theory revisited. In: Scheidt, R. J. and Windley, P. G. (eds) *Environment and Aging Theory: A Focus on Housing*, 1–31. Westport, CT: Greenwood Press.

Lawton, M. P. (2001) The physical environment of the person with Alzheimer's disease. *Aging and Mental Health* **5**(1), S56–64.

Lawton, M. P. and Nahemow, L. (1973) Ecology and the aging process. In: Eisdorfer, C. and Lawton, M. P. (eds) *The Psychology of Adult Development and Aging*, 619–674. Washington, DC: American Psychological Association.

Lawton, M. P. and Simon, B. B. (1968) The ecology of social relationships in housing for the elderly. *Gerontologist* **8**, 108–115.

Lazarus, R. S. (1966) *Psychological Stress and the Coping Process*. New York: McGraw-Hill.

Lazarus, R. S. and DeLongis, A. (1983) Psychological stress and coping in aging. *American Psychologist* **38**, 245–254.

Le Grand, J., Mays, N. and Mulligan, J.-A. (eds) (1998) *Learning from the NHS Internal Market: A Review of the Evidence*. London: King's Fund.

Lechner, V. M. and Neal, M. B. (1999) *Working and Caring for the Elderly*. London: Routledge.

Leder, D. (1984) Medicine and paradigms of embodiment. *Journal of Medicine and Philosophy* **9**, 29–43.

Lehmann, P. and Wirtz, C. (2004) *Household formation in the EU. Statistics in focus: population and social conditions. Theme 3-5/2004*. Luxembourg: Eurostat.

Lehr, U. (1972) *Psychologie des Alterns*. Heidelberg: Quelle & Meyer.

Lehr, U. (1988) Arbeit als Lebenssinn auch im Alter [Work as a meaningful activity in old age]. In: Rosenmayr, L. and Kolland, F. (eds) *Arbeit – Freizeit – Lebenszeit*, 29–46. Opladen: Westdeutscher Verlag.

Lehr, U. (1994) Psychologische aspekte des Alterns. In: *Das Alter: Einführung in die Gerontologie*, 202–229. Stuttgart: Enke.

Leibfried, S. (1990) Sozialstaat in Europa? Integrationsperspektiven europäischer Armutsregimes [Welfare states in Europe? How to integrate European regimes to fight poverty]. In: *Nachrichtendienst des Deutschen Vereins*, **10**.

Lerner, R. M. and Busch-Rossnagel, N. A. (1981) Individuals as producers of their development: conceptual and empirical bases. In: Lerner, R. M. and Busch-Rossnagel, N. A. (eds) *Individuals as Producers of their Development: A Life-span Perspective*, 1–36. New York: Academic Press.

Leroi, A. M., Bartke, A., De Benedictis, G., Franceschi, C., Gartner, A. *et al.* (2005) What evidence is there for the existence of individual genes with antagonistic pleiotropic effects? *Mechanisms of Ageing and Development* **126**(3), 421–429.

Leventhal, H., Leventhal, E. A. and Schaefer, P. M. (1992) Vigilant coping and health behavior. In: Ory, M. G., Abeles, R. P. and Lipman, P. D. (eds) *Aging, Health, and Behavior*, 109–140. Newbury Park, CA: Sage.

Levy, B. R. (2003) Mind matters: cognitive and physical effects of aging self-stereotypes. *Journal of Gerontology* **58B**, P203–211.

Lewin, K. (1951) *Field Theory in Social Science*. New York: Harper.

Lewis, J. (1992) Gender and the development of welfare regimes. *Journal of European Social Policy* **2**(3), 159–173.

Li, K. Z. H., Krampe, R. T. and Bondar, A. (2005) An ecological approach to studying aging and dual-task performance. In: Engle, R. W., Sedek, G., von Hecker, U. and McIntosh, D. K. (eds) *Cognitive Limitations in Aging and Psychopathology*, 190–218. New York: Cambridge University Press.

Li, R. and Orleans, M. (2002) Personhood in a world of forgetfulness: an ethnography of the self-process among Alzheimer's patients. *Journal of Aging and Identity* **7**(4), 227–244.

Li, S.-C., Lindenberger, U., Hommel, B., Aschersleben, G., Prinz, W. *et al.* (2004) Transformations in the couplings among intellectual abilities and constituent cognitive processes across the life span. *Psychological Science* **15**(3), 155–163.

Lieberman, M. A. and Tobin, S. S. (1983) *The Experience of Old Age, Stress, Coping and Survival*. New York: Basic Books.

Light, L. L. (2000) Memory changes in adulthood. In: Qualls, S. H. and Abeles, N. (eds) *Psychology and the Aging Revolution: How We Adapt to Longer Life*, 73–98. Washington, DC: American Psychological Association.

Lindenberger, U. and Baltes, P. B. (1994) Sensory functioning and intelligence in old age: a strong relation. *Psychology and Aging* **9**, 339–355.

Lindenberger, U., Marsiske, M. and Baltes, P. B. (2000) Memorizing while walking: increase in dual-task costs from young adulthood to old age. *Psychology and Aging* **15**, 417–436.

Linstone, H. A. and Turoff, M. (1975) *The Delphi Method: Techniques and Applications*. Massachusetts: Addison–Wesley.

Lio, D., Scola, L., Crivello, A., Colonna-Romano, G., Candore, G. *et al.* (2003) Inflammation, genetics, and longevity: further studies on the protective effects in men of *IL-10*-1082 promoter SNP and its interaction with TNF-alfa-308 promoter SNP. *Journal of Medical Genetics* **40**(4), 296–299.

Litwak, E. and Longino, C. F., Jr (1987) Migration patterns among the elderly: a developmental perspective. *Gerontologist* **27**(3), 266–272.

Lloyd-Sherlock, P. (ed.) (2004) *Living Longer: Ageing, Development and Social Protection*. London: Zed Books.

Lowe, R. (1993) *The Welfare State in Britain since 1945*. London: Macmillan.

Lynott, R. J. and Lynott, P. P. (1996) Tracing the course of theoretical development in the sociology of aging. *Gerontologist* **36**, 749–760.

Lyon, P. and Pollard, D. (1997) Perceptions of the older employee: is anything really changing? *Personnel Review* **26**, 245–258.

Maas, H. S. and Kuypers, J. A. (1974) *From Thirty to Seventy*. San Francisco: Jossey–Bass.

MacIntyre, A. (1984) *After Virtue*. Notre Dame, IN: University of Notre Dame Press.

Magai, C. and Consedine, N. S. (2004) Introduction to the special issue: attachment and aging. *Attachment and Human Development* **6**, 349–351.

Mahieu, S. (2004) Zorgen wij voor onze ouders zoals zij voor ons gezorgd hebben? Gehechtheid, zorg en filiale maturiteit: demensies van de relatie tussen volwassen kinderen en hun bejaarde ouders. Unpublished doctoral disseration, Catholic University of Leuven, Belgium.

Mannheim, K. (1952) The problem of generations. In: Kecskemeti, P. (ed.) *Essays on the Sociology of Knowledge*, Chapter VII, 276–320. London: Routledge & Kegan Paul.

Manton, K. G., Stallard, E. and Corder, L. (1997) Changes in the age dependence of mortality and disability: cohort and other determinants. *Demography* **34**, 135–137.

Marcellini, F., Mollenkopf, H., Szeman, Z., Ciarrocchi, S., Kuesera, C. *et al.* (2005) Mobility and the built-up environment. In: Mollenkopf, H., Marcellini, F. and Ruoppila, I. (eds) *Enhancing Mobility in Later Life*, 221–242. Amsterdam: IOS Press.

Marcoen, A. (2005) Parent care: the core component of intergenerational relationships in middle and late adulthood. *European Journal of Ageing* **2**, 208–212.

Marcus, C. C. (1992) *House as a Mirror of Self: Exploring the deeper meaning of Home*. Berkeley, CA: Conari Press.

Mares, M. (1995) The aging family. In: Fitzpatrick, M. and Vangelisti, A. (eds) *Explaining Family Interaction*. California: Sage.

Markson, E. W. and Taylor, C. A. (2000) The mirror has two faces. *Ageing and Society* **20**, 137–160.

Markula, P. (2003) The technologies of the self: sport, feminism and Foucault. *Sociology of Sport* **20**, 87–107.

Markus, H. R. and Kitayama, S. (1991) Culture and the self: implications for cognition, emotion, and motivation. *Psychological Review* **98**, 224–253.

Markus, H. R. and Wurf, E. (1987) The dynamic self-concepts: a social psychological perspective. *Annual Review of Psychology* **38**, 299–337.

Markus, H. R., Mullally, P. R. and Kitayama, S. (1997) Selfways: diversity in modes of cultural participation. In: Neisser, U. and Jopling, D. A. (eds) *The Conceptual Self in Context*, 13–61. Cambridge: Cambridge University Press.

Marottoli, R. A., Ostfeld, A. M., Merrill, S. S., Perlman, G. D., Foley, D. J. *et al.* (1993) Driving cessation and changes in mileage driven amongst elderly individuals. *Journal of Gerontology* **48**(5), S255–260.

Marshall, V. (1996) The state of aging theory in aging and the social sciences. In: Binstock, R. H. and George, L. (eds) *Handbook of Aging and the Social Sciences*, 12–30. San Diego, CA: Academic Press.

Marshall, M. (2001) Dementia and technology. In: Peace, S. and Holland, C. (eds) *Inclusive Housing in an Ageing Society*, 125–243. Bristol: Policy Press.

Marshall, V. W. (1986) Dominant and emerging paradigms in the social psychology of ageing. In: Marshall, V. W. (ed.) *Later Life: The Social Psychology of Aging*, 9–31. California: Sage.

Marshall, V. W. and Tindall, J. A. (1978) Notes for a radical gerontology. *International Journal of Aging and Human Development* **9**(2), 163–175.

Martin, G. M., Austad, S. N. and Johnson, T. E. (1996) Genetic analysis of ageing: role of oxidative damage and environmental stresses. *Nature Genetics* **13**, 25–34.

Martinez, D. E. (1998) Mortality patterns suggest lack of senescence in hydra. *Experimental Gerontology* **33**, 217–225.

Maslow, A. H. (1964) *Motivation and Personality*. New York: Harper & Row.

Masunaga, H. and Horn, J. (2001) Expertise in relation to aging changes in components of intelligence. *Psychology and Aging* **16**, 293–311.

Matthews, S. (1986) *Friendships Through the Life Course*. Beverly Hills: Sage.

Matza, D. (1969) *Becoming Deviant*. Englewood Cliffs, NJ: Prentice-Hall.

Maurer, T. J. and Rafuse, N. E. (2001) Learning, not litigating: managing employee development and avoiding claims of age discrimination. *Academy of Management Executive* **15**, 110–121.

Maylor, E. A. (1994) Ageing and the retrieval of specialized and general knowledge: performance of masterminds. *British Journal of Psychology* **85**, 105–114.

Maynard, A. (1993) Intergenerational solidarity in health care: principles and practice. In: Hobman, D. (ed.) *Uniting Generations: Studies in Conflict and Co-operation*. London: Age Concern.

McAdams, D. P. (1995) What do we know when we know a person? *Journal of Personality* **63**, 365–396.

McAdams, D. P. (1996) Personality, modernity, and the storied self. *Psychological Inquiry* **7**, 295–321.

McAdams, D. P. and West, S. G. (1997) Personality psychology and the case study: introduction. *Journal of Personality* **65**, 757–783.

McCann, R. and Giles, H. (2002) Ageism in the workplace. In: Nelson, T. D. (ed.) *Ageism: Stereotyping and Prejudice Against Older Persons*, 163–200. Cambridge, MA: MIT Press.

McCarthy, J. R., Edwards, R. and Gillies, V. (2003) *Making Families: Moral Tales of Parenting and Step-parenting*. Durham: Sociology Press.

McCrae, R. R., Costa, P. T., Ostendorf, F., Angleitner, A., Hrebickova, M. *et al.* (2000) Nature and nurture: temperament, personality and life span development. *Journal of Personality and Social Psychology* **78**, 173–186.

McCreadie, C. and Tinker, A. (2005) The acceptability of assistive technology to older people. *Ageing and Society* **25**(1), 91–110.

McEvoy, G. M. and Cascio, W. F. (1989) Cumulative evidence of the relationship between employee age and job performance. *Journal of Applied Psychology* **74**, 11–17.

Mead, G. H. (1934) *Mind, Self and Society*. Chicago: University of Chicago Press.

Medawar, P. B. (1952) *An Unsolved Problem of Biology*. London: Lewis.

Meinz, E. J. (2000) Experience-based attenuation of age-related differences in music cognition tasks. *Psychology and Aging* **15**, 297–312.

Meyer, S. and Mollenkopf, H. (2003) Home technology, smart home, and the aging user. In: Schaie, K. W., Wahl, H.-W., Mollenkopf, H. and Oswald, F. (eds) *Aging Independently: Living Arrangements and Mobility*, 148–161. New York: Springer.

Miesen, B. M. (1992) Attachment theory in dementia. In: Jones, G. M. and Miesen, B. M. (eds) *Caregiving in Dementia: Research and Applications*, 38–56. London: Tavistock.

Miller, D. W., Leyell, T. S. and Mazachek, J. (2003) Stereotypes of the elderly in US television commercials from the 1950s to the 1990s. *International Journal of Aging and Human Development* **58**, 315–340.

Ministry of Social Affairs and Health (Finland) (eds) (2002) *The Many Faces of the National Programme on Ageing Workers*. Helsinki: Edita Prima.

Minkler, M. (1999) Introduction. In: Minkler, M. and Estes, C. L. (eds) *Critical Gerontology: Perspectives from Political and Moral Economy*, 1–13. Amityville, NY: Baywood Publishing.

Mollenkopf, H. and Fozard, J. L. (2004) Technology and the good life: challenges for current and future generations of aging people. In: Wahl, H.-W., Scheidt, R. and Windley, P. (eds) *Annual Review of Gerontology and Geriatrics. Aging in Context: Socio-physical Environments*, vol. 23, 250–279. New York: Springer.

Mollenkopf, H. and Kaspar, R. (2002) Attitudes to technology in old age as preconditions for acceptance or rejection. In: Guerci, A. and Consigliere, S. (eds) *Vivere la Vecchiaia/Living in Old Age: Western World and Modernization*, vol. 2, 134–144. Genova: Erga edizioni.

Mollenkopf, H., Marcellini, F., Ruoppila, I., Szeman, Z., Tacken, M. *et al.* (2002) The role of driving in maintaining mobility in later life: a European view. *Gerontechnology* **1**(4), 231–250.

Mollenkopf, H., Marcellini, F., Ruoppila, I., Baas, S., Ciarrocchi, S. *et al.* (2003) *The MOBILATE Follow-up Study 1995–2000. Enhancing outdoor mobility in later life: personal coping, environmental resources, and technical support.* DZFA research report 14, Heidelberg: German Centre for Research on Aging (DZFA). Website: www.dzfa.uni-heidelberg.de/english_version/ asoeg/ m_mobilate.html.

Mollenkopf, H., Kaspar, R., Marcellini, F., Ruoppila, I., Szeman, Z. *et al.* (2004) Quality of life in urban and rural areas of five European countries: similarities and differences. *Hallym International Journal of Aging* **6**(1), 1–36.

Mollenkopf, H., Marcellini, F., Ruoppila, I., Szeman, Z. and Tacken, M. (eds) (2005) *Enhancing mobility in later life – personal coping, environmental resources and technical support. The out-of-home mobility of older adults in urban and rural regions of five European countries.* Amsterdam: IOS Press.

Montepare, J. M. and Lachman, M. E. (1989) 'You're only as old as you feel': self-perceptions of age, fears of aging, and life satisfaction from adolescence to old age. *Psychology and Aging* **4**, 73–78.

Montepare, J. M. and Zebrowitz, L. A. (1998) Person perception comes of age: the salience and significance of age in social judgements. *Advances in Experimental Social Psychology* **30**, 93–161.

Montepare, J. M. and Zebrowitz, L. A. (2002) A social–developmental view of ageism. In: Nelson, T. D. (ed.) *Ageism: Stereotyping and Prejudice Against Older Persons*, 77–125. Cambridge, MA: MIT Press.

Montgomery, A., Barber, C. and McKee, P. (2002) A phenomenological study of wisdom in later life. *International Journal of Aging and Human Development* **54**, 139–157.

Moody, H. R. (1988) Toward a critical gerontology: the contribution of the humanities to theories of aging. In: Birren, J. and Bengtson, V. L. (eds) *Emergent Theories of Aging*, 19–40. New York: Springer.

Moody, H. R. (1993) Overview: what is critical gerontology and why is it important? In: Cole, T. R., Achenbaum, W. A., Jakobi, P. L. and Kastenbaum, R. (eds) *Voices and Visions of Aging: Toward a Critical Gerontology*, xv–xxi. New York: Springer.

Moos, R. H. (1981) Environmental choice and control in community care settings for older people. *Journal of Applied Social Psychology* **11**, 23–43.

Moos, R. H. and Lemke, S. (1984) *Multiphasic Environmental Assessment Procedure: A User's Guide.* Palo Alto, CA: Center for Health Care Evaluations, Dept of Veterans Affairs and Stanford University Medical Center.

Moos, R. H. and Lemke, S. (1985) Specialized living environments for older people. In: Birren, J. E. and Schaie, K. W. (eds) *Handbook of the Psychology of Aging*, 864–889. New York: Van Nostrand.

Moos, R. H. and Lemke, S. (1992) *Sheltered Care Environment Scale Manual.* Palo Alto, CA: Center for Health Care Evaluations, Dept of Veterans Affairs and Stanford University Medical Center.

Moos, R. H. and Lemke, S. (1996) *Evaluating Residential Facilities: The Multiphasic Environmental Assessment Procedure.* Thousand Oaks, CA: Sage.

Morrow, D. G., Leirer, V., Altiteri, P. and Fitzsimmons, C. (1994) When expertise reduces age differences in performance. *Psychology and Aging* **9**, 134–148.

Morrow, D. G., Menard, W. E., Stine-Morrow, E. A. L., Teller, T. and Bryant, D. (2001) The influence of expertise and task factors on age differences in pilot communication. *Psychology and Aging* 16, 31–46.

Morrow, D. G., Ridolfo, H. E., Menard, W. E., Sanborn, A. and Stine-Morrow, E. A. L. (2003) Environmental support promotes expertise-based mitigation of age differences on pilot communication tasks. *Psychology and Aging* **18**, 268–284.

Mroczek, D. and Spiro, A. (2003) Modelling intraindividual change in personality traits: findings from the Normative Aging Study. *Journal of Gerontology* **58B**, P153–165

Muiras, M.-L., Müller, M., Schächter, F. and Bürkle, A. (1998) Increased poly(ADP-ribose) polymerase activity in lymphoblastoid cell lines from centenarians. *Journal of Molecular Medicine* **76**, 346–354.

Mullan, P. (2000) *The Imaginary Time Bomb: Why an Ageing Population is Not a Social Problem.* London: IB Tauris.

Müller-Höcker, J. (1989) Cytochrome-c-oxidase deficient cardiomyocytes in the human heart: an age-related phenomenon. A histochemical ultracytochemical study. *American Journal of Pathology* **134**, 1167–1173.

Müller-Höcker, J., Seibel, P., Schneiderbanger, K. and Kadenbach, B. (1993) Different *in situ* hybridization patterns of mitochondrial DNA in cytochrome c oxidase-deficient extraocular muscle fibres in the elderly. *Virchows Archives A* **422**, 7–15.

Müller-Schneider, T. (2001) Freizeit und Erholung. In: Schafers, B. and Zapf, W. (eds) *Handworterbuch zur Gesellschaft Deutschlands*, 227–237. Opladen: Leske & Budrich.

Murphy, C. T., McCarroll, S. A., Bargmann, C. I., Fraser, A., Kamath, R. S. *et al.* (2003) Genes that act downstream of DAF-16 to influence the lifespan of Caenorhabditis elegans. *Nature* **424**, 277–284.

Murphy, E., Dingwall, R., Greatbatch, D., Parker, S. and Watson, P. (1998) Qualitative research methods in health technology assessment: a review of the literature. *Health Technology Assessment* **2**(16).

Murray, H. A. (1938) *Explorations in Personality. A Clinical and Experimental Study of Fifty Men of College Age.* Oxford: Oxford University Press.

Naafs, J. (1993) Maatschappelijke beeldvorming over odueren en ouderenbeleid. In: Blom, M. M., Kuin, Y. and Hendriks, H. F. J. (eds) *Ouder worden '93*, 291–294. Utrecht: NIZW.

Naegele, G., Barkholdt, C., de Vroom, B., Anderson, J. G. and Krämer, K. (2003) *A New Organisation of Time Over Working Life.* European Foundation for the Improvement of Living and Working Conditions: Dublin.

National Statistics (2002) Ethnicity: age distribution. Website: www.statistics.gov.uk/cci/nugget_print. asp?ID=272. Date accessed 22/5/2006.

Nelson, T. D. (ed.) (2002) *Ageism, Stereotyping and Prejudice Against Older Persons.* Cambridge, MA: MIT Press.

Netten, A. (2005) *Evaluation of the Extra-care Housing Initiative.* Website: www.refer.nhs.uk/.

Nettleton, S. (1995) *The Sociology of Health and Illness.* Cambridge: Polity Press.

Neugarten, B. L. and Hagestad, G. O. (1976) Age and the life course. In: Binstock, R. H. and Shanas, E. (eds) *Handbook of Aging and the Social Sciences*, 35–55. New York: Van Nostrand Reinhold.

Neyer, F. J. and Lang, F. R. (2003) Blood is thicker than water: kinship orientation across adulthood. *Journal of Personality and Social Psychology* **84**, 310–321.

Nocon, A. and Pearson, M. (2000) The roles of friends and neighbours in providing support for older people. *Ageing and Society* **20**, 341–367.

Nourhashemi, F., Andrieu, S., Gillette-Guyonnet, S., Vellas, B., Albarede, J. L. *et al.* (2001) Instrumental actvities of daily living as a potential marker of frailty: a study of 7364 community dwelling elderly women (the EPIDOS Study). *Journal of Gerontology* **56A**, M448–453.

Nuttin, J. (1984) *Motivation, Planning, and Action: A Relational Theory of Behavior Dynamics.* Hillsdale, NJ: Erlbaum.

O'Connor, B. P. and Rigby, H. (1996) Perceptions of baby talk, frequency of receiving baby talk, and self-esteem among community and nursing home residents. *Psychology and Aging* **11**, 147–154.

O'Connor, B. P. and Vallerand, R. J. (1994) Motivation, self-determination, and person–environment fit as predictors of psychological adjustment among nursing home residents. *Psychology and Aging* **9**, 189–194.

O'Connor, J. (1973) *The Fiscal Crisis of the State.* New York: St Martin's Press.

O'Hanlon, A. and Coleman, P. G. (2004) The influence of early and current attachment relationships on attitudes and experiences of ageing. In: Goossens, L., Hutsebaut, D. and Verschueren, K. (eds) *Ontwikkeling en Levensloop. Liber Amicorum Alfons Marcoen.* (353-373) Leuven, Belgium: Universitaire Pers Leuven.

O'Malley, L. and Croucher, K. (2005) Housing and dementia care: a scoping review of the literature. *Health and Social Care in the Community* **13**(6), 570–577.

O'Rand, A. M. (1996) The precision and the precocious: the cumulation and disadvantage over the life course. *Gerontologist* **36**, 230–238.

O'Rand, A. M. (2000) Risk, rationality, and modernity: social policy and the aging self. In: Schaie, K. W. (ed.) *Social Structures and Aging*, 225–249. New York: Springer.

O'Reilly, P. and Caro, F. G. (1994) Productive aging: an overview of the literature. *Journal of Aging and Social Policy* **3**(6), 39–71.

Oatley, K. and Jenkins, J. M. (1996) *Understanding Emotions*. Oxford: Blackwell.

Oberg, P. and Tornstam, L. (2001) Youthfulness and fitness: identity ideals for all ages? *Journal of Aging and Identity* **6**, 15–29.

OECD (1990) *Labor Force Statistics*. Paris: OECD.

OECD (1996) *Ageing in OECD Countries: A Critical Policy Challenge* [Social Policy Studies 20]. Paris: OECD.

Oeppen, J. and Vaupel, J. W. (2002) Demography: broken limits to life expectancy. *Science* **296**, 1029–1031.

Oliver, M. (1990) The ideological construction of disability. In: Oliver, M. (ed.) *The Politics of Disablement*, Chapter **4**, 43–59. Basingstoke: Macmillan.

Oliver, M. (1992) Changing the social relations of research production? *Disability, Handicap and Society* **7**(2), 101–114.

Oliver, M. (1996) *Understanding Disability*. Basingstoke: Macmillan.

Omran, A. R. (2001) The epidemiologic transition. *Bulletin of World Health* **79**, 161–170.

Open University and Help the Aged (2006) *ROAD: Research on Age Discrimination*. Website: http://road.open.ac.uk. Date accessed 22/5/2006.

OPOCE (2002) *The Life of Women and Men in Europe: A statistical Portrait*. Luxembourg: Office for the Official Publications of the European Communities.

OPOCE (2003) *Health in Europe: Results from 1997–2000 Surveys*. Luxembourg: Office of the Official Publications of the European Communities.

Oppenheim, A. N. (1992) *Questionnaire Design, Interviewing and Attitude Measurement*, new edn. London: Pinter Publishers.

Oswald, F. (2003) Linking subjective housing needs to objective living conditions among older adults in Germany. In: Schaie, K. W., Wahl, H.-W., Mollenkopf, H. and Oswald, F. (eds) *Aging Independently: Living Arrangements and Mobility*, 130–147. New York: Springer.

Oswald, F. and Rowles, G. D. (2006) Beyond the relocation trauma in old age: new trends in today's elders' residential decisions. In: Wahl, H.-W., Tesch-Römer, C. and Hoff, A. (eds) *New Dynamics in Old Age: Environmental and Societal Perspectives*, 127–152. Amityville, New York: Baywood Publishing.

Oswald, F. and Wahl, H.-W. (2003) Place attachment across the life span. In: Miller, J. R., Lerner, R. M., Schiamberg, L. B. and Anderson, P. M. (eds) *Human Ecology: An Encyclopedia of Children, Families, Communities, and Environments*, Santa Barbara, CA: ABC-Clio Press. Vol.2: I-Z, S. 568–572.

Oswald, F. and Wahl, H.-W. (2005) Dimensions of the meaning of home. In: Rowles, G. D. and Chaudhury, H. (eds) *Coming Home: International Perspectives on Place, Time and Identity in Old Age*. New York: Springer. 21–46.

Oswald, F., Schilling, O., Wahl, H.-W. and Gäng, K. (2002) 'Trouble in paradise'? Reasons to relocate and objective environmental changes among well-off older adults. *Journal of Environmental Psychology* **22**(3), 273–288.

Oswald, F., Wahl, H.-W., Mollenkopf, H. and Schilling, O. (2003) Housing and life satisfaction of older adults in two rural regions in Germany. *Research on Aging* **25**(2), 122–143.

Oswald, F., Wahl, H.-W. and Kaspar, R. (2005) Psychological aspects of outdoor mobility in later life. In: Mollenkopf, H., Marcellini, F., Ruoppila, I., Szeman, Z. and Tacken, M. (eds) *Enhancing Mobility in Later Life. Personal Coping, Environmental Resources, and Technical Support: The Out-of-Home Mobility of Older Adults in Urban and Rural Regions of Five European Countries*, 13–19. Amsterdam: IOS Press.

Oswald, F., Wahl, H.-W., Naumann, D., Mollenkopf, H. and Hieber, A. (2006) The role of the home environment in middle and late adulthood. In: Wahl, H.-W., Brenner, H., Mollenkopf, H., Rothenbacher, D.

and Rott, C. (eds) *The Many Faces of Health, Competence and Well-being in Old Age: Integrating Epidemiological, Psychological and Social Perspectives*, 7–24. Heidelberg: Springer.

OWN Europe (2006) Older Women's Network, Europe. Website: www.own-europe.org/. Date accessed 22/5/2006.

Pacolet, J., Bouten, R., Lanoye, H. and Versieck, K. (2000) *Social Protection for Dependency in Old Age: A Study of the Fifteen EU Member States and Norway.* Aldershot: Ashgate.

Palmore, E. (2000) Ageism in gerontological language. *Gerontologist* **40**, 645.

Park, D. C. (2000) The basic mechanisms accounting for age-related decline in cognitive function. In: Park, D. C. and Schwarz, N. (eds) *Cognitive Aging: A Primer*, 3–21. Philadelphia, PA: Psychology Press.

Park, R. E., Burgess, E. W. and McKenzie, R. D. (1925) *The City.* Chicago: Chicago University Press.

Parker, C., Barnes, S., McKee, K., Morgan, K., Torrington, J. *et al.* (2004) Quality of life and building design in residential and nursing homes. *Ageing and Society* **24**, 941–962.

Parmelee, P. W. and Lawton, M. P. (1990) The design of special environments for the aged. In: Birren, J. E. and Schaie, K. W. (eds) *Handbook of the Psychology of Aging*, 3rd edn, 465–489. San Diego, CA: Academic Press.

Parsons, T. (1951) *The Social System.* New York: Free Press.

Passuth, P. and Bengtson, V. (1988) Sociological theories of ageing: current perspectives and future directions. In: Birren, J. E. and Bengtson, V. L. (eds) *Emergent Theories of Aging*, 335–355. New York: Springer.

Passuth, P. and Bengtson, V. (1996) Sociological theories of aging: current perspectives and future directions. In: Quadagno, J. and Street, D. (eds) *Ageing for the Twenty-first Century.* New York: St Martin's Press.

Pastalan, L. A. and Carson, D. H. (eds) (1970) *Spatial Behavior of Older People.* University of Michigan Institute of Gerontology.

Pasupathi, M. and Löckenhoff, C. E. (2002) Ageist behavior. In: Nelson, T. D. (ed.) *Ageism: Stereotyping and Prejudice Against Older Persons*, 201–247. Cambridge, MA: MIT Press.

Pawelec, G., Barnett, Y., Forsey, R., Frasca, D., Globerson, A. *et al.* (2002) T cells and aging. January 2002 update. *Frontiers in Bioscience* **7**, d1056–1183.

Peace, S. (1990) *Researching Social Gerontology: Concepts, Methods and Issues.* London: Sage.

Peace, S. (2002) The role of older people in social research. In: Jamieson, A. and Victor, C. R. (eds) *Researching Ageing and Later Life: The Practice of Social Gerontology*, vol. 14, 226–244. Buckingham: Open University Press.

Peace, S. M. and Holland, C. (eds) (2001a) *Inclusive Housing in an Ageing Society.* Bristol: Policy Press.

Peace, S. M. and Holland, C. (2001b) Housing in an ageing society. In: Peace, S. M. and Holland, C. (eds) *Inclusive Housing in an Ageing Society*, 1–26. Bristol: Policy Press.

Peace, S., Holland, C. and Kellaher, L. (2006) *Environment and Identity in Later Life.* Maidenhead: Open University Press.

Peeters, A., Bouwman and Knipscheer, K. (2004) The Netherlands: quality of life in older age – II. In: Walker, A. (ed.) *Growing Older in Europe*, 201–218. Maidenhead: Open University Press.

Pensions Commission (2004) *Pensions: Challenges and Choices.* London: Stationery Office.

Pensions Commission (2005) *A New Pensions Settlement for the Twenty-first Century.* London: Stationery Office.

Perenboom, R. J. M., Mulder, Y. M., van Herten, L. M., Oudshoorn, K. and Hoeymans, N. (2002) *Trends in Healthy Life Expectancy, Netherlands 1983–2000* [report PG/VGZ 2002.206]. Leiden: TNO Prevention and Health.

Perren, K., Arber, S. and Davidson, K. (2004) Neighbouring in later life: the influence of socio-economic resources, gender and household composition on neighbourly relationships. *Sociology* **38**(5), 965–984.

Perry-Jenkins, M., Repetti, R. L. and Crouter, A. C. (2000) Work and family in the 1990s. *Journal of Marriage and the Family* **62**, 981–998.

Petersen, A. (2001) Biofantasies: genetics and medicine in the print news media. *Social Science and Medicine* **52**(8), 1255–1268.

Pettersen, K. I. (1995) Age related discrimination in the use of fibrinolytic therapy in acute myocardial infarction in Norway. *Age and Ageing* **24**, 198–203.

Phillips, J., Bernard, M., Phillipson, C. and Ogg, J. (2000) Social support in later life: a study of three areas. *British Journal of Social Work* **30**, 837–853.

Phillipson, C. (2006a) Aging and globalization: issues for critical gerontology and political economy. In: Baars, J., Dannefer, D., Phillipson, C. and Walker, A. (eds) *Globalization and Inequality*, 43–58. Amityville, NY: Baywood Publishing.

Phillipson, C. (2006b) Ageing and globalization. In: Vincent, J. A., Phillipson, C. and Downs, M. (eds) *The Futures of Old Age*, 211–217. London: Sage.

Phillipson, C. (1982) *Capitalism and Construction of Old Age*. London: Macmillan.

Phillipson, C. (1990) The sociology of retirement. In: Bond, J. and Coleman, P. (eds) *Ageing in Society: An Introduction to Social Gerontology*, 144–160. London: Sage.

Phillipson, C. (1998) *Reconstructing Old Age: New Agendas in Social Theory and Practice*. London: Sage.

Phillipson, C. (2003a) From family groups to personal communities: social capital and social change in the family life of older adults. In: Bengtson, V. and Lowenstein, A. (eds) *Global Aging and Challenges to Families*. New York: Aldine de Gruyter.

Phillipson, C. (2003b) Globalization and the reconstruction of old age: new challenges for critical gerontology. In: Biggs, S., Lowenstein, A. and Hendricks, J. (eds) *The Need for Theory: Social Gerontology for the 21st Century*, 163–180. Amityville, NY: Baywood Publishing.

Phillipson, C. and Ahmed, N. (2006) Transnational communities, migration and changing identities in later life: a new research agenda. In: Daatland, S. O. and Biggs, S. (eds) *Ageing and Diversity: Multiple Pathways and Cultural Migrations*, 157–179. Bristol: Policy Press.

Phillipson, C. and Smith, A. (2005) *Extending Working Life: A Review of the Research Literature* [research report 299]. London: Department for Work and Pensions.

Phillipson, C., Bernard, M., Phillips, J. and Ogg, J. (2001) *The Family and Community Life of Older People*. London: Routledge.

Pillemer, K. and Lüscher, K. (eds) (2004) *Intergenerational Ambivalences: New Perspectives on Parent–Child Relations in Later Life*. Oxford: Elsevier.

Pillemer, K., Suitor, J. J. and Wetherington, E. (2003) Integrating theory, basic research, and intervention: two cases studies from caregiving research. *Gerontologist* **43** (special issue 1), 19–28.

Pina, D. and Bengtson, V. (1995) Division of household labour and well-being of retirement-aged wives. *Gerontology* **35**(3), 308–317.

Pinquart, M. and Sorensen, S. (2000) Influences of socio-economic status, social network and competence on subjective well-being in later life: a meta-analysis. *Psychology and Aging* **15**(2), 187–224.

Pollack, O. (1948) *Social Adjustment in Old Age*. New York: Social Science Research Council.

Polverini, F. and Lamura, G. (2004) Italy: quality of life in older age in Italy – I. In: Walker, A. (ed.) *Growing Older in Europe*, 179–200. Maidenhead: Open University Press.

Poon, L. W., Jang, Y., Reynolds, S. G. and McCarthy, E. (2005) Profiles of the oldest-old. In: Johnson, V. L., Bengtson, P. G., Coleman, P. G. and Kirkwood, T. (eds) *The Cambridge Handbook of Age and Ageing*, Cambridge: Cambridge University Press.

Powell, J. L. and Biggs, S. (2000) Managing old age: the disciplinary web of power, surveillance and normalization. *Journal of Aging and Identity* 5, 3–13.

Price, C. (2002) Retirement for women: the impact of employment. *Journal of Women and Aging* **14**, 41–57.

Price, D. and Ginn, J. (2006) The future of inequalities in retirement income. In: Vincent, J. A., Phillipson, C. and Downs, M. (eds) *The Futures of Old Age*, 81–89. London: Sage.

Promislow, D. E. L. (1994) DNA-repair and the evolution of longevity: a critical analysis. *Journal of Theoretical Biology* **170**, 291–300.

Rabbitt, P. M. A. (1993a) Does it all go together when it goes? *Quarterly Journal of Experimental Psychology* **46A**, 385–434.

Rabbitt, P. M. A. (1993b) Crystal quest: a search for the basis of maintenance of practised skills into old age. In: Baddeley, A. and Weiskrantz, L. (eds) *Attention: Selection, Awareness and Control*. Oxford: Clarendon Press.

Rabbitt, P. M. A. (1999a) Why I study cognitive ageing. *Psychologist* **12**, 180–181.

Rabbitt, P. M. A. (1999b) Measurement indices, functional characteristics, and psychometric constructs in cognitive ageing. In: Perfect, T. J. and Maylor, E. A. (eds) *Models of Cognitive Aging*, chap. 6. Oxford: Oxford University Press.

Rabbitt, P. M. A., Diggle, P., Smith, D., Holland, F. and McInnes, L. (2001a) Identifying and separating the effects of practice and of cognitive ageing during a large longitudinal study of elderly community residents. *Neuropsychologia* **39**, 532–543.

Rabbitt, P. M. A., Osman, P., Stollery, B. and Moore, B. (2001b) There are stable individual differences in performance variability, both from moment to moment and from day to day. *Quarterley Journal of Experimental Psychology* **54A**, 981–1003.

Rabbitt, P. M. A., McInnes, L., Diggle, P., Holland, F., Bent, N. *et al.* (2004) The University of Manchester longitudinal study of cognition in normal healthy old age, 1983 through 2003. *Aging, Neuropsychology and Cognition* **11**, 245–279.

Rahhal, T. A., May, C. P. and Hasher, L. (2002) Aging, source memory and source significance. *Psychological Science* **13**, 101–105.

Ramian, K. (1987) The resident oriented nursing home: a new dimension in the nursing home debate: emphasis on living rather than nursing. *Danish Medical Bulletin* (special suppl. 5), 89–93.

Randall, W. L. and Kenyon, G. M. (2001) *Ordinary Wisdom: Biographical Aging and the Journey of Life*. Westport, CT: Praeger.

Ranzijn, R., Keeves, J., Luszcz, M. and Feather, N. T. (1998) The role of self-perceived usefulness and competence in the self-esteem of elderly adults: confirmatory factor analyses of the Bachman revision of Rosenberg;s Self-Esteem Scale. *Journal of Gerontology* 33B, P96–104

Rapp, M., Krampe, R. T. and Baltes, P. B. (2006) Adaptive task prioritization in aging: selective resource allocation to postural control is preserved in Alzheimer disease. *American Journal of Geriatric Psychiatry* **14**(1), 52–61.

Reday-Mulvey, G. (2005) *Working Beyond Sixty*. Basingstoke: Palgrave.

Regnier, V. and Pynoos, J. (1992) Environmental intervention for cognitively impaired older person. In: Birren, J. E., Sloane, R. B. and Cohen, G. D. (eds) *Handbook of Mental Health and Aging*, 2nd edn, 763–792. San Diego, CA: Academic Press.

Reich, J. W. and Zautra, A. J. (1990) Dispositional control beliefs and the consequences of a control-enhancing intervention. *Journal of Gerontology* **45**, 46–51.

Reichard, S., Livson, F. and Peterson, P. G. (1962) *Aging and Personality: A Study of Eighty-seven Older Men*. New York: Wiley.

Rhodes, M. (ed.) (1997) *Southern European Welfare States*. London: Frank Cass.

Ridley, R. J. (1982) Changes in motivation in the elderly person. In: Raynor, J. O. and Entin, E. E. (eds) *Motivation, Career Striving, and Aging*, 371–378. Washington: Hemisphere Publications.

Riley, M. W. (1987) On the significance of age in sociology. *American Sociological Review* 52, 1–14.

Riley, M. W. (1998) Successful aging. *Gerontologist* **38**(2), 151.

Riley, M. W. and Riley, J. W. (1992) Individuelles und gesellschaftliches Potential des Alterns. In: Baltes, P. B. and Mittlestraß, J. (eds) *Zukunft des Alterns und gesellschaftliche Entwicklung*, 437–459. Berlin: de Gruyter.

Riley, M. W. and Riley, J. W. (1994) Structural lag: past and future. In: Riley, M. W., Kahn, R. L. and Foner, A. (eds) *Age and Structural Lag: Society's Failure to Provide Meaningful Opportunities in Work, Family, and Leisure*, 15–36. New York: Wiley.

Riley, M. W. and Riley, J. W. (2000) Age integration: conceptual and historical background. *Gerontologist* **40**, 266–270.

Riley, M. W., Johnson, M. and Foner, A. (1972) A sociology of age stratification. In: Riley, M. W., Foner, A., Moore, M. E., Hess, B. and Roth, B. K. (eds) *Aging and Society*, vol. 3. New York: Russell Sage Foundation.

Riley, M. W., Kahn, R. L. and Foner, A. (eds) (1994) *Age and Structural Lag. Society's Failure to Provide Meaningful Opportunities in Work, Family, and Leisure*. New York: Wiley.

Riley, M. W., Foner, A. and Riley, J. W. (1999) The aging and society paradigm. In: Bengston, V. L. and Schaie, K. W. (eds) *Handbook of Theories of Aging*, 327–343. New York: Springer.

Ritchie, J. and Spencer, L. (1994) Qualitative data analysis for applied policy research. In: Bryman, A. and Burgess, R. G. (eds) *Analyzing Qualitative Data*, 173–194. London: Routledge.

Robbins, S. B., Lee, R. M. and Wan, T. H. (1994) Goal continuity as a mediator of early retirement adjustment: testing a multidimensional model. *Journal of Counselling Psychology* **41**, 18–26.

Robertson, A. (1991) The politics of Alzheimer's disease: a case study in apocalyptic demography. In: Minkler, M. and Estes, C. (eds) *Critical Perspectives on Aging: Political and Moral Economy of Growing Old*, Chapter **9**, 135–150. Amityville, NY: Baywood Publishing.

Robertson, A. (1997) Beyond apocalyptic demography: towards a moral economy of interdependence. *Ageing and Society* **17**, 425–446.

Robins, W., Trzesniewski, K. H., Tracy, J. L., Gosling, S. D. and Potter, J. (2002) Global self-esteem across the life-span. *Psychology and Aging* **17**, 423–434.

Robinson, J. D. and Skill, T. (1995) Media usage and portrayals of the elderly. In: Nussbaum, J. and Coupland, J. (eds) *Handbook of Communication and Aging Research*, 359–391. Mahwah: Lawrence Erlbaum.

Robinson, W. S. (1951) The logical structure of analytical induction. *American Sociological Review* **16**, 812–818.

Rodin, J. and Langer, E. J. (1977) Long-term effects of a control-relevant intervention with the institutionalized aged. *Journal of Personality and Social Psychology* **35**, 897–902.

Rodin, J., Timko, C. and Harris, S. (1985) The construct of control: biological and psychosocial correlates. In: Eisdorfer, C., Lawton, M. P. and Maddox, G. L. (eds) *Annual Review of Gerontology and Geriatrics*, vol. 5, 3–55. New York: Springer.

Rodriguez, V. R., Egea, C. and Nieto, J. A. (2002) Return migration in Andalusia, Spain. *International Journal of Population Geography* **8**(3), 233–254.

Roelfsema, P. (2003) Samen ouder worden: Langetermijnvisie op het ouderenbeleid in voorbereiding. *Geron* 5(2), 32–37.

Rogers, W. A. (2000) Attention and aging. In: Park, D. C. and Schwarz, N. (eds) *Cognitive Aging: A Primer*, 57–73. Philadelphia: Psychology Press.

Rook, K. (1990) Social relationships as a source of companionship: implications for older adults' psychological well-being. In: Sarason, B., Sarason, I. and Pierce, G. (eds) *Social Support: An Interactional View*. New York: Wiley.

Rose, H. and Bruce, E. (1995) Mutual care but differential esteem: caring between older couples. In: Arber, S. and Ginn, J. (eds) *Connecting Gender and Ageing*. Buckingham: Open University Press.

Rosenthal, G. (2004) Biographical research. In: Seale, C., Gobo, G., Gubrium, J. F. and Silverman, D. (eds) *Qualitative Research Practice*, Chapter 3, 48–64. London: Sage.

Rosow, I. (1974) *Socialization to Old Age*. Berkeley: University of California Press.

Rossman, G. B. and Wilson, B. L. (1985) Numbers and words: combining qualitative and qualitative methods in a single large-scale evaluation study. *Evaluation Review* **9**, 627–643.

Rothbaum, F., Weiss, J. R. and Snyder, S. S. (1982) Changing the world and changing the self: a two-process model of perceived control. *Journal of Personality and Social Psychology* **42**, 5–37.

Rothermund, K. and Brandtstädter, J. (2003) Coping with deficits and losses in later life: from compensatory action to accommodation. *Psychology and Aging* **18**, 896–905.

Rothman, K. J. (1976) Causes. *American Journal of Epidemiology* **104**, 587–592.

Rowe, J. W. and Kahn, R. L. (1998) *Successful Aging*. New York: Pantheon.

Rowe, J. W. and Kahn, R. L. (1987) Human aging: usual and successful. *Science* **237**, 143–149.

Rowles, G. D. (1978) *Prisoners of Space*. Colorado: Westview Press.

Rowles, G. D. (1983) Geographical dimensions of social support in rural Appalachia. In: Rowles, G. D. and Ohta, R. J. (eds) *Aging and Milieu: Environmental Perspectives on Growing Old*, 111–130. New York: Academic Press.

Rowles, G. D. and Watkins, J. F. (2003) History, habit, heart and hearth: on making spaces into places. In: Schaie, K. W., Wahl, H.-W., Mollenkopf, H. and Oswald, F. (eds) *Aging Independently: Living Arrangements and Mobility*, 77–96. New York: Springer.

Rowles, G. D., Oswald, F. and Hunter, E. G. (2004) Interior living environments in old age. In: Wahl, H.-W., Scheidt, R. and Windley, P. (eds) *Annual Review of Gerontology and Geriatrics. Aging in context: socio-physical environments*, vol. 23. New York: Springer.

Rowles,G.D & Chaudhury, H (eds) (2005) Home and Identity in Later Life: International Perspectives, S21-46, New York:Springer.

Roy, A. and Harwood, J. (1997) Underrepresented, positively portrayed: the representation of older adults in television commercials. *Journal of Applied Communication Research* **25**, 39–56.

Royal Commission on Long Term Care (1999) *With respect to old age: long term care – rights and responsibilities.* London.

Rubinstein, R. L. (1989) The home environments of older people: a description of the psychosocial processes linking person to place. *Journal of Gerontology* **44**(2), S45–53

Rubinstein, R. L. and Parmelee, P. W. (1992) Attachment to place and respresentation of life course by the elderly. In: Altman, I. and Low, S. M. (eds) *Human Behavior and Environment. Vol. 12 – Place Attachment*, 139–163. New York: Plenum Press.

Runyan, W. M. (1984) *Life Histories and Psychobiography: Explorations in Theory and Method.* New York: Oxford University Press.

Ryan, E. B., Giles, H., Bartolucci, G. and Henwood, K. (1986) Psycholinguistic and social psychological components of communication by and with the elderly. *Language and Communication* **6**, 1–24.

Ryan, E. B., Hummert, M. L. and Boich, L. H. (1995) Communication predicaments of aging: patronizing behavior toward older adults. *Journal of Language and Social Psychology* **14**, 144–166.

Ryff, C. D. (1986) The subjective construction of self and society: an agenda for life-span research. In: Marshall, V. W. (ed.) *Later Life: The Social Psychology of Aging*, 33–74. California: Sage.

Ryff, C. D. (1989) Beyond Ponce de Leon and life-satisfaction: new directions in the quest of successful aging. *International Journal of Behavioral Development* **12**, 35–55.

Sachweh, S. (1998) Granny darling's nappies: secondary babytalk in German nursing homes for the aged. *Journal of Applied Communication Research* **26**, 52–65.

Sackmann, A. (1996) Generations, inter-cohort differentiation and technological change. In: Mollenkopf, H. (ed.) *Elderly People in Industrialised Societies: Social Integration in Old Age By or Despite Technology?*, 289–308. Berlin: Edition sigma.

Salthouse, T. A. (1984) Effects of age and skill in typing. *Journal of Experimental Psychology: General* **113**, 345–371.

Salthouse, T. A. (1991a) *Theoretical Perspectives on Cognitive Aging.* Hillsdale, NJ: Erlbaum.

Salthouse, T. A. (1991b) Expertise as the circumvention of human processing limitations. In: Ericsson, K. A. and Smith, J. (eds) *Toward a General Theory of Expertise: Prospects and Limits*, 286–300. New York: Cambridge University Press.

Salthouse, T. A. (1996) The processing-speed theory of adult age differences in cognition. *Psychological Review* **103**, 403–428.

Salthouse, T. A. and Maurer, T. J. (1996) Aging, job performance, and career development. In: Birren, J. E. and Schaie, K. W. (eds) *Handbook of the Psychology of Aging*, 4th edn, 353–364. New York: Academic Press.

Salthouse, T. A., Babcock, R. L., Skovronek, E., Mitchell, D. R. D. and Palmon, R. (1990) Age and experience effects in spatial visualization. *Developmental Psychology* **26**, 128–136.

Savishinsky, J. S. (2000) *Breaking the Watch: The Meaning of Retirement in America.* Ithaca, NY: Cornell University Press.

Schaie, K. W. (1967) Age changes and age differences. *Gerontologist* **7**, 128–132.

Schaie, K. W. (1988) Ageism in psychological research. *American Psychologist* **43**(3), 179–183.

Schaie, K. W. and Achenbaum, W. A. (eds) (1993) *Societal Impact on Aging.* New York: Springer.

Schaie, K. W. and Willis, S. L. (1986) Can decline in intellectual functioning be reversed? *Developmental Psychology* **22**, 223–232.

Scharf, T. (1998) *Ageing and Ageing Policy in Germany.* New York: Berg.

Scharf, T. and Wenger, C. C. (1995) *International Perspectives on Community Care for Older People.* Aldershot: Avebury.

Scharf, T., Phillipson, C., Smith, A. and Kingston, P. (2002) *Growing Older in Socially Deprived Areas.* London: Help the Aged.

Scharf, T., Phillipson, C. and Smith, A. E. (2004) Poverty and social exclusion: growing older in deprived urban neighbourhoods. In: Walker, A. and Hagan Hennessy, C. (eds) *Growing Older: Quality of Life in Old Age*, 81–106. Maidenhead: Open University Press.

Scharf, T., Phillipson, C. and Smith, A. (2005) *Multiple Exclusion and Quality of Life Amongst Excluded Older People in Disadvantaged Neighbourhoods*. London: Office of the Deputy Prime Minister, Social Exclusion Unit, HMSO.

Scharf, T. and Bartlam, B. (2006) Rural Disadvantage: Quality of life and disadvantage among older people – a pilot study, CR 19, London: Commission for Rural Communities.

Scheidt,R., J. and Windley, P.G (eds) (1998) Environment and Aging Theory: A focus on housing. Westport,CT: Greenwood Press.

Scheidt, R. J. and Windley, P. G. (2003) Physical environments and aging: critical contributions of M. Powell Lawton to theory and practice. *Journal of Housing for the Elderly* **17**(1/2).

Scheidt, R. J. & Windley, P. G. (2006). Environmmental gerontology: Progress in the post-Lawton era. In J. E. Birren & K. W. Schaie (Eds.), *Handbook of the psychology of aging* (6th ed., pp. 105–125). Amsterdam: Elsevier.

Schlag, B. (2003) Safety and accidents among older drivers: the German perspective. In: Schaie, K. W., Wahl, H.-W., Mollenkopf, H. and Oswald, F. (eds) *Aging Independently: Living Arrangements and Mobility*, 205–219. New York: Springer.

Schmähl, W. (2000) Paradigmenwechsel mit unsicherem Ausgang: Ammerkungen zu Reformvorschlagen zur Altersicherung [Change in paradigm with insecure consequences: remarks on proposals on how to reform the old age income security systems in Germany]. *Wirtschaftsdienst* **80**, 464–469.

Schmidt, D. and Boland, S. M. (1986) Structure of perceptions of older adults: evidence for multiple stereotypes. *Psychology and Aging* **1**, 255–260.

Schmidt, J. (2002) *Wohlfahrtsstaaten im Vergleich* [Welfare states compared], 2nd edn. Opladen: Leske & Budrich.

Schmitz, U., Saile, H. and Nilges, P. (1996) Coping with chronic pain: flexible goal adjustment as an interactive buffer against pain-related distress. *Pain* **67**, 41–51.

Schooler, K. K. (1982) Response of the elderly to environment: a stress–theoretical perspective. In: Lawton, M. P., Windley, P. G. and Byerts, T. O. (eds) *Aging and the Environment: Theoretical Approaches*, 80–96. New York: Springer.

Schröder-Butterfill, E. (2004) Inter-generational family support provided by older people in Indonesia. *Ageing and Society* **24**(4), 497–530.

Schroots, J. J. F. (2002) Prolegomena van een ontogenetische psychologie. In: Schroots, J. J. F. (ed.) *Handboek psychologie van de volwassen ontwikkeling & veroudering*, 1–38. Assen: Koninklijke van Gorcum.

Schubert, R., Littmann-Wernli, S. and Tingler, P. (2002) *Corporate Volunteering: Unternehmen entdecken die Freiwilligenarbeit*. Bern: Haupt.

Schulte, B. (1997) Juridicial instruments of the European Union and the European Communities. In: Beck, W., van der Maesen, L. and Walker, A. (eds) *The Social Quality of Europe*, 45–68. The Hague: Kluwer International.

Schultz, R. and Heckhausen, J. (1996) A life span model of successful aging. *American Psychologist* **51**(7), 702–714.

Schulz, E., Leidl, R. and König, H.-H. (2004) The impact of ageing on hospital care and long-term care: the example of Germany. *Health Policy* **67**, 57–74.

Schulze, G. (1992) *Die Erlebnisgesellschaft*. Frankfurt: Campus.

Schwarz, N., Park, D., Knäuper, B. and Sudman, S. (eds) (1999) *Cognition, Aging, and Self Reports*. Philadelphia: Psychology Press.

Seligman, M. E. P. (1975) *Helplessness: On Depression, Development, and Death*. San Francisco: Freemann.

Seligman, M. E. P. (1991) *Learned Optimism*. New York: Knopf.

Selwyn, N., Gorard, S., Furlong, J. and Madden, L. (2003) Older adult's use of information and communications technology in everyday life. *Ageing and Society* **23**, 561–582.

Settersten, R. A. (2005) Linking the two ends of life: what gerontology can learn from childhood studies. *Journal of Gerontology* **60B**, S173–180.

Settersten, R. A. and Dobransky, L. M. (2000) On the unbearable lightness of theory in gerontology. *Gerontologist* **40**(3), 367–372.

Shanas, E. (1971) *Disengagement and Work: Myth and Reality*. International Center of Social Gerontology.

Shaver, P. R. and Mikulciner, M. (2004) Attachment in the later years: a commentary. *Attachment and Human Development* **6**, 451–464.

Shilling, C. (2003) *The Body and Social Theory*. London: Sage.

Shweder, R. A. (ed.) (1998) *Welcome to Middle Age! (And Other Cultural Fictions)*. Chicago: University of Chicago Press.

Simmons, B. A. (2001) Women's retirement, work and life paths: changes, disruptions and discontinuities. *Journal of Women and Aging* **13**, 53–70.

Simon, R. (2002) Revisiting the relationship among gender, marital status and mental health. *American Journal of Sociology* **107**, 1065–1096.

Simpson, J. A. and Rholes, W. S. (1998) Introduction. In: Simpson, J. A. and Rholes, W. S. (eds) *Attachment Theory and Close Relationships*, 3–21. New York: Guilford Press.

Singer, T., Lindenberger, U. and Baltes, P. B. (2003) Plasticity of memory for new learning in very old age: a story of major loss? *Psychology and Aging* **18**, 306–317.

Singer, W. (1995) Development and plasticity of cortical processing architectures. *Science* 270, 758–764.

Sinnott, J. D. (1998) *The Development of Logic in Adulthood: Postformal Thought and Its Applications*. New York: Plenum.

Small, B. J., Hertzog, C., Hultsch, D. F. and Dixon, R. A. (2003) Stability and change in adult personality over 6 years: findings from the Victoria Longitudinal Study. *Journal of Gerontology* **58B**, P166–176.

Smart, B. (1985) *Michel Foucault*. London: Routledge.

Smart, C. (2004) Retheorising families [review essay]. *Sociology* **38**(5), 1007–1042.

Smith, A. E., Sim, J., Scharf, T. and Phillipson, C. (2004) Determinants of quality of life amongst older people in deprived neighbourhoods. *Ageing and Society* **24**(5), 793–814.

Smith, H. W. (1975) *Strategies of Social Research: The Methodological Imagination*. Englewood Cliffs, NJ: Prentice-Hall.

Smith, J. (1999) Planning for life goals: anticipating future life goals and managing personal development. In: Brandtstädter, J. and Lerner, R. M. (eds) *Action and Self-development: Theory and Research Through the Life Span*, 223–255. Thousand Oaks, CA: Sage.

Smith, J. and Baltes, P. B. (1997) Profiles of psychological functioning in the old and oldest old. *Psychology and Aging* 12, 458–472.

Smith, J. and Baltes, P. B. (1999) Trends and profiles of psychological functioning in very old age. In: Baltes, P. B. and Mayer, K. U. (eds) *The Berlin Aging Study: Aging from 70 to 100*, 197–226. Cambridge: Cambridge University Press.

Smith, J., Dixon, R. A. and Baltes, P. B. (1989) Expertise in life planning: a new research approach to investigating aspects of wisdom. In: Commons, M. L., Sinnott, J. D., Richards, F. A. and Adams, C. (eds) *Adult Development: Comparisons and Applications of Developmental Models*, vol. 1, 307–331. New York: Praeger.

Smith, M. W., Czaja, S. J. and Sharit, J. (1999) Aging, motor control and the performance of computer mouse task. *Human Factors* **41**, 389–397.

Smits, C. H., de Vries, W. M. and Beekman, A. T. F. (2005) The CIDI as an instrument for diagnosing depression in older Turkish and Moroccan labour migrants: an exploratory study into equivalence. *International Journal of Geriatric Psychiatry* **20**, 436–445.

Sommer, C., Künemund, H. and Kohli, M. (2004) *Zwischen Selbstorganisation und Seniorenakademie: Die Vielfalt der Altersbildung in Deutschland* [Between self organization and organized learning: the variety of continuing education for the third age in Germany]. Berlin: Weissßensee Verlag.

Staats, S. (1996) Youthful and older biases as special cases of a self-age optimization bias. *International Journal of Aging and Human Development* 43, 267–276.

Stainton Rogers, W. (1991) *Explaining Health and Illness*. Hertfordshire: Harvester Wheatsheaf.

Statistics Netherlands (2004) Website: www.cbs.nl. Date accessed 1/10/2004.

Statsbase (2000) Website of the Government Statistical Service: www.statsbase.gov.uk/.

Staudinger, U. M. (1996) Psychologische Produuktivität und Selbstentfaltung im Alter. In: Baltes, M. M. and Montada, L. (eds) *Produktives Leben im Alter*, 344–373. Frankfurt: Campus.

Staudinger, U. M. (2005) Personality and ageing. In: Johnson, M. L., Bengtson, V. L., Coleman, P. G. and Kirkwood, T. B. L. (eds) *The Cambridge Handbook of Age and Ageing*, 237–244. Cambridge: Cambridge University Press.

Staudinger, U. M., Marsiske, M. and Baltes, P. B. (1995) Resilience and reserve capacity in later adulthood: potentials and limits of development across the life span. In: Cicchetti, D. and Cohen, D. (eds) *Developmental Psychopathology. Vol. 2 – Risk, Disorder and Adaptation*, 801–847. New York: Wiley.

Staudinger, U. M., Lopez, D. F. and Baltes, P. B. (1997) The psychometric location of wisdom-related performance: intelligence, personality and more? *Personality and Social Psychology Bulletin* **23**, 2100–2114.

Stearns, P. (1977) *Old Age in European Society*. London: Croom Helm.

Steele, H., Phibbs, E. and Woods, R. (2004) Coherence of mind in daughter caregivers of mothers with dementia: links with their mothers' joy and relatedness on reunion in a strange situation. *Attachment and Human Development* **6**, 439–450.

Sternberg, R. J. (ed.) (1990) *Wisdom: Its Nature, Origins and Development*. Cambridge: Cambridge University Press.

Sternberg, R. J. (2001) Why schools should teach for wisdom: the balance of theory of wisdom in educational settings. *Educational Psychologist* **36**, 227–245.

Sternberg, R. J. and Wagner, R. K. (1986) *Practical Intelligence: Nature and Origins of Competence in the Everyday World*. Cambridge: Cambridge University Press.

Stevens, N. (2001) Combating loneliness: a friendship enrichment programme for older women. *Ageing and Society* **21**(2), 183–202.

Steverink, N., Lindenberg, S. and Ormel, J. (1998) Towards understanding successful ageing: patterned change in resources and goals. *Ageing and Society* **18**, 441–467.

Steverink, N., Westerhof, G. J., Bode, C. and Dittmann-Kohli, F. (2001) The personal experience of growing old: resources and subjective well-being. *Journal of Gerontology* 56B, P364–373.

Steverink, N., Lindenberg, S. and Slaets, J. P. (2005) How to understand and improve older people's self-management of well-being. *European Journal of Ageing* **2**, 235–244.

Strauss, A. L. (1987) *Qualitative Analysis for Social Scientists*. New York: Cambridge University Press.

Strauss, A. L. and Corbin, J. (1990) *Basics of Qualitative Research*. Newbury Park, CA: Sage.

Strawbridge, W. J., Shema, S. J., Cohen, R. D., Roberts, R. E. and Kaplan, G. A. (1998) Religiosity buffers effects of some stresses on depression but exacerbates others. *Journal of Gerontology* **53B**, S118–126.

Strehler, B. L. (1962) *Time, Cells, and Aging*. New York: Academic Press.

Sturm, W. (1992) *Alte Tage*, 2nd edn. Köln: Keipenheuer & Witsch.

Sundström, G. (1987) A haven in a heartless world? Living with parents in Sweden and the United States, 1880–1992. *Continuity and Change* **2**, 145–185.

Szinovacz, M. (2000) Changes in housework after retirement: a panel analysis. *Journal of Marriage and the Family* **62**(1), 78–92.

Szinovacz, M., DeViney, S. and Davey, A. (2001) Influences of family obligations and relations on retirement: variations of gender, race and marital status. *Journals of Gerontology* **56**(1), S20–27.

Tacken, M. and van Lamoen, E. (2005) Transport behaviour and realised journeys and trips. In: Mollenkopf, H., Marcellini, F. and Ruoppila, I. (eds) *The MOBILATE Project: Enhancing Outdoor Mobility in Later Life* [final report], 251–281. Heidelberg: German Centre for Research on Aging (DZFA).

Taranto, M. A. (1989) Facets of wisdom: a theoretical synthesis. *Journal of Aging and Human Development* **29**, 1–21.

Tashakkori, A. and Teddlie, C. (2003) *Handbook of Mixed Methods in Social and Behavioural Research*. Thousand Oaks, CA: Sage.

Taylor, C. (1989) *Sources of the Self: The Making of Modern Identity*. Cambridge, MA: Harvard University Press.

Taylor, P. (2002) Improving employment opportunities for older workers: developing a policy framework. Summary of EU expert presentation, 21–22 March, Brussels.

Taylor, P. (2003) A new deal for older workers? The employment situation of older workers in the United Kingdom. In: Maltby, T., de Vroom, B., Mirabille, M.-L. and Overbye, E. (eds) *Ageing and Transition in Retirement. A Comparative Analysis of European Welfare States.* Aldershot: Ashgate.

Taylor, R. W., Barron, M. J., Borthwick, G. M., Gospel, A., Chinnery, P. F. *et al.* (2003) Mitochondrial DNA mutations in human colonic crypt stem cells. *Journal of Clinical Investigation* **112**, 1351–1360.

Taylor-Gooby, P. (ed.) (2001) *Welfare States Under Pressure.* London: Sage.

Tchernina, N. V. and Tchernin, E. A. (2002) Older people in Russia's transitional society: multiple deprivation and coping strategies. *Ageing and Society* **22**, 543–562.

Tews, H. P. (1991) *Altershilder: Üher Wandel und Beeinflussung von Vorstellungen zum Alter.* Köln: Kuratorium Deutsche Altershilfe.

Thane, P. (1988) The growing burden of an ageing population. *Journal of Public Health* **7**, 373–387.

Thane, P. (2000) *Old Age in English History: Past Experiences, Present Issues.* Oxford: Oxford University Press.

Thayer, P. W. (1997) A rapidly changing world: some implications for training systems in the year 2001 and beyond. In: Quiñones, M. A. and Ehrenstein, A. (eds) *Training for a Rapidly Changing Workplace: Applications of Psychological Research*, 15–30. Washington, DC: American Psychological Association.

The Lancet (1991) Intensive care for the elderly. *The Lancet* **337**, 209–210.

Thomae, H. (1970) Theory of aging and cognitive theory of personality. *Human Development* **13**, 1–16.

Thomae, H. (1975) The 'developmental-task approach' to a theory of aging. *Zeitschrift fur Gerontologie* **8**, 125–137.

Thomae, H. (ed.) (1976) *Patterns of Aging: Findings from the Bonn Longitudinal Study of Aging.* Basel: Karger.

Thomae, H. (1983) *Alternsstile und Altersschicksale.* Bern: Huber.

Thomae, H. (1988) *Das Individuum und seine Welt: Eine Personlichkeitstheorie* [The individual in its world: a theory of personality], 2nd edn. Gottingen: Hogrefe.

Thompson, J. B. (2000) The globalization of communication. In: Held, D. and McGrew, A. (eds) *The Global Transformations Reader.* Cambridge: Polity Press.

Threlfall, M. (2003) European social integration: harmonization, convergence and single social areas. *Journal of European Social Policy* **13**(2), 121–139.

Timmer, E., Bode, C. and Dittmann-Kohli, F. (2003) Expectations of gains in the second half of life: a study of personal conceptions of enrichment in a life span perspective. *Ageing and Society* **23**, 3–24.

Timmer, E., Steverink, N. and Dittmann-Kohli, F. (2002) Cognitive representations of future gains, maintenance, and losses in the second half of life. *International Journal of Aging and Human Development* **55**, 321–339.

Tinker, A. (2002) Mobility and transport: with a particular focus on older people getting around outside the home. In: Pieper, R., Vaarama, M. and Fozard, J. L. (eds) *Gerontechnology. Technology and Aging – Starting in the Third Millenium*, 290–303. Aachen: Shaker.

Tobin, S. S. (1991) *Personhood in Advanced Old Age: Implications for Practice.* New York: Springer.

Toffler, A. (1970) *Future Shock.* London: Bodley Head.

Tomassini, C., Glaser, K., Wolf, D., Broese van Groeneou, M. and Grundy, E. (2004) Living arrangements among older people: an overview of trends in Europe and the USA. *Population Trends* **115**, 24–34.

Tornstam, L. (1989) A meta-theoretical reformulation of the disengagement theory. *Aging: Clinical and Experimental Research* 1, 55–63.

Torres, S. (1999) A culturally relevant theoretical framework for the study of the successful ageing. *Ageing and Society* 19, 33–51.

Torres, S. (2001) Understanding of successful ageing in the context of migration: the case of Iranian immigrants in Sweden. *Ageing and Society* **21**, 333–355.

Tough, A. (1971) *The Adult's Learning Projects* [Research in Education series no. 1]. Toronto: Ontario Institute for Studies in Education.

Townsend, P. (1957) *The Family Life of Old People.* London: Routledge & Kegan Paul.

Townsend, P. (1981) The structured dependency of the elderly: creation of social policy in the twentieth century. *Ageing and Society* **1**, 5–28.

Townsend, P. (1986) Ageism and social policy. In: Phillipson, C. and Walker, A. (eds) *Ageing and Social Policy*, 15–44. Aldershot: Gower.

Tulle, E. (2003) Sense and structure: towards a sociology of old bodies. In: Biggs, S., Lowenstein, A. and Hendricks, J. (eds) *The Need for Theory: Critical Gerontology for the 21st Century*, 91–104. Amityville, New York: Baywood Publishing.

Tulle, E. (2004) Rethinking agency in later life. In: Tulle, E. (ed.) *Old Age and Agency*, 175–189. Hauppauge, NY: Novascience.

Tulle, E. and Mooney, E. (2002) Moving to 'age-appropriate' housing: government in self in later life. *Sociology* **36**, 683–701.

Tulle-Winton, E. (2000) Old bodies. In: Hancock, P., Hughes, B., Jagger, K., Paterson, R., Russell, E., Tulle-Winton, E. and Tyler, M. (eds) *The Body, Culture and Society: An Introduction*, 64–83. Buckingham: Open University Press.

Turner, B. S. (1996) *The Body and Society*. London: Sage.

Twigg, J. (2003) The body and bathing: help with personal care at home. In: Faircloth, C. (ed.) *Aging Bodies: Images and Everyday Experience*, 143–169. Walnut Creek, CA: AltaMira Press.

Uhlenberg, P. and de Jong Gierveld, J. (2004) Age segregation in later life: an examination of personal networks. *Ageing and Society* **24**, 5–28.

United Nations (1956) *The Aging of Populations and its Economic and Social Implications* [Population Studies no. 26]. United Nations, sales no. 1956.XIII.6.

United Nations (1999) *Population Aging 1999*. United Nations, sales no. E.99.XIII.11.

United Nations (2002) *World Population Ageing: 1950–2050* [executive summary]. New York: UN Department of Economic and Social Affairs, Population Division. Website: www.un.org/esa/population/publications/worldageing19502050/index.htm. Date accessed 22/05/2006.

United Nations Secretariat (ed.) (2003) *World Population Prospects: The 2002 Revisions – Highlights*. New York: UN Department of Economic and Social Affairs, Population Division.

Uotinen, V. (1998) Age identification: a comparison between Finnish and North American cultures. *International Journal of Aging and Human Development* **46**, 109–124.

Ursic, A. C., Ursic, M. L. and Ursic, V. L. (1986) A longitudinal study of the use of the elderly in magazine advertising. *Journal of Consumer Research* **13**, 131–133.

Vaillant, C. and Vaillant, G. (1993) Is the U-curve of marital satisfaction an illusion? *Journal of Marriage and the Family* **55**, 230–239.

van Berlo, A. (2002) Smart home technology: have older people paved the way? *Gerontechnology* **2**(1), 77–87.

van den Biggelaar, A. H. J., de Craen, A. J. M., Gussekloo, J., Huizinga, T. W. J., Frölich, M. *et al.* (2004) Inflammation underlying cardiovascular mortality is a late consequence of evolutionary programming. *FASEB Journal* **18**, 1022–1024.

Van Gennep, A., Vizedom, M. B. and Cassee, G. L. (1960) *The Rites of Passage*. London: Routledge & Kegan Paul.

Van Selm, M. and Westerhof, G. J. (2004) Lachwekkend of respectabel? Beeldvorming van ouderen in televisiereclame revisited. Paper presented at the 7th National Congress of the Nederlandse Vereniging voor Gerontologie, Ede, Netherlands.

Van Selm, M., Westerhof, G. J. and Thissen, T. (1996) Ouderen in tv-reclamespots: lachwekkend of respectabel [Portrayal of the elderly in Dutch TV commercials]. *Tijdschrift voor Gerontologie en Geriatrie* **6**, 237–242.

van Tilburg, T. G., de Jong Gierveld, J., Lecchini, L. and Marsiglia, D. (1998) Social integration and loneliness: a comparative study among older adults in the Netherlands and Tuscany, Italy. *Journal of Social and Personal Relationships* **15**, 740–754.

Vasil, L. and Wass, H. (1993) Portrayal of the elderly in the media: a literature review and implications for educational gerontologists. *Educational Gerontology* **19**, 71–85.

Verhaeghen, P. and Marcoen, A. (1996) On the mechanisms of plasticity in young and older adults after instruction in the method of loci: evidence for an amplification model. *Psychology and Aging* **11**, 164–178.

Verhaeghen, P., Marcoen, A. and Goossens, L. (1992) Improving memory performance in the aged through mnemonic training: a meta-analytic study. *Psychology and Aging* **7**, 242–251.

Victor, C. (2002) Using existing research and statistical data: secondary data analysis. In: Jamieson, A. and Victor, C. R. (eds) *Researching Ageing and Later Life: The Practice of Social Gerontology*, vol. 4, 51–65. Buckingham: Open University Press.

Victor, C. R., Scambler, S. J., Bond, J. and Bowling, A. (2004) Loneliness in later life. In: Walker, A. and Hennessy, C. H. (eds) *Growing Older: Quality of Life in Old Age*, vol. **6**, 107–126. Maidenhead: Open University Press.

Victor, C. R., Scambler, S. J., Bowling, A. and Bond, J. (2005) The prevalence of, and risk factors for, loneliness in later life: a survey of older people in Great Britain. *Ageing and Society* **25**, 357–375.

Vincent, J. (1995) *Inequality and Old Age*. London: UCL Press.

Vincent, J. A. (2003a) *Old Age*. London: Routledge.

Vincent, J. A. (2003b) Old age, sickness, death and immortality: a cultural gerontological critique of biomedical models of old age and their fantasies of immortality. Presented at the 4th International Symposium on Cultural Gerontology, Tampere, Finland: 'The cultural in gerontology: challenges, approaches and methods'.

Vincent, J. A., Phillipson, C. and Downs, M. (2006) *The Futures of Old Age*. London: Sage.

Vladeck, B. C. (1980) *Unloving Care: The Nursing Home Tragedy*. New York: Basic Books.

Von Faber, M. (2002) *Maten van suces bij ouderen: Gezondheid, aanpassing en sociaal welbevinden*. Rotterdam: Optima.

von Zglinicki, T. (2002) Oxidative stress shortens telomeres. *Trends in Biochemical Sciences* **27**, 339–344.

von Zglinicki, T., Bürkle, A. and Kirkwood, T. B. L. (2001) Stress, DNA damage and ageing: an integrative approach. *Experimental Gerontology* **36**, 1049–1062.

von Zglinicki, T., Serra, V., Lorenz, M., Saretzki, G., Lenzen-Großimlighaus, R. *et al.* (2000) Short telomeres in patients with vascular dementia: an indicator of low antioxidative capacity and a possible prognostic factor? *Laboratory Investigation* **80**, 1739–1747.

Wadsworth, M. (2002) Doing longitudinal research. In: Jamieson, A. and Victor, C. R. (eds) *Researching Ageing and Later Life: The Practice of Social Gerontology*, Chapter **7**, 99–116. Buckingham: Open University Press.

Wadsworth, M. E. J., Mann, S. L., Rodgers, B., Kuh, D. L. J., Hilder, W. S. *et al.* (1992) Loss and representativeness in a 43-year follow-up of a national birth cohort. *Journal of Epidemiology and Community Health* **46**, 300–304.

Wahl, H.-W. (2001) Environmental influences on aging and behaviour. In: Birren, J. E. and Schaie, K. W. (eds) *Handbook of the Psychology of Aging*, 5th edn, 215–237. San Diego, CA: Academic Press.

Wahl, H.-W. and Lang, F. R. (2004) Aging in context across the adult life: integrating physical and social research perspectives. In: Wahl, H.-W., Scheidt, R. and Windley, P. G. (eds) *Annual Review of Gerontology and Geriatrics. Aging in Context – Socio-physical Environments*, vol. 23, 1–35. New York: Springer.

Wahl, H.-W. and Mollenkopf, H. (2003) Impact of everyday technology in the home environment on older adults' quality of life. In: Charness, N. and Schaie, K. W. (eds) *Impact of Technology on Successful Aging*, 215–241. New York: Springer.

Wahl, H.-W. and Weisman, G. D. (2003) Environmental gerontology at the beginning of the new millenium: reflections on its historical, empirical, and theoretical development. *Gerontologist* **43**(5), 616–627.

Wahl, H.-W., Oswald, F. and Zimprich, D. (1999) Everyday competence in visually impaired older adults: a case for person–environment perspectives. *Gerontologist* **39**, 140–149.

Wahl, H.-W., Scheidt, R. and Windley, P. G. (eds) (2004) *Annual Review of Gerontology and Geriatrics. Aging in Context – Socio-physical Environments*, vol. 23. New York: Springer.

Wainwright, S. P. and Turner, B. S. (2003) Aging and the dancing body. In: Faircloth, C. (ed.) *Aging Bodies: Images and Everyday Experiences*, 259–292. Walnut Creek, CA: AltaMira Press.

Waldman, D. A. and Avolio, B. J. (1986) A meta-analysis of age-differences in job performance. *Journal of Applied Psychology* **71**, 33–38.

Walker, A. (1980) The social creation of poverty and dependency in old age. *Journal of Social Policy* **9**, 49–75.

Walker, A. (1981) Towards a political economy of old age. *Ageing and Society* **1**(1), 73–94.

Walker, A. (1982) Dependency and old age. *Social Policy and Administration* **16**, 115–135.

Walker, A. (1990) The economic 'burden' of ageing and the prospect of intergenerational conflict. *Ageing and Society* **10**(4), 377–396.

Walker, A. (1993) *Age and Attitudes. Main Results from a Eurobarometer Survey*. Brussels: Commission of the European Communities.

Walker, A. (1996) *The New Generational Contract*. London: UCL Press.

Walker, A. (1997) *Maßnahmen zur Bekampfung von Altersbarrieren in der Erwerbstätigkeit: Ein europäischer Forschungsbericht*. Dublin: Europäische Stiftung zur Verbesserung der Lebens – und Arbeitsbedingungen.

Walker, A. (1999a) Attitudes to population ageing in Europe: a comparison of the 1992 and 1999 Eurobarometer Surveys. Website: www.shef.ac.uk/socst/staff/staff_page_elements/a_walker/attitudes.pdf. Date accessed 9/8/2005.

Walker, A. (1999b) Public policy and theories of aging: constructing and reconstructing old age. In: Bengston, V. L. and Schaie, K. W. (eds) *Handbook of Theories of Ageing*, 361–378. London: UCL Press.

Walker, A. (2000) Public policy and the construction of old age in Europe. *Gerontologist* **40**, 304–308.

Walker, A. (ed.) (2004) *Growing Older in Europe*. Maidenhead: Open University Press.

Walker, A. (2005) *Growing Older: Understanding Quality of Life in Old Age*. Maidenhead: Open University Press.

Walker, A. and Foster, L. (2006) Ageing and social class: an enduring relationship. In: Vincent, J., Phillipson, C. and Downs, M. (eds) *The Futures of Old Age*. London: Sage.

Walker, A. and Maltby, T. (1997) *Ageing Europe*. Buckingham: Open University Press.

Walker, A. and Naegele, G. (1999) *The Politics of Old Age in Europe*. Buckingham: Open University Press.

Walker, A. and Wong, C. K. (eds) (2005) *East Asian Welfare Regimes in Transition*. Bristol: Policy Press.

Wallace, D. C. (1992) Mitochondrial genetics: a paradigm for aging and degenerative diseases? *Science* 256, 628–632.

Walsh, D. A. and Hershey, D. A. (1993) Mental models and the maintenance of complex problem-solving skills in old age. In: *Adult Information Processing: Limits on Loss*, 553–584. San Diego, CA: Academic Press.

Wang, X., Merzenich, M. M., Sameshima, K. and Jenkins, W. (1995) Remodelling of hand representation in adult cortex determined by timing of tactile stimulation. *Nature* **378**, 71–75.

Wanless, D. (2006) *Securing Good Care for Older People: Taking a Long Term View*. London: King's Fund.

Warnes, A. (2001) The international dispersal of pensioners from affluent countries. *International Journal of Population Geography* **7**(6), 373–388.

Warnes, A. M., Friedrich, K., Kellaher, L. and Torres, S. (2004) The diversity and welfare of older migrants in Europe. *Ageing and Society* **24**(3), 307–326.

Waugh, N. C. and Norman, D. A. (1965) Primary memory. *Psychological Review* **72**, 89–104.

Weber, R. P. (1990) *Basic Content Analysis*, 2nd edn. Newbury Park, CA: Sage.

Webster, J. D. (2003) An exploratory analysis of a Self-Assessed Wisdom Scale. *Journal of Adult Development* **10**, 13–22.

Weidekamp-Maicher, M. and Reichert, M. (2004) Germany: quality of life in older age – II. In: Walker, A. (ed.) *Growing Older in Europe*, 159–178. Maidenhead: Open University Press.

Weisman, G. D. (1997) Environments for older persons with cognitive impairments. In: Moore, G. and Marans, R. (eds) *Environment, Behavior and Design*, vol. 4, 315–346. New York: Plenum Press.

Weisman, G. D. (2003) Creating places for people with dementia: an action research perspective. In: Schaie, K. W., Wahl, H.-W., Mollenkopf, H. and Oswald, F. (eds) *Aging Independently: Living Arrangements and Mobility*, 162–173. New York: Springer.

Weisman, J., Lawton, M. P., Sloane, P. S., Calkins, M. and Norris-Baker, L. (1996) *The Professional Environmental Assessment Protocol*. Milwaukee, WI: School of Architecture, University of Wisconsin.

Wenger, G. C. (1989) Supporting networks in old age: constructing a typology. In: Jefferys, M. (ed.) *Ageing in the 20th Century*, 166–185. London: Routledge.

Wenger, G. C. (1997) Review of findings on support networks of older Europeans. *Journal of Cross-Cultural Gerontology* **12**, 1–21.

Wensauer, M. and Grossmann, K. E. (1995) Qualität der Bindungsrespräsentation, soziale Integration und Umgang mit Netzwerkressourcen in höheren Erwachsenenalter. *Zeitschrift für Gerontologie und Geriatrie* **28**, 444–456.

Wentura, D., Rothermund, K. and Brandtstädter, J. (1995) Experimentelle analysen zur verarbeitung belastender informationen: differential – und alternpsychologische aspekte [Experimental studies on the processing of negative information: differential and age-related aspects]. *Zeitschrift für Experimentelle Psychologie* **42**, 152–175.

Werner, H. (1957) *Comparative Psychology of Mental Development.* New York: International Universities Press.

Westendorp, R. G. (2004) Are we becoming less disposable? *EMBO Reports* **5**, 2–6.

Westendorp, R. G. (2006) What is healthy aging in the 21st century? *American Journal of Clinical Nutrition* 83 (suppl.), S404–409.

Westendorp, R. G. and Kirkwood, T. B. (1998) Human longevity at the cost of reproductive success. *Nature* **396**, 743–746.

Westendorp, R. G., van Dunne, F. M., Kirkwood, T. B., Helmerhorst, F. M. and Huizinga, T. W. (2001) Optimizing human fertility and survival. *Nature Medicine* **7**, 873.

Westerhof, G. J. (1994) *Statements and Stories: Towards a New Methodology of Attitude Research.* Amsterdam: Thesis Publishers.

Westerhof, G. J. (2001a) Arbeit und Beruf im persönlichen Sinnsystem. In: Dittmann-Kohli, F., Bode, C. and Westerhof, G. J. (eds) *Die zweite Lebenshälfte: Psychologische Perspektiven – Ergebnisse des Alters-Survey*, 195–245. Stuttgart: Kohlhammer.

Westerhof, G. J. (2001b) Freizeittaetigkeiten im persönlichen Sinnsystem. In: Dittmann-Kohli, F., Bode, C. and Westerhof, G. J. (eds) *Die zweite Lebenshälfte: Psychologische Perspektiven – Ergebnisse des Alters-Survey*, 247–277. Stuttgart: Kohlhammer.

Westerhof, G. J. (2003) De beleving van het eigen ouder worden: multidimensionaliteit en multidirectionaliteit in relatie tot succesvol ouder worden en welbevinden. *Tijdschrift voor Gerontologie en Geriatrie* **34**, 96–103.

Westerhof, G. J. and Barrett, A. E. (2005) Age identity and subjective well-being: a comparison of the United States and Germany. *Journal of Gerontology* **60B**, S129–136.

Westerhof, G. J. and Bode, C. (2006) The personal meaning of individuality and relatedness: gender differences in middle and late adulthood. In: Daatland, S. and Biggs, S. (eds) *Ageing and Diversity: Multiple Pathways and Cultural Migrations*, 29–44. Bristol: Policy Press.

Westerhof, G. J. and Dittmann-Kohli, F. (2000) Work status and the construction of work-related selves. In: Schaie, K. W. and Hendricks, J. (eds) *The Evolution of the Aging Self: The Societal Impact on the Aging Process*, 123–157. New York: Springer.

Westerhof, G. J., Kuin, Y. and Dittmann-Kohli, F. (1998) Gesundheit als Lebensthema. *Zeitschrift für Klinische Psychologie* **27**, 136–142.

Westerhof, G. J., Dittmann-Kohli, F. and Thissen, T. (2001a) Beyond life satisfaction: qualitative and quantitative approaches to judgements about the quality of life. *Social Indicators Research* **56**, 179–203.

Westerhof, G. J., Katzko, M., Dittmann-Kohli, F. and Hayslip, B. (2001b) Life contexts and health-related selves in old age: perspectives from the United States, India and Zaire. *Journal of Aging Studies* **15**, 105–126.

Westerhof, G. J., Dittmann-Kohli, F. and Bode, C. (2003a) The aging paradox: towards personal meaning in gerontological theory. In: Biggs, S., Lowenstein, A. and Hendricks, J. (eds) *The Need for Theory: Social Gerontology for the 21st Century*, 127–143. Amityville, NY: Baywood.

Westerhof, G. J., Barrett, A. E. and Steverink, N. (2003b) Forever young: a comparison of age identities in the United States and Germany. *Research on Aging* **25**, 366–383.

Whitbourne, S. K. (1985) The psychological construction of the life span. In: Birren, J. and Schaie, K. W. (eds) *Handbook of the psychology of aging*, New York: Van Nostrand Reinhold.

Whitbourne, S. K. (2001) *Adult Development and Aging: Biopsychosocial Perspectives.* New York: Wiley.

Wicclair, M. R. (1993) *Ethics and the Elderly.* Oxford: Oxford University Press.

Wiese, B. S., Freund, A. M. and Baltes, P. B. (2000) Selection, optimization, and compensation: an action-related approach to work and partnership. *Journal of Vocational Behavior* **57**, 273–300.

Wilkin, D. (1987) Conceptual problems in dependency research. *Social Science and Medicine* **24**, 867–873.

Wilkin, D. and Thompson, C. (1989) *Users' Guide to Dependency Measures for Elderly People.* Sheffield: University of Sheffield, Joint Unit for Social Services Research.

Willcocks, D., Peace, S. and Kellaher, L. (1987) *Private Lives in Public Places.* London: Tavistock.

Williams, A. and Nussbaum, J. F. (2001) *Intergenerational Communication Across the Life Span.* Mahwah, NJ: Lawrence Erlbaum.

Williams, G. C. (1957) Pleiotropy, natural selection and the evolution of senescence. *Evolution* **11**, 398–411.

Williams, R. (1990) *A Protestant Legacy. Attitudes to Death and Illness Among Older Aberdonians.* New York: Oxford University Press.

Williams, R. G. A. (1983) Concepts of health: an analysis of lay logic. *Sociology* **17**, 185–205.

Williamson, S. N. and Crumpton, L. L. (1997) Investigating the work ability of older employees. *International Journal of Industrial Ergonomics* **20**, 241–249.

Willis, S. L. (1990) Current issues in cognitive training research. In: Lovelace, E. A. (ed.) *Aging and Cognition: Mental Processes, Self-awareness and Interventions*, 263–280. Amsterdam: North-Holland.

Willis, S. L. (2001) Methodological issues in behavioural intervention research with the elderly. In: Birren, J. E. and Schaie, K. W. (eds) *Handbook of the Psychology of Aging*, 5th edn, 78–108. San Diego, CA: Academic Press.

Willis, S. L., Cornelius, S. W., Blow, F. C. and Baltes, P. B. (1983) Training in research in aging: attentional processes. *Journal of Educational Psychology* **75**, 257–270.

Wilmoth, J. R., Deegan, L. J., Lundström, H. and Horiuchi, S. (2000) Increase of maximum life-span in Sweden, 1861–1999. *Science* **289**, 2366–2368.

Wink, P. and Helson, R. (1997) Practical and transcendent wisdom: their nature and some longitudinal findings. *Journal of Adult Development* **4**, 1–15.

Woods, R. T. (2001) Discovering the person with Alzheimer's disease: cognitive, emotional and behavioural aspects. *Aging and Mental Health* **5** (suppl. 1), S7–16.

Woollacott, M. H. and Shumway-Cook, A. (2002) Attention and the control of posture and gait: a review of an emerging area of research. *Gait and Posture* **16**, 1–14.

World Bank (1994) *Averting the Old Age Crisis.* Oxford: Oxford University Press.

World Health Organization (1980) *International Classification of Impairment, Disabilities and Handicaps.* Geneva: WHO.

World Health Organization (1998) World Atlas of Ageing. Kobe, Japan: Who Centre for Health Development.

World Health Organization (2001) *International Classification of Functioning and Disability (ICIDH-2).* Geneva: WHO. Website: www.who.int/classifications/icf/en/. Date accessed 5/6/2006.

Wrong, D. (1961) The oversocialized concept of man in modern sociology. *American Sociological Review* **26**, 183–193.

Yang, L., Krampe, R. T. and Baltes, P. B. (2006) *Basic forms of cognitive plasticity extended into the oldest-old:* Retest learning, age, and cognitive functioning. Psychology and Aging, **21**, 372–378.

Yashin, A. I., Begun, A. S., Boiko, S. I., Ukraintseva, S. V. and Oeppen, J. (2002) New age patterns of survival improvement in Sweden: do they characterize changes in individual aging? *Mechanisms of Ageing and Development* **123**, 637–647.

Yeatts, D. E., Folts, W. E. and Knapp, J. (2000) Older workers' adaptation to a changing workplace: employment issues for the 21st century. *Educational Gerontology* **26**, 565–582.

Yin, R. K. (1984) *Case Study Research: Design and Methods.* London: Sage.

Zingmark, K., Norberg, A. and Sandman, P.-O. (1995) The experience of being at home throughout the life span: investigation of persons aged from 2 to 102. *International Journal of Aging and Human Development* **41**(1), 47–62.

Index